KV-662-077

DISPOSED OF
BY LIBRARY
HOUSE OF LORDS

Politics & Power Four

EDITORIAL BOARD

Diana Adlam   Lorraine Culley
Barry Hindess   Paul Hirst
Alan Hunt   Phil Jones
Alan MacDougall   Chris Nawrat
Geoff Roberts   Nikolas Rose
Dan Smith

Politics & Power Four

Routledge & Kegan Paul
London, Boston and Henley

First published in 1981
by Routledge & Kegan Paul Ltd
39 Store Street
London WC1E 7DD
9 Park Street
Boston, Mass. 02108, USA and
Broadway House
Newtown Road
Henley-on-Thames
Oxon RG9 1EN

Printed in Great Britain by
Thomson Litho Ltd, East Kilbride

Books for review should be sent to Geoff Roberts
3a Southend Lane, London SE6

Articles, responses and contributions to debate
should be sent to
Politics & Power, 37 Beversbrook Road, London N19

© Editorial Board 1981
No part of this book may be reproduced in any form without
permission of the publisher, except for the quotation of
brief passages in criticism.

ISBN 0 7100 0984 4

ISSN 0144-0918

Contents

The Editorial Board
Politics & Power Four

In a series of articles on the theme of police, law and justice, this
issue of *Politics & Power* puts in question prevalent positions on the
left concerning political struggles in and around the law. At a time
when such issues are once more at the forefront of political debate,
these articles, from a number of distinct positions, argue for the
necessity of a strategy not of opposition to the institutions and
practices of police and law, but of their constructive and radical
reform.

Other articles in this issue deal with a range of problems which
face progressive politics in Britain today. Problems in the politics
of psychiatry, race and employment, defence policy and taxation are
considered and conventional positions questioned.

Of particular note is an interview with Sue Slipman, formerly a
member of the Communist Party and now a member of the Social Democratic
Party. This interview considers an important and topical development,
the formation of the SDP. It is included not because we agree with
Sue Slipman or the SDP, but because of the political importance of the
issues raised by this development. Thus it is presented for the
centrality of the problems it considers, rather than because it provides a set of definitive answers.

It is in this light that *P&P* endeavours to present and encourage
serious and sustained debate on the many issues where no clear lines
of political strategy have yet been established. Thus a feature of
this issue is a number of responses to earlier articles. Mike Prior
and Dan Smith carry forward the debate on feminism, and men's relation
to feminism, which formed a major theme of our last issue; Simon Watney
responds critically to David Fernbach's analysis of ten years of gay
liberation; Barry Hindess disputes Peter Hain's argument that a priority
for the left should be to establish the Labour Party as an organisation
for mass politics.

The editorial board would welcome further articles, responses and
contributions to debate. These should be sent to
Politics & Power
37 Beversbrook Road
London N19

Alan Hunt
The Politics of Law and Justice

INTRODUCTION

Law and justice are important. The need to state such a truism is a
mark of the extent to which the left in Britain has over a long period
of time failed to recognise that law and justice have a significant
political dimension. But I would argue further that political questions
revolving around law are becoming increasingly important and, indeed,
central to the political problems of the present.

The left *does* have a politics of law; the real problem is that it is
deficient in a number of major respects. It is, first, rudimentary, for
law is given little priority either in the theory or the practices of
the left. Second, these responses, whether theorised or part of a less
articulated set of attitudes, are significant impediments to the
development of a politics of law. Third, responses which the left
invokes in different circumstances are frequently incompatible and even
contradictory; it is little wonder that it is confused, and even less
surprising that the positions it takes up meet with very limited popular
support. It will therefore be necessary to examine in some detail the
varieties of left positions with respect to law and justice and to
explore and criticise their implications. The arena of law and justice,
studded as it is with highly significant values and symbols, has been
handed over without effective resistance to the right, thus allowing
them to make effective and powerful interventions with wide-ranging
political consequences.

This paper argues that law must be regarded as an *arena of struggle*,
a field in which different class and political positions engage, with
consequences that are not deducible from any general theory of law. It
thus rejects any instrumentalist theory of law, which presents law as
being available to any particular class or dominant group as an instrument or means of effecting their will or furthering their interests.
This does not imply that law is neutral, equally available to all political or social forces. The social and political 'limits' to intervention in law are a pressing political concern, and they are determined
in each historical period as the outcome of struggle, whether that
struggle is waged consciously or not.

The designation of law as an arena of struggle implies the rejection of a general politics of law, for such an approach would require law to be a unitary phenomenon. On the contrary, a politics of law requires specific political evaluation of possibilities and tactics with respect to each and every instance of legal regulation. However, consistency and coherence with reference to particular instances of legal struggle are necessary; I argue that one of the weaknesses of prevailing positions on the left is that they frequently lack both internal consistency and coherence in respect of related areas of legal struggle.

Once the weaknesses in the positions taken up on the left have been identified, my final section will be concerned to set out, first, a general framework within which a progressive politics of law and justice can be advanced and, second, to discuss a number of the more pressing contemporary issues of the politics of law. In this latter task I advance a number of positions which conflict with what have tradition- ally come to be regarded as socialist or progressive positions.

The objective of this paper is not to engage in discussion of speci- fic areas of legal and social policy. It is clear from the foregoing that such an exercise cannot be undertaken through derivation from general theoretical considerations. Whilst consideration of individual areas of legal intervention require detailed empirical investigation, these run the risk of lapsing into a narrow empiricism if conducted outside the context of wider theoretical and political considerations. For this reason this paper focuses attention on some of these more important and often neglected considerations.

THE IMPORTANCE OF LAW

Law is important and socialists must take it seriously.[1] Let me briefly examine some areas in which this importance for socialist politics is manifested.

Law is important in that it exhibits a symbolic or ideological dimen- sion. Law mobilises important ideological symbols. The process of the legalisation and legitimation gives both direct advantage and encourage- ment to some social forces and the corresponding delegitimation of criminalisation hampers, penalises or discourages other social forces. For example, an understanding of the recent history of abortion law reform can be facilitated by an understanding of the symbolic dimensions of the 'victories' and 'defeats' recorded in the various stages of legis- lative process. An important question is whether the symbolic dimensions of law are direct effects of the legislative process itself or require a more complex analysis in which, for example, the symbolic content of law is significant with respect to the extent to which it facilitates the mobilisation of political action and sentiment.[2]

Law displays and invokes an array of ideologically significant terms. The language of law, both technical and popular, is studded with appeals to 'rights', 'duties', 'equality', 'justice' and so forth. Indeed much of the history of political thought, in both its academic and popular forms, abounds with appeal to legal concepts and ideas.[3] It is import- ant to recognise that the very terms of political argument and debate are unavoidably 'legalistic'. For example, there has been considerable discussion of the problems inherent in invoking 'rights' with its con- sequential invocation of the atomised 'legal subject'. Yet no amount

of critical commentary removes the appeal to 'rights' from the language
of politics and therefore from the terms within which politics are fought
out.[4]

The importance of law is further underlined by discussions pointing
towards its growing centrality. From different theoretical and political
perspectives it has been contended that one of the significant characteristics of contemporary capitalist democracies is that law is increasingly
becoming a primary mechanism of social control or social order. There
are at least three versions of the 'centrality of law' thesis. Recent
Marxist discussions, initiated by Althusser's discussion of 'ideological
state apparatuses', suggest that law is increasingly becoming a primary
form of social regulation. There has been increasing attention to the
significance of the 'juridification' of social relations, the two-fold
process whereby wider areas of social life become subject to legal regulation and control and social relations themselves come to be treated
and regarded in legalistic terms.

From a diametrically opposed perspective neo-conservatism has identified, albeit in different terms, the same trend. Indeed conservative
theorists have quite consciously set out to attack the modern extension
of legal regulation, by emphasising 'the limits of law'.[5] The third
version of the 'centrality of law' thesis is to be found in the much
wider middle ground focusing variously on the welfare state, social
justice and corporatism. It is clear that almost the full spectrum of
political and theoretical discussion agrees that law has become more
important or central in contemporary capitalist democracies as an
expanding mechanism for the regulation of social life.

Law is important also for the part that it plays in the formation
of popular consciousness. Anyone who has spent any time on the doorstep
canvassing must recognise that it is no invention of the opinion polls
or the popular tabloids that people in very large numbers persistently
refer to 'crime' as an area of concern, fear or anxiety. The prevalence
of and the attention given to 'street crime', that is visible offences
against person and property, play an important part in the way people
form and express their attitudes towards the condition of contemporary
social life and the quality of life. The specific focus of attention
shifts, often with a considerable volatility, heightened by and through
the mass media. One very obvious form of this process is the identification of an enemy/villain to be scapegoated (e.g. black muggers, trade
union pickets, football hooligans, the Yorkshire Ripper).[6] There are
equally powerful yet less personalised and less studied forms of social
anxiety embodied in reaction to street vandalism, car thefts and house-
breaking, etc.

The political importance of popular responses to 'law' and its
correlative 'crime' lies in the two interconnected dimensions referred
to above, at the immediate level the specific anxiety/fear involved in
the particular problem and the deeper social anxiety about changes in
the wider pattern of social life which often underlies it. For example,
concern surrounding youth vandalism and football hooliganism also
expresses disquiet at the transformation of inter-generational relations, the decline in the cohesion of family life and parental control
and, beyond the problem of generations, a more profound concern with
declining levels of 'social responsibility' and 'community'. It is
necessary to insist on the reality of the specific and to avoid dis-
missing popular reaction as a manifestation of false consciousness or

of a traditional ideology. The general failure of the left to say anything about the immediate level of the 'crime phenomenon' itself is a
manifestation of political weakness and failure of political response.
    The popular response to crime tends to be politically articulated
towards the right. Yet it is necessary to insist on the contradictory
nature of popular responses, for this points towards a general political
basis for a progressive response to problems of crime. In *Policing the
Crisis* the 'social anxiety' surrounding mugging is presented as embodying
a 'traditional concensus' which is a *cross-class consensus*, composed of
a number of interwoven commonsense notions, such as 'respectability',
'work', 'social discipline', 'respect for authority', and, perhaps most
powerful of all, the sense of 'Englishness'. I do not want to take
issue with the detailed constituents of this imagery, but it is less
than clear that all of these elements are traditionalist. Interwoven
is another notion which, whilst present in their analysis is never
fully discussed, that of 'social responsibility'; it appeals to ideas
about how people should behave, about care and concern for others.
Now as social historians have so often observed, progressive sentiments
and response often deploy images of a pre-existing ideal state or golden
age. Indeed a persistent theme in the appeal to social responsibility
is a view that in 'the good old days' people were more responsible,
caring, etc. Yet that appeal bears a positive morality about how things
should be and in its more optimistic phases of how things could be. It
is the progressive thrust and potential of concepts of social responsibility that set out the basis for a progressive politics of law, and to
which, therefore, I will return.

THE LEFT AND THE POLITICS OF LAW

The responses of the left fail to take law seriously and are a major
barrier to effective intervention in legal politics. The positions
taken up are pervasive and their crippling effect has to be recognised
before a progressive politics of law and justice can be developed. It
is therefore necessary to consider the varieties of left positions or
responses. Whilst I am critical of the range of positions customarily
associated with the left, it is also necessary to register the presence
of some long-standing and serious progressive traditions[7] in the politics
of civil liberties or, perhaps more accurately, the politics of political
liberties. I shall however argue that this important strand of progressive politics is not without problems.
    The fundamental problem with left responses is that they manifest
themselves as deductions or derivations from general theories of law
and the state. This both causes and reinforces a reluctance to come
to grips with more concrete issues in the broad field of the politics
of law.[8] Where concrete issues are discussed there is a pronounced
tendency for this to be done in a manner which is in fact the simple
application of the general theory which points to the class-discrimina-
tory character of law in general. The result is a complacency of
circularity, in which the general theory is celebrated and the concrete
presented as its proof.
    My objection to the derivation of legal politics from general theory
requires some comment because it appears to conflict with what is frequently claimed as a strength and virtue by the Marxist left, that it is

precisely the existence of the general theory, Marxism, which makes it
possible to avoid the pitfalls of pragmatism, reformism and opportunism.
The problem is not general theory as such, but the nature of the presumed
direct connection between the theoretical concepts (e.g. 'capitalism')
and the concrete (e.g. law in Britain in the 1980s), in which the concrete is treated as an expression or embodiment of the theoretical category. Such a position constantly veers towards idealism and is a
barrier to the detailed analysis of the concrete or empirical reality.[9]

The general theory most commonly deployed by the left is in its
simplest form the 'class-state, class-law' thesis. It has its intellectual and political roots in Marxist theory of the state, particularly in
the version that has had such widespread impact through Lenin's *State
and Revolution* in which the state is a mechanism of class rule. This
theory of the state unproblematically links law to the state as one of
its major instruments or agencies. Law is but an expression of the
needs and will of a dominant class. However much it may be argued that
such a theoretical position does not grasp the fullness or complexity
of Marxist theory, it is powerful and extensive in its influence; and
it has considerable textual support. For example, *The Communist
Manifesto* proclaims: 'Your [bourgeois] law is merely the will of your
class, erected into legislation - a will whose content is defined by the
material conditions of the existence of your class.'[10] The 'class-state,
class-law' thesis provides the general framework within which the left
develops its politics of law. It expresses itself in several variants
which are either loosely combined or differentially accentuated.

The first variant is a conspiracy theory in which the emphasis is
upon the capacity of law to mask or hide its specifically class character.
Law is thus frequently presented as the emanation of a state endowed
with extensive foresight and long-term planning objectives; there is a
strong tendency to see the state itself as the embodiment of political
will and intention. A recent example of this tendency has been the
emphasis on the campaign against the Criminal Justice (Scotland) Bill
which suggests a conscious strategy of the 'ruling class' to use this
legislation as a dry run for an attempt to impose increased police powers
upon the rest of the United Kingdom.[11]

An important pressure towards conspiratorial views of law arises from
verions of ideology theory which emphasise the legitimizing function of
the legal ideology through which legal provisions are expressed. Legitimation tends to be seen as a conscious state policy facilitated by the
formalism through which law invokes 'equality', 'fairness', and other
legal symbols. Its classic expression is Anatole France's ironic decla-
mation on French law 'which forbids both rich and poor from sleeping
under the bridges of the Seine'.[12] It is an easy but nevertheless
dangerous slippage to move directly from functional analysis of law to
assumptions about the political intentions of classes and legislatures.
It is not that law is neutral, above classes or politics, but that there
are risks of oversimplification in reading off or deducing class and
political intentions either about law in general or about specific
legislation.

The second variant of the class law thesis insists, both with respect
to the content of law and to its administration, that law is class
discriminatory. This critique operates by exposing the gap between the
universalistic claims of law and its discriminatory reality. It leads
to two very different versions of legal politics. One is essentially

negative, in the form of the expose of legal inequality. It is a counsel
against holding any illusions about the possibility of law realising the
ideals of equality and fairness, for class discrimination is seen as the
inevitable and unavoidable face of law in a class divided society. The
alternative political orientation is one which emphasises the necessity
and possibility of legal reform. The class discriminatory character of
the institutions and practice is highlighted in order to demand a strategy of reform aimed at the gap between legal ideals and legal reality.
This position is well exemplified by the movement to extend legal
services; it starts by emphasising inequality of access and it demands
administrative and financial arrangements designed to widen and simplify
access to legal services. This orientation has been the organising
theme of the 'law centres movement' to make legal services available to
the communities disenfranchised by the existing distribution and operation of the legal profession. This position is not necessarily wedded
to a simplistic piecemeal or accumulative reform strategy. Its more
radical thrust stresses the contradiction between the ideological commitment of bourgeois democracy to ideals of equality and the fundamental
inequality in capitalist society. By working on this tension, through
demands which seek to realise ideologically legitimate goals, it seeks
to bring about a heightened political consciousness of the inherent
limitation of capitalism and bourgeois democracy, and to create some
of the conditions for a more substantive social equality.

It is important to stress that the 'class state - class law' position
does not give rise to a single political expression. Yet it tends towards
a rejectionism in which the possibility of a progressive politics of law
is so circumscribed by its class nature that little significance is
attached to struggle in the legal field. The gap between rejectionism
and legal reformism tends to be viewed in the light of the dichotomy
between 'reform' and 'revolution', although it is important to note that
wider support from the left is given to specific reform campaigns whenever these are seen as having politicising or radical potential.

The 'class state - class law' position also finds other manifestations.
One which relies on the most explicitly 'revolutionary' inspiration
counterposes 'bourgeois justice' to 'proletarian justice'. In some
versions it is little more than an apology for the legal practice of
'actual socialism'; but even in its non-apologist interpretation it dismisses the ideals of bourgeois law, which are doomed to remain 'pure
ideology' and which must be replaced with other goals and organisational
principles. Individual rights and liberties are irredeemably bourgeois
in character and are counterposed by appeal to goals of class and social
justice to be realised by proletarian institutions and practices. The
goal of class justice is seen as requiring an escape from the formalism
of bourgeois law through informal and popular institutions pursuing
goals of substantive justice untrammelled by too much concern with
proceduralism.

One of the most common manifestations of the generalised 'class law'
thesis attributes the genesis of crime and anti-social behaviour more
generally to the very nature of capitalist society itself. The etiology
of crime is traced to the anti-social, dehumanising character of capitalist social relations, and the conclusion is drawn that it is not the
individual law-breakers but capitalism itself or 'society' which is
'responsible' for or 'causes' crime. 'Don't blame the individual, blame
society' becomes the general slogan of the left or, as expressed in one

placard seen on a demonstration, 'Fight Crime, Smash Capitalism'. It is
a perspective in which the advent of socialism is seen as leading to the
long-term eradication of crime.[13]
     This line of thought has disastrous consequences for the left's
political response to crime. The slogan 'blame society, not the criminal'
persistently deflects the left's response to crime-related problems
towards long-term social reform programmes directed towards the removal
of the social conditions which are seen as giving rise to crime; in so
doing the left tends to have little to offer by way of immediate or
short-term response to crime phenomena themselves. When this is associated with an anti-correctional attitude, discussed below, it gives
rise to the popular picture that the left has nothing to say about the
response to the law-breaker. In the light of the importance attached
above to popular responses to the most readily visible forms of 'street
crime', this is a serious absence. It is especially noticeable in
relation to youth offences, whether it be football hooliganism or street
vandalism: the left emphasises youth employment and the lack of youth
facilities, yet has very little to say about what should be done either
to minimise the incidence of offences or with regard to the appropriate
response towards the offenders themselves.
     The reluctance to blame the offender has origins in a long-standing
distrust of the assumption of free-will and moral responsibility that
underpin classical criminology, and is reinforced by a libertarian
hostility to the demand for social order. It is taken for granted that
the demand for 'law and order' is *inherently* reactionary. The immediate
and unavoidable consequence is that the whole political space of debate
concerning social and moral order is ceded without a struggle to the
right. For a period, in the late 1960s and early 1970s, radical deviancy theory provided a veritable celebration of disorder in which the
denial of value consensus, coupled with a moral relativism, collapsed
not only the distinction between normalcy and deviancy, but that between
social and anti-social conduct. Deviancy was celebrated as a form of
primitive rebellion against the existing social order; Taylor, Walton
and Young produced that 'any acts of deviance must be taken to be acts
of resistance (however inarticulately expressed or formulated)'.[14] This
period found a political rapport with the political commitment to 'the
underdog' as the bearer of revolutionary potential articulated by Marcuse
and Fanon. For radical deviancy theory it was prisoners, prostitutes
and gypsies that elicited moral solidarity. These heady days of radicalism waned for even in the earlier period the realisation existed that
the property that was the site of the struggle for possession was invariably the property of the worker, just as it was the worker's personal
safety that was violated by crimes of violence. Yet the hostility to
'order' has been retained and is shared by much of the left. The content
of this agreement lies in the association of 'order' and the 'status quo';
yet what is adopted in the equation is not a necessary connection but
one which is the result of the highly successful assertion of this
identity in conservative theory and rhetoric.
     The tendency of the left to 'blame society, not the individual' is
reinforced by a pervasive hostility to 'correctionalism', since law in
general is viewed as repressive so necessarily are punishment and other
agencies of social control (e.g. social workers, schools, psychiatrists,
etc.) all geared to relocating offenders/deviants within capitalist
social relations. This approach is of course reinforced by the evident

lack of 'success', when judged against reformatory criteria, of the conventional range of punitive sanctions. This hostility is particularly
directed towards the prison system where the general patterns of high
recidivism are buttressed by a critique of the disciplinary processes
employed.

The reservation or hostility towards prisons and correctionalism more
generally leads the left to share with sections of liberal opinion a
general call for the reduction of the prison population, opposition to
imprisonment for young offenders and first offenders which has been the
dominant legislative trend for over a decade. Yet the left exhibits a
greater scepticism than mainstream liberal thought with regard to
'alternatives to prisons', for example, parole, halfway houses, community service, etc., which are viewed as exhibiting continuity with traditional correctionalist concerns.[15] This hostility to both 'old' and
'new' correctionalism leads the left to a profound silence, an absence
of policy, an embarrassed shuffle or a diversionary attack on the evils
of capitalist society when pressed by the question 'but what should we
do with offenders?'

However, anti-correctionalism does not provide the whole of the penal
policy of the left. There are a number of fields in which the left has
no such hesitancies about the need to punish firmly and demonstrably.
The left has persistently called for the imposition of punitive sanctions on fascists and racists.[16] Is this response in contradiction with
the generalised anti-correctionalism or does it have a distinguishable
rationale? I would suggest that it is a mixture of two elements. First,
an incoherent reliance on simple political criteria, thus expressing gut
hostility to racism and fascism but running the risk of legitimizing the
adoption of a 'political penology' directed against the left. Secondly,
and more coherently, it insists on the presence of an individual responsibility for 'political' action. It sees fascist or racist action as
conscious and deliberate, thus both requiring and justifying punitive
response while insisting that 'non-political' acts cannot be regarded as
attracting the same level of 'responsibility'. What is significant about
this rationale is that it is an application of principles of 'classical
criminology' premised upon the insistence on the moral responsibility of
individuals for their own conduct. To point to this connection with
classical liberal thought is not intended to argue against holding
fascists 'responsible' for their conduct, but to point to the need to
re-examine the general premises on which the left's responses are based.

The left also departs from anti-correctionalism with respect to 'the
crimes of the powerful', for which it demands the application of the
full rigour of the law. Here the focus on the crimes of the powerful
serves to illustrate the class discriminatory character of the law; the
content of the law biased such that important areas of anti-social
conduct, oppressive or exploitative action are not criminalised. In
recent years a pervasive symbol has been the hounding of supplementary
benefit recipients in contrast to the judicial and political encouragement of tax evasion. Pointing the finger at the crimes of the powerful
has contradictory implications. On the one hand it is a potent symbol
of class inequality, and it invokes a positive criterion for law enforcement based on the *degree of social harm* occasioned. For example,
the financial value of the crimes of the powerful far outstrip the
relative triviality of the crime of the poor.[17] Yet crimes of the
powerful frequently are 'crime without victims' in that the losses are

suffered by the state, financial institutions, or are widely dispersed in
the 'social costs' incurred.   In contrast working-class crime is often
more immediate, being inflicted on individual members of the community.
'Social cost' does not provide an unproblematic criterion of moral responsibility' we may wish to maintain that to rob an old age pensioner *is*
worse than to defraud a multi-national corporation.   But does it provide
a basis for a coherent penal philosophy?   The focus on ruling class
crime can serve as a mechanism of deflection; to point to the widespread
nature of tax evasion is not in itself a response to the political question of what attitude should be taken up towards violations of social
security regulations.   Does pointing the finger at tax evasion exonerate
petty social security fiddles?   Can we legitimately fail to censure
working-class crime whilst the universal criminality of capitalism and
imperialism is still rampant?[18]
     The 'class-state, class-law' position has had harmful and pervasive
consequences for socialist politics of law; some of the variants give
rise to less flawed political conclusions, but even these entail either
a general political passivity or an incapacity to confront problems of
law, crime and order.

THE POLITICS OF CIVIL LIBERTIES

The left has a second perspective on the politics of law which is organised around 'the defence of civil liberties'.   What is noticeable, and
in some respects surprising, is the limited extent to which the demand
for defence of civil liberties has been discussed, let alone theorised,
by the left.   The liberal political and philosophical tradition has had
a virtual monopoly over both the terms and the content of the debate.
     The left has recently been forcefully invited to give its attention
to the arena of justice and its relation to civil liberties.   This
challenge has been laid down with customary publicist flair by Edward
Thompson.   His concern is that 'the ambivalence *within the "Left"* towards
civil liberties is the most alarming evidence that the libertarian nerve
has become dulled'.[19]   I share his concern about 'ambivalence' on the
left.   But he is profoundly in error to place the responsibility at the
door of Althusser and structuralist Marxism.   The 'ambivalence' of the
left is of much older lineage; responsibility lies in the extent to
which the left has operated, as I have argued, by appeal to both the
'class-state, class-law' position and the espousal of civil liberties.
The underdeveloped state of the left analysis of civil liberties has
often tended to give an apparently greater political weight to 'class
law' analysis resulting in either a rejection of civil liberties (as
Thompson complains) or, as I want to suggest, an equally problematic
tactical adoption of civil libertarian positions.
     Thompson, however, has done more than direct attention to the question
of civil liberties.   He has also provided a theoretical and historical
account which, if accepted, provides a powerful political case for giving
a major place in socialist strategy to the struggle to protect and
advance civil liberties.   The seeds of his theory of civil liberties
are found throughout his major historical writings, in particular in
The Making of the English Working Class and *Whigs and Hunters*.   He argues
that these liberties were born in the struggle against absolutism; they
were pioneered by independent, radical and republican activists and

thinkers.   This tradition was not simply the creature of a struggle by
the bourgeois against the old order, although many aspects were taken up
and articulated in the creation of the modern bourgeois state.   But they
remained most active and potent in a radical tradition which retained a
political and intellectual independence.   Although often repressed and
sometimes quiescent, they persisted and were revitalised by the developing working class and formed an important inspiration for Chartism and
later for trade unionism.   The signpost of the historical independence
of the civil libertarian tradition is expressed most graphically in
Thompson's imagery of the 'free-born Englishmen'.   An important 'proof'
of the irreducibility of civil liberties to bourgeois ideology lies in
his defence of the jury as the classical embodiment of an independent
banner of liberty: 'The jury system is not a product of "bourgeois
democracy" (to which it owes nothing) but a stubbornly maintained democratic *practice*.'[20]

Thompson's appeal is thus to an independent radical political tradition which is currently at greatest risk not only because of state sponsored attempts to extinguish it but, perhaps most importantly, because
the left is in danger of abandoning it.   His position is by no means
idiosyncratic.   Tony Benn has also advanced a very similar position:
'Our liberties have been won by political and industrial campaigns ...
democratic development has not been achieved by courtesy of the judges.'[21]
Even more evocative of Thompson is Benn's argument that the reassertion
of civil libertarian demands in the present 'will strike a chord in the
collective memory of our own people'.[22]

The civil liberties perspective advanced by Thompson has wider repercussions for political strategy.   It separates him decisively from that
element of the socialist tradition which sees capitalism as the last of
a succession of forms of class society which it is the historical role
of the socialist revolution to replace.   Rather Thompson's scenario is
one which emphasises greater elements of continuity between the bourgeois
and the socialist revolution; in the course of the bourgeois revolution
(but not reducible to it) the people embarked on a struggle for liberty
and democracy which it is the socialist project to *complete*, to rescue
from the limitations imposed within capitalist social relations.   Civil
liberties are, therefore, not a political gloss to socialism, even less
a tactical expedient: rather they are a central and constitutive element
of socialism itself.

Thompson's is the *strongest* and most thorough-going espousal of civil
liberties on the socialist left.   But he should not be thought to be
alone; however, a number of other socialist positions are *weaker* versions
of the commitment to civil liberties.   There are two important variants.
The first is often difficult to fully separate from Thompson's.   It
stresses, in the words of Tony Benn, 'liberties won by political and
industrial campaigns' but it sees these as victories won by the working
class *against* the bourgeoisie which during the struggles of the 19th
century were forced to concede civil liberties which were inimical to
its class interests.   The bourgeoisie is thus presented as having a pre-
disposition to anti-democratic and anti-civil libertarian positions.   It
follows that the need to struggle for civil liberties can be summed up
as the need to 'defend hard-won rights' which are always at risk of
being snatched back.

This position has some rather ambiguous implications.   Like Thompson
it stresses the historical connection between the working class and the

struggle for civil liberties, but it tends to ignore or under-play the
role of other classes and social forces. More seriously, it produces a
very strange and ultimately unsatisfactory account of the relationship
between capitalism and bourgeois democracy in which the political forms
most characteristic of advanced capitalism are presented as the product
of struggle by the working class and as having been conceded grudgingly
by the capitalist class even though they have subsequently succeeded in
turning these structures and practices to their own advantage in securing the conditions for their class rule. At its worst this weak civil
liberties position comes down to a *tactical* defence of civil liberties
both to expose the anti-democratic nature of the capitalist state and
also because the preservation of civil liberties provides the 'most
favourable conditions' for prosecuting the general struggle against
capitalism. Such a political line is tactical because it requires no
commitment to the principles or practices defended; thus making it all
the easier to dispense with them later once the immediate objective of
overthrowing capitalism has been achieved.

The second version of this position has a markedly more positive
thrust and places much less emphasis upon the defensive character of
civil liberties politics. The struggle for civil liberties is presented
as a *continuing* struggle for the creation of new liberties and rights,
extending beyond the scope of 'formal political liberties' into fields
which allow the struggle for rights of substance in the organisation of
production and distribution. The most distinctive demands of this type
are exhibited in calls for 'the right to work' and in the 'industrial
democracy' movement. Such demands are also very much a part of the
commitment of the left to ideas of 'distributive justice' to be discussed below.

The civil liberties politics of the left may also be informed by
another tradition. The Leninist theory of monopoly capitalism insists
that one of the significant features of this final stage of capitalism
is that it marks the abandonment of bourgeois democracy. 'The political
superstructure of this new economy, of monopoly capitalism (imperialism
is monopoly capitalism) is the change *from* democracy *to* political reaction.'[23] This theory of the trajectory of contemporary capitalism is
widely diffused beyond those who would either accept or recognise its
Leninist origin. It allows two rather divergent lines of political
practice. One accepts the inevitability of the anti-democratic direction
of modern capitalism and sees each new onslaught on civil liberties as
confirmation of an 'iron law' of increasing authoritarianism; in its
most extreme form this position sees the direction of modern capitalism
as the drift towards fascism. The second version has undergone considerable development in recent years and is embedded in the 'authoritarian
statism' theory advanced by both Poulantzas and Stuart Hall.[24] Without
discussing this theory fully it is necessary to note its implications
for the politics of civil liberties: it finds expression in a commitment
to 'the democratic road to socialism' which emphasises the importance
of strategies which seek to achieve a defence of formal civil liberties
alongside a transformative commitment to the development of popular
democratic practices with an emphasis upon new forms of direct or
participatory democracy.

The multiplicity of forms of the politics of civil liberties to be
found on the contemporary left reveals the general lack of sustained
attention to developing a coherent and comprehensive political strategy.

Often these different positions are found in various combinations or even more frequently different versions are invoked at separate stages in political argument. There is an inevitable sense of confusion which is the direct result of the failure on the part of the left to examine systematically the basis of its positions on questions of civil liberty. Beyond the inherent problems of such confusions is the more important consequence: the position on civil liberties is seen, both by the left itself and more importantly by the audience it addresses, to lack conviction and consistency and thus providing some confirmation to the criticism levelled by both liberals and conservatives that the left has an inadequate and unacceptable position on problems of civil liberties.

THE PROBLEM OF RIGHTS

The language of rights provides an organising framework in and through which political struggles are fought out. All political issues involve, usually quite directly, appeals to rights; whether it be the 'right to work' or 'the right to a fair profit', 'a woman's right to choose' or 'the right to life', politics and political demands invoke appeals to rights or to the analogous language of 'freedom'. So persistent is this appeal to rights that it makes little or no sense to dismiss this reality, as some on the left seek to do, by arguing that 'rights' are merely ideological masks disguising naked interests. Equally unhelpful is the tendency to counterpose collective to individual rights, the former being seen as politically progressive, the latter 'bourgeois'. What is problematic about individual rights is not that they may be secured by or on behalf of particular persons by resort to legal institutions. Indeed collective rights are no rights at all unless they can be secured by particular persons. All too often the espousal of collective rights, e.g. in defence of denial of rights in actual socialist states, is an actual denial of rights *as such*. Whilst there is scope for arguing about the political priority of competing rights, socialism is at risk of lapsing into authoritarianism if it constructively denies the importance of rights.[25]
    The left however exhibits a pervading ambivalence towards rights. On the one hand it frequently organises its campaigns and demands around the politics of rights; Tony Benn even appeals to 'the idea of inherent rights implanted by the very fact of human existence'.[26] But on the other hand it exhibits systematic doubt and in many cases hostility towards rights which are seen as inherently bourgeois categories riddled with individualism and subjectivism. Before considering the way in which the left deploys 'rights' in political argument, I want first to consider the question of the theoretical hostility to rights as such since this has important theoretical and political ramifications, not least in providing some measure of justification to the critique from the right that socialists are not and cannot be committed to rights and their defence.
    The theoretical objection to the discourse of rights has its roots in the extent to which rights are necessarily conceived as being given or assigned to 'legal subjects', individuals as citizens, who exercise their proprietorial rights in relations with other legal subjects. The Soviet jurist Pashukanis insists that the very concept of the legal subject as possessor of rights is a direct consequence of the existence

of commodity relations and provides the form for the resolution of conflicts between the parties to commodity relations. Even if Pashukanis
is not followed in equating rights with the very existence of capitalist
relations, objections to the language of rights remain. First, the concept of rights abstract from the socio-economic relations within which
people live and act, and in lifting them outside this reality it cloaks
them with property in a right which they may exercise, through the
institutions and procedures of law, against other individuals. Thus
'rights' are seen as inherently *abstract*. Second, rights invoke the
'legal subject', the atomised individual as citizen; thus rights are
seen, not only as abstract, but as individualised.[27] Finally, rights
either explicitly or implicitly refer to some view about the basic or
fundamental character of people which provides grounds for giving priority to certain classes of claims as constituting rights; in other words
the concept of rights is seen as invoking some ontological view of the
character of the species, where different ontological views clash they
express themselves by giving priority to different rights.[28] The
general objection then is that the idea of rights involves some reference to the essence or universal nature of people.

For some or all of the above reasons, the left has exhibited a certain caution or reluctance in making use of the appeal to rights. Now
the general power and persistence of the politics of rights has resulted
in political activists not being too concerned about the philosophical
problems of the slogans they use. But these intellectual concerns are
not without importance precisely because the left, especially in its
Marxist expressions, has generally been concerned with its theoretical
rigour and consistency.

I will explore one theoretical attempt to purge 'rights' of its
abstract, individualised and ontological features by considering Paul
Hirst's essay 'Law, Socialism and Rights'.[29] He recognises the political
importance of rights and seeks to avoid the simple equation of rights
within the bourgeois form of law (this is especially important to his
argument that it is essential to reject notions of the withering away of
law under socialism). Having considered the objections to the concept
of rights, he proposes an alternative conception which is purged of
these deficiencies. His alternative requires rights to be conceived as
'specific capacities sanctioned by laws ... they serve certain socially
determined policy objectives and interests ... they have no inherent
unity or a single point of reference',[30] and he suggests that 'the composition of legislation must be discussed on grounds that go beyond existing rules of law', thus seeking to go beyond a narrowly positivist view
of law[31] to include, for example, reference to extra-legal considerations of the policy objectives embedded in statutes.

The general formulation proposed by Paul Hirst is a view that insists
that rights have no autonomous existence, they are created by legislation or law-making activity. Without entering too fully into the controversies of jurisprudence, it must be recognised that this position is
open to major objection. Hirst's definition of rights as the creation
of legislation requires us to accept that it is the legislature that
determines what rights to create or to remove. Consider the following
examples: (i) the government, in the wake of hostility to street demonstrations, proposes legislation banning all demonstrations and this is
passed by the legislature; (ii) a future parliament passes legislation,
which in pursuit of a more egalitarian education removes the right of

parents to exercise any choice in the school their children will attend.
Forget whether we approve or disapprove of either piece of legislation,
can we say that the extinction of the 'right' in question will prevent
political action in favour of 'the right to demonstrate' or 'parents
right to choice'. To insist, as Hirst does, that the only rights that
can be said to exist are those present in current legislation is to view
rights as being in the gift of the current political majority in the
legislature. Yet the political reality is that rights are not coterminous with the content of legislation. The 'right to demonstrate' or 'the
right to choice' will in an important sense be more active and powerful
in the act of their repeal; it is a hostage to authoritarianism to insist that the legislative act can by itself extinguish the right in question. This should be particularly problematic for Hirst given his in-
sistance, with which I concur, on the necessity of rights of opposition,
criticism, etc., in socialist societies. The extinction of such rights
through the practices of legal institutions in socialist states does not
extinguish these 'rights'; rather it makes more essential, as he himself
argues, that the necessary institutions able to defend these rights and
to restrict their violation be created within a socialist state with
democratic aspirations.[32]

Hirst's attempt to tighten the definition of rights and to avoid the
pitfalls of ontology and abstractness fail because of the inherent statism of the positivist position which he adopts. His conclusion largely
negates the purpose of his own discussion, to take rights seriously in
the context of a stress on the concreteness of law as an 'instance of
regulation' with respect to which definite struggles for and against
particular policy objectives occur; in stressing the concreteness of
legal regulation he ends by reducing law to the technical content of
legal rules and procedures.

In developing a theory of rights it is necessary to make use of a
concept of rights which explicitly spans both their legal form, as
specifically created powers and capacities assigned to legal agents, and
their character as expressions of particular social policy objectives.
Thus we can distinguish between 'legal rights' and 'socio-political
rights', but while insisting that this distinction embodies a continuity
rather than a stark legal/non-legal boundary. Thus 'legal rights' designate not only the capacities created but also the policy objectives
embodied in legislative form. This allows us, with reference to any
particular area of law, to identify along a continuum legal capacities
which are capable of giving full or satisfactory effect to social policy
objectives. Using Hirst's own example of the Abortion Act 1967, we may
study the degree to which the legal capacity conferred on women to seek
an abortion is limited by the particular organisation and procedures of
medical services and of the legal statuses of doctors, charities, etc.,
and the relationship to an analysis of the policy objectives embodied
in the 1967 Act. This type of analysis makes it possible to analyse
areas of legislation where the capacities created are ineffective in
securing policy objectives (e.g. race relations legislation, equal pay
legislation etc.), but where the creation of the 'right' is significant
in lifting the policy objective to a higher level by virtue of its incorporation in legislation. Here we may note the significance of the role
played in the politics of legislation by the symbolic dimension and of
the role of secured social policy rights in effecting political mobilisation for continuing struggles for implementation.[33]

Outside the sphere of actual legal regulation 'social rights' express social policy objectives and differentiate rights from mere claims, in that the appeal to rights facilitates the articulation of coherent grounds for the policy objective in terms of related socio-political conceptions. The existence of social rights is therefore not dependent on the content of legal provision; they are advanced as claims on the legal system and/or on other agencies of decision.

The use of notions of legal and social rights can embrace both the specific consequence of designated legal capacities and at the same time can include the socio-political dimension. It allows theoretically important distinctions to be made whilst at the same time facilitating the expression of popular conceptions of rights. The left can and must abandon its ambivalence towards rights; they are a field of engagement between alternative social policies and political objectives, and are at the same time important sources of mobilisation and for securing political advances (and defeats of course!).

THE POLITICS OF JUSTICE

The rhetoric of justice plays an important part in political struggles. Contending political forces articulate and justify their actions through appeals to justice and this in turn contributes to their capacity for political mobilisation. The contemporary left exhibits an ambivalence towards justice, which needs to be explored. The right exhibits no such inhibitions or self-doubts and it has tended to secure a *de facto* monopoly of the banner of justice which has further reinforced the equivocal response of the left. I advocate a strategy which seeks to wrest from the right political slogans with important mobilising capacity by breathing new substance and life into them, and integrating their present application with the political goals of socialism.

The hesitancy of the left towards justice has a number of dimensions. The first has its roots in the opposition of Marxism to any theory founded on the primacy of a moral doctrine, whether it be justice or any other ideological category.[34]

This tradition has had lasting reverberations in producing not an absence of political references to justice, but their use only at the most general and rhetorical level. The most characteristic form of this invocation of 'justice' is as a condemnation of capitalist society as 'unjust' and the sketching out of the possibility of the essential justice of future socialist society. The experience of 'actual socialism' has in most sections of the left diminished the unproblematic juxtapositioning of the contrast between capitalism and socialism as that between injustice and justice. Rather the general thrust of argumentation tends frequently to seek other forms of expressing the opposition between capitalism and socialism. This caution is further reinforced by the long historical association of 'justice' with liberal individualist theories to such an extent that the term has often become synonymous with this variant in liberal political and legal philosophy.

Before considering left interventions in discussion on justice and their political ramifications, some comments are necessary on the contemporary crisis of liberal theories of justice. At its centre lies an increasing disillusionment with a narrow identification of justice with 'procedural justice' or 'legal justice'. Procedural justice identifies the arena of justice as *internal* to legal systems and revolves around the primacy attached to the principle of 'treating like cases alike', and its consequent individualisation in the atomised environment of the legal action before a court. The heightened awareness of social inequality in all its diverse forms attacks the doctrine of 'treating all alike' at its philosophical and political achilles heel.

In the light of these debates, the recent adoption of the 'justice model'[35] by several progressive trends is of considerable interest. It reflects a widespread dissatisfaction with existing, reformist and rehabilitary approaches to punishment. In calling, as a consciously progressive demand, for the readoption of the classical view that the only basis for punishment is that the offender's act 'deserves' to be punished it is recognised that the reality of inequality poses a considerable difficulty. This difficulty concerns whether it can ever be just to punish the disadvantaged in an injust society. The force of this concern has tended to push the left towards an abstentionist position where it has been very close to opposition to punishment itself.[36] I argue that the left must recognise the necessity of punishment in liberal democracies marked by substantial injustice, precisely in order to make possible political and legal challenges to the specific forms of injustice which characterise capitalist society. The specific objects for legal regulation are, of course, subject to detailed political argument and debate. But a socialist approach must deploy the demand for justice and, in the process, transform the content of justice itself.

Aside from the general left ambivalence concerning justice, there have been present over a long period of time associated ideas which, in a variety of combinations and emphases, demarcate a distinctive social-democratic theory of justice. A central organising role is played by the objective of 'equality' which is seen, not in opposition to liberty, but as a prior condition.[37] This emphasis on equality is central to social-democratic conceptions of justice and it is substantially congruent with more radical versions of the liberal theory of justice, such as that presented by Ronald Dworkin.[38] The focus on equality avoids a direct commitment to a levelling egalitarianism; egalitarian objectives identified as the realisation of social justice are seen as the cumulative result of the provision of equality of opportunity. These ideas are very closely linked to an insistence on the central role of the welfare state as operating in such a manner as to improve individual life chances freed of the vagaries inherent in the operation of the market economy. This conception of the role of the welfare state goes well beyond the much more restricted notion inherent in the tradition from the Poor Laws through to Beveridge where the objective is that of minimum provision. Concern with equality of opportunity focuses attention on such arenas as educational and health provision as positive arenas of compensatory activity. This thrust has, in the more recent period, been reinforced by the rise of wider fields of compensatory legislation, in particular concerning sex and race equality, and even more explicitly with the growth of positive discriminatory legislation (a trend which has been more important in the United States than in Britain).

There has also been a strong strand of utilitarian thought within the social democratic tradition of justice. The objective of the maximisation of human wellbeing, when the majority are in major respects disadvantaged, give rise to a concern with the aggregation of social benefit, that is with the sum total of benefits or advantage provided to the disadvantaged majority. Maximisation through aggregation reveals the inherent tension within utilitarian thought and politics between individualism and collectivism. Social democratic views of justice exhibit a range of positions within this tension; in some instances justice is conceived as the provision of universal individual rights and benefits; in others it is more collectivist, arguing for the interests of the majority, and placing a lower priority on individual rights. The question of justice should sharpen our awareness of the problems generated by majoritarian democracy; it is this problematic area which has given rise to the assault on 'elective despotism' from the right, but the problems posed in the relationship between majorities and minorities are central problems for all varieties of democratic roads to socialism.

A more radical strand to socialist politics of justice has been the demand for a 'popular justice', which would dispense with the exercise of justice from above by the state or by professionalised judiciary. Popular justice is concerned with direct participation in the processes of social control with a minimum degree of procedural formalism. There has been an interest in the forms of popular participation developed, for example, in China and Cuba,[39] and in the examination of the applicability of participatory politics of justice in pre-revolutionary conditions, for example, developments in Portugal after 1974.[40] The central concern has been with the potentialities of pre-figurative legal politics, that is with strategies designed to create some of the elements of the structures and practices of a socialist system of justice within the framework of capitalist society. Thompson's defence of the participatory character of the jury trial is in this sense pre-figurative since it implies a goal of an extended popular participation in legal processes; so also are calls for a strengthening and democratisation in lay participation in the magistrates courts in Britain.[41]

However, some problems concerning popular justice as pre-figurative politics should be considered. The first is that, as de Sousa Santos' discussion of Portugal shows, such developments are only possible because of the generalised crisis of the legal system, or more widely, what he calls 'the global situation of dual powerlessness'.[42] In stable capitalist democracies the degree of existing forms of popular participation is very limited (e.g. jury, lay magistrates, lay participation in tribunals, etc.) although these elements can, and indeed should, be defended. A more difficult task is posed in interventions in professionalised legal structures. The extent to which there is a general hostility to such structures and the opportunities they present, articulated most systematically by Bankowski and Mungham,[43] has inhibited serious discussion of transformative possibilities. Attention has been focussed, particularly through the law centres movement, on the provision of more effective legal services and representation *within* existing institutions. The general political conclusion must be that there are very limited opportunities for parallel popular justice, but that political attention needs to be focused on transforming and democratising strategies.[44]

One final comment on the topic of popular justice concerns the question of 'delegalisation'; it is assumed in much of the literature that the complexity of law, in both its procedural and substantive form, is an inherent barrier to popular participation. There has therefore been a general assumption at work which posits the necessity of simplification

and the introduction of broader criteria in the process of adjudication
which dismantle the barriers between legal, moral and political wrongs.
The more important question is whether the abandonment of distinctions
between legal, moral and political are in principle desirable. Such an
objective runs the risk of the reduction of all forms of social control
to political control. The practices of 'actual socialism' provide evidence of the dangerous consequences of that reduction. Retention of a
distinctive form of legal regulation clearly separated from other regulatory processes is necessary if formal sanctions are to be applied
since a degree of certainty, predictability, etc. seems to be an essential condition of civil liberty. Expansion of the arena of popular
participatory social control should be clearly separated from processes
of legal control, for example, through the express exclusion of most,
if not all, the range of sanctions associated with legal systems. The
range of fields of social control subject to legal regulation should be
restricted, but this should be distinguished from a more general 'delegalisation' of the whole field of social control.

It is in the context of the discussion of the trends within both
liberal and socialist traditions that the position adopted by E.P.
Thompson in his discussion of the rule of law is all the more startling.
At a time when the liberal theory of justice has become aware of the
limitation of legal (or procedural) justice and there has been a widespread shift to concern to the problems of social justice, we find
Thompson expressing commitment to the rule of law. It has not been
sufficiently widely recognised that his is a surprisingly narrow view
of the rule of law which equates it with adherence to procedural justice.
These comments are made not to deny Thompson's conclusion but to point
to the rather limited frame of reference which his intervention has
stamped upon the debate amongst socialists. This is reinforced by one
important feature of the civil liberties response which focuses its
concern primarily on what are perhaps most accurately identified as
'political liberties'. The positive feature of this in relation to the
politics of justice is that it provides a potentially powerful intervention with respect to the relations between state and individual. It is
a powerful alternative both to the statist tendencies of social democracy
discussed above, but also against the prevailing judicial ideology,
forcefully expressed by Hailsham, who poses the judiciary as the protective barrier between the leviathan of the modern state and the hapless
individual; thus reproducing the same passivity as the statism which it
opposes.

It seems clear that legal or procedural justice is not enough. The
real problem is to achieve an integration of the wider socialist concern
with social justice with the maintenance of legal justice. Justice is
necessarily concerned with how particular persons are treated; this is
equally true for questions of social justice since it is always concrete
individuals or organisations (and never classes as such) that are involved. The challenge for the socialist politics of justice is to
realise an integration of two rather separate and divorced traditions;
this integration cannot proceed on the basis of simple conflation
because at its root lies the importance of overcoming the contradiction
between individualism and collectivism.

CONCLUSION

This paper has examined a range of issues that are fundamental to the
development of a socialist politics of law and justice. It has not been
intended to arrive at specific policy suggestions on individual topics.
Rather a major object has been to argue for these issues to take their
proper place in the priorities of socialist politics. It has therefore
been essential to examine those elements in current socialist responses
which inhibit or prevent that development. It has also been a conscious
intention to bring together a number of strands discussed in more specialist and academic forums and to make the issues more accessible to a
wider audience. The central focus of the argument, the focus on 'the
politics of law', has been directed to advocating an interventionist
strategy. Such a strategy rejects both the view that law is a technical
field above and beyond politics and also the view that a general critique
of capitalism is a sufficient basis for arriving at socialist analysis
and socialist politics of law. In particular it has been important to
examine in some detail the political problems inherent in what has been
called the 'class state - class law' position. The argument is that the
prevalence of the unexamined political consequences constitutes a major
inhibition to the development of a meaningful socialist intervention in
this field. No such inhibition has affected the political right who
have been successful over a long period of time in achieving a virtual
monopoly of the politics of law and justice. Even the considerable
growth of the last decade of socialist and radical work in criminology
and the theory of law has in the main failed to realise a viable political position.
     The reasons for this failure are complex and result from the interweav-
ing of a wide range of positions which it is hoped to have gone some way
towards identifying. The substance of this critique of left positions
is threefold. The left has been widely influenced by an abstentionist
position which has led it not to give political priority to wide areas
of legal development which have played an important part in determining
the character of the regulative framework of modern capitalist democracies.
     Secondly, the left has often resorted to an oppositionism with funda-
mentally negative political results. A very important exemplification
of this opposition is to be seen in the reaction of the left to the
recent Royal Commission on Criminal Procedure. The left has been
entirely correct in identifying the fundamental weakness of the Commission's proposals in its failure to address itself adequately to the
question of 'safeguards' to the abuse of police powers and its preparedness to rely on internal police organisational and disciplinary procedures. Yet the left has engaged in this purely negative or oppositional
response which has its root in a very simple and obvious failure. None
of the active left commentators, whether it be the Labour Party or the
specialist bodies such as the NCCL or Legal Action Group (LAG) see it
as any part of their concern or responsibility to improve the effectiveness of policing. This failure ensures that their opponents are able
to effectively marginalise the validity of the criticism made. This
attitude towards policing is a classic example of the abstentionism of
the left; the effectiveness of policing is seen as someone else's problem, the left contents itself with problems of abuse of police powers,
civil liberties, etc. Such a position is strategically incorrect but

also tactically inept because not only does it marginalise the important
criticisms made but it also leaves uncontested the view promulgated by
the right and by the police themselves that an extension of police powers
of arrest, search, detention, etc. are central to improving the effectiveness of policing. The result is that opposition to the extension of
police powers is widely interpreted as opposition to effective policing.

The third general criticism of the left's positions is that they
generally *deflect* from the immediate political issues posed in the politics of law towards a general critique of capitalism and assumptions
that the development towards or the advent of socialism resolves the
problem. Popular concerns or anxieties are thus largely ignored and
real social problems are identified as indexes of the evils of capitalism and not as a field for current action.

The really difficult problem for socialists is developing a political
response which both addresses the immediate and pressing issue on the
political agenda whilst at the same time making the connection with its
contribution to kindling and mobilising a perspective that things could
be other than they are, that other forms of social organisation and
relations are both desirable and possible. There is no simple prescriptive solution but one essential condition is largely absent, namely an
awareness of this as the fundamental problem of socialist politics. Of
themselves neither immediate policies nor sustaining a vision of socialism are solutions to the question posed.

The requirements of an interventionist politics of law require certain
changes for the left which are likely to appear at first sight unpalat-
able; this unpalatability arises from the impossibility of an abstentionist or oppositionist position. Some of the more important examples have
been touched upon. For example, a left politics concerned with issues
of policing, sentencing and administration of punishment is an unavoidable necessity. The brief discussion of the justice model indicates that
although not without problems it offers one framework within which
socialist consideration of some of these issues can be developed, however much this may offend deeply embedded assumptions of hostility to
punishment itself.

I have suggested that the notion of social responsibility provides
a criterion for evaluation of legal policies which can assist in identifying both political objectives and in specifying a progressive legal
principles. But it also provides a basis for political mobilisation
for specific objectives. It does carry the explicit recognition that
it involves the struggle for social responsibility within capitalist
social relations, not as an objective that is to be postponed to the
future socialist society. It can be used not only to assess existing
legal regulation, but also to determine alternative fields of legal
regulation.

The principle of social responsibility provides also a potentially
coherent basis for intervention in the politics of policing. It provides a basis not only for assessment of existing policing practices
but also for mobilising forms of popular and community participation in
the broad field of social control and regulation. It may be that an
alternative extra-institutional popular justice or direct community
self-policing is not a political possibility within institutionally
stable capitalist democracies. Yet it provides a basis for the development and mobilisation around the content and direction of policing.
In so doing it provides the basis for a perspective of transformation

of both practices and institutions consistent with the requirements of pre-figurative politics.

Finally it has been a central strand of the argument that the extension of a socialist politics of law requires an entirely different and more rigorous approach to the question of rights and justice. We must contest the dismissal of these questions, which has been the main feature of the existing discussions. The widespread popular caution towards the left with respect to the content and form of its commitment to rights and to justice is not just a product of hostile anti-progressive propaganda. We must insist on the necessity of a politics of rights and justice which advances from the basis of existing bourgeois legality. This approach is certainly hostile to abolitionist attitudes on the left and argues that positions which express concern with 'transcending' bourgeois legality[45] are not in fact political, or for that matter theoretical, solutions. Individual and collective rights and justice cannot be counterposed, nor should socialism elevate collectivism at the expense of individual rights. Rather what is needed is a struggle to transform the content of rights and the terms in which interests are identified and given priority.

We require an *extension* of existing rights in the course of which the content of rights and their priority is transformed. This does not imply that all individuals will accept and approve this transformation and indeed the very need for law and legal regulation lies precisely in the capacity to secure enforcement. This transformation is never one of a change from a capitalist to a socialist content for such a manner of assessing the content of particular rights or forms of justice has no meaning; there is no inherent political litmus test of socialist or capitalist content of rights or justice.

There will be a protracted struggle to secure political and legal legitimacy through concrete forms of legal regulating during the transition from and extension of bourgeois legality. Such a struggle is a necessary constituent of a socialist politics of law and justice consistent with an overriding political commitment to a democratic road to socialism.

NOTES

1 The call to 'take seriously' is becoming a pronounced theme in both socialist and liberal politics. It extends from Dworkin's concern for 'taking rights seriously', Ronald Dworkin, *Taking Rights Seriously*, London, Duckworth, 1978, to renewed concern amongst socialists with problems of democracy and legality.
2 The classic treatment of the symbolic dimension is Gusfield's *Symbolic Crusade*, Urbana, University of Illinois Press, 1966, while Sheingold in *The Politics of Rights*, New Haven, Yale University Press, 1974, attributes primacy to the mobilising potential of legal rights.
3 See A. Skillen, *Ruling Illusions*, Hassocks, Harvester Press, 1977.
4 Much of the recent debate has been given a particular inflection as a result of the enthusiastic rediscovery of the writings of the early Soviet legal theorist Pashukanis. Pashukanis' writings are to be found in P. Beirne and R. Sharlet, *Pashukanis: Selected Writings on Marxism and Law*, London, Academic Press. For discussion of

Pashukanis see papers by Bob Fine and Sol Picciotto in Fine *et al.*, *Capitalism and the Rule of Law*, London, Hutchinson, 1979, and by Paul Hirst, *On Law and Ideology*, London, Macmillan, 1979.

5   See in particular F. Hayek, *Law, Legislation and Liberty* (3 volumes), London, Routledge and Kegan Paul (1973, 1976 and 1979), and also Iredell Jenkins, *Social Order and the Limits of Law*, Princeton, Princeton University Press, 1980.

6   These processes have been much focused upon in the literature of deviancy theory and of media studies as analyses embodying and expanding on the title of Stan Cohen's book *Folk Devils and Moral Panics*, London, Paladin, 1973.

7   The National Council for Civil Liberties (NCCL) has a long tradition and or more recent origin is the Legal Action Group (LAG) and of State Research. A much more recent trend has been the appearance of a number of left studies which take very seriously the politics of law: E.P. Thompson's *Whigs and Hunters*, London, Penguin, 1975; 'Introduction' to J. Friedman, *Review of Security and the State*, State Research, London 1978 and *Writings by Candlelight*, London, Merlin, 1980; Stuart Hall *et al.*, *Policing the Crisis*, London, Macmillan, 1978; Jock Young, 'Left Idealism, Reformism and Beyond', in B. Fine *et al* (eds.), *Capitalism and the Rule of Law*, London, Hutchinson, 1979; and Frank Burton, 'Questions of Juvenile Justice' and Mike Collison, 'Questions of Violence in Party Political Criminology', both in P. Carlen and M. Collison (eds.), *Radical Issues in Criminology*, Oxford, Martin Robertson, 1980.

8   The multiplicity of elements I perceive in left responses may result from lack of sufficient detailed scrutiny of the press and publications of the left; here is a field in much need of more detailed research to examine what I am conscious is lacking in my discussion, that is a sense of historical change or development in positions taken up by the left.

9   It is to make this general point about the dangers of deductions from general theory that recent Marxist literature frequently invokes Lenin's definition of Marxism as 'the concrete analysis of concrete conditions'. Lenin, 'Kommunismus', *Collected Works*, Vol. 31, p.166.

10 Marx, 'Communist Manifesto', *Marx-Engels Selected Works*, Vol.I p.49.

11 A sophisticated version of this 'dry run' theory is advanced strenuously despite rather limited evidence in R. Baldwin and R. Kinsey, 'Behind the Politics of Police Powers', 7 *British Journal of Law and Society*, 242-65, 1980.

12 See Jock Young's attack on Marxist espousal of Anatole France's dictum in 'Left Idealism, Reformism and Beyond', in B. Fine (ed.) *Capitalism and the Rule of Law*, London, Hutchinson, 1979.

13 Significantly this thesis still underlies much of the official criminology of Eastern Europe.

14 Taylor, Walton and Young, *The New Criminology*, London, Routledge and Kegan Paul, 1973, p.252.

15 See Andrew Scull, *Decarceration*, New Jersey, Prentice-Hall, 1977, for an attempt to establish a critique of the movement away from imprisonment in terms of the imperatives of capitalist economic and political requirements.

16 There has been sharp internal controversy within the NCCL over the demand for bans on marches and meetings of far right organisations.

17 See on the 'costs' of the crimes of the powerful Frank Pierce, *Crimes of the Powerful*, London, Pluto, 1976.
18 Herman and Julie Schwendinger, 'Defenders of Order or Guardians of Human Rights?' in Taylor, Walton & Young, *Critical Criminology*, *op.cit.* make precisely such a case for the criminalisation of capitalism itself and come very close to the legitimation of 'normal crime'. See in particular page 135.
19 E.P. Thompson, 'The Secret State' in *Writings by Candlelight*, London, Merlin, 1980, p.165.
20 *ibid.*, p.169. It should perhaps be pointed out that, whilst it in no sense invalidates Thompson's conclusions, the historical origins of the jury lie not in a democratic inspiration, however much it may have become suffused with that tradition, but in the system of collective criminal responsibility which the Norman monarchs and barons imposed upon an obdurate and resentful populace.
21 Tony Benn, 'Democracy and Human Rights', London, Haldane Society, p.3.
22 *ibid.*, p.13.
23 Lenin, 'A Caricature of Marxism', *Collected Works*, Vol.23, p.43.
24 See Poulantzas, *State, Power, Socialism*, London, New Left Books, 1978, in particular Part IV; Stuart Hall *et al*, *Policing the Crisis*, see note 7.
25 The importance of 'rights' in political mobilisation is stressed in a valuable study by Stuart Scheingold (see note 2). He argues that mobilisation remains even though 'the myth of rights' has often resulted in an overestimation of the progressive capacity of legislation to secure specific rights.
26 Tony Benn, *op.cit.*, p.2.
27 Even when there is legal recognition of group or collective entities, and they are deemed to have rights, it is significant that the notion of 'legal personality' endows the collectivity with the attributes of the individual legal subject.
28 For example the controversy between Dworkin and Rawls as to whether 'liberty' or 'equality' is to be given priority as the basis of the theory of rights involves competing ontological views.
29 Paul Hirst, 'Law, Socialism and Rights', in Carlen, P. and Collison, M. (eds.), *Radical Issues in Criminology*, Oxford, Martin Robertson, 1980, pp.58-105.
30 Hirst, *ibid.*, p.104.
31 That is a position which defines law as being restricted to the rules laid out in the existing legislation (whether formulated by parliament or the judiciary); in its simplest form, the law is the rules laid down by the lawmakers.
32 My argument against the positivist definition of rights is consistent with the position argued with great vigour in the name of radical liberalism by Ronald Dworkin, *Taking Rights Seriously*. It is not necessary to apologise for invoking a liberal defence of 'rights against the state'. The real problem that follows is the nature and extent of the divergence between the concrete rights which liberals and socialists seek to promulgate.
33 See on symbolic dimension of legislation Gusfield, *Symbolic Crusade*, Illinois, University of Illinois Press, 1963; Carson, W. 'Symbolic and Instrumental Dimensions of Early Factory Legislation', in Hood, R. (ed.), *Crime, Criminology and Social Policy*, London, Heinemann, 1974; and comments on Scheingold above, note 25.

34 The issues touched on here are complex both with respect to the
    interpretation of Marx's text and their intellectual location; for
    a useful discussion of Marx's treatment of 'justice and its implica-
    tions' from a number of contrasting positions see M. Cohen *et al*
    (eds.) *Marx, Justice and History*, Princeton, Princeton UP, 1980.
35 See, in particular, A. Von Hirsch, *Doing Justice: The Choice of
    Punishments*, New York, Hill & Wang, 1976 and American Friends
    Committee, *Struggle for Justice*, New York, Hill & Wang, 1971.
36 The worst excesses of the libertarian phase were particularly evident
    in 'the new criminology' and its offshoots subsequently labelled by
    Jock Young for example as 'left idealism' in 'Left Idealism, Reform-
    ism and Beyond', in B. Fine *et al* (eds.), *Capitalism and the Rule of
    Law*, London, Hutchinson, 1979.
37 John Rawls, *A Theory of Justice*, Oxford, Oxford UP, 1972.
38 R. Dworkin, *Taking Rights Seriously*, London, Duckworth, 1978, which
    presents the most systematic statement of the priority of 'equality'
    over 'liberty'.
39 See H. Pepinsky, 'The People v. the Principle of Legality in the
    People's Republic of China', *Journal of Criminal Justice* (1973);
    J. Berman, 'The Cuban Popular Tribunals', *New Columbia Review*(1969).
40 B. de Sousa Santos, 'Popular Justice, Dual Power and Socialist
    Strategy', in Fine *et al* (eds.), *Capitalism and the Rule of Law*.
41 R. Pearson, 'Popular Justice and the Lay Magistracy', in Z. Bankowski
    and G. Mungham, *Essays in Law and Society*, London, Routledge and
    Kegan Paul, 1980, pp.73-94.
42 B. de Sousa Santos, *op.cit.*, p.158.
43 Z. Bankowski and G. Mungham, *Images of Law*, London, Routledge and
    Kegan Paul, 1976.
44 It should be noted that these issues concerning legal apparatuses
    in important respects parallel the more developed area of concern
    with 'policing the police' and it may be that the issue posed of
    popular and political 'controls' on official apparatuses offers a
    point of entry for the consideration of transforming and democratis-
    ing legal institutions.
45 For example as expressed by Jock Young in his conclusion to 'Left-
    idealism, Reformism and Beyond', *op.cit.*, p.28.

Robert Reiner
The Politics of Police Powers

THE LEFT AND THE POLICE

Until relatively recently the Left has tended to neglect issues of crime,
civil liberties and policing. This is surprising in view of the centrality of the *state* in theoretical discussions of the reproduction of the
capitalist social order, and the prospects for socialism. The police,
as supposed guardians of the public against crime and defenders of the
status quo against subversion, figure crucially in even the minimalist
'watchman state' conceptualisations of conservatives. The organisation
of the police, the agency charged with the domestic monopoly of the
legitimate means of violence, the heart of the state's specific character,
ought to be an important political concern to the Left. That it has not
been so is probably due to the deforming consequences of two influential,
albeit contradictory, facets of socialist thinking about the state. The
first is a kind of folk-Leninism which sees the state machinery as so
irredeemably formed on a capitalist mould that it cannot be 'perfected'
but must be smashed and destroyed. The second, polar opposite view sees
the State as a mere *instrument* of the ruling class which only needs to
be taken over by a socialist revolution for it to function to different
ends. From either perspective there is little interest in specific
analyses of the workings of the police or any other concrete apparatus
of the State.

In the last three years, however, there has been a profound change in
the attitudes of the Left towards questions of 'law and order', and these
have become central concerns. The clearest indications of this are the
recent interventions of such assorted theorists as Stuart Hall[1] and Paul
Q. Hirst,[2] and somewhat earlier the path-breaking polemic by Edward
Thompson.[3] Feeding these more general statements has been a new stream
of radical journalism documenting the changing practices of the state
apparatuses, among which the excellent bi-monthly *State Research* bulletin
has been the most outstanding example.[4]

THE POLITICISATION OF THE POLICE

The stimulus for this upsurge of Left interest in the police has undoubtedly been a change in the material character of police forces in the last
15 years - their growing politicisation. This has taken two interrelated forms. First, the police have emerged as an overtly political
pressure group, lobbying for enhanced powers and changes in legal and
social policy which they would regard as making their law enforcement
job easier.[5] This has occurred at all levels of the police force, spear-
headed by the 'Marksist revolution' at Scotland Yard during the early
1970s. Robert Mark's new policy of cooperation with (selected) sections
of the media was part of a coherent package aimed to publicise internal
reforms as a shield from effective external control.[6] The starting
signal for the new wave of police punditry was Mark's notorious 1973
Dimbleby lecture on BBC TV, with its attacks on suspects' rights. Since
then several police chiefs, notably Manchester's James Anderton and
Mark's successor at Scotland Yard, David McNee, have become media super-
stars, as in a rather different way has Devon and Cornwall's John
Alderson, the thinking man's copper. More recently, the Association
of Chief Police Officers, the representative body for senior police,
has also adopted a more public profile, partly to prevent competitive
jostling for the limelight by individual police chiefs. The media have
gladly lent themselves to propagation of preaching by what Thompson has
called 'the Church of Scotland Yard as by Law Established'.[7]

THE POLICE AND ELECTORAL POLITICS

The grassroots of the police force, as organised in the Police Federation, have also become vocal advocates of police power and authoritarian
legal and social changes.[8] In 1975 they launched a 'law and order
campaign' aimed at reversing what they saw as an unwelcome liberalisa-
tion of society. This was shelved by the pressures of the 1976-77 pay
dispute, but revived in February 1978 specifically to influence the
1979 General Election, as Chairman Jim Jardine made clear in his speech
re-launching the campaign:
    We are anxious to make it a big election issue. We want the
    political parties to give serious and urgent thought to the problems
    of law and order and to say what they are going to do to stem the
    tide of lawlessness in their manifestoes [sic] ... We are strictly
    non-political and we will not become involved in campaigning on
    behalf of any party.
Belying this latter reassurance was the announcement later that month
that:
    The Conservatives ... decided to mount a Commons challenge to the
    Government on law and order... Recent studies have suggested
    that, together with immigration, law and order is the issue on
    which the Conservatives stand to make a big impact with the
    electorate.
    ('Tory Law and Order Challenge', *Daily Telegraph*, 23 February 1978)
Throughout the run-up to the May 1979 General Election there was to be
a similar symbiosis between the tone and content of public declarations
on 'law and order' by police spokesmen and Conservative politicians.
The Labour Party leadership chose to fall in line with the terms of

the debate set by the police-Tory axis. Parliamentary 'confrontations' on the 'law and order' issue between Merlyn Rees and Willie Whitelaw resembled rehearsals for 'Annie Get Your Gun' - 'Anything you can do, I can do better'. For example, in a Commons debate on 27 February 1978 on an Opposition motion to reduce the Home Secretary's salary because of his 'astonishingly complacent approach to the problem of serious crime', Mr Rees replied to Mr Whitelaw's salvoes with the assertion that 'the Opposition had a tendency whenever there was a sign of an election ... to tell the electorate that only they were concerned with law and order. That was unhelpful and untrue'. He then recounted his government's record of spending on the criminal justice system to refute Tory charges of neglect. There was no suggestion of any funda-mental divergence of policy.

Throughout 1978 and early 1979 there was a stream of similar much publicised declarations by police spokesmen (both chief constables and Federation representatives) and Tory politicians as part of what the media dubbed the 'great debate' on law and order. The high points which marked the increasingly explicit political involvement of the police occurred near to the election.

On 19 April 1979, the ex-Commissioner of the Metropolitan Police hit the headlines with his article comparing the relationship between the Labour Party and the trade union movement to 'the way the National Socialist German Workers' Party achieved unrestricted control of the German State'. He alleged that 'Socialism is changing the nature of our society irreversibly'. (For a full report of Mark's article see 'Mark's Broadside at Labour', *Daily Mail*, 19 April 1979, pp.1-2.) Mark's intervention met predictably bitter Labour Party and trade-union rebuttals. Prime Minister Jim Callaghan, for example, responded: 'We should be pretty careful before we allow policemen, however eminent their record, to dictate to us what the law should be.' (See reports of Labour Party reaction in 'Drop it, Sir Robert', *Evening Standard*, 19 April 1979, p.1, and 'Jim Puts in the Jackboot', *Evening News*, 19 April 1979, p.1.) The Conservative response was essentially to support the substance but deprecate the 'extremist' tone of Sir Robert's remarks. Willie Whitelaw, for example, said Sir Robert 'exaggerates some of the points against the Labour Party'. The Conservative-supporting newspaper the *Daily Mail* similarly stated: 'The *Daily Mail*, while respecting his integrity and conviction, feels he is overstating his case' (19 April 1979, p.6). This did not deter them from giving 'The gospel according to Sir Robert Mark' (as they called it) maximum publicity.

The most significant police intervention of all came on 20 April (less than two weeks before the 3 May election), when the Police Federation placed a long advertisement in most of the national press. Headed in bold type 'LAW AND ORDER', it was 'an open letter to all General Election candidates from the Police Federations of the United Kingdom'. It told the candidate:

> We wish to place before you policies formulated by the elected
> representatives of those who, in the course of their daily duty,
> face the crime and violence which has become endemic in our
> society. As a prospective Member of Parliament you will no
> doubt encounter questions concerning the role of our police
> forces and debate matters which involve the liberty and
> security of our fellow citizens. We feel sure that all who

responsibly aspire to represent others by election to Parliament
will be seriously concerned with the intolerable growth of
serious crime.
The advertisement then quoted some 'Facts which Speak for Themselves',
documenting a five-fold increase since the War in recorded crime, and
the present extent of violent crime, juvenile offences and assaults
against the police. Not content to let these facts speak for themselves,
the Federation drew the conclusion: 'Is this remarkable when the average
cost of police services is 38½p per week per head of the population,
compared to £2.69 for education and £2.15 for defence?' The Federation's
credo and solutions were then outlined:

> We Believe - There is no excuse for crime. Our laws and courts
> must reflect that concept. Crimes of violence must be met with
> the severest penalties. The powers of Juvenile Courts must be
> restored to allow them to determine the appropriate punishment
> for offenders. Sufficient secure accommodation must be provided
> for those sentenced to detention. It is the duty of Government
> and politicians to uphold the rule of law and to support the
> police in their efforts to apply it. The best insurance against
> crime is the existence of a properly manned, well equipped,
> trained and efficient police service. Since 1975 the Police
> Federations have been conducting a campaign to draw attention
> to these crucial questions. We do urge you to give the deepest
> consideration to our views and to lend support to our proposals.

The similarity between police and Conservative public pronouncements
was underlined when, four days after the Federation advertisement, Willie
Whitelaw outlined a six-point plan to tackle the problems of law and
order ('Tories' law and order pledge', *Guardian*, 25 April 1979). These
matched all the points in the Police Federation credo, promising tougher
action against 'violent young thugs', increasing the powers of magistrates
to sentence juveniles to detention and providing more secure accommodation
facilities to allow this, castigating Labour for not supporting the police
and the rule of law, and promising to implement 'at the earliest opportunity' the full police pay award which had been 'phased and delayed' by
Labour. Despite the clear way in which the public pronouncements of
police officers and Conservative politicians lent support to each other,
the Police Federation claimed that it was not involved in party politics.
Chairman Jardine maintained that the £21,000 series of advertisements had
not been intended to sway voters in the election ('Police "not out to sway
voters", *Guardian*, 21 April 1979). If so, one wonders why this large
expenditure was indulged in.
The advertisement did pay handsome dividends, however, when on the
first working day after the Conservative election victory (9 May) Police
Federation representatives were summoned with urgency to Downing Street
to be told that the new government would redeem their pledge to give the
police their full pay increase (an extra 20%) immediately without phasing.
Three months later, the fruits of the commitment to maintain the real
value of police pay in accordance with the Edmund-Davies Committee
recommendations were realised when a further 13½% was awarded, making
the police a most attractive occupation in financial terms. 'A new
agency for helping university graduates find jobs concluded last year
that police work was the best-paid job a university graduate could take'
('Our blue chip boys', *Guardian*, 10 May 1979). Although not totally
exempt from the effects of the Conservative government's swingeing public

expenditure cuts, the police received clear 'special case' treatment in
the protection of their pay and manpower position. It is no wonder that
the first post-election issue of *Police* (the Federation magazine) carried
a cover cartoon depicting Willie Whitelaw in the guise of the traditional
British Bobby 'Old Bill' singing:

I'll not hesitate to introduce the right Law

To stamp out crime and get true justice done;

And I'll see to it that - sure as my name's Whitelaw -

The Policeman's lot is made a happy one.

As if to symbolise the amity between the police and the new Conservative government, in July the Federation broke with past tradition (which
had been that their Parliamentary Adviser was drawn from the Opposition
party), and reappointed Eldon Griffiths, a Conservative MP noted for
abrasive speeches on 'law and order'. They justified this by,

his very close links to the Federation, his vast experience, and

his commitment to the policies which the Police Federation has

been putting forward on law and order... The Government's mandate

includes several major reforms which coincide with our policies

and no one in the House would be better qualified to put forward

our views.

There was some concern within the Federation that it thus 'appears to
have nailed its flag for all to see to the Conservative Party mast', but
the leadership defended its decision which was probably popular with most
members who do not support Labour.[9] It is a widespread belief among
policemen that they are better served by Tory than by Labour governments,
which reinforces their ideological conservatism.[10] There is, however, no
convincing evidence that in the past the Labour Party has provided less
generously for 'law and order' than the Conservatives.[11]

THE POLITICS OF POLICE WORK

The other aspect of police politicisation is the more overtly political
character of much police work in the last decade. This is manifested in
three interrelated areas: public order, pre-emptive policing and surveillance, and the increasingly acerbic relationship between police and blacks.

1 Police and public order

During the 1970s the preparedness of the police to cope with public order
situations has been both expanded and refined.[12] Without any public
discussion or debate, internal changes within all police forces have
produced *de facto* 'third forces', specially trained and readily mobilisable to cope with riots and other crowd-control problems. The Metropolitan Special Patrol Group (SPG), originally formed in 1965 as a mobile
reserve, has clearly developed a para-military role in dealing with
public order, as well as terrorism. Most provincial forces now have
similar units (usually with different names) all of whom are specially
trained in riot control, use of firearms and sometimes CS gas. Since
1974 most forces have also formed Police Support Units (PSU) to help in
controlling crowds, strikes, and demonstrations. These comprise men
specially trained for public order duties, including the use of shields,
but normally engaged in ordinary policing at local level. However, they
are readily mobilisable to deal with problems arising outside their own

force under mutual aid arrangements. In addition to the SPGs and PSUs,
many other ordinary police officers now receive riot training. The
intensity of this is suggested by the plea at the 1978 Police Federation
Annual Conference that training be made less realistic because of an un-
acceptably high level of injuries to police on courses. Although it is
true that the British police response to riots remains rather lower in
profile than most foreign forces, there has undoubtedly been a considerable stiffening of strategy. There are frequent rank-and-file calls for
other protective equipment to be added to the riot shields introduced in
1977, and sometimes arguments for offensive weapons too. The unpreced-
ented severity of the April 1980 Bristol and the April 1981 Brixton riots
will strengthen these police demands. In addition to these structural
changes in riot control tactics, ACPO and the Police Federation have
urged that there should be greater police powers to ban or control
political demonstrations, such as a requirement of advance notice
(periods suggested vary from 3 to 7 days) and an extension of powers to
include static meetings.[13] These police demands are clearly a major
influence on the Government's 'green paper' on public order published on
24 April 1980, and are likely to be adopted.

2   *Changes in routine policing*

The second aspect of the politicisation of police work is the radical
shift in the organisation and character of routine policing consequent
upon a set of interdependent changes since 1965, frequently referred to
as a 'police revolution'.[14] The main themes are centralisation, technological innovation and specialisation. The panda car driver, constantly
in contact with headquarters via personal radio, has replaced the foot-
patrolling bobby as the basis of the system.[15] Police forces have become
fewer, larger and less subject to local control.[16] Computers are now of
major importance in policing, for both 'command and control' and information processing.[17] The political consequences of these changes are twofold. First, the new pattern of 'fire-brigade policing' has augmented
rather than displaced the 'action perspective' which most sociologists
have discovered as the central value of police subcultures. The result
is a more abrasive quality in police-public encounters, lamented by
many police officers themselves, and leading to the frequently raised
nostalgic pleas to 'put the bobbies back on the beat'. Second, there
has been an emphasis on the formal gathering and routine central processing of information, as a part of a new *pre-emptive* interpretation of
preventive policing. This was built into the unit beat system from the
start with the central role given to the collator, the local officer
responsible for coordinating the low-level information provided by
patrolling and neighbourhood constables. As Duncan Campbell has demonstrated, this largely consists of hunches based on the political and
personal proclivities of individuals who arouse the idiosyncratic suspicions of local police, which when centralised and readily available
in computer systems acquire a more dangerous status as hard data.
    In this 'pre-emptive' view, any citizen, certainly any socially
    uncharacteristic citizen, is a target for suspicion and observa-
    tion. This quite explicit development in police planning has
    virtually put the whole of society under surveillance.[18]

3 *Police-black relations*

The third strand of the more overtly political character of policing is
the critical state of police-black relations. As Stuart Hall has summed
it up:

> Since the late 1960s, a sort of war of attrition has been going on
> between the police and black people in areas of high urban population;
> and, despite the consistent adverse publicity which this has attracted,
> those who know these communities at first hand will attest that it
> shows little sign of abating.[19]

Words sadly confirmed by subsequent events at Bristol and more recently
Brixton. The source of animosity to the police lies in the twin beliefs
that blacks are harassed by heavy policing - SPG blitzes on inner-city
areas with high black concentration, disproportionate stops and searches
and arrests on catch-all, resource charges like the notorious section 4
of the 1824 Vagrancy Act ('sus') - while at the same time the police are
less concerned to devote resources to investigating and preventing racialist attacks than to protecting the 'democratic rights' of racist marchers.
There certainly seems strong statistical evidence of a disproportionate
arrest rate for blacks, in particular for offences, like 'sus', where
there is, as a Home Office study put it, 'considerable scope for selective
perception by police of potential or actual criminals'.[20]

The police are obviously extremely sensitive to these charges, and
chief constables regularly point with pride to the doubtless sterling
work of their community relations officers, though the peripheral nature
of their activities is widely conceded. Firm evidence of racial discrimination in attitude as opposed to practice is harder to come by. When I
interviewed a sample of rank-and-file police in the division responsible
for St Paul's, Bristol, in 1973, no less than 35% quite spontaneously
cited racial problems as one element which had made their job more difficult.[21] The standard perception was one which combined a denial of prejudice with a clear preconception of blacks as inclined to crime and
hostile, often dangerous, to the police. The ambivalence was summed up
by one sergeant's remark that 'I don't exercise a colour bar, but I must
admit that if my daughter were to marry a coloured man, I would most
certainly object'. It has become commonplace to mitigate such statements
by the observation that they are widespread attitudes shared by the population at large, from which the police are drawn. As Stuart Hall has
commented trenchantly: 'This is an utterly cynical and quite unacceptable
proposition. The same thing could be said of the criminal population...
But no Chief Constable could afford to be so cavalier about the criminalisation of his own force.'[22] Simon Holdaway has argued by contrast that
'the *quality*, the techniques of policing blacks, are essentially the same
as those used to police the white population. The problem therefore is
that of normal policing, not one of police/race relations'.[23] Whether
or not there is any evidence of covert or intentional discrimination,
'normal policing', even if the absence of the over-determining effects
of police racism, would bear disproportionately on blacks given their
areas of residence and socio-economic circumstances.

THE ROYAL COMMISSION ON CRIMINAL PROCEDURE DEBATE

Given the already aroused interest of the Left in issues of 'law and order' due to the changes just outlined, the publication in January 1981 of the report of the Royal Commission on Criminal Procedure has acted as a stimulus to considerable debate.[24] The Commission had originally been announced to Parliament by James Callaghan on 23 June 1977, and began work in February 1978. Its establishment was the outcome of years of conflicting pressure concerning the vexed questions of criminal proced-ure. The growth of a police 'law and order' lobby urging restrictions on suspects' rights has already been described. Their views were reflected in the controversial 11th Report of the Criminal Law Revision Committee 1972, which had recommended the end of the 'right to silence' by suggesting that a court should be allowed to conclude that a suspect's silence in response to police questioning is indicative of guilt.[25] The strength of objections from the Bar Council and civil libertarians to these proposals led to their being shelved, but pressure from the police continued. On the other hand, civil liberties groups had for years been arguing that the rights of suspects (as encapsulated for example in the 'Judges' Rules', the non-statutory administrative directions concerning procedures for questioning and taking statements) were routinely violated.

The immediate trigger for the Commission's establishment was probably the publication in 1977 of Sir Henry Risher's report on the Confait case.[26] Fisher had found that in the Metropolitan Police several of the Judges' Rules were honoured more in the breach than in the observance; indeed the very existence of many of these rules (for example about suspects' rights to speak to a solicitor and the police duty to inform him of these rights) were unknown to many police officers, even some quite senior ones. Fisher suggested that the reform of the Rules should be conducted in the light of a broader enquiry - 'something like a royal commission' - to analyse criminal procedure. The hint was taken up shortly afterwards.

The Report was greeted with almost universal condemnation by the Left and civil liberties groups immediately upon publication. Indeed, the tone was set a week before its official appearance in a *New Statesman* article by Harriet Harman of the NCCL based upon a leaked copy of the Report.[27] Harman concluded that the Report constituted a 'triumph of the "law and order" lobby', and she supported the views of two dissident members of the Commission (inown to be Jack Jones and Rev. Wilfred Woods) who are referred to several times as dissenting from proposals which widened police powers. The essence of Harman's criticism was that 'while the new powers which the police are to receive are spelt out in uncompromis-ing detail, the nature of any compensating obligations remains extremely vague'. This line was echoed by, for example, Roy Hattersley as Labour Shadow Home Secretary,[28] the *Guardian*,[29] Robert Kilroy-Silk representing the civil liberties group of the Labour Party,[30] Ole Hansen and Tony Gifford of the Legal Action Group,[31] the Young Liberals,[32] and many other groups of Left or civil liberties lawyers.[33] The only voices identified with the Left and civil liberties groups who have broadly defended the Report are Martin Kettle,[34] Walter Merricks (a member of the Royal Commission as well as of NCCL and LAG[35]) and Michael Zander[36] (whose support of the Social Democrats undermines any association with the Left but who has a long record of research and activity in the civil liberties

field). In my view, despite the weight of opinion condemning the Report
out of hand, the latter approach is more fruitful - to broadly welcome
it while arguing for particular modifications. The Report raises issues
at three distinct levels: (a) its general theoretical framework; (b) the
specific proposals it makes; (c) the relationship of these to broader
questions of police organisation, legislative reform and social change.

THE ROYAL COMMISSION'S THEORETICAL FRAMEWORK

The theoretical framework of the Report does have serious inadequacies,
but these derive from the terms of reference given it, and the assumptions are simply stood on their head by much of the criticism. The
basic concept of the Report is that 'a fundamental balance' must be
struck between 'the rights of the individual in relation to the security
of the community'. This notion of a conflict between the 'communal'
interest in reducing crime and maintaining order on the one hand, and
the rights of individual suspects on the other, was built into the
Commission's terms of reference. These instructed it to have regard
'both to the interests of the community in bringing offenders to justice
and to the rights and liberties of persons suspected or accused of crime'.
The trouble with this formulation is that there is no evidence to support
the implication that reducing the rights of suspects would contribute to
the 'communal' interest in security from crime. (Quite apart from the
more abstract point that civil liberties are as much a 'communal' interest as security, and that the sharp individual/society dichotomy is
questionable).

Even if we concede the tenuous argument that conviction of criminals
is an important deterrent (because of its specific incapacitating or re-
habilitative effects on the offender and/or the general example to other
potential criminals) the law and order lobby's claims that the 'failure
rate' (i.e. acquittal rate) of criminal procedure is too high cannot be
sustained.[37] Most defendants accused of crime are convicted. In magistrates' courts over 90% of prosecutions result in conviction, while even
in Crown Courts 83% of all defendants (in 1978) were convicted (65%
after guilty pleas, 18% after being found guilty by the jury following
a not guilty plea). Nor is there any evidence that 'serious' or 'professional' criminals benefit to any significant extent in terms of being
acquitted more often. So much for the claim by the Chairman of the
Police Federation that if someone had drawn up the rules of criminal
procedure 'and sent the idea to the makers of Monopoly as a new board
game, Waddington's would have turned it down because one player, the
criminal, was bound to win every time'.[38] It seems inherently unlikely,
to say the least, that any marginal increases in conviction rates
brought about by changes in criminal procedure could have any effect
on overall rates of crime. (In any case the evidence does not suggest
that such *bêtes noirs* of the law and order brigade as the right to silence are significant factors in determining the acquittal rate, as few
suspects avail themselves of these rights.) Indeed, several studies of
police effectiveness suggest that (in the words of two members of the
Home Office Research Unit) 'the evidence is strong that the capability
of the police to affect levels of crime through deterrent strategies is
limited'.[39]

If the notion of a balance between communal interests and individual
rights cannot be sustained, it is nonetheless an accurate reflection of
the conflicting lobbies whose contradictory arguments generated the
Report. Although members of the Commission have denied vehemently that
considerations of political acceptability motivated their deliberations,
this is disingenuous. Explicit calculations of what different groups
would wear were not necessary, for the conflict between their viewpoints
was written into the Commission's terms of reference. But if the idea
that suspects' rights undermine the communal interest in law and order
cannot be maintained, much of the response of the Left has merely stood
this fallacy on its head (even if they have questioned the 'fundamental
balance' concept, as for example Harriet Harman does). Their arguments
imply that any extension of police power is necessarily disruptive of
the communal interest and would threaten the positive police-public
relations which are generally regarded as essential to law enforcement.
The Report is interpreted as increasing police power, and objected to
accordingly.

This response seems to me misguided in two ways. First, at the level
of principle, I would argue against regarding any extension of particular
police powers as necessarily undesirable. While the content and administration of criminal law in a class society reflects the interests of
the dominant class, at the same time it also protects the basic conditions of existence of individuals in all classes. As Thompson has
cogently argued:

> There are exalted theorists who suppose that cat's eyes are placed
> in the road by fairies, that missing persons materialise of their
> own accord, and that the police are nothing but an organ of the
> state with the function of repressing the proletariat... In any
> known society, some of the functions of the police are as necessary
> and legitimate as those of firemen and of ambulance-men; and these
> legitimate functions include not only helping old ladies across
> the road ... but enforcing the law and protecting citizens against
> offenders... A wholly indiscriminate attitude of 'bash the fuzz'
> is ... sentimental ... self-indulgent, and counter-productive.[40]

More specific to the recommendations of the Report, the elision from
an expansion of specific police *powers* to an overall increase in police
power must be questioned. It is clear that the Report recommends increases in specific police powers, but whether the package as a whole
involves a net increase in police power is debatable. It is both a
question of textual interpretation and how the proposals are concretely
implemented and work in practice. To clarify this we shall have to move
from the overall framework of the Report to its specific recommendations.

THE SPECIFIC PROPOSALS OF THE ROYAL COMMISSION

The Report examines two aspects of criminal procedure: (i) the investigation of offences; (ii) the prosecution of offenders. The second part of
the Report recommends the establishment of a new independent official,
'the Crown prosecutor', who would take all decisions on the conduct of
a case, after the initial police decision to institute proceedings.
This official would be appointed and supervised by a local 'police and
prosecution authority', an extension of the existing police authority,
subject to overall supervision nationally by either the Home Secretary

or the Attorney General. This removal of prosecutorial decisions from
the police has been generally welcomed by the civil libertarian critics
of the Report (as well as its supporters of course), and condemned by
the police.

I shall concentrate on the Report's first half, on the investigation
process, for it is these sections which have attracted the attacks of
civil libertarians (and a cautious welcome from the police). However,
the proposals in the second half do involve a new element of accountability for police decisions which should be borne in mind (although some
North American experience suggests that supposedly independent prosecutorial agencies can degenerate into mere rubber-stamping extensions of
the police bureaucracy).

In analysing the investigation process (broadly the powers of search,
arrest, detention and interrogation), the Commission operationalises its
concept of 'fundamental balance' into three specific criteria: are the
arrangements (i) fair and clear; (ii) open and accountable; (iii) workable and efficient? Whatever reservations there may be about the notion
of 'fundamental balance', it is hard to object to these more concrete
criteria of evaluation, although it is arguable that in some respects
the proposals do not succeed in meeting them.

In considering the proposals it is necessary to emphasise that they
are norms and suggested institutional arrangements, not concrete practices. They outline an *ideal*, a benchmark against which to judge actual
practices of policing, plus a set of 'safeguards', procedures for checking whether or not there is deviation from the standards. There is
clearly a problematic relationship between the law (whether the substantive laws the police are supposed to enforce or the procedural rules
governing legitimate means of doing so) and concrete police practice.
As Doreen McBarnet has argued, studies of the police have been 'dominated
by interactionist rather than structuralist sociology, the key to police
action is found in the informal, the situational and the subjective'.[41]
She provides a corrective to this by demonstrating how the legal rules
governing police powers tend to be so elastic that practices which viol-
ate idealised notions of the due process of law are nonetheless perfectly
in accord with the concrete rules. Thus attention must be paid to the
law itself as setting the parameters within which informal organisational
and interactional processes can operate. While this admonition to analyse
the rules of law themselves is valuable as a corrective to a purely situational and interactionist approach, the extent to which police behaviour
actually accords with the rules always remains problematic.

Critics of the Report have essentially operated with a double standard in approaching the package of police powers and safeguards proposed.
It is assumed that all police powers will be used to the hilt, and probably even exceeded, while the procedures for controlling police abuse
will remain merely words on paper. The interpretation of the Report as
involving a net increase in police power rests on that assumption. But
the activation of both formal powers and controls depends upon, first,
the structural and situational determinants of police action and, second,
the extent of mobilisation of civil libertarians to make a reality of
the proposed safeguards, as well as to press for wider legal and social
reforms which are quite in accord with the Report itself.

It is true that the Report recommends the extension of police powers
in several directions. These usually take one of two forms: (i) standardisation and rationalisation of confused and piecemeal existing powers.

An example is the replacement of the 'stop and search' powers derived
from a haphazard miscellany of individual statutes ranging from control
of firearms to protection of birds' eggs by a single power to stop a
person on 'reasonable suspicion' and search for stolen goods or other
things which are prohibited in a public place. (ii) Formalising police
practices in areas where the existing law is murky or largely inoperat-
ive, for example the dubious status of people 'helping the police with
their enquiries' who have not been charged.

At present the law requires that a person taken into custody for a
serious offence should be brought before a magistrates' court 'as soon
as practicable', and, for any other offence, within 24 hours. In theory
anyone detained by the police can apply for a writ of *habeas corpus* to
test the legality of his detention. In practice this right is seldom
invoked, and even more rarely upheld. Although the majority of suspects
are either released or charged fairly soon (75% within 6 hours according
to the Commission), a substantial proportion (20%) are kept for 24 hours,
and 5% longer than that. The Commission proposes that after 6 hours'
detention, if the suspect has not yet been charged, an officer unconnected
with the investigation and over the rank of inspector should have to be
satisfied that grounds for detention still exist. These grounds must
be formally recorded, and the suspect informed of them. After 24 hours'
detention a suspect must be either released or charged. In serious cases,
however (defined in para. 3.7, and a group which few would quarrel with
substantially), if the police want to prolong detention beyond 24 hours,
they must bring the suspect before a magistrates' court, sitting in private, but at which the suspect would be legally represented, to seek an
extension.

There is no doubt that most of the powers conferred on the police by
the Report sanction activities the police already engage in *sub rosa*.
This has attracted particular ire from critics, who seem to be postulating what might be called a law of inevitable increment: whatever powers
the police have they will exceed by a given margin. As Ole Hansen
puts it:

> If the police are breaking the law now, why trust them with wider
> powers without imposing adequate sanctions - if they exceed their
> present powers why should they not exceed wider powers?'[42]

This overlooks the extent to which current abuses may result partly
from the inconsistent or vague state of the law itself and its failure
to provide adequate powers for what are sometimes quite reasonable police
activities, which contributes to a more general contempt for the letter
of the law in police culture. But more crucially, it assumes that the
controls suggested by the Commission will necessarily be ineffectual so
that the rationalisation and formalisation of specific police powers
will involve a net gain in police power.

It is by no means clear that the Commission's package does involve an
overall extension of police power. As an illustration let us examine
its proposals on arrest powers. At present powers of arrest derive
from the common law (to deal with breaches of the peace), magistrates'
warrangs, and, most frequently, from section 2 of the Criminal Law Act
1967 which gives a police officer the power to arrest, without warrant,
anyone he reasonably suspects of committing an 'arrestable offence',
i.e. one carrying a potential penalty of 5 years' imprisonment or more.
The Commission proposes abandoning the distinction between arrestable
and non-arrestable offences (which anyway departs in many cases from

common-sense conceptions of seriousness), and substituting instead a 'necessity principle'. An arrest would only be legitimate if one or more of the following five 'necessity' criteria are met (otherwise the suspect should be brought to court by summons): the suspect refuses to identify himself so that a summons cannot be served; to prevent continuation or repetition of the offence; to protect the accused, or some other person or property; to secure, preserve or obtain evidence; the person is un-likely to appear in court. The majority of the Commission feel that the substitution of the 'necessity principle' for the 'arrestable offence' as the criterion for arrest would result in fewer arrests, although 'some Commissioners' favoured leaving the law as it is, believing that the proposals would lead to more arrests. As a matter of textual analy-sis, the proposals constitute something more complex than the extension of arrest powers which critics have implied. The police gain the power to arrest even for previously non-arrestable offences if the necessity criteria obtain, but they lose the power to arrest even for previously arrestable offences when the necessity criteria do not apply. The critics argue that the criteria are sufficiently elastic to be stretched to cover any case where the police, for whatever reason, wish to arrest someone. It should be emphasised that this is already true, given the battery of mainly common-law derived vague 'resource charges' such as breach of the peace.[43] If interpreted in line with the Report's intentions, the necessity criteria would not permit arrest in many instances where this now occurs.

THE PROBLEM OF SAFEGUARDS

Whether the proposals do work in practice as intended depends on the safe-guards suggested. Critics have argued that the safeguards rely primarily on internal police procedures. In fact the Commission does at several points argue that existing machinery for external accountability, such as HM Inspectors of Constabulary, the Complaints Board, local police authori-ties, and civil proceedings against police should be used more vigorously or have their powers extended. It does, however, regard (probably cor-rectly) these issues of external accountability as outside its terms of reference. The focus is on accountability within the police hierarchy and to the courts. But the innovations in internal police accountability are clearly geared to providing adequate data for the external machinery to work. The purpose of the innovations is to ensure three things which are essential for the machinery of independent accountability: (i) Police powers and suspects' rights must be clear, unambiguous and made known to suspects; (ii) Records should be made immediately of the reasons for any exercise of police powers, and these should be made available if their legality is in question; (iii) A specific senior officer should be per-sonally responsible for all serious matters such as welfare of suspects or prolongation of detention.

This tightening of internal police discipline is not supposed to be adequate by itself, but to supply the data for the possibility of external accountability. See, for example, what the Report says about 'stop and search' powers (paras. 3.24 - 3.28):

Clarification of powers will help but the principal safeguard must be found in the requirement for and stricter application of the criterion of reasonable suspicion.... The grounds for search

should be given to the person stopped and searched and they should
be recorded.... A copy of the record should be made available
within a reasonable period on request by the person who has been
searched. Supervising officers should have a specific duty to
collect and scrutinise figures of searches and results. They
should watch for signs that searches are being carried out randomly, arbitrarily or in a discriminatory way. And HM Inspectors
of Constabulary should give attention to this matter on their
annual inspections of each force. Numbers of stops and searches
should be contained in the chief constable's annual report,
which will make the broad application of the powers subject to
scrutiny by the police authority.... The record of the reasons
for the stop and search and the availability of a copy on request
will increase the effectiveness of controls after the event, since
they will be produced if the legality of the action is challenged,
or if civil proceedings or a complaint against the police ensue.
This lengthy citation demonstrates the interdependence of internal and
external controls which is the Report's intention, not reliance on
internal controls alone.

THE EXCLUSION OF EVIDENCE

The main specific failure of the Report in providing safeguards is,
according to critics, the rejection of an automatic exclusionary rule
(as obtains in the USA) whereby evidence obtained through improper
police behaviour cannot be presented in court. The Report rejects this
on its interpretation of the American experience. There are three main
reasons given: (a) The harmful effects on public confidence in the law
and on police morale when, in the words of Chief Justice Cardozo, 'the
criminal is to go free because the constable has blundered', and patently guilty people are released on minor procedural technicalities;
(b) the delays in trials due to interminable wrangles about admissibility of evidence; (c) research by Dallin Oaks concludes that the exclusionary rule is ineffective as a deterrent to police misconduct.[44]
The Report recommends that evidence gained through police 'violence,
threats of violence, torture or inhuman or degrading treatment' should
be automatically excluded as a mark of 'society's abhorrence of such
conduct'.
    In cases of less severe breaches of the rules governing police behavi-
our, 'the judge should point out to the jury or the magistrates be
advised of the dangers involved in acting upon a statement whose reliability can be affected by breach of the code' (paras. 4.132-3). But
the evidence should still be placed before the jury to assess. The
Commission's argument is far from convincing on this point. As G.R.
Baldwin pointed out in an important letter to the *Guardian*, the Commission
misinterpreted Oaks' evidence.[45] This refers mainly to hard evidence
obtained by illegal searches. In such instances the Commission's arguments are most cogent, and the case for the exclusionary rule weak. But
with regard to statements or confessions obtained through violations of
due process the issue is whether these have any evidential value whatsoever. Furthermore, Oaks' arguments imply that the exclusionary rule may
be effective as a deterrent against police violations of the code for
interrogation. There thus seems to be a strong case for automatic

exclusion of uncorroborated statements obtained in breach of the code of interrogation suggested by the Commission. This ought to be urged vigorously when and if legislation is proposed.

Perhaps the clearest indication of the overall potential of the Report, however, is an examination of a recent controversial case. On 9 March 1981 the *Guardian* published on its front page a disturbing report on how an innocent young black man, Errol Madden, had been forced by police pressure during interrogation to sign a confession to a crime he had not committed, the theft of two Dinky toys from a shop.[46] The case against Madden was dismissed by magistrates because he had been fortunate enough to keep a receipt establishing that he had purchased the cars. The *Guardian* report quoted Harriet Harman of the NCCL who argued that the case illustrated the inadequacies of the safeguards proposed by the Royal Commission, and the need for an exclusionary rule to reject uncorroborated statements obtained in violation of the interrogation code (a point I agree with).

However, a subsequent letter from Walter Merricks (on 13 March) showed how on the contrary the case could never have arisen under the new procedure suggested by the Commission: (a) The initial search was without good reason. Under the Report's recommendations the reason would have had to be recorded at once, and given to Madden, which may well have deterred the search in the first place; (b) Madden was not informed of his right to see a solicitor on arrival at the police station. Under the proposals he would have had to sign the custody sheet declaring he was waiving this right. In addition it recommends ways of ensuring adequate availability of solicitors through developing duty solicitors' schemes; (c) Under the proposals the confession itself would have to be tape-recorded; (d) Mr Madden had attended a school for the educationally subnormal, and the Commission recommends such especially vulnerable people should never be interviewed alone. Had he been, the Court would have had to look for corroborating evidence before accepting the statement as reliable; (e) The independent Crown prosecutors recommended by the Report might not have proceeded with the charge given all the dubious circumstances surrounding the 'confession'. Overall, the case illustrates how the safeguards recommended by the Report could be useful in protecting against abuses which are now possible. However, this would only be true if the proposals were implemented as the package they are intended to be. The danger to be averted is that Left opposition to the Report should not allow it to be prised apart, and the proposals rationalising police powers introduced without the safeguards. (This does not preclude detailed argument about, for example, broadening the exclusionary fule.)

THE WIDER CONTEXT OF THE ROYAL COMMISSION

It must be acknowledged that the scope of the Report is limited, given its terms of reference. The extent of danger presented by the increases in police powers suggested, and the effectiveness of the safeguards, depend partly upon changes in the wider context of criminal procedure. These can be classified under four broad heads: (a) changes in external police accountability; (b) changes in internal police organisation; (c) changes in substantive criminal law; (d) changes in society.

POLICE ACCOUNTABILITY

Conventional rhetoric makes much of the democratic character of the
British police, based on their supposed accountability to the public.
As Mark put it in his Dimbleby lecture:
> The fact that the British police are answerable to the law, that
> we act on behalf of the community and not under the mantle of
> government, makes us the least powerful, the most accountable
> and therefore the most acceptable police in the world.[47]

In practice the police have always tended to resist any concrete mechanisms of external control, and the claim amounts to little more than an
assertion of some peculiar, mystical bond and rapport between British
police and 'community'. The fact that in civil liability cases the
courts have declared that the police do not stand in a master-servant
relationship to police authorities has been used as the basis for the
development of the doctrine of police 'independence', the much broader
fiction that constables should be immune from external direction and
control in all law enforcement matters (an issue which has never been
directly tested in the courts).[48]

At present there are three main channels of external accountability
of the police. None is as effective as it could be, and current initiatives to strengthen them should be supported: (a) legal accountability;
(b) the independent Police Complaints Board; (c) local police authorities and the Home Secretary.

LEGAL ACCOUNTABILITY

The prime channel of accountability of police in Britain is supposed to
be 'the law'. In concrete terms, there are four ways in which the
courts may operate to regulat police conduct: (i) In serious complaints
alleging criminal misconduct the Director of Public Prosecutions may
recommend prosecution; (ii) civil action can be brought for damages in
cases of wrongful arrest, trespass, assault, etc; (ii) a writ of *habeas
corpus* can be sought for illegal detention; (iv) judges have discretion
to exclude evidence obtained in violation of due process of law. In
practice none of these operates satisfactorily.

The DPP has stated recently that it is the policy of his department
to demand stricter standards of evidence before recommending the prosecution of police officers than other suspects, because of the difficulty
of persuading juries not to give special credence to police testimony.[49]
The burden of proof in civil actions is the lesser standard of 'balance
of probabilities' but the problems of cost, time and access to lawyers
mean that such actions are rarely resorted to (and rarely successful).
The same is true of *habeas corpus*. Recent judicial decisions have
whittled away the control functions of judicial discretion to exclude
evidence. In Sang's case, the Law Lords decided that judges could not
exclude illegally obtained evidence other than confessions.[50] As Lord
Diplock put it: 'It is not part of the judge's function to exercise
disciplinary powers over the police or prosecution as respects the way
in which evidence to be used at the trial is obtained by them.' So much
for police accountability to law, at any rate given the present attitudes
of the judiciary.[51]

Some of the Royal Commission's recommendations are explicitly intended to give teeth to judicial control. First, the precise enumeration of suspects' rights and placing these on a statutory basis. Second, the requirement that the reasons for the exercise of any police powers must be recorded explicitly at the time, which should overcome some of the problems of evidence which occur when the testimonies of police and suspect clash without any independent corroboration.

THE POLICE COMPLAINTS BOARD

After many years of pressure to introduce an independent element into the investigation of complaints against the police, resisted by most police opinion, the 1976 Police Act established the Police Complaints Board. This receives a copy of the investigating officer's report on any complaint made under the procedures instituted by Section 49 of the 1964 Police Act, together with a memorandum stating whether the deputy Chief Constable has decided to bring disciplinary charges against the officer. The Board, after studying the papers, can recommend, and, if necessary, direct that disciplinary charges be brought.

The Board, a political compromise, was greeted with dismay by both the police (it prompted Mark's resignation) and civil libertarians. The latter deplored the impeccably establishment character of the Board's members, the lack of independent *investigation* powers, and the greater facilities for police officers to sue complainants for libel which was won by the Police Federation during the political wrangling preceding the Act. When the number of complaints reaching the Board fell far short of initial expectations, this was widely attributed by critics to lack of public confidence in the Board, and to the warning in the leaflet advising potential complainants that they might be sued by the police officer for defamation.[52] Suspicions were aroused also by the tiny number of cases where the Board recommended displinary proceedings.[53]

There are signs more recently, however, that the Board may become a more effective body. The 1980 Triennial Report of the Board which reviewed its progress set out several recommendations to improve its functioning. The most important suggested that in the crucial area of complaints alleging police assault (20% of the total, and the largest single category), its powers were severely limited. 'Assaults which are alleged to have occurred during arrest or while in custody are unlikely to be witnessed by civilians, and where there is a denial supported by one or more police colleagues and no corroborative evidence to support the allegation, neither criminal nor disciplinary action against a police officer is likely.'[54] To remedy this, the Board recommended the establishment of a national specialist team of investigating officers, recruited from all forces on 2-3 year secondment, who would look into allegations of assault resulting in serious injury. They would be responsible to an independent, experienced lawyer or judge. This proposal was examined by a Home Office working party, largely packed by police representatives, as well as the DPP who supported them. Although the party was chaired by Lord Plowden, the retiring chairman of the Complaints Board which had suggested the scheme, and it was supported by the Home Office, the idea was rejected.[55]

This police victory may prove pyrrhic. On 8 April 1981 no less respectable an organ than *The Times* leaked the findings of an unpublished
Home Office study on its front page. This showed that there were
serious defects in the system of investigating complaints of assault
by police, and that the Board's recommendations were eminently justified.
Despite the predictable chorus of police denial, pressure seems to be
mounting effectively for a more vigorous and independent scrutiny of
allegations of serious police misconduct.
     The Royal Commission on Criminal Procedure had argued strongly that
public confidence in its safeguards required the implementation of the
Police Complaints Board's proposals (para. 4.119). Its own recommendations for a more open system of recording police investigative decisions
were intended to facilitate subsequent scrutiny by the Board. The Royal
Commission's chairman, Sir Cyril Philips, has recently been appointed
chairman of the Complaints Board. He committed himself to a tougher
policy from the Board, declaring that 'the existing board has kept so
low a profile that it has climbed into a ditch'.[56] He criticised police
pressure on people to withdraw complaints, and promised to appoint
younger Board members, and representatives of ethnic minorities. Altogether the indications are that a strong body of influential opinion now
regards the effective independent investigation of serious complaints
against the police as a priority for public confidence in the system.

POLICE AUTHORITIES

For all the rhetoric about the democratic accountability of the British
police, they are virtually impervious to any control by elected political
bodies, and adamant in remaining so. In theory there is some tenuous
accountability in all forces to the police authority. In provincial
forces this consists of two-thirds elected councillors and one-third
local magistrates, in the Metropolitan Police the authority is the Home
Secretary. The Police Act of 1964 defines the general duty of the
police authority as being 'to secure the maintenance of an adequate and
efficient police force for the area' (section 4.1).
     The precise relationship, constitutionally and in practice, between
police authority, chief constable and Home Office is a complex and much
debated matter.[57] Although the 1964 Act purports to clarify and rationalise the situation, it fails to do so. Its statements are self-contra-
dictory or vague at the crucial points. The police authorities are
explicitly empowered to appoint the chief constable, to secure his
retirement (subject to the Home Secretary's agreement) 'in the interests
of efficiency', and to receive an Annual Report from the chief constable.
They may also ask the chief constable to submit further reports on
'matters connected with the policing of the area' (Section 12.2).
However, the chief constable can refuse to give such a report if he
deems it inappropriate, and the dispute is to be referred to the Home
Secretary as arbiter. Nor is the Act clearer about the possibility of
the police authority being able to instruct the chief constable on general policy concerning law enforcement in the area, as distinct from the
immediate, day-to-day direction and control of the force. Again in
cases of conflict it is for the Home Secretary to arbitrate.
     Altogether the Act, together with the organisational changes in
policing already discussed (amalgamation, technological advance,

professionalisation, growth of the police lobby), have strengthened the
power of the chief constable and the Home Office at the expense of the
local authority. The police authorities pay the piper (or more precisely
share policing costs 50:50 with central government) but don't call any
tunes. They determine the force's establishment and rank structure, and
appoint the chief constable (both subject to Home Office approval). But
the chief constable has sold responsibility for deployment of the force,
as well as for appointment, promotion and discipline. The authority can
dismiss the chief constable for good cause, but subject to Home Office
veto. The evidence is that police authorities do not even use the
limited powers envisaged by the 1964 Act, deferring normally to the
chief constable's supposed professional expertise.[58] In recent years,
on the rare occasions where conflict between police authority and chief
constable has arisen, this has been quashed in favour of the latter,
although in the 19th century there are numerous examples of Watch
Committees successfully exerting their political muscle over chief
constables.[59]

Recently there have been several initiatives from the Left campaigning for police authorities to exercise their dormant powers as well as
seeking an expansion of these. The police retort has been that policing
should be kept out of politics, a disingenuous plea in view of their own
politicisation in recent years. Jack Straw, Labour MP for Blackburn,
introduced an unsuccessful private member's Bill on police authorities
in November 1979. However, this may well be revived with greater success
in future, especially if there is a change in government, for there is
likely to be a commitment to expanding the police authorities' role in
the next Labour manifesto. Straw's Bill aimed to increase the influence
of police authorities (democratically elected by the local community,
removing the JP element) over general police policy issues (e.g. the
balance between panda cars and foot patrols, whether to have an SPG,
etc.) as distinct from day-to-day operational decisions, which would
remain the chief constable's prerogative (albeit with the authority
using more energetically its existing powers to call for after-the-event
reports). The authority would also have control of appointments, promotion and dismissal of ranks above superintendent (whose responsibilities
are now frequently equal to those of chief constables a decade ago).
As safeguards against corruption and local 'tyrannies of the majority',
the Bill proposes that a chief constable could delay any suggested
policy change for six months, and can appeal to the Home Secretary to
overrule the police authority.

Particular controversy has arisen over the Metropolitan Police, for
whom the authority is the Home Secretary, so that Londoners do not have
even the limited form of financial accountability available in the
provinces. Last year, the Labour-controlled Borough of Lewisham
threatened to withhold £5.5m from the Metropolitan Police, unless there
was greater accountability, a revolt which fizzled out when councillors
were informed that each could be made personally liable for up to
£147,000.[60] In March 1980 Jack Straw introduced another unsuccessful
Bill aiming to create a Greater London police authority to control a
reorganised Greater London police force, from which the national policing
functions now carried out by Scotland Yard would be hived off into a new
National Police Agency. Pending successful national legislation to
alter the constitutional position of the Metropolitan and other police
forces, the Labour Party's manifesto for the May GLC elections pledged

to establish 'a police committee to monitor the work of the police forces
as a prelude to it gaining power to control the police'. The Labour
Party is also committed by the manifesto to campaign for a more powerful
local police authority, as well as other police reforms such as disband-
ing the SPG, ending surveillance of political and trade union activists
and destroying non-crime related files, and giving the police the right
to unionise.

There are dangers for the Left in the cry for 'community control' of
police. Most obviously, the concept of community itself is misleading,
overlooking both questions of conflict within and between local areas.
However, the more limited goals of Straw's Bill avoid these problems to
the extent that the greater influence of elected authorities would be
balanced by the continued power of the chief constable and Home
Secretary, answerable to Parliament. But the idea is no panacea. The
contradictions of policing a society divided on lines of class, ethnic
group and gender will remain. The great advance is that policing
decisions would be recognised as sometimes involving political issues
and can be openly debated. Instead of being shrouded in the mystique
of 'professional expertise', police policy would have to be publically
justified and literally account-able. This much is clearly envisaged by
the Royal Commission on Criminal Procedure, even though it regards the
broader issue of accountability as beyond its purview. A more vigorous
utilisation by the police authority of its existing powers is clearly
pre-supposed by the argument that better police record-keeping on, for
example, stops and searches would enable authorities to monitor these
(Para. 3.26). A greater role for local authorities is also explicitly
envisaged in the discussion of the proposed police and prosecution
authorities with the role of supervising both police and prosecution
agancies, subject to central coordination (Paras. 6.48 - 6.60).

CHANGES IN INTERNAL POLICE ORGANISATION

Controlling police abuse by safeguards and after-the-event accountability, while of importance, can, like any strategy of deterrence, only
have a limited efficacy in the absence of changes in the basic character
of policing. This in turn depends on the internal structure of police
organisations, as well as wider legal and social reform.

The basic thrust of change in this century has made a mockery of one
of the central shibboleths of the English police, that they 'have never
been recognised either in law or by tradition, as a force distinct from
the general body of citizens'.[61] The police have become more 'professionalised', increasingly drawing on young recruits with no outside
work experience, and with ever greater reliance on specialisation and
technology. The problems in maintaining or restoring the still influential and desirable ideal of the policeman as 'citizen in uniform' is that
the contra-trend towards professionalisation has structural as well as
organisational roots. If the contradictions of society generate
increasing conflict and crime, then policing will involve characteristics of temperament, as well as skill and training, which are not universal. Of course, 'conflict' and 'crime' are not unproblematic concepts,
and traditional police responses may not always, or even frequently, be
appropriate. But how should situations like an embassy siege, a ghetto
riot or a hunt for a rapist or mass murderer be handled? There is of

course no general answer, and the fundamental social changes to which the Left would aspire may progressively erode the sources of some of these problems. But not tomorrow. What I am trying to indicate is that the Left has not really begun to think of how the hard problems of policing should be handled, beyond rather pious and long-term hopes that they will somehow be qualitatively transformed by socialism, a perspective which blocks any further discussion of what to press for now. A common assumption is that specialist, para-military groups like the SPG should simply be disbanded. Certainly there is an overwhelming case for not using such units in day-to-day policing, and probably not for most crowd control situations. But there are times where a highly trained and disciplined unit is necessary precisely to limit the extent of possible violence, although it is crucial that its activities be democratically accountable.

At the same time, there are many changes which are possible in routine policing to make the 'citizen in uniform' ideal more of a reality. Unionisation of the police would bring the rank-and-file into contact with the labour movement from which it is at present segregated by statute.[62] In many European countries the police unions, affiliated to the wider labour movement, are a progressive influence within the force. The difference from the English Police Federation is illustrated by their recent condemnation of the main French police union sending delegates to a London meeting of the Anti-Nazi League.[63] (American experience, however, suggests that independent police unions without labour affiliations may be an even more reactionary pressure group than the relatively shackled Police Federation.) During the pay dispute of 1977-78 there was a considerable upsurge of rank-and-file support for unionisation, but this fizzled out after the Edmund-Davies Committee in 1978 recommended very generous inflation-proof pay rises, with only token changes in representative machinery.[64] The most significant reform was the recommendation of facilities for Federation consultation on force policy, through creation of local Joint Negotiating and Consultative Committees (Para. 254) and attendance as observers at police authority meetings (Para. 247). In the absence of full unionisation, however, these may prove retrograde steps if they merely provide platforms for a narrow police view. Given the Edmund-Davies proposals, however, it is unlikely that there will be any significant rank-and-file support for unionisation in the foreseeable future.

There is certainly a strong case for attempting to recruit more black police to try and alleviate present tensions. American experience suggests that, while individual black officers vary in their performance (and some take on the white police culture with a vengeance), on the whole black officers have been a progressive force fighting racism within police departments.[65]

There is also a strong case for greater direct involvement of *all* citizens in policing. At present the only civilian input into operational policing is the volunteer Special Constabulary, who are by their very nature self-recruited from sections of the population with the most conservative conceptions of 'law and order'. There is no intrinsic reason why all citizens should not be expected to participate in routine policing of their areas as a regular communal duty. (National Service? Although it is imperative that it be seen as an *adult* not teenage, once-and-for-all duty). An obvious danger is the possibility of co-optation into police culture. But the considerable gain would be a

breaking-down of the barriers of secrecy surrounding the police station,
an essential requirement for any meaningful accountability, and for the
prevention of covert police violence and pressure being brought to bear
on suspects.

LEGAL AND SOCIAL CHANGE

It is a truism, but nonetheless important to emphasise, that no combination of organisational change and external accountability can eliminate
the pressures generating police abuse. This requires both reformulation
of substantive criminal law and broader movements towards a more just
and democratic society. It is, of course, beyond the scope of this
paper to suggest a complete agenda for social reform, but the limited
proposals outlined must be viewed in the context of such an aspiration.

    A more limited goal must be the decriminalisation of 'victimless' or
'consensual' crimes, such as drug offences and prostitution, long a
favourite target of liberal criminologists.[66] From a historical perspective such offences have always been the prime breeding ground for
police abuse, and criminalisation as a form of control of activities
between consenting participants generates a proliferation of derivative
major criminal enterprises.

    More broadly, however, even the successful implementation of a pro-
gramme of reform in policing which controlled abuses would at best
produce a criminal justice system satisfying a standard of formal
justice. To the extent that there remain class, ethnic, gender and
other social divisions, this would still reproduce the substantive
injustices of the wider society. Social justice cannot be achieved by
means of the criminal justice system alone.

NOTES

1   See for example his 1979 Cobden Trust Human Rights Day Lecture
    'Drifting Into A Law and Order Society', now available as a pamphlet
    from the Trust.
2   Most explicitly in his article 'Law, Socialism and Rights' in
    P. Carlen and M. Collison (eds.), *Radical Issues in Criminology*,
    Oxford, Martin Robertson, 1980.
3   Above all in 'The Secret State', his influential introduction to
    The Review of Security and the State Vol.1 (London, Julian Friedman,
    1978) and his *New Society* series 'The State of the Nation',
    8 November - 13 December 1979. These essays are all reprinted in
    Thompson's collection *Writing by Candlelight* (London, Merlin Press,
    1980).
4   Tony Bunyan, one of the State Research Collective, pioneered this
    approach with his invaluable *The History and Practice of the Political
    Police in Britain* (London, Julian Friedman, 1976 - 2nd. ed. Quartet
    Books, 1977). Other examples include Martin Kettle (of *New Society*),
    Duncan Campbell and Rob Rohrer (of the *New Statesman*), all of whom
    have published many excellent pieces of investigative journalism on
    the police and civil liberties. Peter Hain has also edited two use-
    ful journalistic appraisals of the police: *Policing the Police*, Vols.
    1 and 2, London, John Calder, 1979 and 1980.

5   This process is traced in detail in R. Reiner, 'Fuzzy Thoughts: The
    Police and Law and Order Politics', *Sociological Review*, May 1980,
    pp.377-413.
6   S. Chibnall, 'The Metropolitan Police and the News Media', in
    S. Holdaway (ed.), *The British Police*, London, Edward Arnold, 1979,
    pp.135-49, lucidly demonstrates the interdependent rationale of
    Mark's policies on corruption control, internal re-organisation,
    relations with the media, advocacy of reductions in suspects' rights
    and opposition to proposals for independent investigation of
    complaints against the police.
7   *Writing by Candlelight*, *op.cit.*, p.202.
8   The background to the Federation's campaign is outline in R. Reiner,
    The Blue-Coated Worker: A Sociological Study of Police Unionism,
    Cambridge, Cambridge University Press, 1978, pp.45-49 and Chapter 11.
9   See discussion in *Police*, July 1979, p.10, and September 1979, p.20.
10 R. Reiner, *The Blue-Coated Worker*, *op.cit.*, pp.60-62.
11 L. McDonald, *The Sociology of Law and Order*, London, Faber, 1976,
    Chapter 6, esp. pp.193-97.
12 The structural developments are pieced together in detail through
    painstaking detective work on the published annual reports of chief
    constables and Her Majesty's Inspectors of Constabulary in 'Policing
    the 80s: The Iron Fist', *State Research Bulletin No.19*, Aug-Sep 1980,
    pp.146-68. The police thinking behind these changes is discussed in
    R. Reiner, 'Forces of Disorder', *New Society*, 10 April 1980, pp.51-54;
    and M. Kettle, 'The Politics of Policing and the Policing of Politics'
    in P. Hain (ed.), *Policing the Police Vol.2*, *op.cit.*, pp.33-59.
13 See 'Police chiefs plan to restrict marches', *State Research No.17*,
    April-May 1980, pp.96-98; 'Tory public order plans', *State Research
    No.19*, Aug-Sept 1980, pp.145-46; 'Right to demonstrate under threat',
    State Research No.20, Oct-Nov 1980, pp.1-3.
14 This was the term used by the Police Federation itself in 1967 to
    welcome one aspect of these changes, the move from the foot-based,
    fixed-point beat to the motorised unit beat system. See R. Reiner,
    The Blue-Coated Worker, *op.cit.*, p.33 and pp.189-91. Peter Evans,
    Home Affairs correspondent of *The Times* used the term 'The Police
    Revolution' as the title of his 1974 book documenting the ongoing
    technological and organisational rationalisation of police forces.
15 The technological and formal organisational changes are, of course,
    filtered through the patrol sub-culture, which may lead to some
    frustration of the intended rationalisation and central control.
    See the example in R. Reiner, *The Blue-Coated Worker*, *op.cit.*,
    pp.191-92.
16 Most of the 125 separate forces in England and Wales examined by the
    1962 Royal Commission on the Police Report are now only divisions or
    sub-divisions under the command of a chief superintendent (or lower
    rank) within one of the 43 surviving mega-forces. Whatever the
    intentions of the 1964 Police Act, the civilian police authorities
    of these forces have little effective influence over them.
17 For a detailed examination of the political consequences of police
    computerisation see Duncan Campbell's excellent 'Society Under
    Surveillance' in P. Hain (ed.), *Policing the Police Vol.2*, *op.cit.*
18 *ibid.*, p.65.
19 S. Hall, 'Drifting Into A Law and Order Society', Cobden Trust Human
    Rights Day Lecture, 1979, p.13. These charges are amply documented

in 'Police Against Black People', Evidence submitted to the Royal
Commission on Criminal Procedure by The Institute of Race Relations,
and published as *Race and Class* Pamphlet No.6, 1979.

20 T. Rees, P. Stevens, D.F. Willis, 'Race, crime and arrests', *Home
Office Research Bulletin No.8*, 1979, p.12.

21 R. Reiner, *The Blue-Coated Worker*, *op.cit.*, pp.225-26.

22 S. Hall, 'Drifting Into A Law and Order Society', *op.cit.*, p.13.

23 S. Holdaway (ed.), *The British Police*, *op.cit.*, p.8.

24 Royal Commission on Criminal Procedure, *Report*, London, HMSO, 1981,
Cmnd. 8092.

25 Criminal Law Revision Committee, *Eleventh Report Evidence (General)*,
London, HMSO, 1972, Cmnd. 4991.

26 *The Confait Case. Report by the Hon. Sir Henry Fisher*, London, HMSO,
1977, HC 90.

27 H. Harman, 'Royal Commission Report', *New Statesman*, 2 January 1981,
pp.6-7.

28 'Police powers: Labour speaks out', *New Statesman*, 10 January 1981, p.2.

29 'Tilting the scale against innocence?', Editorial, 9 January 1981,
p.10.

30 'Proposals "take liberties with our freedom"', *Guardian*, 9 January
1981, p.4.

31 'Changes "will increase tension"', *Guardian*, 9 January 1981, p.4;
T. Gifford, 'Why the Commission's Report was a cop-out', *Guardian*
19 January 1981; *Legal Action Group Bulletin*, February 1981, pp.26-33.

32 J. Hughes, 'Towards 1984', *The Liberator*, March 1981, p.6.

33 'Lawyers denounce "Police Power" call', *Morning Star*, 9 January 1981,
p.1.

34 M. Kettle, 'A conflict of evidence', *New Society*, 1 January 1981,
pp.16-17, and 'Controlling the police', *New Society*, 8 January 1981,
pp.52-53.

35 W. Merricks, 'How we drew the thin blue line', *New Statesman*,
9 January 1981, pp.12-13.

36 M. Zander, 'Royal Commission: no grounds for suspicion', *Guardian*,
12 January 1981, p.7; 'The fears of the loudest critics seem exaggerated', *Guardian*, 28 January 1981, p.9. Malcolm Dean, the
Guardian's social policy correspondent, also defended the Report
in similar terms: 'The Commission that did its homework', 14 January
1981, p.9, all articles which go against the paper's initial critical
editorial response.

37 The studies rebutting this claim are usefully surveyed in M. Zander,
'What is the evidence on law and order?', *New Society*, 13 December
1979, pp.591-94.

38 Speech to 1979 Annual Conference, reported in *Police*, June 1979, p.12.

39 R.V.G. Clarke and J.M. Hough (eds.), *The Effectiveness of Policing*,
Farnborough, Gower, 1980, p.8.

40 E.P. Thompson, *Writing by Candlelight*, *op.cit.*, pp.174-75.

41 D.J. McBarnet, 'Arrest: The Legal Context of Policing' in S. Holdaway
(ed.), *The British Police*, *op.cit.*, p.25.

42 Letter to *New Society*, 22 January 1981, p.161.

43 See the examples in D.J. McBarnet, 'Arrest: The Legal Context of
Policing', *op.cit.*, p.33. The Report explicitly welcomes the Commons
Home Affairs Sub-Committee's recommendation that the most notorious
resource charge of all, 'sus', be repealed (Para. 3.88).

44 D.H. Oaks, 'Studying the Exclusionary Rule in Search and Seizure', *University of Chicago Law Review*, 1970.
45 11 February 1981, p.9.
46 'How the innocent can still "confess"', *Guardian*, 9 March 1981, p.1.
47 R. Mark, *Policing A Perplexed Society*, London, Allen and Unwin, 1977, p.56.
48 G. Marshall, *Police and Government*, London, Methuen, 1965, and 'Police Independence: A Note on its Origin, Nature and Limits', unpublished paper delivered at the 1981 Annual Conference of the Political Studies Association.
49 'DPP admits many guilty police go free', *Guardian*, 7 February 1981.
50 R.V. Sang, 1979, 3 Weekly Law Reports, p.263.
51 Judicial reluctance to review police conduct critically is documented more fully in N. Blake, *The Police, The Law and the People*, London, Haldane Society, 1980, Chapter 4.
52 For a critique of the Board see D. Humphry, 'The Complaints System' in P. Hain (ed.), *Policing the Police Vol.1, op.cit.*
53 In 1979 disciplinary proceedings were brought in only 127 of 7,365 cases processed by the Board. In only 18 of these did the Board challenge the police conclusions.
54 *Police Complaints Board Triennial Review Report 1980*, London, HMSO, p.13.
55 'Call for extra powers to pursue police complaints', and Editorial: 'A mouse on a loose leash', *Guardian*, 19 March 1981.
56 'Tougher system for police checks blocked', *Guardian*, 19 March 1981.
57 See the following works by G. Marshall: *Police and Government, op.cit.*; 'The Government of the Police Since 1964' in J. Alderson and P. Stead (eds.), *The Police We Deserve*, London, Wolfe, 1973; and 'Police Accountability Revisited' in D. Butler and A. Halsey (eds.), *Policy and Politics*, London, Macmillan, 1978, pp.51-65. H. Levenson, 'Democracy and the police', *Poly Law Review*, Spring 1981, pp.41-50, provides a useful general overview.
58 M. Brogden, 'A Police Authority: The Denial of Conflict', *Sociological Review*, 25:2, 1977, pp.325-49; M. Kettle, 'Quis custodiet ipsos custodes?',
59 M. Dean, 'Who watches the police?', *Guardian*, 28 January 1981, p.9; 'Merseyside Police: A Councillor Speaks Out', *State Research No.16*, February-March 1980, pp.58-60; 'S. Yorks: Police Criticised', *State Research No.18*, June-July 1980, pp.128-29.
60 'The Control of London's Police', *State Research No.17*, April-May 1980, pp.88-90; 'London: Bill Aims For Greater Accountability', *State Research No.18*, June-July 1980, pp.124-26; D. Clark, 'London's police: how can we police them?', *The Leveller*, 17 April 1981, pp.16-17.
61 The words of the *Report of the Royal Commission on Police Powers and Procedure 1929* (Cmnd. 3297), endorsed in 1962 by the *Final Report of the Royal Commission on the Police* (Cmnd. 1728), p.10.
62 The issue of police unionism is discussed more fully in R. Reiner, *The Blue-Coated Worker, op.cit.*, and 'Police, Class and Politics', *Marxism Today*, March 1978.
63 'Big row with French police on Anti-Nazis', *Daily Telegraph*, 2 April 1981, p.2.

64 *Committee of Inquiry on the Police*: Reports 1 and 2 on 'Negotiating
   Machinery and Pay', July 1978, Cmnd. 7283; Report 3 on 'The Structure
   and Role of Police Staff Associations', July 1979, Cmnd. 7633.
65 R. Reiner, 'Fuzzy Thoughts', *Sociological Review*, May 1980, pp.388-89.
66 See for example E.M. Schur, *Crimes Without Victims*, Englewood Cliffs,
   N.J., Prentice-Hall, 1965; and N. Morris and G. Hawkins, *The Honest
   Politician's Guide to Crime Control*, Chicago, University of Chicago
   Press, 1970, Chapter 1.

Phil Jones
Police Powers and Police Accountability: The Royal Commission on Criminal Procedure

That the report of the Royal Commission on Criminal Procedure (RCCP)
should prove controversial was hardly surprising. It was examining
fundamental issues: the balance, to paraphrase its own terms of reference, between the interests of the community in policing and the liberties of the individual. It was examining such issues in the context
of a conflict of views concerning contemporary policing: between those
who questioned the police handling of interrogations, their treatment
of suspects etc., and those who argued that the work of the police was
made increasingly difficult because of the restraints imposed by the
requirements of criminal procedure. Finally, it was examining such
issues at a time when questions of policing were increasingly at the
heart of the political arena. Popular anxiety at the level of crime
was manifestly growing, crime was increasingly registered as an index
of social disorganisation within the popular news media, attachment to
'law and order' politics had become a symbol of political virility for
sections of the Thatcherite right, and prominent police chiefs were
visibly campaigning for an increase in powers of draconian proportions.
Meanwhile calls to increase democratic accountability of the police
were increasingly forthcoming from the left.

A controversial report then was to be expected. Indeed, the Royal
Commission had in a sense been created as a site for the representation
and potential resolution of controversies within the arena of criminal
justice. Royal Commissions are to an extent an anachronism. They are
an institution which predate the emergence of policy analysis in the
Civil Service, the development of research within the Universities and
the growth of well organised, well-informed pressure groups. Nevertheless they are an institution which, on occasion, can function to canal-
ise the activities of pressure groups, focus and finance the work of
researchers, generate new analyses and, perhaps critically, they can
short-circuit the potentially fraught channels of communication between
departments, agencies and pressure groups.

Such a short-circuiting process the Home Office sorely needed. It
had long been concerned with the chaotic structure of criminal procedure
and with the endeavours of the police to justify illicit policing practices through reference to that chaotic structure. Events throughout the

1970s were, however, to demonstrate that reform would not be possible
through the usual mechanism of policy analysis, departmental deliberation, pressure group consultation and political compromise. Relations
between the Home Office, pressure groups and the police had become too
strained for that, as the furore generated around the Eleventh Report
of the Criminal Law Revision Committee revealed.

The report published in 1972 was a disaster. It was underpinned by
the concern to impel suspects to produce evidence and, accordingly, it
proposed to abolish suspects' rights to silence. It was disastrous
because this proposal took on a symbolic status, producing an opposition
that damned a report which deserved greater attention, it discredited a
relatively useful committee of respected lawyers, it unified the criminal
justice lobby, and it opened the stage to police campaigners typified by
Robert Mark. Mark was to use the Dimbleby Lecture in 1973 to lobby in
favour of greater autonomy and discretion for the police, an autonomy
which explicitly implied an erosion of suspects' rights, and he, and
other prominent chief constables, were to sustain their campaigns
throughout the 1970s.

These campaigns, however, coincided with demands from civil libertarians for more control over the police, which exacerbated the ever tense
relationship between the latter and sections of the criminal justice
lobby. Such campaigners were assisted by the exposure of widespread
corruption in the Metropolitan police, by a succession of celebrated
cases on wrongful identification that culminated in the Devlin Inquiry's
call for statutory safeguards for the suspect, by academic studies that
revealed the importance of confessions in plea-bargaining and, finally,
by the Fisher report on the Confait murder case. In this case three
youths, including a vulnerable mentally handicapped boy, were found
guilty of an offence which subsequent evidence revealed they could not
have committed. The Fisher Inquiry showed that the defendants had been
wrongly convicted on the basis of uncorroborated confessions extracted
in breach of the Judges' Rules and administrative directions to the police. After making detailed criticisms of the law relating to police
investigations and criminal prosecutions, the report suggested that a
Royal Commission be considered.[1]

If controversy, though, was built into the very structure of the
RCCP, the nature of the controversy that greeted its publication was
somewhat unusual.

The publication of the report was prefigured by a leak of its contents
in the *New Statesman*, accompanied by an analysis in which Harriet Harman,
legal officer of the NCCL, described the report as a 'victory for the
"law and order" lobby'. This was followed on the day of publication
with the adoption of oppositional postures by various groups within the
civil liberties wing of the criminal justice lobby: the Law Centres
Federation, the Haldane Society of Socialist Lawyers, the Legal Action
Group, and the NCCL all expressed critical misgivings. Their stance
appeared to take on added justification as Richard du Cann QC, chairman
of the Bar Council, expressed 'concern', saying that he had 'grave
reservations', and it was further legitimised as the police gave a
cautious welcome to the proposals.[2]

What was unusual, in this context, was the support given by writers
otherwise known for their support of civil libertarian positions.
Michael Zander, writing in the *Guardian*, described the report as a
'major step towards significantly better safeguards for the accused',

and he characterised the libertarian response as that of a 'knee-jerk
reaction'. Martin Kettle, Home Affairs correspondent of *New Society*,
wrote in a similar vein and described those who had written off the
report as 'fools'. For him the report provided 'the most authoritative
modern rejection of a whole series of existing police practices and
demands'. Meanwhile Walter Merricks, a Commission member, took the
relatively unusual step of writing a series of spirited defences of the
report, written as a long-standing NCCL member and Law Centre worker,
and explicitly concerned to take on the libertarian opposition.[3]

The controversy is of considerable interest. It provided the opportunity for a whole range of questions concerning contemporary policing to be
debated and strategic perspectives considered. Before examining the
issues raised by the report and in the subsequent debate it is necessary
to give a brief outline of the report's proposals.

The report's recommendations fall into four groups. It contains a
set of proposals that clarify, regularise, or extend police powers in
relation to search, arrest, detention and interrogation. It then provides, in relation to these powers, a set of safeguards. It is this
part of the report's proposals, which interconnects proposed powers with
suggested safeguards, that is often referred to as a package. It proposes the introduction of a Crown Prosecution department to take over
the case from the moment the charge has been formulated and the evidence
prepared. Finally, it makes a set of recommendations that are concerned
with the preparation of cases for trial, including a proposal to abolish
committal hearings.

There has been a certain amount of criticism that focuses on the
latter elements of the proposals. It has been argued, rightly in my view,
that if a prosecution department is not to be a mere cipher that rubber-
stamps cases already sealed and packaged by the police, then it must
have powers to examine evidence, interview witnesses and suggest alternative lines of inquiry when it is not satisfied with the police case.
The Commission's proposals fall far short of this. It has also been
suggested, I think wrongly, that the committal hearing, largely nowadays
a formality, is an essential safeguard in a criminal process that is
already dominated by the removal of procedural safeguards consequent
upon the development of plea bargaining. It is largely, though, in
relation to the first two elements of the proposals, the package, that
the criticism and controversy has been generated.

The major issue, given that the Report presents an interconnected
package of reforms, is whether the Report should be opposed outright or
whether it provides the basis for a critical intervention.

The charge of the libertarian opposition is that the proposals involve
unwarranted extensions of police powers as part of a package that provides
inadequate safeguards. The critics differ on points of emphasis in their
critique of the extension of police powers proposed, but they are unified
in their objection to the suggested safeguards. These, it is said, are
inadequate because the police are being asked, in effect, to police
themselves, a proposition that is ridiculed as patently absurd.

The interventionists accept that there are problems within the proposals as they stand, but argue that the Report leaves certain crucial
options open. The proposals, it is said, provide a framework for discussion, they leave room for differing emphases and alternative proposals
and thus provide a structure within which intervention is possible to
secure the protection of suspects' rights, and to check the more severe
claims and practices of the police.

     In this review I want to discuss these issues and explore further a
series of questions that underpin them. My own position on the substantive proposals is neither for nor against them in any simple way. In this
respect it is near to the position of Dr Leonard Leigh, author of *Police
Powers in England and Wales*, who argues that there is much in the Report
which 'deserves praise and speedy implementation, but there are [also]
aspects of it which ... ought to be rejected in any free society'.[4] I
tend, therefore, to agree with the interventionist position that there
are problems in the RCCP proposals, but that these can be challenged and
checked to produce a significant set of reforms. I shall develop this
argument in the course of the paper but I shall also consider problems
in the way in which the libertarian opposition have presented their objections, in the manner in which the advocates have formulated their
support, and in the way in which the report's recommendations and
analyses are structured.
     The argument of the libertarian opposition is twofold. It is that
the proposals envisage an extension of police powers that is unwarranted
and that the safeguards are inadequate. It is argued also, almost as a
supplement to the main charge, that the proposals and the safeguards
taken as a whole reduce public control over the police and render them
ever more remote from the framework of democratic accountability. The
point is not developed - it is made essentially in the form of a polemic.
It is a crucial point, however, for all reforms are profoundly affected
by the structure within which they occur and by their connection with
related structures. In making this connection polemically, there is a
failure adequately to analyse the relationship and thus an underestimation of the possibilities present within the proposals of the RCCP.
     There is a similar failure amongst the interventionists. Precisely
because reforms are shaped by the structures within which they occur
they are rarely adequate in themselves, they need to be linked with
other reforms if their potential is to be realised in a positive direction. In failing to consider the close and important connection between
the structure of safeguards and the structure of accountability, the
interventionists fail to present an adequate analysis of the possibilities and, it should be said, the problems implicit in the RCCP strategy.
     My analysis, then, will give particular attention to the relationship
between the proposals of the RCCP and the existing structure of accountability. It will be developed in two sections: the first will consider
the redefinition of legal powers recommended, the second will consider
the structure of suggested safeguards and their relationship to mechanisms of accountability. There is, however, a preliminary question
which needs to be considered concerning the evaluative framework of the
report.
     The report of the RCCP is prefaced by a discussion of what is called
the 'fundamental balance'; the balance, that is, between 'the interest
of the community in bringing offenders to justice and the rights and
liberties of persons suspected or accused of crime'. In the course of
this discussion it develops an evaluative framework that introduces
three 'principles' as its criteria of evaluation: the principles of
fairness, openness and workability. The question that now needs to be
considered is whether the notion of balance, and the Commission's interpretation of it, necessarily structures the report according to a
policing perspective. Or does it effectively transcend the apparent
antinomies of balance and provide an evaluative structure which permits

a broader range of possibilities? The former is suggested by the libertarian opposition, the latter is implied by the Commission.

THE FRAMEWORK OF THE REPORT

The Commission's consideration of the concept of a fundamental balance
and its endeavour to develop a set of evaluative principles was an
essential part of its attempt to produce a report outside the terms which
had produced a stalemate in the politics of criminal justice. The principles it developed were in part a strategic choice but were also to
an important extent imposed on it. The very notion of a balance was not
invented by the Commission but was part of its terms of reference, and
it was clearly unhappy with the need to produce an equation between
what it saw as false antinomies.
    Thus the RCCP does not identify the interests of society with the
interests of the police, as the libertarian opposition has argued;
rather it explicitly criticised the Criminal Law Revision Committee for
doing precisely that in its Eleventh Report. It argues, moreover, that
insofar as there is a need to register a balance, this arises because
of the deadlock that exists between utilitarian and libertarian conceptions of criminal justice. This, though, is not a philosophical statement. These opening sections of the report certainly appear naive if
read as an exercise in philosophy - but then it is even more naive to
read it as philosophy. The report is not engaging here in abstract
speculation on the nature of criminal justice, it is making an intervention in which positions within the arena of criminal justice are
characterised through the philosophies they represent.
    'Utilitarians' are those forces which are primarily concerned with
the 'right result', with securing convictions, with pursuing the community interest in effective policing. 'Libertarians', in contrast, argue
that certain rights are 'inviolable', that a 'right result' necessarily
involves a consideration of the processes by which it was arrived at.
Such a position is usually constructed in the language of individual
rights but it can be argued equally through a defence of the community
interest in justice.
    The Commission sought to overcome such philosophies and the political
positions associated with them by abandoning the terrain of rights. It
argues that rights are not inviolable but negotiable and that a considered use of checks and balances may in fact be a more effective means
of enforcing 'rights' than the use of such 'rights' as the organising
principles of reform.
    Constructing such checks and balances, is, however, a difficult
exercise. The Commission felt there was no way that it could construct
a compromise between the two opposing positions. It was not the function of a Commission, it argued, to construct such a compromise; moreover such an endeavour would have to assume that 'the positions occupied
by the opposing groups were solidly based on an objective knowledge
about how pre-trial procedures work in practice'.
    It sought to overcome these problems by commissioning research to
provide information previously lacking, and it supplemented this with
visits and consultations at home and abroad. It sought, too, to develop
its own criteria for assessing its research and the evidence submitted
to it. The principles it developed were those of fairness, openness

and reliability. However, if the libertarian opposition is wrong to
argue that the Report is structured by a policing perspective on 'the
fundamental balance', it is not at all clear that the Commission's own
concepts resolve the problem of the stalemate. The point, as Bernard
Smythe argues, is that 'hidden within the notions of fairness and workability are the very factors which the Commission admits have created
an unbridgeable gap between the libertarians and the utilitarians'.[5]
The concept of openness invoked does little to resolve the problems.

Fairness is interpreted by the Commission to mean that those who
have rights should be informed of them, that rules which we expect the
police to observe should be clear, and that such rules should be applied
equitably to all people. But, as the *Criminal Law Review* notes, of
itself 'fairness' provides no benchmark against which to measure whether
there are too many or too few controls on the police, too many or too
few rights for the individual.[6]   The concept of 'workability', it observes, is similarly vacuous. 'Workability' can refer to the need of
the police to be effective in arrest, interrogation and prosecution,
but it can also refer to the protection of individual rights.

'Openness' refers to the view that all decisions should be subject
to review. They should be known to the suspect. They should be written
down so that they will be available for inspection by supervising
officers. Once written down they should be open, if need be, to
challenge by the suspect and by the courts. They will also, thus, be
reviewable by the police authority, by central government and ultimately
by Parliament.

Two perspectives seem to inform the Commission's particular emphasis
on openness. The first stresses a form of accountability that is
characterised as 'explanatory and co-operative', as distinct from the
more typical 'subordinate and obedient' mode of accountability. The
second emphasises the importance of standards, codes and guidelines as
a means of regulating police decision-making.

The existence and nature of the police presents a clear problem for
liberal conceptions of accountability. These classically conceive the
relationship between the supervisor and the supervised in what Geoffrey
Marshall characterises as the 'subordinate and obedient mode'.[7]   In
this the responsibility of the supervised to the supervisor is typically
accompanied by administrative control in which the supervisor may issue
directions and impose vetoes. If the police were an executive body
such a relationship would be appropriate and they should in principle
be answerable to some elected body. But this raises the spectre of
partisan influence within law enforcement which is untenable within the
liberal position. However, the police, because they exercise considerable decision-making capacities, are not akin to the judiciary which in
liberal theory are independent of political control. The police are
clearly not 'impartial' in the judicial sense, they do not simply
administer rules.

Marshall suggests that if we are to develop adequate notions of
police accountability we need to differentiate between a series of
police decision-making capacities: between (i) the decision to prosecute
in individual cases; (ii) the decision to prosecute in particular areas,
i.e. motoring offences as distinct from public order offences; (iii)
decisions concerning police deployment, policing technologies, policing
styles etc. For the last a subordinate and obedient mode of accountability is clearly applicable; directions and veto power should be

appropriate. They might not be appropriate though as a means of regulating the other decision-making capacities. Here there is a need for a style of accountability that is explanatory and cooperative; one which rests not on the ability to issue orders but on the capacity to request information, answers and reasons and then to debate. The Commission's emphasis on the maintenance of records, the insistence on the necessity of review, is clearly conceived to aid such a process.

However, while police work is often seen as culminating in an arrest and subsequent prosecution, there is a whole range of such work that does not necessarily take this form. The need to regulate the exercise of police 'discretion' in the field has been central to the influential work of K.C. Davies. He argues that police discretion is both inevitable and essential, but is concerned to combat excessive or unnecessary discretion and with how to ensure that necessary discretion is effectively controlled. An important emphasis in his work is the stress on the need to reform both procedural and substantive law so that neither imply excessive discretionary power. Thus he argues that it is essential to regulate procedure so that stop and search powers are carefully defined but also to reform laws concerning 'victimless crimes', for example, which usually endow the police with considerable discretion. Regulating police discretion, though, centrally involves subjecting police discretion to public scrutiny and regulation. This involves as a crucial aspect the preparation of standards and guidelines, it means that 'the police should prepare proposed rules on the basis of staff studies, publish them, invite written comments from any member of the public, revise on the basis of the comments and then publish the final rules. They should freely amend the rules from time to time to keep up with the developing understanding and changing conditions.'[8]

The RCCP's principle of 'openness', as will become clearer later, is clearly informed by such perspectives. It is concerned with providing means to develop standards to regulate police stop and search powers, to regulate arrest, and, through the preparation of a code, to regulate interrogation. Such an emphasis clearly underpins the imperative to record decisions so that they are reviewable and open to scrutiny.

Codes, guidelines and standards are only effective if there are detailed and clear rules which specify exactly what is and what is not allowed. The Commission, however, frequently leaves the content of standards to be worked out by the police, by the Inspectorate or by the Judges. As Bernard Smythe suggests, its concept of openness 'requires underpinning by clearly defined and acceptable rules and, above all, effective sanctions and remedies'.[9] At fault, in part, is the concept of accountability that is utilised. Mechanisms of accountability are essentially mechanisms of delimitation.[10] The form of accountability is important, but so too is the range of decisions regulated and this needs clear specification. For a mechanism of accountability to be effective, whatever the form of the link between supervisor and supervised, there is a need to specify the powers clearly and to specify equally clearly how they are to be regulated. The Commission does not do this; in explicitly disavowing detail in the name of principle it creates a range of possibilities. It leaves it open to police authorities how they will review the proposed records, it leaves it open to HM Inspectorate how it will report its inspections, it accordingly leaves much open to the police.

Neither the concept of the 'fundamental balance', nor the way in which
it is utilised, structure the report in such a way that it necessarily
endorses a policing view. Nor do the evaluative principles. The Commission's notions of 'fairness' and 'workability' are inadequate. On the
one hand each simply restates the antinomies of 'utilitarianism' and
'libertarianism', on the other, the antinomies remain unresolved within
them. Meanwhile the principle of 'openness' is one which operates not
to delimit decision-making possibilities but to endorse them. It is
this which makes it possible to see the mechanisms of accountability,
the safeguards, simply as *internal* police reviews. I shall argue that
this view of the safeguards is inadequate and locate them within a range
of mechanisms of accountability. But first let us examine the redefinition of legal powers proposed by the Commission.

AN EXTENSION OF POLICE POWERS?

The argument that the proposals of the RCCP involve an extension of
existing police powers is a central element in the opposition to the
Report. It is an argument that while simple to assert is difficult to
assess because of the range of considerations involved. 'Power' is not
a singular entity, it involves a range of capacities subject to varying
levels of delimitation. Nor is it exercised across a single dimension.
As we have seen in discussing principles of accountability, police
decision-making capacities exist at distinct levels, they are endowed
through a variety of authorisations and they are subject to diverse
forms of accountability. Analysing police power in this context involves assessing not a simple addition to an existing structure but
the variable effect of a series of interventions within a dynamic
configuration.

I shall not, then, attempt to consider here to what extent an
'increase' in legal *powers* involves an 'increase' in police *power*. I
shall focus instead on two rather simpler questions which are involved
in the arguments of the opposition to the report. The first is whether
the report can be taken as a 'victory for the "law and order" lobby'
(*New Statesman*). I argue here that if we take McNee's much publicised
'shopping list' as the touchstone of the 'law and order' position then
we find that, in the concept of the 'grave offence', considerable concessions have in fact been made. This is not the case, however, in
the main body of the RCCP proposals and here I shall examine a second
question: whether the redefinition of *legal* powers involves an extension
of such powers beyond what exists at present.

'Grave offences'

The proposal to define a category of 'grave offences' and to create a
set of separate powers to deal with problems in this area is at first
sight an imaginative one. There have always been problems in utilising
a single set of rules to deal with the broad range of behaviours defined
as criminal. The notion of the 'grave offence' apparently provides a
means of dealing with those who argue for wholesale changes in the law
on the basis that current procedures set up an obstacle course for the
police in their endeavours to deal with serious crime. Distinguishing
'grave offences' from 'normal' offences and creating separate regimes

for each appears to provide a means of dealing with these objections without abandoning all of the standards traditionally provided by the law of criminal procedure. There is always the danger, though, that in such an endeavour the standards for those charged with 'grave offences' will be surrendered. The Commission clearly succumbed to this danger.

The 'grave offence' is defined to include serious crimes against the person, damage to property, dishonesty, drugs offences, blackmail, or perversion of the course of justice. In such cases there would be a power temporarily to detain persons in the vicinity of a grave offence who may be able to assist in the apprehension of offenders, or in securing or recovering property or persons. There would be power to search premises and seize evidence before a charge has been made. Finally, suspects who have been charged with committing a grave offence can be detained for long periods, during which time they can be held without legal advice and without their family or friends being notified as to there whereabouts. Leigh describes such powers as appalling.

The proposals recommend that suspects should be brought before a magistrate after 24 hours, that the magistrate, sitting in private, should fix a period of not more than 24 hours in which the person should be charged, or if still uncharged, be brought before him again. At any subsequent appearances they would have the same power, but after two appearances the suspect would have the right to appeal. Provision should be made for such a suspect to see a lawyer, but the latter should only be concerned with the suspect's health and the conditions of custody. The police would continue to have a discretion to refuse access to solicitors but it should be exercised in exceptional cases only. Then it should be used only where there is reason to believe that consulting a solicitor 'may cause delay resulting in risk to life or property ... interference with evidence or witnesses, the disposal of the proceeds of crime or the escape of accomplices'. In such a case, though, the refusal of access to a solicitor must be authorised by a different and relatively senior officer and the specific grounds for refusal must be recorded.

It is an understatement to describe these powers as draconian; they involve considerable concession to the demands of the police. In his evidence to the RCCP, Commissioner McNee called for restrictions on police powers of search to be lifted. Under his proposals once a search warrant for premises was granted the police would be able to seize *any* property whether or not it related to the offences specified in the warrant. Powers of search without warrant in a public place would also be extended. The police would be entitled to look for 'any article which has been or is intended to be used to cause injury to the person or damage to property' and they would get the right to search a person 'if by reason of a person's presence at a location an officer believes that such a search may assist in the prevention of serious crime or danger to the public'. What is involved in these proposals, as Martin Kettle suggests, is a shift to an earlier, less specific and more speculative stage in the process of evidence gathering.[11] Such a shift was also evident in McNee's proposals that a senior police officer should be empowered to authorise general and block searches of motor vehicles and their passengers, and, in the proposal that a senior police officer should be able to apply to a judge to order compulsory fingerprinting of 'every person or category of person living or working in any area'.

In relation to detention, McNee argued that once having arrested a
person the period of time available should be extended to 72 hours with
the opportunity to gain further extensions of up to 72 hours on the
approval of a single magistrate. In this period he wants to increase
the pressure to talk by weakening the Judges Rules through the abolition
of the existing caution and through destroying the right to silence.
This is not matched by any concessions on tape-recording; indeed McNee's
evidence contains a lengthy attack on its use. Nor is it matched by any
concessions on the right of suspects to see lawyers. For McNee, the duty
of a lawyer to his client and that of the police to further the interests of the public are diametrically opposed.

On balance Kettle may well be right to argue that the RCCP contains
'the most authoritative modern rejection of a whole series of existing
police practices and demands',[12] but it is difficult to say this of the
proposals for dealing with 'grave offences'. If such a category is to
be accepted it needs, as Walter Merricks has argued,[13] to be vigorously
and carefully defined. Wherever possible the availability of powers in
such cases should depend on application to a High Court judge, and particularly where detention is proposed for longer than a 24-hour period.
Magistrates are already too compliant and ready to rubber stamp police
requests, as the Commission itself observes in another section of the
report. This tendency would definitely be exacerbated if the magistrate
were to sit in private.

It is difficult, moreover, to see how the proposals concerning access
to solicitors would work. 'Is there,' Leonard Leigh asks, 'to be a
blacklist of solicitors, a request for which sets warning bells jangling
in the mind of the Inspector. May a suspect be dissuaded from obtaining
speedy access to all solicitors if he asks for the wrong one - or simply
prevented from having access to all solicitors depending on the nature
of his crime and his past associates.'[14] The RCCP admits, in its discussion of 'normal' cases, that the problem of dishonest solicitors is
a problem that should be dealt with by professional discipline - it
should not, therefore, affect rights. Lord Salmon does, indeed, suggest
that where a suspect does ask for his own solicitor, which is unusual,
then a phone call to the Law Society could inform the police whether or
not the solicitor is of high repute. If he is not, or if the suspect
has no solicitor, then the police should be able to refer the suspect
to a local solicitor - probably one of those available under the duty
solicitor schemes that the RCCP envisages developing.[15]

But these are details on dangerous ground. There is, in fact, little
evidence to suggest that such proposals concerning grave offences are
justified. It is true that there are anomalies in the law concerning
rape and murder, but these could be rectified without the innovations
recommended. And while it is in relation to the professional criminal
that such powers have usually been demanded, there is little evidence to
suggest the necessity of special changes in criminal procedure. Michael
Zander showed in 1972 that, in fact, the worse the prior criminal record,
the higher was the statistical chance of there being a conviction. His
study was subsequently criticised by John Mack for defining professional
criminals too broadly. Mack distinguished between the 'Main Group', the
'Lesser Group' and the 'Small Fry' and showed that the Main Group was
more successful in avoiding charges than the others. In fact, though,
the difference was of an order of only 10% and no less than three-
quarters of the charges against top criminals proved successful.

Baldwin and McConville in their study produced similar results and concluded: 'the picture that emerges is, thus, hardly one of professional
criminals exploiting the system: rather the evidence suggests that they
are, for the most part, unable to extract much advantage from it.[16]

'Normal crimes'

Let us turn from this rather unsavoury set of recommendations to those
that concern 'normal' crimes and consider whether the redefinition of
police powers involves an extension of such powers beyond those which
exist at present. My emphasis here will be on the extent to which
the redefinitions depart from existing law and practice. This is an
approach which differs slightly from that of the opponents of the RCCP
and needs to be clarified for the opposition has tended to invoke two
yardsticks as a means of criticising the report: existing law or existing practice. Each is problematic.
     McConville and Baldwin are a clear example of the first. They argue
that the recommendations involve a threat to three fundamental principles
of English criminal law.[17] The fundamental principles said to be bet-
rayed are: (i) citizens should be protected from random searches and
from searches based upon mere generalised suspicion; (ii) the police
have no powers, short of arrest, to detain citizens pending inquiries;
(iii) defendants should be protected from interrogation evidence which
is - or may be - unreliable because of the behaviour of the interrogators.
This is an effective and perfectly justifiable form of criticism provided that the principles are adequately secured in the existing law.
It will become clear, though, that they are not. English law provides
imperfect means of protecting these principles and in the case of each
principle there are considerable problems in developing adequate forms
of regulation. The proposals of the RCCP are at worst on a par with
the existing situation and at best a considerable improvement.
     Most critics, however, recognise that the existing law provides no
such protection; that in practice the principles are abused and the law
inadequate as a means of regulation. The critics then cite existing
practice as the problem to be remedied, they invoke experiential evidence
which reveals the problems as self-evident and use this as the yardstick
of criticism. This again would be an appropriate way of proceeding if
adequate alternative means of resolving the problems were offered.
Frequently they are not.
     We can demonstrate these points by considering the law concerning
stop and search, and then go on to examine the law of arrest and that
regulating detention and interrogation. Each is crucial to the critic's
case.

Stop and search powers

On first examination the RCCP proposals on the law regulating stop and
search practice seem appalling. Police practice in this area has been
an incessant cause of aggravated relations between the police and the
public, especially in areas with large ethnic minorities. If we take
the proportion of arrests to searches as the 'success' rate, the
Commission's own figures provide evidence to indict such policing.
Stops under Section 66 of the Metropolitan Police Act 1839, for example,
produced an arrest rate of only 13% and 12% in two one-month periods

in 1978 and 1979, while stops under the Misuse of Drugs Act 1971 produced
a 23% arrest rate.

In response   the   Commission's proposals seem both inadequate and
likely to exacerbate the situation. It proposes a single statute consol-
idating existing powers and making available a new general power to stop
and search for possession of stolen goods. A police officer, it is proposed, should have the power to stop and, if need be, search any person
in a public place whom he, on 'reasonable grounds', suspects of conveying
stolen goods or of being in possession of anything the possession of
which in a public place is, of itself, a criminal offence. As a safeguard to regulate these search powers it is proposed that a record of
the reasons for the search be made by the searching officer. A copy of
this should be made available on request so that the suspect can use it
as a basis for testing the legality of the search or in making a complaint. The record is to be used too as a means of regulation by
supervising officers and HM Inspectorate, who are to ensure that searches
are not being carried out at random, arbitrarily or in a discriminatory
way.

The criticisms are twofold. First, it is argued that the redefined
power of search extends police powers to stop and search to include the
power to stop and search for offensive weapons. Since offensive weapons
can be defined to include almost any article, the danger is that this
will justify yet more random searches which the proposed safeguards will
be inadequate to stop. Thus, second, it is argued that the safeguards
are inadequate. The reasons recorded, it is plain, could easily become
a formality, those searched are unlikely to be aware of their rights to
a copy of the record, and there will be a tendency only to record the
stop and searches that lead to charges; meanwhile the suspect is unlikely to prolong contact with the police by requesting a copy of the
record.

There are undoubtedly problems in the Report's proposals. The
Commission recognised that there was a risk of random searches 'because
of the wide range of articles that can be classified as offensive
weapons'. It resisted the demand of McNee for a general power to search
gangs of youth either at seaside towns or on their way to football
matches. But it is difficult not to feel that the Commission was
passing the buck in suggesting that the solution lay in Parliament
removing the imprecision in the definition of offensive weapons. It is
also difficult to have confidence that the Commission's distinction
between searches for detection of offences and those used as means of
controlling potential threats to public order will be effective in
practice.

But there are also problems in the critique. It is staggering to
discover that there is no power to stop and search for offensive weapons
at present. It is not at all clear, moreover, that a low police success
rate can be measured in terms of a low proportion of arrest, for police
practice can have a whole series of objectives other than arrest. The
critical question is how to regulate such powers and this the current
law patently fails so to do. It is in fact in such a state that a
recent commentary has observed: 'The limits on police rights of search
remain obscure, concealed in vague terms allowing considerable leeway.'[18]

The major problem has been the way in which statutes authorise the
police to search upon 'reasonable grounds' of suspicion. This is a
much lower standard of suspicion than that which is required to arrest

suspects, and it is open to arbitrary, discriminatory and necessarily subjective interpretations. But unless one is to restrict the power to search the person so that it can only take place subsequent to an arrest (the position of the NCCL and critics such as Brian Hogan),[19] then it is difficult to think of another formula. The key problem then becomes how to give it some kind of substantive content. This was attempted by the Advisory Committee on Drug Dependency in its 1971 Report, but it failed to find any objective basis on which to define 'reasonable suspicion'.[20] A majority sought to provide a positive definition which included a series of traits associated with the action prohibited. A minority sought to define it on an exclusionary basis such that the fact that a person was searched merely because he was young and long-haired, for example, would be insufficient in itself to justify a search. Both approaches were rejected by the Committee as too restrictive, inflexible and difficult to implement. How, then, given these difficulties, should the RCCP's proposals be assessed?

First, it should be said that the failure to arrive at any formula for assessing the reasonableness of alleged suspicion is to be regretted. On the other hand, though, the proposals are an improvement on the existing situation. The requirement to record reasons opens up the possibility of developing standards of what is and what is not to count as reasonable suspicion. While the police and the Home Office will have a view on what such standards should be, so too should those supporting a more restrictive view. Indeed a start could be made with the demand, suggested by Lord Salmon, that an immediate record be provided, by requiring the reasons justifying the stop and search to be written in the police notebook, and a carbon copy to be given instantaneously and as a matter of course to the suspect.[21] This would at least prevent the construction of reasonable criteria on an *ex post facto* basis by the police.

Arrest and detention

There are evident problems, too, in the Commission's proposals to clarify the existing law regulating arrest. The clarification involves extending the definition of arrestable offences (offences, that is, the suspected committal of which lead to instant arrest) to include all imprisonable offences. It involves, further, the creation of a power of arrest in offences which carry only a fine or penalty if the suspect withholds his/her name and address.

The critics are right, I think, to suggest that this latter clarification will present the police with an arbitrary power of arrest, but they are wrong to suggest that overall there will be an increase in powers of arrest. The existing definition of arrestable and non-arrestable offences was clearly indefensible, and although the Commission chose the widest solution, the proposed power of arrest will be subject to the 'necessity principle'. According to the Commission, arrest constitutes such an invasion of liberty that it can only be justified where it is deemed absolutely necessary. It argues that wherever possible, recourse should be had to appearance notices rather than to arrest, while arrest should be subject to the necessity criteria the Commission elaborates. The idea is that an arresting officer should record the reasons for the arrest on a new custody sheet and that this should be reviewed by a senior officer at the station.

There is a clear danger here that, while some policemen will operate
the test fairly, others will 'find little difficulty in making the cap
fit to suit convenience'.[22] The more serious objection to the proposals,
though, lies in the danger that the Commission has, by implication, proposed a power to detain citizens pending inquiries. Elsewhere the
Commission refused to regularise the situation known euphemistically as
'helping the police with their inquiries', yet they include within the
necessity principle the justification of arrest where it is necessary
'to obtain ... evidence from the suspect by questioning him'. They thus,
with no apparent discussion, effectively create the power to arrest and
detain a citizen simply because the police want to question him or her.
Of course, questioning may allay suspicion, as the Commission's research
demonstrates, but the difficulty in creating such a power is that it
requires little evidence to create suspicion and a lot to dispel it.
There is a clear danger, as Leigh suggests, that 'the police will use
coercive measures more or at least no less frequently than they do at
present'.[23]

The criticism is well placed, but overlooks the parlous state of
current police practice and ignores the totality of the Report's recommendations. At present there is no power to arrest pending inquiries.
Suspects, however, are detained. They are detained in a limbo with no
legal rights and they are detained for considerable periods. They have
no right to a caution as they have not been arrested nor, indeed, will
they have been charged. They have no right to see a solicitor and
their interrogation is not regulated by the Judges' Rules. Even if
arrested the position is far from satisfactory.

There is no right, as is often believed, to be brought before a
court within 24 hours, only a requirement that an arrested person be
brought before the court 'as soon as is practicable'. In theory pro-
longed detention can be challenged in the courts by a writ of habeas
corpus but in practice this is very rarely used in cases of police
detention. Nor is there a right to see a solicitor, merely an un-
enforceable administrative direction to the police from the Home Office
to permit a suspect to telephone a solicitor 'provided that no hindrance
is reasonably likely to be caused to the processes of investigation or
the administration of justice'.

The Commission proposes to change all this in a quite dramatic
fashion. Arrest would only lead to detention for a maximum of 24 hours,
it would be reviewed after six hours, and there would be a proposed
right to see a solicitor. The right to legal advice is to be made
effective in that it 'should not be dependent upon the suspect's happening to be aware that he has the right or upon his having his own solicitor or upon the convenience of the police'. It is recommended, further,
that the caution be simplified and that it be given at an earlier point
than is presently required. These are important gains in themselves
but they also need to be read in relation to the proposed power to
detain for questioning, if such a power is indeed implied. Formalising
the current practice would not then be the regressive step it appears
to be because the act of arrest carries with it these safeguards. What
is undoubtedly problematic, however, is the abrogation of such rights
in relation to 'grave offences'.

Interrogation

If the law regulating stop and search powers and the law of arrest can
be said to be in a critical state, so too can that regulating interrogation. It is widely accepted that the law in this area is riddled with
inconsistencies, that although it may contain formal rights for the
accused it offers little protection in practice. Criticism of police
interrogation practices, and of the widespread ignorance of the Judges'
Rules which was revealed, was central to the Fisher Report, the appearance of which was a catalyst for the appointment of the RCCP. It was an
area, too, that was a particular focus of the Commission's research.
As in other areas, though, the Commission's recommendations have disappointed its critics.

The Commission proposes that the Judges' Rules be abolished and replaced with a code of practice to be drawn up by the Home Office and
incorporated in subordinate legislation. The code should cover 'all
aspects of the treatment of a suspect in custody', it should be concerned with the problem of access to legal advice, the taking of statements, the use of tape recorders, the giving of cautions and with
securing the special treatment of suspects. It should provide guidance
to control the length, timing and circumstances of questioning so as to
avoid the current vagueness associated with the Rules' requirement that
a statement be 'voluntary', and it should provide for the comfort and
refreshment of suspects.

As I have already indicated, detention is to be subject both to a
practice of review and to a time limit, while the right of access to
legal advice is to be made effective. To improve the accuracy of the
record, it is argued that tape recording should become general practice.
In the interim, it is suggested, note-taking techniques should be
improved, but this, it is recognised, is inadequate. Accordingly it
is proposed that a taped summary of the interview be recorded at the
end of each interview. With the completion of the summary the suspect
should be allowed to comment on this, and on how he or she has been
treated.

The recommendations, it has been argued, are riddled with weaknesses.
Improving the accuracy of note-taking will no doubt help to reduce the
incidence of courtroom exchanges concerning records that are inaccurately
recorded as a result of incompetence and inadvertence, but the real problem relates not to accuracy but to the situation where a suspect denies
making a damaging admission to the police. Improved note-taking will
provide no answer to this problem, which is why reformers have tended
to demand tape-recording. The Commission's generally favourable approach
to tape-recording is commendable, but there are dangers in its interim
proposals. There is a danger, firstly, that 'verbals' - alleged admis-
sions made at the point of arrest - will remain admissible and thus
remain contested; there is a danger, further, that a suspect, faced
with a crisp, coherent and clear summary of an interview, will indicate
assent, only later realising what it is that is being assented to. The
pitfalls for the inarticulate, the tired and the confused are only too
evident.

Most of the criticism, however, has centred on the proposed abolition
of the principle, based on the Judges' Rules, that a statement should
no longer be excluded as evidence because it is involuntary. The
Commission rejected the use of this term as too vague, and suggested

that the Judges Rules should be replaced by a statutory code. Evidence
obtained in breach of the code should not be excluded, although it is to
be so excluded if there is violence, threats of violence, torture or
inhuman or degrading treatment. Reliance is to be placed instead upon
police supervision, discipline and civil actions. Additionally, where
the code is broken, the judge should bring this to the attention of the
jury, or the magistrates should be advised, and it should be pointed out
that there are dangers of acting upon a statement whose reliability
might be affected by a breach of the code.

Criticism has taken two forms. The first is to defend the existing
rules. The second is to argue that the proposed enforcement mechanisms
are inadequate and that there is a need for an exclusionary rule to
enforce the terms of the code.

The existing rules provide that a statement made by a suspect shall
be admissible in evidence against him only 'if it shall have been voluntary, in the sense that it has not been obtained from him by fear or
prejudice or hope of advantage exercised or held out by a person in
authority or oppression'. Lord Salmon criticises the RCCP proposals
through a defence of this provision. The only word that is unclear, he
argues, is oppression, which needs clarification, the rest is crystal
clear. The question as to whether a statement made by an accused was
made voluntarily, i.e. not as a consequence of a threat or a promise
held out by a person in authority, depends only on the evidence. It is
a question, he argues, 'which has caused considerable difficulty, but
if tape-recording is introduced immediately, as I am sure it ought to
be, the question should present no difficulty at all'.[24]

The Commission's approach to the problem of interrogation flowed
largely from its research findings. The concern to establish its conclusions on the basis of original research was one of the notable features of the Commission. Indeed, the work of Paul Softley and Barrie
Irving was the first such work to take place in English police stations.[25]
Their research provided the basis for the time limits on detention that
the Commission proposed. Thus Softley's sample showed that 72% of
suspects were released within 6 hours and a further 27% within 24 hours.
Irving's sample revealed similar findings, with 32% released within 6
hours and a further 61% within 24 hours; the reason for the longer hours
of detention is that many suspects were held overnight prior to interview
because of shift patterns. Most interviews it was found were completed
in less than an hour, and in only 1.5% and 7% of cases respectively were
suspects detained for longer than 24 hours. As Tom Hadden suggests, in
a useful review of the evidence, 'There is little evidence here of
systematic oppression'.[26] However, there are clear weaknesses in both
studies. Both suffer from what Hadden calls the 'observer effect' and
the 'ordinary case' effect. The first refers to the fact that the
presence of a researcher almost certainly eliminated any real possibility that there would be serious malpractice, while the second refers to
the small size of the samples and the absence from them of persons suspected of any really serious crimes which, again, must have reduced the
likelihood of the researchers coming across really oppressive conduct
on the part of the police.[27]

Neither of these defects, though, affects the main argument of the
research, which was not so much concerned with obvious malpractices but
with the difficulties in defining 'voluntariness'. Thus they were concerned to show that the typical interrogation did not conform to the

model prescribed in the Judges' Rules. The reality of the interrogation, the studies demonstrate, is that a number of techniques are regularly used by the police to solicit confessions: indications that suspects will be kept longer in custody if they do not cooperate; reference to the availability of other evidence which may or may not be forthcoming; appeals to the suspect's good nature and self-esteem; and, where other methods fail, resort to persistent high pressure interrogation but stopping short of serious threats or ill-treatment. It is a reality which strongly conflicts with the image conveyed by the Judges' Rules which, as Softley comments, 'convey an image of a suspect announcing to an astonished and suitably silent police officer, waiting patiently by his side, "I wish to make a statement"'.[28] Irving comes to similar conclusions, and both in his review of the psychological literature and in his case study stresses that the social and psychological pressures on the suspect, the authority of the police, and the violation of the suspect and his natural anxiety and stress, make it unrealistic even to attempt to apply the basic legal rule that any statement made in police custody must be shown to be voluntary before it is admitted in evidence. As far as he was concerned the notion that a statement in such conditions can be voluntary is psychological nonsense.

Nevertheless there are clear dangers in the Commission's position. To argue that the police station is coercive by nature does not necessarily mean that the voluntariness principle should be removed. Doreen McBarnet rightly suggests that 'it would be equally logical to extend the voluntariness principle to *exclude* questioning in the police station'.[29] It is hard, in fact, to be other than cynical at the Commission's suggestion that police officers should be made aware of the 'powerful psychological forces' at play during interrogation. Here much will depend on the Code of Practice and it is to be regretted that the detail of this is to be left to the Home Secretary.

The *New Law Journal* trenchantly argued the second fundamental objection to the Commission's proposals: 'Providing a more rational basis for both individual rights and police powers within the interrogation context is only one half of the problem,' it wrote. 'The other half is making the imposed standards enforceable and that calls for effective sanctions against non-compliance. The existing sanctions, such as police disciplinary measures and the use of civil proceedings have been shown to be almost wholly ineffective. A radically new approach to the problem was to be called for.'[30]

Before examining the RCCP's approach to the provision of safeguards I will summarise the argument so far. I have examined both the conceptual framework developed by the Commission and its redefinition of legal powers in three areas: the law of stop and search, the law of arrest, and that regulating detention and interrogation. In considering each, a series of problems has been examined. It is not at all clear, however, that the framework of the Report produces a structure within which the interests of society are identified with those of the police, nor is it clear that the proposals would amount to a definite extension of police legal powers.

The major exception here is the creation of a separate legal regime to deal with 'grave offences'. The case for this has not been made out and the powers proposed would involve a considerable departure from the existing situation. But for the rest, despite the problems considered, there is much to applaud in this part of the package. A new and

markedly improved regulation of detention and interrogation is proposed,
reasons are to be recorded for any stop and search of the person, suspects
are to be notified of their rights in custody, arrest is to be subject
to review, the conclusion of interrogations are to be taped and the
Commission further recommends that fingerprinting no longer be routine,
that limitations be imposed on strip searching, and that the use of
telephone tapping by the police be brought under statutory control.
Insofar as there are problems, these are frequently due to the openness
of the proposals, but it is indeed precisely such openness that provides
the opportunity for a critical intervention.

THE 'SAFEGUARDS' AND ACCOUNTABILITY

The second element in the criticism by the libertarian opposition concerns the adequacy of the safeguards. They are inadequate, it is said,
because it is naive to expect the police to police themselves and it is
this that the Commission is seen to propose. It is argued, further,
that the only adequate safeguard would be an automatic exclusionary
rule. Such a rule would prohibit the introduction into a trial of any
evidence that had been obtained unlawfully. The Commission recommends
such a rule where evidence has been obtained by violence, threats of
violence, torture or inhuman or degrading treatment. It also recommends
it when evidence of another non-grave offence is seized during a search
of premises that goes beyond the terms of the authorising warrant. For
the critics, such a rule should also apply when evidence has been obtained as a result of a breach in the code of interrogation. The
Commission's proposal in such cases is that there should not be automatic exclusion of evidence but rather a discretion; it suggests, that
is, that it should be 'left to the jury or magistrates to assess the
reliability of confession evidence upon the facts presented to them'.
    In this section I will consider both the Commission's arguments
against the use of an automatic exclusionary rule and the overall structure of the safeguards. I shall argue that there are considerable weaknesses in the Commission's arguments against the rule but that the
overall structure of safeguards proposed could entail a radically new
departure. To support this proposition I will relate the structure of
safeguards to the existing structure of accountability.

The exclusion rule

The Commission develops three different kinds of argument against the
use of an automatic exclusionary rule. It opposes it because of its
effect upon the conduct of trials, it opposes it on grounds of principle,
and it opposes it on the basis of the American experience with such a
rule, which suggests that such a rule would be ineffective. Indeed, in
considering the American experience the Commission suggests that the
rule was introduced to deal with a constitutional structure that is
totally different, and that in America there was a failure of the police
to discipline themselves. As the situation is different here, they
argue, there is no need for such a rule.
    It is clear that the RCCP was very concerned about the effect of an
automatic exclusionary rule on the trial process. American evidence
and the experience of the breathalyser law in this country were both

drawn upon to suggest that such a rule would lead to interminably lengthy
trials punctuated by continual legal arguments concerning the admissibility of evidence. Its operation would often result in technical acquittals
of those who were transparently guilty. It would, indeed, turn the trial
of a defendant into a trial of the police. Thus from one procedure, a
criminal prosecution, would be produced another, for inquiring into the
behaviour of the police. This would be an awkward and indirect form of
procedure, one that would operate to benefit a person incriminated by
illegally obtained evidence, and it would do nothing to recompense the
injury suffered by the victim of an illegal search that turns up nothing
incriminatory.

Underlying this objection is the issue of principle. Three distinct
principles have been differentiated as informing arguments for the operation of different versions of the rule.[31] The 'reliability' principle
is that which informs the current practice of the English judiciary.
It assumes that the sole purpose of the criminal trial is the determination of truth in assessing criminal charges. It follows, therefore,
that evidence should be admitted or excluded solely on the grounds of
reliability. Confession evidence, for example, might be excluded as
unreliable if it had been obtained as a result of torture, but equally
it might not. It would be a question of fact for the judge or jury to
decide at their discretion. It would be compatible with the principle
to insist that such evidence should only be admitted if it was corrobor-
ated by other evidence.

Exponents of the 'protective principle' agree that the main function
of the criminal trial is to determine the truth of criminal charges, but,
they argue, where a legal system declares certain standards for the conduct of a criminal investigation, then it should respect those rights
by ensuring that the suspect is not prosecuted on the basis of evidence
obtained by improper methods. Accordingly evidence obtained through
torture, for example, should be excluded not because it is potentially
unreliable but because it has been secured by methods which abrogate
the standards the system should protect. While adherence to the reliability principle is compatible with a discretionary exclusion rule,
adherence to the protective principle is compatible with what is called
the 'reverse onus' exclusionary rule. This would lead to automatic
exclusion of any illegally obtained evidence unless the prosecution can
satisfy the court that it should be admitted in the public interest, on
the grounds of, for example, the triviality of the breach. Such a rule
would be objected to by those concerned with reliability because it
would justify exclusion for a breach of certain standards regardless
of their effect on reliability. It should be rejected also by
exponents of the third principle.

The third approach is to argue for the automatic exclusionary rule
as a means of discipling the police. This is the so-called 'disciplinary principle', according to which the police would lose their particular case through their wrongful behaviour and hence will be deterred
from acting in the same way in the future. Aside from those objections
to an automatic exclusionary rule so far mentioned, the Commission
objected to a disciplinary justification on two bases: first, the
research does not show unequivocally that an exclusionary rule deters
the police from illegal conduct; second, the rule has been developed
in the United States because of the 'vast abnegation of responsibility'
to discipline themselves by the law enforcement agencies.

The first argument depends to a large extent on the research by
Dallin H. Oaks.[32] He shows that there are a number of risks consequent
upon adoption of the rule that can be counterproductive. The rule can
tempt the police to 'twist' the facts in order to prevent the exclusion
of evidence and the release of persons they 'know to be guilty'. There
is also the danger that the police can utilise the rule to immunise a
criminal from prosecution by deliberately overstepping legal bounds in
obtaining vital evidence. The rule, then, can be manipulated by a corrupt
police but more importantly it is ineffective, and almost necessarily so.
This is because the penal effect of the rule is felt only when a crime
comes to court and there is an attempt to introduce illegally obtained
evidence in order to secure a conviction. As a consequence the rule is
unlikely to be an effective deterrent against official misconduct if
that misconduct is not directed towards acquiring evidence or if it is
not likely to result in a prosecution. That is to say, as Chief Justice
Warren pointed out, the rule is ineffective 'where the police either
have no interest in prosecuting or are willing to forego successful
prosecution in the interests of securing some other goal'.[33]

For the police there are of course a whole series of goals beyond
that of securing arrest and conviction. These include: arrest or confiscation as a punitive sanction (i.e. in gambling and drug law violations), arrest for the purpose of controlling prostitutes, arrest of
drunks for their own safety, search for the purpose of recovering stolen
property, arrest and search and seizure for the purpose of 'keeping the
lid on' in a high crime area or for the purposes of satisfying a public
outcry for visible enforcement. The rule will have no deterrent effect
in such cases because the concern of most of the challenged conduct is
with the maintenance of order rather than the prevention of crime.
This is particularly so in the area of 'victimless crimes', such as
gambling, drugs, liquor prohibition and cases concerning sexual immoral-
ity. In such crimes the gravity of the offence (as measured by the
penalties involved) is relatively insignificant, the density of subcultures is high and detection, accordingly, difficult, and yet there
is frequently public demand for visible enforcement. In such cases the
police are less likely to be interested in convictions and much more
likely to make illegal intrusions to secure control. It is in such
areas, too, that the opportunities for police corruption and other malpractices are high.

All this points to an underlying factor that militates against the
effectiveness of the exclusionary rule. The rule conceived as a deterrent suffers, like any deterrent, from the fact that its effect will be
neutralised where there are strong competing pressures. In the case of
the exclusionary rule such competing pressures lie in the needs of the
situation as interpreted through competing norms of police behaviour.
Thus, as Jerome Skolnik has argued on the basis of his observations of
city policing in America, 'norms located within police organisation are
more powerful than court decisions in shaping police behaviour'. [34]
Even if a police officer's conduct was illegal and resulted in the loss
of a conviction, Skolnik observed, the officer was assured of the
sympathy of his superiors so long as he acted 'in conformity with the
administrative norms of police organisation'.[35] Albert J. Reiss and
Donald J. Black make essentially the same point. They argue that there
is a conflict between the appellate criteria for the exclusion of
evidence, which 'articulate a moral order - a system of values and

norms' and that of the police who 'are organised to articulate a behaviour system - to maintain law and order.... [Thus] their organisational
concern is less for the legitimacy of norms than for the rather immediate end of enforcing behaviour standards'.[36]

The Commission clearly objected to the use of an automatic exclusionary rule on the basis of all three arguments surveyed above, but it is
equally clear that questions of principle predominated. Thus, although
it emphasises the problems attendant upon trials within trials and
stresses the American experience, it is largely on the basis of principle that it puts forward its own proposals. The principles which it
endorses are a combination of reliability and protection. Thus automatic
exclusion should operate to mark 'society's abhorrence' of violence,
torture etc, and it should operate because of 'the right of members of
the public to be free from general searches must be respected'. But no
other rule should be protected through automatic exclusion, nor should
there be a discretion to exclude evidence on any ground other than its
reliability.

This is much to be regretted. Even accepting the Commission's arguments that the exclusionary rule is neither appropriate nor effective
as a disciplinary measure, their juxtaposition of the protective and
reliability principles still leaves much to be desired. This is because,
as the *Criminal Law Review* points out, the code of interrogation 'recognises rights which deserve far more protection than they are likely to
receive from a discretion to exclude evidence solely on grounds of
reliability'.[37] The Commission is surely right to suggest that the
advantage of the protective principle is that it allows a judge not to
exclude evidence when the breach is trivial but to exclude it where a
suspect's rights are seriously infringed. Yet, according to the
Commission's recommendations, a series of important rules could be
broken - the wrongful withholding of legal advice, failure to use a
tape-recorder, failure to interrogate according to the code of practice,
or even failure to interview young persons or the mentally handicapped
under the special conditions recommended - but in each case the breach
would only be relevant if it produced unreliable evidence.

The Commission moreover not only applies the principles badly, but
it also uses inadequate means of protection. As we have seen, it would
be compatible with the reliability principle to exclude evidence where
it was uncorroborated and it would be compatible with the disciplinary
principle to introduce a reverse onus exclusionary rule. The Commission's arguments against each are lame. It dismisses the former as
impracticable and simply suggests that greater care should be taken in
checking the details of confessions. It dismisses the latter on the
grounds that it would be difficult to interpret consistently and that
it would not reduce trials within trials. It is clear, though, that
their own proposals will not resolve the problem of trials within trials.
Indeed, one procedure - for testing reliability - will increasingly be
used for another - attempting to safeguard standards. It is hard to
see how such a process could be effectively resisted.

It is not at all clear, moreover, that the disciplinary approach is
ineffective. Oaks in fact explicitly exempted confession evidence from
his findings because 'the predominant incentive for interrogation is to
obtain evidence for use in Court. Consequently, police conduct in this
area is likely to be responsive to judicial rules governing the admissibility of evidence'.[38] In addition, Oaks' more general arguments

have been rejected by other American analysts. Their work has been
reviewed by Jim Driscoll, who argues that there is now 'convincing evidence that it [the automatic exclusionary rule] has fostered a significant and increasing improvement in the standard of police behaviour in
the United States'.[39] Oaks' research was primarily concerned with
arrest, conviction and property confiscation data related to gambling,
narcotics and weapons offences in Cincinnati in the five years prior to
and after the *Mapp* decision which introduced the rule. He concluded
that *Mapp* had some effect on gambling offence investigations but no
discernible influence on the remaining police activities studied.
Driscoll compared these conclusions with other research of the same
period and found that '*Mapp* had an uneven impact following its announcement and that its reception varied according to the local political/
legal culture'.[40] Recent studies have confirmed this conclusion.

Canon, for example, made a comprehensive analysis of changes in
police practices between 1967 and 1973. He found a significant adherence to *Mapp* and again concluded that its effect was determined by
'such factors as police training and policies and the attitudes of
political and legal officials'.[41] The studies were confirmed by reports
to the US Comptroller General and by the US Department of Justice which
also showed that it was mistaken to conclude that guilty offenders were
acquitted on technicalities as the evidence considered by the RCCP
suggested. While it was indeed true that evidence might be excluded
by the operation of the rule, other evidence was usually available to
secure a conviction. Driscoll also examined changes in police practices
and concluded that 'as early as 1966 several police departments had
modified their arrest, interrogation and search and seizure policies,
had provided additional training for their personnel and had established
additional liaison between themselves and the prosecution departments'.[42]
Finally, Driscoll considered the Commission's argument tnat it was
only the differences between the systems which made the exclusionary
rule necessary in the United States and unnecessary here. He suggests,
in conclusion, that England and Wales, 'with a unified legal system,
relatively homogeneous police organisation and greater police commitment to the outcome of prosecutions may well provide a more fertile
environment for the rule than the United States'.[43]

These points are useful but inconclusive. They are compatible with
arguments for an automatic exclusionary rule but they are also compatible with a rule requiring alternative corroboration or a reverse onus
exclusionary rule. Indeed, given that Driscoll's argument concentrates
on the effect of the rule on police training, it may well be that the
Commission's own proposals will be more, or at least as, effective in
achieving this and more consonant with the legal and political culture.
Let us turn then to consider the proposed safeguards and their relationship to the existing structure of accountability.

The safeguards

The Commission's proposed safeguards. as I suggested earlier, are
developed as a result of its belief in the efficacy of guides, standards and codes as a means of regulation. It places considerable emphasis
on the maintenance of records as a means of regulating stop and search,
it establishes a set of criteria - the necessity principle - to regulate
arrest and provides for a form of review, and it rejects the Judges'

Rules and calls for a comprehensive code to regulate interrogation.
These forms of control are developed partly because of a belief that
judicial control through the exclusionary rule is ineffective and undesirable, but more positively because of their general belief in favour
of 'contemporaneous controls and good supervision' as against reviews
long after the event. The Commission, in developing this view, notes
that 'it is not possible for the cell block, charge office and interview
rooms of a police station to be open to members of the public to come
and go as they please', and argues that if suspicion of what goes on
behind these closed doors is to be diminished, then 'satisfactory means
of supervision and review' are required.

To consider whether the Commission has provided such means of review,
or whether it has simply provided a structure in which the police police
themselves, it is necessary to consider the existing structure of review:
through the law, through the complaints procedure and through the system
of political accountability. The problem with the legal controls and
with the complaints system is that they provide an inadequate form of
ex post facto review designed to regulate individual malpractices. The
structure of political accountability, on the other hand, provides an
inadequate means of regulating police decision-making in general. I
shall argue that the review mechanisms proposed by the Commission fit
logically into this structure, providing the possibility of an adequate
review at a more intermediate level. Its effect could be either to
render the existing mechanisms more effective or at the very least to
generate demands for more effective mechanisms.

Legal accountability operates through four devices. It can exclude
evidence obtained in breach of the law. English judges have always been
reluctant so to do. It can, through the writ of habeas corpus, provide
a means of regulating detention. This, again, is inadequately enforced.
When the Divisional Court is presented with a prima facie case of unlawful detention the matter is adjourned for the prosecution to be represented, by which time the defendant has either been charged or released.
The law can also provide a means of civil redress for damages where
legal powers are abused. The difficulties here are notorious. Delay
is a major problem but so too is the considerable difficulty in marshal-
ling satisfactory evidence. Finally, the police may be prosecuted where
they commit criminal offences. The DPP, however, has said that he will
not prosecute unless there is a 50% chance of conviction. Juries, he
claims, are reluctant to convict police officers and so he finds it more
difficult to say that the 50% rule has been satisfied in the case of a
police officer than in any other case.[44]

The Commission's proposals are designed to deal with a number of
these problems. We have considered its view of the exclusion rule at
length; we have also seen that it proposes new procedures for review of
detention that should rectify some of the problems inherent in habeas
corpus. Finally, its emphasis on the production of contemporaneous
records should help resolve some of the difficulties that arise when
there is a conflict of evidence in legal disputes. The proposals are
not unproblematic. It could have produced more stringent exclusionary
requirements, its proposals concerning detention are subject to considerable abuse in the case of 'grave offences', and it could have proposed
a simpler civil law remedy. Thus it could have recommended a summary
procedure for civil redress and it could have considered a new tort concerning harsh and oppressive treatment of persons in custody.[45]

The Commission's recommendations taken as a whole, however, are a vital first step in strengthening legal review. They may also provide a means of strengthening the police complaints procedure. The present system of investigating complaints was set up by the Police Act 1964 and it was modified by the Police Act 1976. This introduced a public element, the Police Complaints Board, but it was concerned not to remove the initial investigation from the police, nor to undermine the chief officer's responsibility for the discipline of his force, nor finally to put a police officer in jeopardy twice in respect of the same complaint. The Board's role then is a limited one. Its work arises when, after the DPP has decided not to prosecute, the Chief Constable decides not to discipline an officer. The Board then reviews the papers and can recommend or direct that disciplinary charges be brought.[46]

The Board, as Maureen Cain has stressed, is clearly a contradictory phenomenon.[47] On the one hand it introduces an independent lay element into the adjudication of complaints, yet at the same time that element is severely circumscribed. It is clear that in its early years the balance lay very much with the police. Robert Mark and the Police Federation opposed its creation and as a major concession the Act provided that the police would be able to sue complainants for libel.[48] Its inception was, in fact, marked by a decline in complaints investigated, and its limited and rather tame role seemed confirmed by the decreased level of complaints both made and investigated.

It is also clear however that the balance has tipped in contradictory directions. In its Triennial Review Report published in 1980, for example, the Board criticised the reluctance of the police to investigate complaints adequately and was so dissatisfied with investigations into unexplained injuries incurred by complainants that it recommended for consideration a proposal to create a specialist body of investigating officers, seconded from all police forces and under the direction of a judicial figure. At the same time a Home Office Research report, as yet unpublished but leaked in *The Times*, confirmed the inadequacies of such investigations.

The position remains contradictory. On the one hand the Home Office working party set up to consider the recommendations was so blatantly packed as to make their rejection inevitable. On the other hand, however, the RCCP endorsed the views of the Triennial Review and stressed that its own reforms depended on an effective and credible complaints procedure. Again it is clear that its own recommendations with their stress on the production of reasons, the keeping of records, and on the practice of supervision will facilitate external review through the complaints process. Thus the emphasis in the Commission's proposals is not that of an internal review alone, but of an internal review connected to this external review. It was, indeed, no coincidence that Sir Cyril Philips (Chairman of the RCCP) was appointed to chair the Complaints Board and no coincidence either that he has adopted an aggressive posture.

The mechanisms of internal review are also connected with the structure of political accountability. The Commission makes this quite explicit when discussing its criteria of openness. Decisions should be recorded, it argues, to 'make possible general oversight of the process by the police authority, by central government, through its inspectorate, and ultimately by Parliament'. Similarly, when emphasising the recording of reasons for search, it stresses that the number of

such searches 'should be contained in the chief constable's annual
report, which will make the broad extent of the application of the
powers subject to scrutiny by the police authority'.

The structure of political accountability, though, is if anything
less adequate than the mechanisms of legal review and the complaints
structure. The place of the police within the constitutional structure
is defined by the Police Act 1964. This Act, which followed the report
of the Royal Commission on the Police (1962), severely diminished the
powers of local police committees and facilitated the centralisation of
the police that has been such a characteristic of the last two decades.
The Act changed the constitution of Police Authorities, which are now
composed of one-third magistrates and two-thirds representatives of the
local authority. It provided for police amalgamations which were
further facilitated by the Local Government Act 1972. As a consequence
police areas are not now necessarily coterminous with county area
boundaries and local control is exercised through a joint authority.

Although it is the duty of the Police Authority to secure the maintenance of an adequate and efficient police force for the area, the Act
provides that the police force shall be under the direction and control
of the chief constable. Both the Home Secretary and the Police Authority may call for reports from the chief constable but the latter may
refuse to give them to the Police Authority 'in the public interest'
or if he judges the matter to be beyond their jurisdiction. The Home
Secretary adjudicates in the case of a dispute between them. Neither
can give the chief constable operational directions.

This is a structure which provides little opportunity for control
either at the local level through councils or centrally through Parliament. Howard Levenson, in fact, reports evidence which shows that in
ten cases the chief constable did not report regularly to the Authority
and in only ten cases did the authority frequently request reports.
The relative independence of Police Authorities, moreover, created
suspicion between them and the county councils.[49] The structure of the
Act produced a system of policing that was decreasingly amenable to
control at the local level and increasingly centralised.

The centralisation was of a form that facilitated the generation of
new practices of policing. The increased operational autonomy given to
chief constables and the increased emphasis on police college thinking
that was evident led to the generation of new conceptions of policing
that were developed at managerial level. But it also facilitated Home
Office control. The Home Office is undoubtedly influential in direct-
ing Police College thinking. Its control over the police begins and
continues with the power over the purse. The Home Office also controls
certain central police services. It is concerned with police research
and development and with promotion and conditions of service.

The new managerial conceptions of policing developed within the
National Police College and through the Home Office have been characterised as indicative of a move towards police professionalism. This is
a conception of policing that emerged in part as a consequence of the
threat presented to the police by other government agencies - the social
work service, for example - in the post-war period, in part as a consequence of manpower problems, and in part as a consequence of the
challenge to police credibility presented by the inquiries into police
malpractices that marked the late 1950s and early 1960s. It was to deal
with this final problem that senior officers became concerned to diminish

the possibility of investigating officers breaking the legal rules governing the securing of evidence in questioning after arrest.[50]

Professional policing was a theory of policing based on three principles. First, the acquisition of specialist knowledge of particular
aspects of policing and the restructuring of the organisation into specialist units. Second, to a significant extent, specialist knowledge was
based on the use of technology, i.e. on a knowledge of vehicular policing,
telecommunications and computerisation. Third, although discretion has
always been an integral feature of policing, the development of professionalism led to the emergence of the principle of 'informed discretion'.
In this the slow build-up of evidence prior to arrest, such that arrest
becomes inevitable, is stressed. It is intended that, as a consequence,
evidence will be gained before arrests are made, that the police will
cease to be action oriented, and that, accordingly, the possibilities of
abusing suspects during questioning after arrest are reduced, because
evidence is gained before not after arrest.

The dangers in such 'pre-emptive' policing practices are clear and
have been copiously documented by Duncan Campbell.[51] Nevertheless such
a strategy, as I have suggested, was conceived, in part, as a means of
ensuring that policing by the lower ranks should operate within the parameters set by the rule of law. The thrust of professional policing was,
however, limited. It was directed at officers whose primary task was
the administration and supervision of the police service. It was not
directed at those engaged in the practical activity of law enforcement,
although it had critical implications for this. Practical policing was
transformed through the technological aspects of the new policing
strategy but, as Simon Holdaway has demonstrated, not through the
development of informed discretion and, accordingly, not through preventing the abuse of suspects.

In a survey of his and other work, Holdaway has argued that as a
consequence 'we should be looking for policies that break into the
structural network of policing to make the work group accountable ...
to render the practices within the charging and questioning process
more visible'.[52] As he suggests, if the low visibility work of policing
is rendered more visible, the process of investigating complaints after
police action may well be improved to a considerable extent.

The proposals of the RCCP flow directly within this trajectory of
development. As I have repeatedly suggested, it is not a set of internal
safeguards that is being proposed, but ones in which internal controls
are closely articulated with external controls. In this instance the
proposal to establish a chain of review through HM Inspectorate to the
Home Office is critical. As with all developments of the recent past,
there is a close interconnection between processes which appear simply
to enhance police autonomy and those which develop the regulatory
capacity of the Home Office. Indeed, Maureen Cain in assessing the
evolution of police professionalism suggested that there were two
possible developments. One would be the emergence of a truly professional police force with the autonomous generation of norms and
practices. The other, which she saw as more likely, is that central
government would influence the norms that apparently emerge from within
the police. In this case 'professionalism disguises central power'.[53]
She characterised the first as a national disaster as it would preclude
accountability, and the second as the worst of all possible worlds
because central government is not fully answerable for police actions.

This conclusion seems to me to be too pessimistic. The latter option does indeed seem to be dominant and it is within this that the RCCP 'strategy' can be located. The situation, and the structure of safeguards, is indeed inadequate, but the introduction of the safeguards could provide an essential precondition for the development of some form of accountability. The advantage of a system of accountability structured around the proposed safeguards is that it has the potential to extend throughout the police service.

CONCLUSION

How then are we to assess the Report of the Royal Commission on Criminal Procedure? Is it, as its oppositionist critics suggest, a report which makes major concessions to the police, which extends their powers considerably and which provides inadequate safeguards as part of an overall package? Or does it, on the contrary, present a check to current police claims and practices, a check which, though not perfect, provides opportunities for a considerable improvement on the conditions of the present?

I have argued that, except in one major instance, it is wrong to suggest that the Report recommends major extensions of police powers. In relation to the law of stop and search, arrest, detention and interrogation - the points at which the critics direct most of their fire - there are indeed problems but they are problems that in most cases could be simply remedied. The Report is open enough in its structure to permit this. There is, however, with the sections concerning 'grave offences', a set of proposals and recommendations which are abhorrent. They need to be strenuously opposed.

It is hard, however, to be very enthusiastic about the safeguards proposed. I tend to agree with the Commission's arguments against the automatic exclusionary rule, but would like to have seen a more judicious combination of the reliability and protective principles with more rigorous rules to enforce them. But I have also shown that it is wrong to characterise the safeguards as simply internal in character. They combine internal and external methods of review, providing fresh means to strengthen the latter. I have also shown that these proposals fit into a trajectory of reorganisation of the police service and that as such they could provide one of the preconditions of increased accountability. There is thus potential, through the safeguards, to set in motion a process that might reveal more than at first glance they would seem to suggest.

NOTES

I would like to thank Nikolas Rose and Barry Hindess for their helpful
criticisms and suggestions.

1   Cf. M. Dean, 'The Commission that did its homework', *Guardian*,
    14/1/81. Background Paper on Suspects Rights, *State Research*, Vol.2,
    no.12. The Confait Case. Report by the Hon Sir Henry Fisher.
2   Cf. *New Statesman*, 2/1/81. *Rights*, Vol.5, No.4, March/April 1980.
    Legal Action Group *Bulletin*, February 1981.
3   Cf. M. Zander, 'Royal Commission: no grounds for suspicion',
    Guardian, 12/1/81. M. Zander, 'The fears of the loudest critics
    seem exaggerated', *Guardian*, 28/1/81. M. Kettle, 'Controlling the
    Police', *New Society*, 8/1/81. D. Hayter and W. Merricks,
    'Commissioner's Reply', *Labour Weekly*, 16/1/81. W. Merricks,
    'How we drew the thin blue line', *New Statesman*, 8/1/81.
4   Leonard Leigh, 'The Royal Commission on Criminal Procedure', *Modern
    Law Review*, May 1981.
5   Bernard Smythe, 'The Royal Commission on Criminal Procedure', *Public
    Law* June 1981, p.187.
6   *Criminal Law Review*, July 1981, p.437.
7   Geoffrey Marshall, 'Police Accountability Revisted', in D. Butler
    and A. Halsey (eds.), *Policy and Politics*, London, Macmillan, 1978.
8   K.C. Davies, *Police Discretion*, Minnesota, 1975, p.168. For a
    discussion cf. Michael Freeman, 'Controlling Police Discretion',
    Poly Law Review, Vol.6, No.2, Spring 1981.
9   Smythe, *op.cit.*, p.187.
10 Cf. Barry Hindess, 'Democracy and the Limitations of Parliamentary
    Democracy in Britain, *Politics & Power* 1.
11 Martin Kettle, 'The Politics of Policing and the Policing of Politics'
    in P. Hain (ed.), *Policing the Police*, Vol.2, John Calder, London,
    1981.
12 Martin Kettle, *New Society*, *op.cit.*
13 Walter Merricks, 'Why NCCL should back Report', *Rights*, *op.cit.*
14 Leigh, *op.cit.*
15 Lord Salmon, 'The balance of criminal justice', *Listener*, 4/6/81.
16 M. Zander, 'What is the evidence on law and order', *New Society*,
    13/12/79.
17 M. McConville and J. Baldwin, 'Justice in Danger', *New Society*,
    30/4/81.
18 Roshier and Teff, *Law & Society in England*, Tavistock, 1980, p.99.
19 Brian Hagan, 'Search', *New Law Journal*, 16/4/81.
20 Powers of Arrest & Search in relation to Drug Offences, HMSO, 1970.
21 Lord Salmon, *op.cit.*
22 Leigh, *op.cit.*
23 *ibid.*
24 Salmon, *op.cit.*
25 Paul Softley, *An Observational Study in Four Police Stations*, RCCP
    Research Series No.4. Barrie Irving and L. Hilgendorf, *Police
    Interrogation: The Psychological Approach*, and Barrie Irving,
    Police Interrogation: a Study of Current Practice, RCCP Research
    Series, Nos.1 & 2, HMSO.
26 Tom Hadden, Book Review, *International Journal of Sociology of Law*,
    1981.

27 *ibid.*
28 Softley, *op.cit.*
29 Doreen McBarnet, 'Balance and clarity', *Criminal Law Review.*
30 'Investigative Powers and the Rights of the Citizen', *New Law Journal*, 15/1/81.
31 A.J. Ashworth, 'Excluding Evidence as Protecting Rights', *Criminal Law Review*, 1977, p.723 et seq.
32 Dallin H. Oaks, 'Studying the Exclusionary Rule in Search and Seizure', *University of Chicago Law Review*, Vol.37, p.665 et seq.
33 Terry v. Ohio, 392 U.S.I. 15 (1968), quoted in Oaks, *op.cit.*
34 Jerome H. Skolnick, *Justice Without Trial*, 1967, p.219, quoted in Oaks, *op.cit.*
35 Skolnick, *op.cit.*
36 Albert J. Reiss Jr. and Donald J. Black, 'Interrogation and the Criminal Process', 374 *ANNALS* 47, 48-39, 1967, quoted in Oaks, *op.cit.*
37 *Criminal Law Review*, *op.cit.*
38 Oaks, *op.cit.*, p.722.
39 Jim Driscoll, 'Excluding illegally obtained evidence - can we learn from the US?', Legal Action Group *Bulletin*, June 1981, p.131.
40 *ibid.*
41 *ibid.*
42 *ibid.*
43 *ibid.*
44 Cf. Howard Levenson, 'Democracy and the Police', *Poly Law Review*, *op.cit.*
45 Cf. Smythe, *op.cit.*
46 Terry Walters, 'Complaints against the Police', *Poly Law Review*, *op.cit.*
47 Maureen Cain, 'An ironical departure': the dilemma of contemporary policing', *Yearbook of Social Policy*, 1976.
48 Cf. Derek Humphrey, 'The Complaint System' in P. Hain (ed.), *Policing the Police*, vol. I, John Calder, 1979.
49 Howard Levenson, *op.cit.*
50 Cf. Simon Holdaway, 'Changes in Urban Policing', *British Journal of Sociology* 28(2), pp. 119-37. Daniel James, 'Police-Black Relations: the Professional Solution', in S. Holdaway (ed.), *The British Police*, Arnold, 1979.
51 Martin Kettle, 'The Politics of Policing and the Policing of Politics' in P. Hain (ed.), *Policing the Police*, vol. 2, John Calder, 1980.
52 Holdaway, 1979, *op. cit.*
53 M. Cain, 'Police Professionalism: its meaning and consequences', *Anglo-American Law Review*, 1(2), 1972.
54 *Criminal Law Review*, *op. cit.*

Deprivation, Participation & Community Action

Community Work Six

Edited by Leo Smith and David Jones

Contributors: Leo Smith, Chris Miller, Charles Allwright, Mark Brangwyn, Fiona Crosskill, Jo Oserio, Mary Turle, Marilyn Taylor, Laurie Bidwell, Bill Edgar, Nick Bailey, Mike Cooper, Charlie McConnell, Dudley Savill, Bryan Simons.

The sixth book in the Community Work Series considers the reasons why the demand for participation in national and local government decision-making has arisen, and also demonstrates the ways in which public participation has been organised. The contributors provide analyses of the factors that lead to effective participation and give examples of good practice, so that community workers and those involved in service and politics at the local level will be better able to develop participation through their work.

0 7100 0827 9   paperback £5,95   Community Work Series

Automatic Poverty

Bill Jordan

Bill Jordan argues that unemployment and the fall in our industrial workforce are best understood as manifestations of a new phase of industrial development: new technology does not always increase national income when it increases productivity, and when it does not - as in Britain - it necessarily reduces both the employment and income of the working class.

0 7100 0825 2   paperback £4.95

RKP ██████████████████████████████████

Paddy Hillyard
From Belfast to Britain: some critical comments on the Royal Commission on Criminal Procedure

INTRODUCTION

Over the last decade a number of very long-established and cherished
principles of the British criminal justice system have been laid to rest.
Some were laid to rest by the parliamentary process, some by stealth and
some by deceit. The abolition by Parliament of unanimous verdicts in
1967, Hailsham's decision during 1973 to remove the occupation of each
potential juror from the jury list and the introduction of jury vetting
by prosecutors some time in the early 1970s are just a few examples of
the modifications to, and abolition of, long-established principles.[1]
It was, therefore, to be expected that the Royal Commission on Criminal
Procedure would also recommend far-reaching and fundamental changes in
principle. The publication of the Commission's report has confirmed
the expectation. The recommendations relating to stop and search,
arrest detention and questioning involve far-reaching changes. As a
package, it will radically modify the existing relationship between the
citizen and the state, strengthen the repressive potential of the police
and courts and introduce into England and Wales a criminal justice which
closely resembles the system introduced into Northern Ireland in the
early 1970s to deal with the widespread problem of political violence.[2]
Many people now live in fear of crime and it may well be argued that
radical modifications to the present system of pre-trial procedures are
essential to deal with crime effectively. The central argument of this
paper is that the modifications proposed will do little to help deal
with the problem of crime, principally because the success of the police
depends on public support and these recommendations are likely to lead
to a worsening of police public relations. The paper draws heavily
on the experiences of Northern Ireland to criticise the recommendations.
The Commission did not consider these experiences because it took the
view that there are 'special problems in dealing routinely with persons
suspected' of political violence.[3] But this very routineness provides
an excellent opportunity to study what happens when serious offences
are committed on a massive scale and pre-trial and trial procedures are
modified. It shows the disadvantages of radically altering existing
procedures. It illustrates very clearly the dangers in terms of public

confidence of extensions of police powers, the inadequacies of relying
upon internal police controls, and the trend towards bureaucratisation
inherent in an Office of Prosecutions. Moreover, it provides some
information on the context of police work in relation to serious crimes
and how the practices of the police can be greatly influenced by outside
political pressures.

The paper begins by criticising the Commission's analysis and its
failure to examine in detail three central topics: the delicate relationship between the police and the public; the extent to which the
police may be misusing their existing powers; and the context of police
work and the reasons why the police may misuse their powers. It then
proceeds to consider a number of the more important proposals in detail,
and drawing on, where appropriate, the lessons from Northern Ireland.

POLICE-PUBLIC RELATIONS

Over the last few years there have been numerous instances indicating
that relations between sections of the public and the police were far
from satisfactory. For some time there has been ample evidence that
certain minority communities were extremely estranged from their local
police forces. The events in St. Pauls, Bristol, and Brixton were simply
expressions of a deep underlying malaise. These problems between the
police and the public, however, have not been confined only to minority
communities; there is also evidence of widespread alienation from the
police in certain working class areas. All this information indicates
that the relationship between the blue-coated worker and the public are
very strained. The Commission shows little concern and in place of a
comprehensive analysis there are only occasional references to the
problem of relationships between the police and the public. Many of
these references stem from a concern shared by a small minority of the
Commission that the proposed extensions in police powers may further
harm relations between the police and the public. Apart from these,
there is only one short paragraph in which the topic is discussed.
Following a discussion of the role of interrogation, the Commission
continues: 'There is, then, a critically important relationship between
the police and the public in the detection and investigation of crime.
This alone makes it essential that the public should have confidence in
the way the police go about the process of investigation, so that ordinary citizens will continue to cooperate in that process. The success of
the police depends upon public support and this should be reflected in
the arrangements for investigation.'[4]
Central questions which are raised include: Has the relationship
between the police and the public been deteriorating in recent years?
Does the use of the present powers of the police alienate sections of
the population? What is the precise contribution of the public in the
detection and investigation of crime? Would this contribution be
severely affected if police powers were extended?
The simplest explanation for this lack of analysis of such core
questions is that the majority of the Commission's members made no
connection between the extension of police powers and the interests
of the community; extensions of police powers were seen as problematic
only in terms of the individuals affected by them. In all the discussions of the very strange and confused notion of 'the fundamental

balance', which constrasts the interests of the community in bringing
offenders to justice and the rights and liberties of the individual,
there is no reference that the extension of powers may conflict with the
interests of the community. As Fine has pointed out, the concept of the
fundamental balance conceals more than it reveals: 'It presupposes
exactly what it should be looking into; namely an identity of interest
between the interest of the community and the powers of the police'.[5]

MISUSE OF EXISTING POWERS BY THE POLICE

The second neglected topic is the extent to which the police are already
misusing their powers. The opening pages of the report point out that
among factors crucial to the government's decision to establish a
Commission were 'the manifestly growing concern about the continuing
rise in the level of crime' and, on the other side, concern that the
use of powers by the police 'was often open to grave question'.[6] In
particular, the Commission noted the disquiet aroused by the Maxwell
Confait case. It was, the report stated, against this background that
the Commission began its work in February 1978. Unfortunately, this
last concern is quickly lost and is never discussed again. Yet the
Commission had available various statistics concerning the three key
areas of the policing - stop and search, questioning and detention -
which suggested that the police were probably misusing some of their
powers and actually misusing others. All these statistics were ignored
as possible signs of police malpractices: they were used only to indicate the extent of police practices. The statistics produce a disturbing
picture.
   The Law and Procedure volume presents statistics for stop and searches
under both the Misuse of Drugs Act 1971 and the Metropolitan Police Act
1839.[7] In 1978 over 18,000 people were stopped and searched for controlled drugs but only about 4,000 or 23% were found to be in possession.
This suggests either that the police do not restrict their searches to
those people whom they reasonably suspect of being in unlawful possession
of drugs, or that their judgment concerning suspicion is totally inaccurate. Whatever the reason, the evidence suggests that the police are
either incompetent or are acting unlawfully. Similar comments can be
made in relation to activities under the Metropolitan Police Act 1839.
In a sample month in 1978 over 40,000 people were stopped and searched
under this Act, and only 13% were subsequently arrested. If this was a
typical month, this suggests that over 200,000 people were stopped and
searched by the Metropolitan Police in 1978. It is remarkable that so
many people should be thought to be wandering around the streets of
London with dishonestly appropriated goods hidden on their beings.
The size of the operation is equivalent to stopping and searching every
person above the age of criminal responsibility in a medium-sized city
on one occasion. It is hard not to avoid the conclusion that the police
are using illegally their various powers of stop and search.
   Further evidence of the possible misuse of powers by the police is
provided by data on arrest. The research carried out for the Commission
showed that somewhere between 10% and 20% of all arrested persons are
released without any proceedings being brought against them.[8] In 1978.
370,000 people were arrested for indictable crimes. This means that some
74,000 people are arrested every year for indictable crimes but then not

prosecuted. There are a number of possible explanations for this high
rate of release: the police may have insufficient evidence to bring a
prosecution; they may not want, for various reasons, to proceed further;
or the person may be innocent of the offence. The Commission tends to
favour this last explanation. It enthusiastically points out that
arrest and subsequent detention 'is used not only to confirm but also
to dispel suspicion'.[9] There is no apparent concern that over 70,000
innocent people are being arrested every year, taken to the police
station, fingerprinted, photographed and then released.

The statistics pertaining to the period during which people are held
in detention also suggest misuse of powers. The Commission sponsored a
number of studies into interrogation. Two of them showed that no-one
was held in custody for more than 48 hours.[10] This was not a particularly surprising result, as the presence of a researcher probably encouraged the police to stick to the law. A more interesting study was
carried out by the Metropolitan Police.[11] They found that in the period
1 October to 31 December 1979, 212 persons out of 48,343 2343 held for
72 hours or more before charge or release without charge. The Commission
notes that this constituted 0.4% of those held, thus suggesting that the
figure made up a very small proportion of those detained. In proportionate terms the figure is very small, but in absolute terms it is considerable. It indicates that over 800 Londoners a year are being held in
police custody for over three days, some of whom are then released
without charge.

While these figures only raise doubts - they do not show categoric-
ally that the police are misusing their powers - other statistics
collected for the Commission are less problematic. Research by Baldwin
and McConville, based on interviews with defendants tried on indictment
showed that one-third of all defendants who pleaded not guilty asked to
see a solicitor - a fundamental right - but the police turned down the
majority of these requests.[12] A study by Zander of convicted prisoners
found that rather less than half said that they had asked to see a
solicitor and three-quarters of them were not allowed to do so.[13]

All these statistics paint a disturbing picture of present police
practices. Thousands of people every year are being subjected to police
powers but are then permitted to go on their way because there is no
evidence for the police to proceed further. The damage of operations
of this scale on police-community relations must be considerable. Many
of those people who are subject to a search in public but not arrested,
or who are arrested but then released, must develop a negative attitude
towards the police and become reluctant or simply refuse to cooperate
in subsequent investigations by the police. It is against this background that the many proposed extensions in police powers must be
considered.

THE CONTEXT OF POLICE WORK

The third topic which receives very little attention in the report is
the context of police work. Throughout, the Commission argues that
contemporaneous controls and good supervision by the police are the
best methods of controlling abuse. But underlying this view is an
assumption that the pressure to break rules arises from the personality
characteristics of the police. It is assumed that they are either over-

zealous or in some circumstances deviant. This assumption is highly
questionable. There is a considerable body of evidence which suggests
that the pressure on the police to break the rules does not stem from
the personality characteristics of policemen but is located within the
organisation of policing.[14] The pressures tend to be developed in response to the perceived seriousness of the crime problem and often deci-
sons concerning particular responses to the problem are decided at a
very high level. In these circumstances exceptional policies are
assumed to be necessary, and if the police are not actually encouraged
to bend the rules they are certainly not discouraged.

To place so much faith in the use of contemporaneous controls and
good supervision by the police themselves is therefore misguided. The
only adequate safeguard to police malpractices, where the pressures stem
from within the organisation, is some form of public accountability over
operational matters. This issue, however, was outside the Commission's
terms of reference and, as it is currently receiving considerable
attention, it will not be discussed further here.[15]

EXTENSION OF POWERS OF STOP AND SEARCH, ARREST AND DETENTION

The Commission proposes two new powers of stop and search. First, it
recommends that a police officer should have the power to stop and if
need be search any person in a public place whom he reasonably suspects
of conveying stolen goods or of being in possession of anything in a
public place - which is of itself a criminal offence. The real significance of this provision is that it creates a new power to stop and
search an individual whom the police suspect of carrying an offensive
weapon. Second, the Commission recommends that a police officer of
senior rank may authorise the setting up of road checks when a person
whose arrest is sought in relation to a grave crime is believed to be
in the area.

The vagueness of the terms in both provisions is considerable. The
crucial concept of an offensive weapon is not defined and could cover
any item from a penknife to a studded belt. Even packages could be seen
as offensive weapons and people carrying them could reasonably be stopped
and searched under the new power. Moreover, the key concept of a 'grave'
crime is only broadly defined:

> ... serious offences against the person or serious sexual offences
> (murder, manslaughter, causing grievous bodily harm, armed robbery,
> kidnapping, rapd); serious offences of damaging property (arson,
> causing explosions); serious dishonesty offences (counterfeiting,
> corruption, and burglary, theft and frauds, where major amounts are
> involved); and a miscellaneous group (the supply, importation or
> exportation of controlled drugs, perversion of the course of
> justice, and blackmail.[16]

There is no attempt to detail the range of offences which should be
included in each of the broad categories of offence. Nor is there any
attempt to say what might be considered a 'major amount'. Similarly,
there is no definition as to what is meant by 'moving in a particular
area'. Every day of the week the police must receive information of
one sort and another which suggests that a person whom they believe has
committed a grave crime is 'moving in a particular area'. Would every
such piece of information permit the setting up of road checks? In any

event, what is an area? Is it a block of houses, a few streets or a
square mile of town? All these and many other key concepts are left
vague.

One of the stated objectives of the Commission was to clarify the
existing law. It went to considerable lengths criticising the vagueness
of existing powers, particularly the concept of 'serious offence' in the
Magistrates' Courts Act 1952. Yet all it does is to replace one set of
vague terms by another. This lack of clarification can only increase
the trend of the police to use their powers randomly and arbitrarily.

The Commission proposes various safeguards to cover both provisions.
It suggests that a person who is stopped and searched should be informed
of the reason for the search, the search should be recorded by the searching officer and a senior officer should supervise and monitor the records.
In addition, it is recommended that a copy of the record should be made
available within a reasonable period on request by the person who has
been searched. While these proposals are a move in the right direction,
they will have only a limited impact and they certainly do not in themselves justify the increases in powers that are proposed. To begin with,
how effective will the monitoring system be in practice? All the monitoring is to be conducted by the police and their perceptions as to what
is satisfactory will be determined by operational considerations and not
by whether the practices appear random, arbitrary or discriminatory.
Moreover, the potential success of monitoring depends in the first place
on the policemen on the street recording every time a person is stopped
and searched. But how realistic is this? If, as I have argued above,
there are strong pressures on the police to produce results, the context
of policing will encourage the police to cut corners and break the rules
if it is thought necessary. The extent to which existing stop and
search provisions are at present misused should have suggested to the
Commission that these types of safeguards are unlikely to be successful.

The Commission also proposes substantial extensions in arrest and
detention powers. At the present time, a police officer may arrest a
person only on reasonable suspicion of committing an arrestable offence.
An arrestable offence is defined as any offence which carries a prison
sentence of five years or more. It is proposed that this definition
should be widened to include any offence which carries a prison sentence.
This extension is to be balanced by a new safeguard which the Commission
describes as 'the necessity principle'. This involves the application
of various criteria to determine whether detention upon arrest should
continue.

The Commission's presentation of this safeguard is most misleading.
It is discussed in a section sub-headed 'Restrictions upon Arrest'.[17]
But the restrictions which are recommended are not in fact to be
applied upon arrest, i.e. at the moment of arrest, but at some subsequent point in time when the person is in the police station. This
careless use of language appears to have confused the majority on the
Commission. In discussing the effects of the proposal it notes that
'the restrictions upon arrest and detention upon arrest proposed are
such as to ensure that arrest will be less frequently and widely used
even if the definition of arrestable offences is widened'.[18] But the
Commission does not in fact recommend any safeguards *at the point of
arrest* but only at the point of detention in the police station. The
implicit assumption is that a policeman in exercising the power of
arrest will bear in mind the criteria which will be subsequently

applied and this will restrict the use of arrest. But the very opposite
may occur: policemen may apply a lower standard of reasonable suspicion,
because they know that there will be an additional check to their
judgment.

Apart from the question of whether or not the 'necessity principle'
will curtail the number of arrests, there is also the question of whether
it will succeed in preventing the unnecessary detention of suspects. It
is proposed that a person should be detained only if there is a likelihood that the person may fail to appear in court or if he or she is unwilling to identify themselves so that a summons may be served, or there
is a need to prevent the continuation of further offences, to protect
the arrested person from harm, and to secure and preserve evidence.
There is also another criterion which is tagged onto the need to secure
and preserve evidence and it is most extensive. If there is a need 'to
obtain such evidence from the suspect by questioning', the person can
also be detained.[19] In other words, the Commission is recommending that
after a person who has been arrested on reasonable suspicion of committing an arrestable offence may be detained solely for the purposes of
questioning. Moreover, the way in which the criterion is presented the
questioning does not have to apply to the offence for which the person
was arrested, but to any offence. This criterion opens the door to
arrest for questioning.

In any event, the potential efficacy of the use of these criteria is
extremely dubious. It is probable that in many cases the police will
tend to err in the direction of caution and interpret these criteria
broadly in order to justify the detention of the suspect. The Commission
notes that the criteria have broadly the same effect as the criteria
under the Bail Act for the purpose of the court's decision to grant
bail. This is hardly a recommendation. Nearly 40% of 63,865 people
who were remanded in custody in 1979 were eventually acquitted according
to recent figures published by the National Association for the Care
and Resettlement of Offenders.[20] These figures provide clear evidence
that the application of the bail criteria by magistrates do not prevent
innocent people being deprived of their liberty prior to trial. There
is no reason to believe that similar criteria applied by the police
will be any more successful at preventing innocent people being deprived
of their liberty at an earlier stage in the criminal justice process.

The Commission makes a number of other proposals concerning detention.
It recommends that after six hours of detention there should be an automatic review by a police officer who is not connected with the investigation. After 24 hours the suspect must be either charged or released.
In other words, the Commission is recommending an absolute limit on
detention and this is probably the only satisfactory method of safeguarding the rights of the suspect. This safeguard, however, is not to
apply to all offences. In the case of grave crimes, the Commission
proposes that further detention after 24 hours may be authorised by a
magistrate sitting in private. The suspect would have the right to
legal representation at the hearing. If the suspect is not charged or
released in this period the police may go back to the magistrate and
ask for another 24 hours' detention. If they need another 24 hours,
they can go back again. This recommendation therefore amounts to indef-
inite detention. Even under the Northern Ireland (Emergency Provisions)
Act and the Prevention of Terrorism Act there are absolute limits after
which the suspect must be released or charged.

It can be argued that this is an academic point because in practice
the magistrates will not permit long periods of detention. But this
must be questioned. The problem with magistrates' supervision of detention is that they are entirely dependent upon the information supplied
to them by the police. The Commission recognised this problem in relation to the authorisation of road checks and rejected the idea that
magistrates should be responsible for this task. It argued that 'for
operational matters such as this the magistrates can do little other
than endorse a police request, so that they would provide no real safeguard'.[21] Yet, only a few pages further on, it is argued that they
provide a safeguard in matters relating to detention.

The problems associated with relying on magistrates to provide an
adequate safeguard for those detained can be best illustrated by considering a concrete example. In March last year the arson campaign in
Wales resulted in a nationwide police operation.[22] Of the 52 people
known to have been detained only four were charged, a number of suspects
were not brought before a magistrate's court 'as soon as possible' and
one was held for three days and another for nearly two. This situation
would not be improved under the above proposals. The magistrate will be
entirely dependent on what the police say. If the police say that important evidence is being brought down from the north of the country or
that the laboratory requires another day to analyse some forensic material, is the magistrate likely to refuse a request for another 24 hours
of detention? It is most unlikely, particularly in the case of grave
crimes. The proposal would have some teeth if the Commission had recommended that magistrates' decisions be monitored and a record kept of the
outcome of all their decisions to extend the period of detention. In
this way they would know whether or not any particular extension was
really necessary.

THE NORTHERN IRELAND EXPERIENCE AND THE EXTENSION OF POWERS OF STOP AND
SEARCH, ARREST AND DETENTION

Extensions of police and army powers in respect of these three key areas
of policing were introduced into Northern Ireland in the early 1970s.
Although the extensions advanced by the Commission differ in some detail
from those introduced into Northern Ireland, nevertheless they are in the
same direction. The ways in which the new powers were used in Ulster
illustrate the dangers of increasing police powers, particularly at a
time when there is considerable external pressure on the police to produce results. The changes were based on the recommendations of the
Diplock Commission[23] which was set up in 1972 to review the legal procedures for dealing with terrorists. They were enacted in the Northern
Ireland (Emergency Provisions) Act 1973.

The Army was given the power to arrest and detain for up to 4 hours
any person suspected of terrorist activity and both the army and police
were given power to stop and question any person as to his identity and
knowledge of terrorist incidents. The Act also gave the police and the
army powers to enter and search houses to search for arms and explosives.
In addition, the powers of arrest were made less demanding than under
the ordinary criminal law. The emergency legislation permits a policemen to arrest without warrant any person whom he suspects of being a
terrorist. There is no need for there to be reasonable suspicion, only

suspicion, and there is no requirement that the policeman has any particular offence in mind, only that the person is a terrorist.

All these powers were extensively misused. The 4-hour detention power
was employed to 'screen' as large a section of the Catholic population
as was possible with the aim of obtaining as much information on social
and other characteristics as possible. All the information was computerised. While the police arrest power did not gain significance until the
ending of internment in 1975 - up to then suspects could simply be picked
up and detained - it was then used on a massive scale to bring in for
questioning anyone who was thought to be involved in terrorism. This, of
course, included the majority of the population in particular areas. The
extent of the misuse can be seen from figures presented to the Bennett
Committee.[24] In the period September 1977 to August 1978, 2,814 people
were detained for more than 4 hours under the Northern Ireland (Emergency
Provisions) Acts 1977 and 1978 and only a little over one-third were
charged; the rest were released.

The misuse of these powers played a fundamental part in antagonising
those who lived in Catholic enclaves and further lessened their confidence in, and support of, the police.

Many people will dismiss these details as irrelevant to policing in
England and Wales. For those that do, it should be remembered that the
present troubles in Northern Ireland began with a minority of the population complaining about social and economic discrimination and the arbitrary and repressive behaviour of the police. While the social, political
and historical circumstances of the minority groups in England and Wales
are clearly very different from Catholics in Northern Ireland, nevertheless there are similarities in their feelings of resentment. Extensions
in police powers of stop and search, arrest and detention, can only exacerbate these feelings and further alienate the minorities from the
police. This can only make more difficult the task of the police in
detecting and investigating.

THE ABOLITION OF THE VOLUNTARINESS RULE AND THE RELAXATION OF THE
EXCLUSIONARY RULE

At the present time conduct during questioning is provided for in the
non-statutory Judges' Rules. They lay down that all statements should
be obtained voluntarily in the sense that they are not 'obtained by fear
of prejudice or hope of advantage exercised or held out by a person in
authority, or by oppression'. If this 'voluntariness' rule is broken,
the judge has a discretion to exclude any statement so obtained. The
Commission recommends the abolition of the voluntary rule and a substantial relaxation of the exclusionary rule. I will deal with each proposal
in some detail.

The principal arguments against the present voluntariness rule are
that: it is vague; there is no correspondence between the legal and
psychological concepts of psychological oppression; and it means, in
practice, that a police officer 'is required under the confusion and
pressures of an investigation to make an assessment of the character,
susceptibilities and mental state of the suspect whom he is interviewing'.[25] This last reason is most strange: it suggests that it is satisfactory for a suspect to make judgments about his involvement in, and
circumstances surrounding, a crime in 'the confusion and pressures of

an investigation', but unsatisfactory for a police officer, under similar
circumstances, to make a judgment about whether or not his questioning
methods are such as to be oppressive.

In place of the voluntariness rule the Commission proposes that, apart
from a code of practice, which is discussed below, there should be no
specific rule governing the questioning of suspects other than that
questioning should not include violence, threat of violence, inhuman or
degrading treatment or torture. In other words, it is proposed that the
police be permitted to move from a situation where they are obliged to
observe a voluntariness rule, however vague this may be and however hard
it is to define accurately, to a situation where they are permitted to
use any technique or method of interrogation short of violence, threat
of violence, inhuman or degrading treatment.

What the Commission has done is to take Article 3 of the European
Convention on Human Rights and add to it violence and the threat of
violence. The Convention's Standard, however, is only a minimum Standard
as Lord Justice McGonigal made clear in a famous judgment in Northern
Ireland concerning the question of admissibility:

> Treatment to come within Article 3 must be treatment of a gross
> nature. It appears to accept a degree of physical violence which
> could never be tolerated by the courts under the common law test
> ... it leaves open to an interviewer to use a moderate degree of
> maltreatment for the purpose of inducing a person to make a
> statement. It appears to me that this is the way the words must
> be construed and that is the effect of the section.[26]

By adding violence and the threat of violence the Commission has extended
the minimum Standard only a little. Threats, inducements of oppressive
techniques designed to disorientate the subjects, all of which are at
present illegal, will be permitted under this proposal. In effect,
licence is being given to the police to use any form of psychological
pressure as well as threats such as 'I will arrest your mother unless
you confess' or 'We will keep you here for the next three days unless
you sign a confession'. The Commission clearly was in support of such
practices. It proudly stated:

> We have concluded that the *regulation of questioning* is not,   [27]
> for a variety of reasons, practicable or *desirable* (italics added)

Although the Commission is against regulating the actual conduct of
questioning, it does support the regulation of the conduct of interviews
and proposes a code of interrogation practice. It makes no attempt,
however, to draw up a code and recommends only in very vague terms
what it should include.

> We would suggest for consideration provisions that required an
> interview to be broken for brief refreshment and for meals after
> specified times; that precluded interviewing at night if the
> suspect had been interviewed for any substantial period in the
> day or immediately after a suspect had been woken up (it would
> be unrealistic to prohibit all interviews at night since if that
> were so a person arrested late in the evening might have to be
> held overnight); that prohibited questioning after a suspect
> had been held incommunicado beyond a specified period; that pre-
> vented interviewing persons substantially under the influence of
> drugs or alcohol; that precluded more than a specified number of
> officers being present at any one time; that set conditions of
> lighting, ventilation and seating for the interview room.[28]

The vagueness of so many of these provisions will permit whoever draws up the code extensive discretion. What does the Commission mean, for example, by the word 'substantial' in relation to the period of inter- viewing during the day? Would it consider one, two or eight hours of interrogation substantial? Apart from the vagueness there are no pro- visions covering interrogation of females, the actual length of any particular interview, or the number of teams of police officers who may interview the suspect at any one time.

While a code of practice for the regulation of interviews is to be welcomed in principle, it is unlikely to have very much effect as the Commission rejects the proposal that breaches of the code should lead to the automatic exclusion of evidence.

The Commission's three arguments against an automatic exclusionary rule are very weak. To begin with, it points out that judges have not seen themselves as having the function of controlling improper police behaviour and they refer to a judgment of Lord Diplock. This is no argument. Because judges do not see themselves as carrying out this function, there is no reason why they should not be given the task.

Secondly, it argues that the use of the automatic exclusionary rule can apply to a small proportion of cases only, because the majority of police conduct does not actually lead to a prosecution. This point is certainly correct, but it is a fallacy then to argue that 'the rule can operate to secure the rights only of a very small minority'.[29] Although not everyone subject to detention and interrogation will end up in court challenging the evidence, this does not mean that a far greater number of people may benefit from an exclusionary rule. The police do not know when they detain and question a suspect whether they will obtain evidence which can be used subsequently in court. On the contrary, the knowledge that misbehaviour may lead to a case being lost is much more likely to help make the police stick to the rules.

The Commission's third argument against an exclusionary rule is that research has shown it to be ineffective. The Commission refers to an American piece of research which concluded that the exclusionary rule operates under conditions that are extremely unfavourable for deterring the police. Although the Commission points out that, as the United States jurisdiction is in so many respects different from our own, the comment should be treated with care. Nevertheless, it concludes that 'the American experience does not offer any encouraging prospect of an automatic exclusionary rule its proponents see for it here'.[30] It therefore rejects its general introduction.

The implications of this decision are considerable. It will mean, among other things, that there will be no automatic exclusion of evid- ence where a suspect's request for a solicitor has been wrongly denied, or where a statement has been obtained either from a young mentally retarded person without any adult being present, or when someone has been interviewed continuously throughout the night. Evidence will be automatically excluded only where there has been a breach of the rule prohibiting violence, threats of violence, torture or inhuman or degrading treatment.

In the absence of any information one way or the other on the possible deterrent effects of an automatic exclusionary rule in England and Wales it is more constructive to keep an exclusionary rule on the expectation that it may have some effect.

Apart from a code of practice, the Commission proposes a number of other contemporaneous controls to safeguard the suspect in detention. But they are unlikely to have much impact. In the first place, it recommends that tape recording should be gradually introduced not to monitor all the exchanges between police and suspect but for making and reading back a summary of the interview. After this has been recorded, the suspect will be invoted 'to offer comments upon it as well as his comments on how he has been treated'. This proposal illustrates again the failure of the Commission to understand the context of police work. It ignores the fact that very few suspects will have the ability to articulate their views into a tape recorder. It also ignores both the pressures to conform and the mental state of suspects after being in police custody. It is incomprehensible how this proposal will lead to a more accurate record of what the suspect wishes to say or provide any safeguard for the suspect.

Secondly, the Commission recommends making more effective the existing rights of a suspect in custody. Every suspect will have the right of access to legal advice except where a person is suspected of a grave crime and 'there is reason to believe that access to a solicitor may cause delay resulting in risk to life or property, or give rise to interference with evidence or witnesses, the disposal of the proceeds of crime or the escape of accomplices'.[31] Again, the imprecise concept of grave crime is used to restrict suspects' rights and again the general criteria are vague. For example, what is meant by risk to property?

Finally, the Commission confirms that all suspects should continue to have the right to have someone notified of their arrest.

The Commission rejects perhaps the only way to safeguard the suspect during questioning: to have a third party present, whether it be a magistrate, solicitor or any other person. The proposals as a whole will do little to improve the present unsatisfactory state of affairs concerning the interrogation of suspects. On the contrary, the relaxation of the exclusionary rule and the abolition of the voluntariness rule will only encourage the police to rely more and more on questioning as the principal method of solving crime and the trend towards more and more outcomes of the criminal process being determined in the police station, rather than in open court, will continue. Justice will become even more invisible.

THE NORTHERN IRELAND EXPERIENCE: THE ABOLITION OF THE VOLUNTARINESS RULE AND THE RELAXATION OF THE EXCLUSIONARY RULE

The Commission's proposals to alter the practice and sanctions relating to questioning follow closely the changes introduced into Northern Ireland in 1973 following the recommendations of the Diplock Commission, which argued that:

> ... the detailed technical rules and practice as to the 'admissibility' of inculpatory statements by the accused as they are currently applied in Northern Ireland are hampering the cause of justice in the case of terrorist crimes and compelling the authorities responsible for public order and safety to resort to detention in a significant number of cases which could otherwise be dealt with both effectively and fairly by trial in a court of law.[32]

Diplock therefore proposed that the law should be changed to allow statements obtained in breach of the common law rules to be admitted in evidence provided that they could not be shown to have been obtained by
subjecting the accused to torture, inhuman or degrading treatment. This
proposal was duly adopted in the Northern Ireland (Emergency Provisions)
Act 1973. The only difference between this provision and the proposals
of the Royal Commission is that violence and the threat of violence is
added to the latter.

The main point to emphasise about the Diplock reforms is that they
were combined with extensions in police powers of arrest and detention.
All the changes were part of a package to make it easier for the police
to obtain confessions. The Commission's proposals are in an identical
form: increased police powers and changes in the rules of questioning
and evidence.

What happened in Northern Ireland, once these changes became significant with the ending of interment in 1975 and the reliance on courts,
provides a salutory lesson for those who argue for wide-ranging changes
in criminal procedure. The politicians were determined that the switch
from the use of internment to the use of the courts for dealing with
those involved in political violence would be successful and as a result
enormous external pressure was put on the police to produce results.
Moreover, with forensic evidence often hard to obtain because of the
nature of the violence, and with witnesses reluctant to come forward,
confession statements were often central for a conviction. The number
of allegations against police behaviour during interrogation began to
increase. The details of the allegations and the subsequent uproar
which they caused need not concern us. The main point is that the
combination of external political pressure, increased police powers and
changes in the admissibility of evidence was disastrous not only for
suspects but also for public confidence in the criminal justice system.
Yet the Commission is recommending a very similar package for England
and Wales.

A NEW PROSECUTION SYSTEM

The final recommendation I wish to consider is the proposal to establish
a statutory based prosecution service for every police area. This will
be headed by a person called the Crown Prosecutor, and he or she will
be responsible for the conduct of all criminal cases once the police
have taken the decision to start proceedings. Ministerial responsibility
for the service will rest with the Attorney-General. These proposals
would create in England and Wales a very similar prosecution process to
that in Northern Ireland.

The Northern Ireland system was established in 1972 following the
recommendations of the MacDermott Committee.[33] It consists of an Office
of Director of Public Prosecutions which is responsible for the conduct
of all serious prosecutions. The initial decisions concerning the
selection of charges and the preparation of files are carried out by
the police. The Director is responsible to the Attorney-General. Apart
from the fact that there is only one central office and that the Director
is only responsible for more serious crimes, the system recommended by
the Commission will be identical to that in Northern Ireland. The
Commission did visit the Office but it made no analysis of the system.

    There can be no doubt that it has achieved the central aim of estab-
lishing the system in the first place - to achieve uniformity in the
selection of charges between different sections of the community - but
there are a number of limitations. To begin with, there is a tendency
for bureaucratic demands to predominate to the detriment of considerations of justice. For example, there is a constant pressure for the
prosecution to obtain a high proportion of guilty pleas as this will
ensure a speedy disposal of the cases. This will be to the advantage
of some suspects in so far as their case will be dealt with speedily.
However, it will be to the disadvantage of those who may be acquitted if
they plead not guilty. Secondly, the Northern Ireland example raises
doubt about the independence of the Office. An analysis of what happens
in practice shows that the Office is not in fact independent of either
the police or, more importantly, the Attorney-General. It can take no
action until the police have selected the charges, compiled a file and
delivered it to the Director of Public Prosecutions. It is only at this
stage that any influence can be exerted. Similarly, the Office is not
totally free of the influence of the Attorney-General. It has been
admitted that in respect of the more serious charges against members of
the security forces in Ulster, the Director discusses the case with the
Attorney-General before proceeding. The establishment of an 'independent' system of prosecution in England and Wales for which the Attorney-
General is responsible will make it more rather than less easy for
political influence to be exerted particularly in relation to prosecutions of a political nature. Although the proposal to establish an
Office is to be supported, more substantial recommendations are necessary if it is to avoid the failures of Northern Ireland.

CONCLUSIONS

A number of more general points can be made in conclusion. In the first
place, the recommendations will do little to help deal with the problem
of crime which in the last instance depends on everyone having confidence in the police. In failing to confront the problems of the present
misuse of powers by the police, as well as the poor relations between
the police and the public in certain areas, it has done little to
encourage support for the police in the detection and investigation of
crime.
    Second, in the place of the existing confusion concerning the extent
of police powers, the Commission has introduced more confusion but only
after radically extending police powers. Finally, the package will
establish in England and Wales a far more repressive, professionalised
and bureaucratised criminal justice system similar to the system in
Northern Ireland. F.L.S. Lyons, the eminent Irish historian, has
pointed out that, in the 19th century, Ireland
    ... was used almost as a social laboratory. That is to say
    experiments in governmental regulation were undertaken to a
    degree that would hardly have been tolerated in England of that
    day.... This was the case, for example, with the creation of a
    national police force, with the beginnings of a rudimentary health
    service, and with the various enterprises by the Board of Works.[34]
Can we now soon add to that list, in the 20th century, a criminal justice
system?

NOTES AND REFERENCES

1   See Harman, H. and Griffith, J., *Justice Deserted*, NCCL, 1979.
2   For a detailed analysis of the operation of the criminal justice
    system in Northern Ireland over the last eleven years see Boyle,
    Kevin, Hadden, Tom and Hillyard, Paddy, *Law and State: The Case of
    Northern Ireland*, Martin Robertson, 1975. Boyle, Kevin, Hadden, Tom
    and Hillyard, Paddy, *Ten Years On in Northern Ireland: The Legal
    Control of Political Violence*, NCCL, 1980.
3   The Royal Commission on Criminal Procedure, *Report*, Cmnd. 8092, HMSO,
    January 1981, p.104.
4   *ibid.*, p.20
5   Fine, Bob, *Rights*, March/April 1981, Vol.5, No.4, p.3.
6   *Report, op.cit.*, p.2.
7   The Royal Commission on Criminal Procedure, *The Investigation and
    Prosecution of Criminal Offences in England and Wales: The Law and
    Procedure*, Cmnd. 8092-1, January 1981, p.80.
8   *Report, op.cit.*, p.43.
9   *Report, op.cit.*, p.43.
10 *Report, op.cit.*, p.52.
11 *Report, op.cit.*, p.53.
12 *Report, op.cit.*, p.97.
13 *Report, op.cit*, p.98.
14 See, for example, Chambliss, W.J. and Seidman, R.B., *Law, Order and
    Power*, Addison Wesley, 1971, Chapter 14.
15 See, for example, 'Controlling the Police?: Police Accountability in
    UK', *State Research No.23*, April/March 1981, pp.110-23.
16 *Report, op.cit.*, p.24.
17 *Report, op.cit.*, p.44.
18 *Report, op.cit.*, p.48.
19 *Report, op.cit.*, p.45.
20 National Association for the Care and Resettlement of Offenders,
    reported in *New Society*, 23 April 1981.
21 *Report, op.cit.*, p.32.
22 See *Operation Fire*, W.C.C.P.L., April 1980.
23 Report of the Commission to consider legal procedures to deal with
    terrorist activities in Northern Ireland, Cmnd. 5185, December 1972.
24 Report of the Committee of Inquiry into Police Interrogation
    Procedures in Northern Ireland, Cmnd. 7497, March 1979.
25 *Report, op.cit.*, p.93.
26 R.V. McCormick (1977) *Northern Ireland Reports 105*.
27 *Report, op.cit.*, p.109.
28 *Report, op.cit.*, p.108.
29 *Report, op.cit.*, p.113.
30 *Report, op.cit.*, p.114.
31 *Report, op.cit.*, p.123.
32 Cmnd. 5185, *op.cit.*, p.31.
33 Report of the Working Party on Public Prosecutions, Cmnd. 554,
    Belfast, 1971.
34 F.S.L. Lyons, *Culture and Anarchy in Ireland, 1890-1939*, Oxford,
    1979, p.9.

And now~ Secondhand books!

Subjects include: The Thirties,
Russian Revolution, biography,
poetry, China, politics, fiction,
Trade Union history, socialism

37 Grays Inn Road, London WC1

Open 9.30~5.30 Sats 10~2   01~242 6166

Stephan Feuchtwang
Collective Action and English Law against Racial Discrimination in Employment*

This article will take up some of the implications of laws against
discrimination and of the Race Relations Act 1976 (RRA 76) in particular.
Its challenges will be set out first by examining the judgements in a
recent case which came before employment tribunals. There are two main
reasons why this case is important. One is that it was a group application, and I will argue that attacks on racialist effects in employment
by means of tribunals will have no deterrent force unless they are taken
collectively. The other is that the case confused the notion of indirect, or effective discrimination. This notion is not written into
the RRA 76 in so many words. But it was current in the deliberations
which preceded the drafting of the Act and is by now common usage in
discussing sexual and racial discrimination in law.[1] The case left the
issues involved unclarified. Yet they are well worth raising and the
notion is worth canvassing. It allows for the identification of racialist or sexist circumstances which are the effects of practices even
though the practices cannot be said to be racist or sexist in nature or
motivation. The issues of interpreting the RRA 76 are still alive,
since no definitive legal judgements in Courts of Appeal have yet been
made on it.

A review of the Act's operation and of what it is intended to remedy
will show how severely limiting the practices of tribunals are and how
restrictive the Act in its present form is compared with what it could
be. But the RRA 76 also sanctions activities outside tribunals and
courts. The range of instruments which are at the disposal of collective and government action outside tribunals will be indicated. But here
too it will be argued that the possibilities are far greater than what
is actually done. If the possibilities are to be realised, forces and
organisational initiatives on the part of employees will have to emerge.
What these might be and with what consequences and policy implications
for the labour movement will be suggested throughout and summarised in
conclusion.

INDIRECT DISCRIMINATION

In September 1978 an Industrial Tribunal started proceedings. A group
of seventeen Asian spray-shop workers accused their employer, Pel Ltd -
furniture manufacturer - and their union, the Furniture, Timber and
Allied Trades Union, of racial discrimination against them. The workers
constituted the entire personnel of one job grade, and one of their
complaints was that they had been unfairly graded in relation to workers
in similarly described jobs. Comparability of grading could be a very
widespread issue and source of grievance, but this was a rare (if not
unique) instance of its being raised as racial discrimination in law -
though not by any means rare in other forms of industrial dispute, nor
rare under sex discrimination law.
    The application concerned a matter which, as the tribunal said,
'accrued over time', and so was a practice rather than a single incident. The tribunal also decided to follow the example of two Employment
Appeals Tribunal (EAT) judgements, under the Sex Discrimination Act and
the Equal Pay Act, that the applicant has only to establish unfavourable
treatment and to be 'self-evidently' of 'a racial group' different from
others treated more favourably, for the burden of proof to shift to the
employer to show that no unlawful discrimination occurred. The discrimination need only be inferred from the facts presented. The defence
against the inference would have to be that the practice in question was
one properly within the normal practices of employment and therefore
that there was no intrusion of judgement of attributes that should
remain private and irrelevant to those practices. Intention to discriminate does not have to be evidenced.
    The state of mind of the respondent is not material in proving many
kinds of unlawful discrimination. But there is a further difficulty in
interpreting the meaning of discrimination. It is a difficulty borne
by the notion of indirect discrimination, which raises and appears to
recognise the possibility that a number of practices, none of which is
unlawfully discriminatory in itself, may have the combined effect of
segregation or of unlawful discrimination. In this case all those practices would have to be raised before the tribunal for remedy. It could
be said that continuation of a disadvantage suffered disproportionately
by a black population constitutes effective discrimination, if the
practices responsible for this continuation were identifiable.[2]
    How is such a multiple cause of racial discrimination to be identified?
The problem here is that discrimination as an effect of multiply-deter-
mined construction cannot be attributed to the intention of an individual subject. But unlawfully discriminatory practices are *presumed* to
emanate from an intention and so are given a singularity and a unity.
That, at least, was the way the Tribunal indicated. The furthest the
Tribunal went toward recognition of the possibility of a multiply-deter-
mined construction of a discrimination effect was to say: 'We have to
look at the incidents which happened and the policy of the respondent
in each application and decide whether the totality of what happened
resulted in discrimination against the applicants' (paragraph 31 of the
Tribunal's Decision). An earlier paragraph (no.29) had introduced the
whole matter of effective discrimination as 'secondary' or 'indirect'
or 'unconscious' discrimination, and to do this it refers to the
'demeanour' of the respondents' witnesses: 'In most instances it will
be a question of assessing the facts in the light of the evidence of

the witnesses including their demeanour and deciding whether from those
facts there can be inferred any elements of discrimination.' Finally in
last paragraph of its decision for the applicants and against the Union,
the Tribunal reasserts the primacy of the legal subject with definite
and very limiting implications for what can be recognised as discrimination: 'On the basis however that people are presumed to intend the consequences of their actions, we have no doubt that the applicants were left
with the feeling that they were in effect second class members of the
union at one time'. In other words, the effect is itself to be supported
by a subjective affirmation.

Accordingly, the Tribunal found for the applicants in its own construction of their case, namely that there had been 'a failure of communcations'
(paragraph 40 and passim). The Union had refused to appoint a shop
steward to represent the seventeen men. The Tribunal commented that
'whilst we appreciate that it may be a fairly small number of people,
we do think that because of all the circumstances including the nature
of the work and the question of communication it would have been helpful
for the applicants to have had some separate representation' (paragraph
35) and 'we do not think that they [the Union officials] realised how
necessary it is to ensure that members of the union, especially who may
have language difficulties, realise exactly where they stand and what
is being done' (paragraph 40). By constructing the validity of the case
around what it calls 'the question of communication', and so reasserting
in another way the primacy of the subjectivities of the parties to the
case, the Tribunal introduces the attributes of 'racial group' so that
they are not only found to be negatively pertinent but positively relevant to the case in the form of special needs.

Even the claim of effective segregation against the Company becomes
a matter of communication: 'We think that there could have been a more
positive employing policy to endeavour to make sure that this element
of segregation or the suspicion of it did not arise within the spray
department.' The segregation is almost reworded as an inducement to
feel segregated. Lack of communication in this instance is identified
with the 'policy' of the personnel department, whose director's absence
from the witnesses called for the defence was of marked significance to
the Tribunal. It concluded: 'We think more could have been done to
establish it [the personnel department] as a positive force especially
in communication between the employing company and its work people, in
particular, so far as we are concerned, the applicants. Altogether it
appears to us that the personnel department by the way they deployed
the company's employment policy were keeping the spray department as
an Asian shop' (paragraph 77).

Within the multiplicity of practices described as the company's
employment 'policy', responsibility for segregation was finally pinned
down to the conduct of a department and the demeanour of an absent
witness.

That a collective legal application succeeded on a count of effective
racial segregation was a notable departure, given the abstraction of an
individual subject and of a particular incident usually associated with
legal action. But it may well be, if the proceedings of this case are
exemplary, that racial segregation and discrimination are charges which
can be brought collectively with ease only because the 'nature' of
their collectivity is defined in terms of set of attributes and needs
that are taken as given, rather than as the effect of a number of

practices. It may be that judicially the fact of belonging to a 'racial
group' does after all *not* have to be demonstrated only in the negative
sense of exclusions suffered as the result of unlawful constructions,
imposed limitations, and wrongful attributions. In the Pel case, the
success of the application was founded in the Tribunal's decision upon
the 'question of communication' which introduced the racial attributes
as proper and necessary considerations in the practices of Union and
Company policies. Language difference, a quite definitely specifiable
condition, becomes an attribute among others of a collective subject of
communication.

The defence can make use of the same possibility, attributing to the
collective subject what might in fact have been the result of employment and recruitment practices. Two instances can be given. Segregation was stated to be due to the Asians' habits of recommending jobs to
each other through 'family connections' and 'from their own community'
(paragraph 53). The claim for parity in pay with higher-paid workers
was said to be due to the collective misunderstanding of the applicants
and strongly implied to be the result of self-induced isolation. Though
the applicants were persuaded to admit that there had been a lack of
knowledge of the national wage structure, they maintained a claim that
they were still graded too low (paragraph 17). The claim was, however,
simply ignored in the Tribunal's decision.

Even this tinkering with intentionality was set aside on appeal by
the Union and the Company. The Employment Appeals Tribunal (EAT) in its
Judgement first insisted on discarding indirect discrimination despite
the fact that the Industrial Tribunal (IT) had quoted (p.6 of the transcript) the relevant clauses of Section 1 (1) of the Act for both direct
and indirect discrimination. The EAT Judgement claims that the solicitor
representing the applicants put the case in the first place under
Section 1 (1) (a). This required proof that the applicants were treated
less favourably than other persons and that this treatment was meted out
on racial grounds. The question of intention is open in the wording
of this clause and depends on the interpretation of 'treatment' and
'grounds'. Treatment seems to indicate more deliberate action than does
mere effect. And though 'grounds' could be inferred just from the fact
that those unfavourably affected were disproportionately members of a
distinct racist categorisation, it can also be taken to imply intention,
ever so unconscious though it be. Section 1 (1) (b) has fewer possible
implications of intention in its wording. It has application of a
'requirement or condition' where 1 (1) (a) has 'treatment'. Then where
1 (1) (a) has 'on racial grounds', it has application 'equally to persons not of the same racial group as that other but ... such that the
proportion of persons of the same racial group as that other who can
comply with it is considerably smaller'.

In any case, having confined its judgement to 1 (1) (a), the EAT
reviewed the points made by the IT on the case against the Union and
then before coming to its decision in favour of union and employer,
namely that there had been an error in law, turned its attention to the
problem of inference of intention:

> We have said on a number of occasions that the cases which come
> before the industrial tribunals will rarely, if ever, have
> evidence of admitted acts of discrimination on racial grounds.
> Sometimes the evidence will point clearly to an act on the part
> of an employer, or another person brought within the framework

of the Act, which will make it clear that there has been
deliberate discrimination. More often it is the task of the
tribunal to look at all the facts and to see whether, on the
facts which have happened, the right inference to draw is that
what has been done has been done on racial grounds and that it
amounts to 'discrimination' within the meaning of the Act.
(p.7 of the transcript)

In order to help it to see whether there has been unfavourable treatment
on racial grounds 'the tribunal is entitled to take account of the attitude of the witnesses and of the history of the matter as the tribunal
did in this case' but, the next sentence concludes, this is in order to
go behind the facts 'to see what really happened *and what the motive
was*' (my stress). In other words, it is not to uncover a 'policy'
resulting from decisions and practices not themselves motivated by unconscious racial discrimination. Nor is it merely to presume for such
a policy, once it can be inferred to exist, a single agent. It is to
find an agent and evidence of its motivation.

Unfavourable treatment may be found. But that is not enough. It
must also be found in the active channelling of treatment by the agent:

We do not for one moment dissent from the view expressed by
the tribunal that the Union had not fully appreciated and taken
care of the problems of these men in this paint shop. But the
tribunal did not ask themselves whether what had happened
amounted to less favourable treatment than the treatment
afforded to other people.
(p.9 of the transcript)

The Company and its managers had been equally forthright and uncommicat-
ive to the whole workforce, the Union had been equally neglectful. The
Asian workers' special needs, or the low grading and comparatively worse
work conditions of the spray shop in the organisation of the factory as
it was may be allowed to have compounded greater disadvantages than
other workers suffered from this indifferent treatment. Possibly, with
greater precision in defining the treatment or neglect as a 'condition'
or 'detriment', effective discrimination in the terms of sub-section
1 (1) (b) could have been shown. But the EAT, having discarded reliance
upon that sub-section, could insist upon inference of discrimination
'on racial grounds' being inference of active differentiation of treatment, originating with the agent responsible for it.

The IT's registering of the fact that the Asian workers 'were still
adamant that their grading was too low' could thus be ignored again even
more easily than when the decision of the IT ignored their claim.

The doctrine of intention upon which the EAT insisted unites the
agent of remedy with the agent which instigated the wrong to be remedied.
A finding of effective discrimination on the contrary identifies a wrong,
and agents whose actions may have contributed to it without necessarily
intending it. They are directed to make changes preventing recurrence
of the wrong that has been called to their attention. If effective or
indirect discrimination were rigorously defined and shown, brooking no
play with intention, agents of change could be identified, as they would
have to be in any case to assign responsibility for remedy, without the
stigma of original ill intention and the implied call for conversion or
suppression of wrongful motive which is beside the point of effect.

The EAT rejected indirect discrimination outright, associating it
with the sub-section of the Act 1 (1) (b) which it summarily discarded.

It discarded it to insist on intent, but did so without any elucidation
of what discrimination without intent would be. This must have confirmed
the Union's opinion of the IT's findings. 'Indirect discrimination'
could not be defined and a finding of indirect discrimination in an
application to which it was the respondent constituted a stigma upon its
reputation. The union issued a statement on the IT's finding, reported
in the *Guardian*, 11.4.79, rejecting the very phrase 'indirect discrimination' with all its tendencies to interpret into the Act the possibility
of merely effective discrimination. At the same time it rejected the
call upon it to cater for the special needs situation of the spray shop
workers, saying that 'indirect discrimination' appears to have consisted
in 'an alleged failure on the Union's part to give specially preferential
treatment to its Asian members over and above the service it would provide for the rest of its members. To call this "discrimination", whether
indirect or not, is, in our view, a travesty of words.'

The slur of racial discrimination, which the words of the Act may
well carry, however they might be interpreted legally, is rejected.
But the union's statement did not apparently include any off-setting
recognition of a task to improve the pay and conditions of low-graded
workers and to cater for such needs Asian workers may have as a result
of difference in language and of past disadvantages.

This may be typical of the weak representation which low-graded
workers, and the black and women workers who are disproportionately
concentrated in the lowest grades, have so far been able to achieve in
trades unions. Discrimination law in the employment field, even in its
minimal aim of removing obstacles to mobility when they have no necessary
connection to the jobs of work, points to concentrations of black and
women workers in the lowest grades as its main challenge. However much
more evenly they are distributed in higher grades of employment, continuation of disproportionate concentrations of black and women workers in
lower grades will bring into question the adequacy of the law and its
enforcement.

Unions have often been the targets for attack in industrial disputes
by black workers, and they are enshrined in the Act alongside employers
as the possible agents of racial discrimination in employment. But the
law is a goad, example or deterrent, and its chief agencies for enforcement and policing the employment field must be organisations of the
employees whose interests are most immediately served by its enforcement.
This challenge to the unions was accepted. The 1976 Race Relations Act
was welcomed by the TUC, unlike the first two Race Relations Acts when
it had recognised no problem of discrimination and covered its indifference to the problem by opposing any legislative invasion of the employment field and its bargaining ethos. Unions had individually begun to
adopt resolutions against racialism since 1973; the TUC produced its
model equal opportunity clause for inclusion in collective agreements
in 1975 and in the same year established committees for Equal Rights
and Race Relations. If the challenge of the discrimination laws is to
be met, there will have to be struggle within the unions representing
the lower grades, in which anti-discrimination policies will have to be
pursued, consequently changing attitudes on differentials in pay,
grading, access to training and possession of acquired knowledge.
Certainly, government enforcement of the law cannot be relied upon to
meet the challenge, as we shall see, and a more numerous and widespread
movement of agencies seeking enforcement of 'equal opportunity' will be

required if even the limited policies described by that phrase can be
implemented.

The significance of the Pel case and the tribunals' judgements is not
simply that the formal possibilities afforded by the Act for collective
action through litigation were not really tested, but also that certain
traditions of legal judgement and procedure may prevent their being
tested and will themselves have to be challenged.

The formal possibilities are

(1) for a group rather than an individual to bring a case, and to do so
    without imputing to it a portmanteau-nature which prevents clear
    differentiation between those characteristics and practices which
    are relevant to a job and those which are not and so should not be
    considered;

(2) for naming agents who can be deemed responsible for changing a
    situation without imputing to them an intentional interest in
    bringing that situation about, though the responsibility might well
    drive them into becoming something different from what they and
    their previous practices had constituted.

The traditions of legal judgement and procedure preventing the realisation of these possibilities are:

(1) classification of laws into public and private and the personalisa-
    tion of cases in common-law thinking;[3]

(2) strong presumption of rational action and therefore of need to show
    the subjective intention of the legal person named as applicant or
    respondent;

(3) procedures of proof which restrict the range of application of a
    finding, which make the burden of inference too great and place it
    too heavily upon the applicant.

Inferring intention is of course a problem in all English law. Here
it is particularly problematic as a way of dealing with effective discrimination. The problem is to distinguish intention to have the effect
from intention in the sense of activating the practices which, in combination, have produced the effect, and to allow the second sense on its
own. Presumed intention for *natural* (i.e. reasonably to be expected)
consequences, and not just any consequences, is part of common law on
tort. It was cited by the IT omitting the 'natural'. But precisely
that term opens the way by proceed by inference without recourse to the
subjectivity of the agents. I will return to both these possibilities
and their frustration. But to put them within a broader context, I will
first review the ways in which collective action other than litigation
can be taken under this and other parts of current English law against
discrimination in employment.

COLLECTIVE ACTION AGAINST RACIAL DISCRIMINATION

The discrimination to be eliminated is any which is activated 'on racial
grounds' or which unfavourably affects 'a racial group'. In other words
it concerns from the start a category of population. That does not mean
that the category is presumed already to have a collective representation
for action, though it does assume some means of collective identification
by which membership of the category can be ascribed. And also it means
that the unfavourable conditions of a section of the population under
jurisdiction have become a matter of legislative policy.

The conditions suffered disproportionately by a section of the population may themselves be made possible only by discrimination. Dangerous
or particularly monotous and badly paid jobs may be kept in existence by
recruiting to them workers showing signs of 'origin' to which are attributed lower than normal needs, and those workers are then by the same
token restricted in their movement out of these poor jobs. Or there may
be preconditions for unfavourable treatment so strong that without their
elimination discrimination will recur. For instance, chain migration
into unattractive jobs with low pay and no prospects traps the immigrant
workers from that place of emigration in those jobs, just because of the
poor prospects of leaving that kind of job are built into the organisation. When to that is added the place of settlement in order to take
this kind of job, the crowded and dilapidated housing, run-down educational and other facilities, the trap is inherited: poor job or no jobs.
The key pre-condition is job organisation. It too, and not just intentional racial discrimination, must be discoverable for legal action.
Disadvantage and disproportionate concentrations of black workers in
the worst jobs were the reasons for strengthening Race Relations legislation in the first place. Their continuation points either to an inadequacy of what has been done through legislation or in what could be
done, and if the latter then to the necessity for action by other means
than legislated instruments and the courts.

This then is the measure by which 'collective action' is to be
defined: the collectivities in the action are any organisations which
can be held responsible for eliminating conditions of discrimination.
The agencies include those who mount or have to respond to legal action,
organisations of employees as well as of employment and of government.
But if the same organisations can be held responsible for continuing or
even initiating discriminatory conditions, then plainly some changes in
the organisations themselves are implied by collective action to eliminate racism.

Even the negative instruction to desist from racial discrimination
entails definite changes. But we can reach some idea of the limits to
which legal action is at present confined, within a fuller scope of
what may in fact be required to end discriminatory conditions in employment. I have elsewhere given some idea of the fullness of that scope.[4]
The argument can be summarised as follows: First, the separation of
those jobs which are usually described as 'secondary' in dual labour
market hypotheses is a strong precondition for racial as well as other
unfavourable discriminations. 'Secondary' means relatively insecure,
low-graded and ill-paid jobs. Secondly, racial discrimination in the
narrow sense of racial categorisation of any kind and its application to
recruitment, transfer and promotion, is itself one among a number of
practices causing a separation of 'secondary' from 'primary' jobs. But
other practices beside that of narrowly racist discrimination are quite
sufficient to produce concentrations of what can then be categorised as
black workers in secondary jobs. They include practices concerning
work organisation itself, as well as the disposition of work according
to the availability of relatively cheap labour supplies; they include
too the bargaining and other practices of differentiation and comparison
in industrial relations; and they include, of course, the regulation of
immigration and civil status. Eliminating racial discrimination in
employment will, accordingly, require changes in all of these. But only
some of the practices and only some of the agencies involved can be

called into remedial action by the instruments and the stimulus of a law,
even though it be a law enforcing social policy.

To see what are the limits of the law, the practices of job demarcation and grading will be applied as a test of what does come within the
scope of legal action against racial discrimination. By demarcation and
grading, or grading in short, is meant first the description of a job,
that is of the tasks involved in it and not in other associated jobs,
the relation of those jobs to the others in terms of learning for them
or responsibility over them, and of ease of movement between then; second,
it means the evaluation of jobs so described, whether evaluation is
formally carried out or not, that is to say the conditions and rewards
attached to them, including closeness of supervision, 'privileges' such
as arrangements to take time off and others more detached from the job
like holidays and training facilities, and, of course, pay and perquis-
ites.

We will see whether the Race Relations Act or an extension of it can
provide:

(1) any power to induce the reorganisation of a workplace to integrate
    jobs which were secondary and separated; or
(2) only a regrading of jobs, as already organised, to ease mobility
    between them; or
(3) only the reversal of a definite act of grading found to be to the
    detriment of black workers.

REVIEW OF THE OPERATION OF THE RACE RELATIONS ACT OF 1976 (RRA 76)

The RRA 76 became operative in industrial tribunals in June 1977. Previous Race Relations Acts and accompanying activities against racial
discrimination in employment had purchased little or no improvement as
measured by distribution of black workers through socio-economic groups
(SEGs) since the Census of 1971. Ann Barber of the unit of Manpower
Studies wrote:[5]

> The proportion of professional and managerial workers among
> overseas born males of Indian and African ethnic origin is shown
> by the NDHS, like the census, to be similar to that of males of
> White ethnic origin while the proportion among males of
> Pakistani-Bangladeshi origin born overseas is lower and that
> among males of West Indian origin born overseas lowest of all.
> The high proportion of skilled manual workers among males of
> West Indian ethnic origin is confirmed and may have continued
> to the second generation....
> For people of West Indian ethnic origin as a whole, without
> distinguishing between those born in the UK and those born
> abroad, ... there is a strong similarity between the distribu-
> tion (for both males and females) shown in the 1971 Census,

the 1974 PEP Survey of Racial Minorities, and the 1977-78 NDHS.
Worse, there was a strong indication that there had been no change
between the situation of black immigrants and that of their children:
'The NDHS distribution (for young people of West Indian origin) is
similar to that of their parents' generation.'[6]

Reporting on a more recent survey of unemployment conducted by the
Policy Studies Institute, David J. Smith commented that:[7]

the minorities are concentrated within low-paid jobs at the lower
occupational levels which are most at risk ... while the same
proportion of the minorities as of whites had found a new job,
a higher proportion had done so only be accepting a job they
thought was inferior to their previous one.

Using very similar tests to those devised and operated by the PEP, the
Nottingham and District Community Relations Council decided to find out
the extent of racial discrimination in the selection of black and white
workers for lower-grade white collar jobs. It discovered that discrimination against black applicants had, between 1973-74 and 1977-79, risen
by one third for both males and females.[8]

Whatever powers the RRA 76 offers, the effectiveness of their use
will not have been measured by these findings. What they do indicate is
the bench-mark against which the effects of the RRA 76 and accompanying
activities can be measured in future surveys. In the lowest grades and
in manual work black workers, including those born in the UK, and
exemplified by West Indian workers, are as disproportionately represented as they were, and in a recession are sinking faster than are
white workers. Black workers are more than twice as likely to be out
of work than the average worker in 1980-81, according to figures
published by the Department of Employment.[9]

In the field of employment the government has used few of the considerable powers at its disposal to implement the RRA 76. There has
never been a move to require more than nominal statements of intent to
observe it by nationalised industries and contractors to government.
The Civil Service Commission's own finding of 'hazards to fairness'
and large-scale disproportions of black employment in the lowest grades
of employment in the civil service has met only with a government
refusal to monitor the continued existence of this state of affairs.

The Commission for Racial Equality (CRE) has so far had no injunctions served on an employer to cease discriminatory practices. Its most
effective form of action in the field of employment has been in helping
individuals bring cases before the industrial tribunals. Nearly all
the cases which have succeeded have been aided by the CRE and its
Community Relations Councils. But cases upheld between June 1977 and
June 1980 came to only 85 out of 457 hearings. And although the number
of applications to industrial tribunals increased, the number of cases
withdrawn before conciliation and before hearings were held increased
even more. Of all the matters which individuals have had enough confidence to apply for remedy to a tribunal, unfair dismissal has been by
far the most common. Industrial tribunals have since 1975 been able,
under the Employment Protection Consolidation Act, to order re-employ-
ment in such cases, but none have. So, has compensation been imposed
instead, and with what satisfaction to the victim or, more strategically,
with what possibility of deterrent effect on the employer? The maximum
which can be awarded on any one count is in the region of £5,000. But
nothing like even that amount has been awarded. Only two awards over
£1,000 were made up to June 1980, including cases upheld as well as
conciliation awards. It appears that there is very little to be gained
in any sense from taking cases of racial discrimination to industrial
tribunals on their present form.

Until now it has been almost impossible to find direct or intended
effective discrimination, though precisely these possibilities raise
the best hope of deterrent effects and more solid remedies in legal

action. This is not to say that effective discrimination cannot be
proved in a tribunal or by a CRE investigation, only that the judicial
traditions of proof and interpretation appear for the moment to be obstacles to legal action which can have exemplary and deterrent effects.
One may look, as does Geoffrey Bindman, a solicitor who had a part in
lobbying for the Race Relations Act in 1968 and its strengthening and
broadening of scope in the RRA 76, to the United States for examples of
much greater willingness by government to use its powers to enforce
equal employment opportunity and among the judiciary to make punitive
awards and so stimulate preventive action on the part of employers to
avoid being taken to law for racial discrimination.[10] Though this has
undoubtedly helped in the United States to bring about greatly increased
proportions of black workers in primary jobs, it must be remembered that
at the same time concentrations of black workers out of jobs or in
secondary jobs are undiminished there too.[11] This is the fact upon
which the question of how discrimination law can effect grading focuses.

ACTION OUTSIDE TRIBUNALS AGAINST RACIAL DISCRIMINATION

Grading has not been given much of a legal and political airing in relation to racial discrimination in Britain, although it has emerged as an
issue in a number of industrial disputes besides the one at Pel. Where
it has so far had prominence in discrimination law has been in cases of
sex discrimination and equal pay. Manipulation of grading by employers
seeking to minimise their obligations under the Equal Pay Act has been
exposed, for instance in the investigation by the Equal Pay and Opportunity Project at the London School of Economics.[12] The effect of legislation against sex discrimination appears to have been to consolidate a
situation in which women are concentrated in lower grades and paid on
lower rates than are men, even though women's pay relative to men's has
improved. Part of that consolidation has been evasive evaluation of a
job's exact contents. The Equal Pay and Opportunity Project found
formally conducted job evaluation to be the most effective way of implementing the Equal Pay Act favourably to women workers. Involvement in
job evaluation by the women concerned, as the Project recommends, would
make implementation of the Act more effective. But even then it does
not touch upon the separation of low-graded jobs in which women workers
are concentrated.
   It is through collective agreements between unions and employers
that the Equal Pay Act has been implemented in most cases, with grades
left as given in everything but the pay attached to them. Unions, women
workers, employers, or the Secretary of State could take a collective
agreement if it applied to men only or to women only to the Industrial
Court and Central Arbitration Committee for the removal of pay discrimination. The Project found that there were many cases of women workers
benefitting from this provision, but nevertheless they remained 'graded
and paid below their skill level in relation to men in the same pay
structure'.[13]
   That is all the Equal Pay Act can do. And yet note that, much more
than the Sex Discrimination and Race Relations Acts, it places a positive obligation upon employers to act. There is no Equal Pay Act for
black workers. Perhaps it is just because of this, namely that there
are no positive obligations to observe or avoid, that the principle of

equal opportunity in grading has not been brought out as a major issue
of racial discrimination.

Even the obligations which have to be found through a case being
brought to a tribunal are hard to enforce. A tribunal's finding that a
practice is discriminatory carries little weight, since it cannot issue
an injunction to cease the practice. That can only be done by a County
Court, and can occur only after the CRE has made an investigation (which
takes months). If after investigation the CRE finds either that a notice
which it has issued after a previous investigation, or a tribunal's
declaration of the existence of a discriminatory practice, has been ignored, it can apply to a court for an injunction. Tribunals are not
given the resources to monitor their decisions. Injunctions - the only
current form of legal obligation to cease a discriminatory practice -
depend entirely on the CRE and its resources. They are not likely to be
increased in the near future. A further problem is the difficulty in
awarding damages even when racial discrimination has been found by a
tribunal. The RRA 76 enables the exaction of damages only where intention to discriminate has been proved.

There are areas in which the discrimination Acts sanction positive
action, but they are not obligatory. Employers, industrial training
boards, the Manpower Services Commission, and other state-designated
training bodies are allowed, but not required, to provide courses especially for members of particular racial categories or for women. In
addition, Section 35 of the RRA 76, more generally than the equivalent
Sections 43-46 of the Sex Discrimination Act 75, allows but does not
require facilities of welfare 'or any ancillary benefits', as well as
training and education, to be provided for the 'special needs' of
persons belonging to a particular 'racial group'.

A positive response has come from only a few employers - central or
local government authorities on whom such demands could be pressed.
The others will not respond without further pressure from the CRE or
organisations of people likely to benefit. To have a further effect,
in other words, the Act would have to call into existence organisations
able to represent 'racial groups' to the CRE and its Councils and to
put pressure on employers. The fact that the discrimination Acts rely
on voluntary acquiescence and are so hard to implement has one good
effect: it shows immediately, rather than after a period of relying on
stronger-sounding laws, that even when elmination of discrimination is
sanctioned by law, it depends on the formation of activist organisations.
But the positive action envisaged by the law at present is in relation
to 'special needs' and provision for them rather than to any reorganisation of grading. That may be to cater for needs which are not, after
all, 'special' to a given minority, although they affect a racial category of population disproportionately. For instance, it is assumed that
a history of cyclical disadvantage has produced the special needs brought
about by cultural differences and the limitations and disparities of
competence for work of different kinds inherent in any immigrant labour
force. This can be remedied by special training facilities. But if, as
I have suggested, part of the problem is the lack of prospects in the
jobs into which that force, and 'black' workers in particular, whether
immigrant *or* settled, are channelled, then the 'needs' are going to
recur for any workers who may end up in those jobs. The needs can be
claimed as soon as they can be categorised as 'minority', 'ethnic' or
'racial'. This does serve the indispensible purpose of defining a

constituency more definite and in many ways more potent than the category 'the low-paid and low-graded' for fighting against the conditions giving rise to the 'need'. But it also tends to divert the fight from the generality of those conditions, which in this case is the lack of access to training in the *jobs* and *their* conditions.

There are no collective agreements applying only to black workers, as there are to only women workers, though there must be some that apply to white workers only. At national and regional levels, in the classification used for national statistics, there are far fewer instances of industries and occupations being filled by a majority of black workers than could be found of industries and occupations in which mainly women work. Such concentrations of black workers occur with far greater frequency at the level of shifts, works, and grades in individual enterprises. Black workers' grades could be made an issue, therefore, but it will require reference directly to individual employers or through larger-scale collective agreements to their effects (or ineffectiveness) at the level of individual firms.

One way in which the grading of black workers, and thence the whole matter of grading by which black workers are concentrated in the lower ranks, could be made an issue is in fact related to the RRA 76, but linked to the implementation of the CRE's Code of Practice and equal opportunity clauses in collective agreements.

The RRA 76 indicates only 'special' needs provision, not the vital provision of training to the system of grading and pay structures in which black workers are concentrated and stuck. Union activities against discrimination have tended to further the RRA 76, not to go beyond it. The equal opportunity policy model cause issued by the Trades Union Congress is all-encompassing and so it is vague. It lacks a sense of direction, but its adoption is a step towards more definite initiatives. It commits the parties to the policy to developing 'positive' promotion of equal opportunity in employment regardless of sex, marital status, creed, colour, race or ethnic origins. Apart from pay and benefits, it mentions such particulars of work organisation as work allocation, shift-work, recruitment, training, promotion, and redundancy. Missing from this list is temporary and short-term employment, and the grading and pay differentiation between comparable jobs. Instead, the model clause, like the discrimination Acts, goes on to lay stress on training and promotion opportunities.

But even there the policy is only to bring these opportunities, as they already exist, to the attention of all eligible employees. The TUC 'Black Workers' Charter, issued in June 1981, adds to this strong recommendations to review indirect discrimination, and to develop courses through Industrial Training Boards in favour of unqualified black workers. This is a definite advance. Stricter job evaluation and a special needs eligibility for training and education, on the lines of the two discrimination Acts, are also current points of TUC propaganda. But none of it promotes what would be better still, extending eligibility to *grades* formerly not included in training schemes, promotion ladders and systems of transfer, where women and black workers are disproportionately concentrated.

The only TUC recommendations for positive action to tackle the isolation of 'secondary' jobs stem from the Equal Opportunities for Women proposals, to open training and promotion schemes to part-time workers and up-grade 'women's work' by applying the concept of equal value and

stricter criteria of skill and job content to job evaluation. In the
case of black workers, it is the positive action recommended to employers
by the CRE's *Equal Opportunity in Employment, Why Positive Action?* (June
1980) which comes nearest to proposals for reducing secondary jobs' isolation. It suggests giving more time off for training during working
hours and provision of subsidies for retraining.

The mechanisms of isolation - short-term hiring, home-working, part-
time working, restricted comparability, exclusion from training schemes
and from promotion and transfer - keep workers in separate and easily
disposable, low-paid, and deadeningly simple and inflexible jobs. The
workers in them can only leave them to enter the dole or to similar
jobs. Black workers already disproportionately caught in these jobs
will remain there unless the mechanisms are dismantled and the separations breached. The equal opportunity policy does not rule out its
extension to such matters, but there would have to be something close
to a new or at least an additional clause specifying a commitment not
just to review but to undertake an investigation and overhaul of work
organisation within a firm or industry. Trades unions may never succeed
in gaining for this the full agreement of employers anxious to retain
flexible and cheap labour supplies and unwilling to devote the bother
and other costs of such a commitment. But they could still include it
in their own policy aims, to be pursued in whatever ways they could.
And any section of low-graded workers can with justification from the
equal opportunity policy press their unions to adopt policies of review
and overhaul of grading, with their active participation.

On the matter of pay alone, and on the national scale, grading and
comparability have in any case become negative issues. Certain developments restricting comparability have had the effect of increasing the
isolation of low-paid, low-graded workers, by making similarly-graded
work immune to pay deals won in analogous agreements. The Clegg
Commission, a semi-governmental research and arbitration body to which
pay claims could be referred for comparability between similar work in
different industries, was beginning to increase ranges and consolidate
them in a review of the national wage structure. It has been disbanded
without much protest. And this is only the most prominent manifestation of effective if undeliberated collusion between Tory market ideology and 'free' collective bargaining policies leading to similar
occupations, similarly graded but in different industries, being paid
at very different rates, and movement between them made difficult.

The implication of increased comparability is a wage structure based
on occupations rather than industries, where the employer pays a standard national wage for the job of work and the financial viability of
the firm or industry does not depend on restricted mobility between
industries or firms enabling them to depress or hold down wages.

To press at the same time, as I am advocating, for an overhaul of
transfer, promotion and training, as well as comparability and standardisation of pay, is to aim for increased mobility and maximum ease and
involvement of workers in judging how and where their capacities can
best be used and developed. Plainly the full implementation of what I
am advocating, though necessary for the elimination of racialism in
employment and just extension of equal opportunity policies, is beyond
the scope of discrimination law and its enforcement alone. It includes
incomes policy and reform of trades union organisation, and more besides.
But it starts with the extension of equal opportunity clauses and of the

apparatuses of the discrimination laws. And it is limited by considerations of what causes concentrations of black workers in the worst jobs
even when there is strong anti-discrimination legislation and increased
representation of black employees in the higher echelons of employment.

An automatic response of trades unions to the existence of low-paid
and low-graded workers is to recruit and organise them in order to
strengthen their bargaining power within a united movement. Unquestion-
ably, organisation and the backing of a union are vital. But there are
different bargaining forces among and within unions which have left pay
differentials and controls of training, transfer and promotion within
any one occupation unaffected for decades. Strengthening of work-place
organisation and alliances across union boundaries between low-paid and
low-graded workers is equally indispensible if this situation is to be
changed.

Even before that occurs, there is often a choice of unions open to a
group of low-graded workers. The unevenness of the pursuit of anti-
racist policies among unions is an index of how crucial that choice can
be for black workers. Here the internal procedures of the union movement in disputes between unions over membership could use criteria of
positive action for equal opportunity. Whichever union the workers consider would press their claims most effectively should be endorsed, even
if this involves a switch of membership. As Christopher McCrudden points
out in a contribution to *A Review of the Race Relations Act 1976*,[15] this
proposal entails pressing for a broadening of the TUC's Disputes
Committee's brief, and to give it investigative facilities.

Beside the organisations of the labour movement, there are bodies
such as Wages Councils upon which representatives of organised labour
sit and which affect low-paid and low-graded workers, regulating minimum
conditions of employment, safety and other work-place conditions where
employees are not unionised. The minimum conditions set are very low,
their enforcement often feeble. But unionisation and collective bargaining is sometimes not the better alternative to remaining under Wages
Council regulations. Unions appoint members to the Advisory Conciliation
and Arbitration Service (ACAS) which makes recommendations to the statutory authorities for Wages Council coverage.[16]

> Current research of some Wages Councils which have been abolished
> seems to indicate that some trades unions may have been too
> optimistic in supposing that collective bargaining would success-
> fully replace the statutory machinery due to the often formidable
> barriers to further organising in particular industries. The
> willingness of the union concerned, based on past experience,
> to represent black workers effectively should be an additional
> factor in ACAS' decision whether to recommend abolition of the
> statutory machinery.

It could in this case be better if the labour representatives fought on
the councils for higher minimum standards and more resources for enforcement.

The perspective I have suggested focuses on employment practices
themselves rather than just on provisions outside the job structure.
Whatever its limitations, it is strategic in scope compared with the
more limited aim of eliminating practices by means of individual hearings and investigations which can be shown to be discriminatory only
when they involve requirements affecting certain physical or cultural
characteristics such as height or turbans. But it is a perspective

which draws from the same evidence which constitutes statistical support
for the occurrence of offences against the Sex Discrimination and Race
Relations Acts. It draws attention to implications and directions in
the reform of practices of employment which equal opportunities policy
even in its present form can take. Union and otherwise organised activists willing to extend the use of present instruments beyond the narrow
limits of their most obvious provisions have plenty of openings in the
interpretation of their wording and there are many instruments of state
besides judicial ones for their enforcement, though their use will also
come up against constraining interpretations and institutions.

For instance, there are, at the disposal of government, contracts or
purchases amounting to a large proportion of the total volume of trans-
actions in the domestic economy. Nominal observation of the Race Relations Act has since 1969 been written into government contracts. To
enforce compliance it was then proposed, on the model of US government
enforcement, that the Department of Employment should require from
contractors statistical information on their minority group employees
and on what steps they were taking to avoid racial discrimination. If
the answers were unsatisfactory, further contracts would be witheld or
at least the matter would be passed on to the CRE for further investigation. Beside contracts, there are powers of licensing, planning permission and granting which could be used to enforce compliance with
equal opportunity policy. The proposal was endorsed by the Treasury
in 1979. But since the Confederation of British Industry's hostile
reaction to the Treasury statement there has been no further action on it.

In the USA, the Office of Federal Contract Compliance in the Department of Labour has had powers of monitoring compliance and seeking
enforcement of equal opportunity since the Second World War and in
Britain a Parliamentary Order of 1946 enforced compliance with a Fair
Wages Resolution through government contracts. But neither have ever
brought about a cancellation, as distinct from non-renewal of contracts.
Their powers are too easily overridden. Different but possibly greater
powers are wielded by the Equal Opportunities Commission (EOC) and the
CRE. Like their US precedent the Equal Employment Opportunity Commission, they can start cases against employers and practices which appear
to have discriminatory effects. But their powers are isolated from
other government powers, and they can only be implemented through the
courts. Labour, party or lobby, might fight to extend the CRE and the
EOC with an inter-departmental inspectorate to ensure compliance with
discrimination law through contracts, licences and the other means.

In present circumstances much depends on the willingness of tribunals
and courts to take a strategic and deterrent view of discrimination law.
In Britain, judicial practices are a far greater hindrance to doing so
than they are in the USA. But by issuing a Code of Practice for employment the CRE could, if the Code passes through the tribulations of the
Secretary of State for Employment and of Parliament, influence the
interpretation of the RRA 76. The Code would (under Section 48(10)) be
admissible as evidence in determining whether a practice departing from
it is unlawfully discriminatory. The Code could also be added to equal
opportunity clauses in collective agreements.

The Consultative Draft issued in February 1980 follows the RRA 76
quite closely. There are sections on respecting cultural and religious
needs, on giving due consideration to the grievance of racial abuse and
provocation, and on catering for communication and comprehension diffi-

culties and for differences in cultural background. All this emphasises
a constituency of special needs entering ready made into employment and
which a plural society, employers included, must respect. Consistent
with this emphasis, and following the same emphasis in the RRA 76, the
draft Code encourages as good employment practice the provision of special training to achieve equal opportunity within the organisation.
Such provision is to be aimed at groups which are under-represented and
members of which have not realised the potential they have because of
past discrimination, and which could then be at employers' disposal.

None of this gets us very far. But the draft Code also encourages
a number of practices concerning what might be called accountability;
that is, accountability of job description, and of recruitment and promotion according to some rational assumption of the true requirements
of the job. The definition and demarcation of the job is unfortunately
taken as given. The Code, and the RRA 76, want only that there be
practices of open description and publication of requirements, and that
the requirements be justifiable by the nature of the job and only by
that nature, nothing more than is required for the performance of its
component tasks. The employer would be held accountable accordingly to
justify any recruitment, promotion or exclusion which has occurred, and
the job vacancy should be publicised without restriction or selectivity.
In pursuit of this principle, present practices of recruitment, transfer
and promotion are named which will have to be changed to become accountable; advertisements of vacancies, apprenticeships and training facilities to selected schools and areas of recruitment, word-of-mouth
recruitment, and union-only channels of recruitment are all suspect.
That is the nearest it comes to challenging grading practices. Job
definition and demarcation and all the other mechanisms for separating
secondary jobs are unchallenged.

STATISTICAL MONITORING

Still, in an emphatic elaboration of the RRA 76 and equal opportunity
policies, the draft Code does stress statistical monitoring. Disproportionate absence from higher or concentration in lower grades of jobs by
black workers is to be treated as presumptive evidence of possibly unlawful discrimination. For example, draft Code paragraph 2.2.5 says
    It may be found that employees of a particular racial group
    are concentrated in particular sections from which transfers
    are unjustifiably and therefore unlawfully restricted.
The draft recommends (p.16) that monitoring 'be discussed and where
possible agreed with trade union and employee representatives.'[17]
Plainly this is essential if, as I have argued, monitoring is a constant
reminder both of the legislative policy and of the inadequacy of present
measures which concentrate on special needs and hardly touch upon
reforms of work organisation and grading themselves. Statistical monitoring can perform a clear demonstration of racialist effects in employment. But more than discussion, and with more than trade union representatives, will be necessary if keeping records classified according to
race is to withstand hostile suspicion on the part of the workers concerned, black and white.

The best guarantee against workers' opposition to monitoring is for
their organisation to carry it out. Next best is for it to keep the

records or be fully informed on where they and all copies of them are
and how they are being used. This may be possible within an enterprise.
It is not possible for the public records of a labour market - the
economically active population in a given location and their proportional
distribution in the occupations of work there. Such records are essential for the comparison which demonstrates disproportions in the distribution of sub-populations classified by race in whole occupations. They
are also essential, classified by race, for comparison with proportions
in any one organisation. This being so, and since public records and
surveys are made anyway, control over records must be of a more remote
nature and it becomes important to say what kind of record is necessary
for the purposes at hand allowing the least possible abuse.

If it should be argued that black workers do not need records to know
their condition, then it must be said that the demonstration of disproportionate numbers of black workers among the worst employed is
necessary to keep at bay another argument. That is the argument that
because white workers in the same grades and in greater absolute numbers
are equally exploited, black workers must be pleading a specious case.
On the contrary, not only are there disproportionate numbers of black
workers amongst the worst employed. They exist as a constituency because
of racism. A separate black movement in Britain will not on its own
achieve the elimination of racism and racialist effects in employment.
On the other hand, racism has brought about a potential for alliance
and mutual support among black workers. Given the traditions of organisation at their disposal, this is a force which any attack on grading
practices needs if it is to be successful.

The public records needed to demonstrate disproportionate concentrations of black workers in the lower grades, and to locate them in
particular industries and occupations regionally and nationally, must
of course divide the population of the economically active into sub-
categories. How should they be defined? The category 'immigrant' is
not useful, either as a euphemism for 'black' of literally as a resident
within a set number of years since entry through Britain's border controls. We are concerned with racism of all kinds and as an effect of
all kinds of practice in employment, not just immigration controls.
The population category should be as close as possible to the cumulative
distinctions made in deliberate racial discrimination, whatever the
explanations of the differences upon which racialist distinctions lean.
This is not a surrender to the doctrine of intention in explaining
racialist effects, but a recognition of the only two alternatives open
to a description of them as racialist. The two are: (1) a description
of the racial categorisations used in deliberate discrimination;
(2) differences which these categorisations use and which might be
thought to exist as their objective references. It is impossible to
list the latter without drawing them together as the real basis of racial
categorisation and so converting distinctions made in all kinds of other
ways into racial distinctions. The RRA 76 does this in its description
of racial groups, 'defined by reference to colour, race, nationality, or
ethnic or national origins' (Section 3(1)). It elides the significance
given by a racial categorisation to any one of the differences registered
in the list with the significance of distinctions which other classifications of skin pigmentation or of cultural and political arrangements
may given.

Rather than this confusion, measures of racialist effects should make
use only of the racist categories themselves, without giving them any
further credence than the fact that they exist as categories in use.
They should use the distinctions made according to racist categories
but without any attempt to register the 'origins' which the distinctions
signify for them. The broadest racist category distinction is that of
colour. In all racist classifications colour marks the weight of alien
distinctiveness given to other signs such as language, diet and any
number of cultural and historical items. Therefore to measure racialist
effects in employment, the major division of the population should be
black and white. Black, in racist classification, is itself the broadest
of many subsidiary categories of and by origin. Although it may not in
most usages include all of 'semitic', 'Eastern', 'coloured', and 'Asian'
for instance, the designation 'black' can be used to cover all these by
reason of the colour factor in racist classification and by the combined
resistance to it. The cultural differences which those categorised as
black or white wish to have respected are matters to be dislodged from
their disposal in racial terms and should be discussed with reference
to each matter raised (food, worship, dress, language, tradition of
organisation, etc.) and by means of the many ways of raising them other
than by categories of origin.
I have argued for records using the category black, and with the
possible addition of sub-categories of 'black', but not for any register
of origins. 'Origins' are not needed for the purpose of demonstrating
the existence of racialist effects in employment. Others, such as
registers to gauge the need for facilities of translation, English
language teaching or accommodation of different religious holidays,
will require the appropriate information and *not* categorisation as white
or black or a racist sub-category. Neither the record to gauge racialist effects nor the registers for language and holiday facilities
require records individualised by name, address or birthplace which
could thereby be linked to other records and so attach to the individual
a large amount of information usable for racial discrimination and other
abuses, though of course in all these records individuals are counted.
On the other hand, health and educational records of patients and students are necessarily individually identifiable and may well include
details of family life and difficult negotiations of cultural differences.
But these again are quite separate records and even they may not need to
include birthplace.
Now, monitoring as encouraged by the CRE's Code is according to the
RRA 76's definition of racial group, and so it recommends 'analysis of
the distribution of employees and job applicants according to ethnic
origin' (paragraph 4.1). Parents' birthplaces is the usual way of
registering ethnic origin. Yet none of the records for measuring racialist effects and registering the need for facilities require this information. Language spoken at home, or chosen form of worship, may be
information required, and if that is what 'ethnic' means why not ask
for the information in that form, and for those records only? Any
information facilitating identification of individuals with another
nationality - principally, that is, by birthplace - carries the possibility of facilitating official harrassment for documentary proof of right
to reside. For the labour population record no such information is
necessary. All that is required is classification according to racist
categories and that means asking either the individual counted or the

enumerator to name the category into which a racial discriminator has or
would put the individual.

Labour market records of comparative distributions of men and women
through occupations and industries have been primary materials for detecting targets of equal opportunity policies. In the same way comparisons
of the distributions of the black with the total population of the economically active in a locality and nationally can serve to direct policies
for the elimination of racial discrimination. They can also be used as
evidence in industrial tribunals to establish the likelihood of absence
of black workers from a firm or from its higher grades being unlawfully
discriminatory. That is, if there are numbers of black workers in the
local population under-represented in the respondent's employment or its
higher grades, this in itself could weigh in the balance of conflicting
facts before a tribunal. Beyond particular firms, for the elimination
of patterns of employment practices, statistics are crucial ways of
showing absence or disproportionate concentrations, in particular
occupations as such or in an occupation within one industry but not in
another.

They point to what could be a great range of targets. What can be
said, though, of the policies so far pursued collectively by employee
organisations and the CRE? Marginal is probably the shortest verdict
on the remedies to racial discrimination being promoted at the moment
by the CRE and the TUC. The test of how much they will attack the problem of grading reveals the shallowness of their penetration to the
employment practices which create and isolate secondary jobs. According to their positive remedies the provision of training is not to be
attached to the lower grades but to special needs; they include no
tackling of work organisation, no methods of reducing pay differentials,
and not even the aim of increasing and maintaining minimum standards of
work conditions in the jobs where black workers are over-represented.
But this is not a fixed limitation. Organisations in and outside the
TUC can extend the movement beyond those implied by 'special needs' -
namely beyond claimant organisations of the ethnic groups' cultural
or communal activities.

COLLECTIVE ACTION IN TRIBUNALS

We have seen that there is not much to be gained by taking a case of
racial discrimination to an industrial tribunal, either for the individual concerned or for the elimination of racialist effects in employment,
not even for ending practices declared unlawful, since the sanctions
against the agents responsible for them are so weak and dilatory. Yet
the possible scope of the RRA 76 and the possible sanctions which could
be exerted through government are greater than the cases so far settled
and the actions taken tell.

We can also see that collective action outside tribunals has been
and may continue to be only marginally effective unless there is a
change of direction in activity. One way of reducing practices in
employment which are racialist is through fighting for a broader interpretation of the RRA 76 so that practices implicated in any one decision
on effective discrimination can be broadened to include practices in
which a number of employees beside the individual applicant can be
joined. Beside designating a practice as effectively discriminatory,

whether intended or not, this would also make the respondent liable to
a multiple of the individual compensation which could be awarded if the
practice did not cease. But the only way in which the interpretation
of the RRA 76 can be thus expanded from its present narrow usage is
through an organised backing of cases through tribunals and to higher
courts where questions of law are settled. No individual stands to gain
by this, and risks great loss. Yet the more cases there are, problem-
atising interpretations of Section 1 (1) (b), the stronger the general
case will become for an authoritative judgement or a legislative clarification, and thereby a chance to overcome the judicial habits prevailing
at the moment in tribunals. From there cases and sanctions can accumul-
ate, directed at employment practices and so going beyond the marginal-
ising pluralism of race relations prevailing in equal opportunities
organisations at the moment.

The is not the only way in which anti-racist activity can become
more effective. Judgement and legislation may well continue to restrict
the scope of government and judicially sponsored action to reduce racialist effects in employment. Political activity, in the sense of active
support for new anti-racist policies, will also and at the same time
have to develop in any case if the present restrictions are to be broken
down.

Lawyers involved in race relations have already raised objections to
the difficulties for applicants posed by tribunal decisions. For
instance, one of the ways 'intention' restricts enforcement of the law
against sex and race discrimination beside those I have already described
in the Pel case was described recently by Geoffrey Bindman. In the *Law
Guardian Gazette* he wrote that 'the very low success rate in industrial
tribunal applications under the Race Relations Act and the Sex Discrimination Act could be due to the burden of proof placed upon the applicant.'[18]
Under the current line of decisions, even when the applicant has successfully shown less favourable treatment and a probable inference of unlawful discrimination, all the respondent need do is deny that racial factors
were in his or her mind and claim a plausible or just vague alternative
ground for the treatment, and the burden of proof is returned to the
applicant.

The demonstration of unlawful discrimination will nearly always have
to be by inference and probability. This is one of the reasons for
having local labour market records and also for demanding the employer's
records. Bindman claims that getting the records has been eased by
judgements in 1979 and 1980. But, as he writes, what still needs to be
achieved is for the respondent to 'retain the burden of proving that
his explanation (and not race) was the more probable'.

Unions and employees generally could well have claims to employers'
accountability and records other than monitoring against the possibility
of sex and race discrimination. They might well demand on both these
and other grounds to have access to records of manning and to participate
in job description and evaluation, and in the drafting of requirements
for recruiting and promotion. Tribunals are one arena in which to
realise part of these demands. But since employers' records will often
not be classified by race, the workers' organisation will have to be
involved in doing its own count and submitting that as evidence.

The difficulties placed by tribunals before anyone seeking more
effective judgements in pursuit of the RRA 76's policy do in any event
go deeper than the burden of proof alone. The doctrine of intention is

part of common law tradition, combining precedent with great specification of the individuality of each case. Laurence Lustgarten made a
similar point in his book on *Legal Control of Racial Discrimination*,[19]
and I will merely quote what he says, for it needs no further exposition.

> Those steeped in the common law see the choices as bounded by
> the poles of compensation and punishment because they restrict
> their focus to the plaintiff and the defendent in individual
> litigation. The deterrent-regulatory view becomes possible only
> when one's focus shifts to encompass the world beyond the specific
> case. The former is an intellectual framework deriving from and
> perhaps appropriate to private law, and has the virtues of
> encouraging meticulous attention to specific facts, individual
> differences and the achievement of justice between persons.
> It is however badly suited to achieving social justice, or even
> to accommodating the reality of collective action and interests.
> The continued suzerainty of common-law thinking - even in cases
> requiring the interpretation of statutes which impose public
> ordering on hitherto private decisions - must subtly but inevitably
> confine their scope and impact.

The point should be taken further than Lustgarten has taken it.
Discrimination law, though formulated in terms of individual rights, is
a distinct type of law. Legal means of achieving social justice do not
adequately describe it. When there are practices which legal and other
investigations find to be socially unjust not because of their intent
but simply because of their effect, then the law becomes a means of
reforming those practices. This includes providing means of (1) judging which practices have the undesirable effect and which agents can
be held responsible for changing them, rather than just an individual
case and its perpetrator; (2) monitoring the effects; (3) deterring
continuation or recurrence of the practices. (The propaganda associated
with the policy embodied in the law is also responsible for encouraging
the reform by indicating the positive effects of compliance.) The
better the undesirable effects can be defined and detected, the more
the law is an instrument of social reform rather than a statement of
rights. The definition in discrimination law includes not only unfavourable conditions (of work, housing and educational facilities, or
their lack), but also a category of population among those who suffer
those conditions in general. This is what differentiates discrimination
law from the mere claim to a right to work, good housing and education,
which states a policy to improve educational facilities, working conditions and housing, and diminish unemployment and homelessness as such.
The fact that some or most of the practices of employment having
racially or sexually discriminatory effects are also those which produce poor working conditions and employment in general does not deny
their being identifiable also as discriminatory. It only shows the
full implications of what is a legally viable concept in more general
and longer-term aims of social or economic policy that cannot be contained in a law.

The way in which the more general rights can be encompassed in a
viable law without the notion of discrimination, that is to say differential provision of the rights in question, is by definition of absolute
minima with which everyone concerned must be provided. This is how the
health, safety and education acts work. Anyone can ask a court or
tribunal to judge a claim that the minimum provisions have not been

made in his or her case. The court finding this to be so places responsibility upon the appropriate authority to make the provision. There is
no finding of culpable practices here as there can be with discrimination
law, just omissions.

Lustgarten hopes to construct a legal right like the right to education out of discrimination law.[20] He wants a fuller interpretation of
the right not to be discriminated against on the grounds of race or sex.
His aim is to turn what is at present only a permissive discretion into
a positive requirement and to facilitate claims on government authorities
to rectify its lapse. The law against sex or race discrimination would
then exist not just to detect definite cases of unlawful discrimination
but also to assume the requirement not to discriminate and to refuse to
tolerate inaction in the face of racial or sexual inequality. Where that
was found, the tribunal or court could place responsibility on government
authorities to act or to induce rectifying action. This would have the
effect of extending laws on rights to minimum standards to the making of
provisions for special needs on the model of the Local Government Grants
(Ethnic Groups) Bill, whereby central government funds would have been
available to local authorities for positive action to remedy the effects
of past disadvantages suffered disproportionately by members of ethnic
groups. (The 1979 General Election stopped parliamentary process on
this Bill after its second reading.) But Lustgarten's reconstruction
would not help the identification and elimination of those employment
practices which have racialist effects.

But the weakness of the RRA 76 in eliminating disablement is as much
a matter for concern as the weakness of its provisioning. It is a weakness protected by the difficulty in bringing to bear a deterrent-
regulatory view of the law as described by Lustgarten. In certain key
appeals (Rookes v. Barnard 1964, and Cassell v. Broome 1972), the Lords
have, according to Lustgarten, encouraged a narrow common-law perspective
relegating any notion of deterrent sanction to criminal law, confining
compensation to purely individual restitution.[21]

One way of enlarging this to a deterrent sanction is to allow some-
think like the American device of a 'class action'. This would be to
allow a litigant whose claims are typical of numerous other persons to
represent their interests in court and is, as Lustgarten says, a logical
corollary of the collective dimensions of the RRA's 'racial grounds' and
inclusion of effective discrimination in its ambit.[22] At present a
tribunal can collect a number of submissions together and treat one as
representative, but a litigant cannot take the initiative and begin an
action in this way.

'Class action' in the USA stems from Rule 23 (a) of the Federal Rules
of Procedure (1970). By it an individual case may represent a class
where 'joinder of all members is impracticable', where 'there are questions of law or fact common to the class', where the claims of the
parties are typical of all claims in the class, and where 'the representative parties will fairly and adequately protect the interest of the
class'. Either an individual or, to protect against victimisation, an
organisation can bring a class action. And the possibility that a class
action will be brought is enough to maintain discovery of records from
an employer in order to develop the action.

To join a 'class action' means that all parties with the same questions of fact or law are bound by the decision. It is not confined to
a single respondent (defendant), but the amount by which differences of

fact or law are counted to be within the same class must be a matter of
dispute. By the same token, whether a case can be taken to court or
tribunal for another decision or by bound by a class action decision
already made must also be a source of dispute. But in the USA it is
not necessary for all those who want or will want eventually to join a
class action even to be cited beforehand, let alone had their cases
submitted individually first for a court or tribunal to decide to join
them.

This joining of an action is not like that of the Pel workers already
grouped in a single shop. The applicants may be dispersed, for instance
black workers disabled from promotion in several places and possibly in
several firms by the same requirement or condition. In English law it
is possible, as in the Pel case, for a group to come together to bring
an action against a single defendant (respondent), and it is also
possible for a court or tribunal to decide to treat an individual case
as a test, representative of a closely defined set of cases. To establish the further possibility of a class action to identify a practice
wherever it occurs and make every corporate body in which it occurs
liable to pay compensation to anyone suffering detriment from that
practice will call for legal reform.

In any case, to sustain a class action, especially against the
resources ofwealthy defendants anxious to reduce or pre-empt its deterrent effects, requires organisational backing - as William Gould's
account of hampering by US employers, government agencies and unions
makes quite clear.[23] Organisational backing will also be necessary to
sustain case pressure and political activity to make the RRA effective
against more than culturally or locally selective recruitment practices.

Grading has been found to be racially discriminatory only in cases
of an individual being moved down a pay-grade or to what should have
been better-paid work while he was placed in a lower grade and paid
accordingly. A collective finding has not yet been made where groups
of black workers have been comparatively ill-paid or less provided
with training and other facilities in jobs similar on evaluative criteria
to others where workers are better paid or provided - whether this is
justified by the employer through formal grading or not. Yet such was
precisely the cause of several industrial disputes, before and since
the RRA 76 came into force. Perhaps the RRA 76 has cast no illusions
that legal action can substitute for other means of raising and settling
industrial disputes. But it must be said that, for both, for industrial
action through tribunals and by other means, to be more than marginally
effective in eliminating racialist effects, organised collective activity
of a kind so far lacking will be necessary.

SUMMARY OF ACTION PROPOSED

In assessing the operation of the RRA 76 I have set it against the extent
of racial discrimination in employment as measured by a number of statistical indexes. They indicate that, despite the operation of the RRA 68
and the few years of the RRA 76, black settlers and their children are
likely to be condemned to the same kinds of residual and unattractive
employment as immigrant workers. Direct discrimination cannot be made
to account for this persistant discriminatory effects. Racial grounds
for an act, even by inference, can be shown only in infrequent and

highly specified cases. I have therefore concentrated on the application
of the RRA 76 to segregation and to the existence of conditions and
requirements which can only be complied with by a disproportionately
small number of members of a 'racial group'. In particular I have concentrated on employment practices which tend to exclude black workers
from training facilities and jobs with career ladders. These practices
include, beside direct racial discrimination, discrimination against the
jobs into which black workers have for one or another reason (immigration, racial discrimination) been channelled. They are, or have become,
separated from jobs with prospects. Sometimes the separation will have
been made by regrading, but in most cases the grading practices already
in existence separate them. It may well be only when a grading event,
rather than a continuing practice, can be shown that the RRA 76 can be
applied. Action through tribunals will in any case never on its own
eliminate racial discrimination. But tribunals are not the only form
of action enabled by the provisions of the RRA 76, and there are other
activities outside its provisions which together could have a more
marked effect or at least be aimed at the more deep-rooted causes of
discriminatory effects. In this article I have suggested what a number
of these might be.

At the moment 'special needs' is the basis for the kind of organisation expected by and appropriate to the RRA 76 and its associated
machinery, in the TUC as well as the CRE. That means communal claimants
and lobbies in a sphere of welfare and education. And communal organisations do, of course, exist. On the other hand the backing of black
workers' industrial actions, in and out of tribunals, would have to come
from trades unions or some more distinctly black and workers' organisation, like the Indian Workers Association. The source of new organisations capable of more direct attacks on the mechanisms which create
secondary jobs and the concentrations of black workers in them will
possibly be groupings of black workers combining communal and union
organisations. Fights by lower-grade black workers for union recognition
by an employer and recognition by unions of the force of their grievances
raised grading as an issue in the first place, in the long run of disputes over more than a decade including the famous disputes at Imperial
Typewriters, Mansfield Hosiery and Grunwicks.

The powers for executing some of the reforms I have suggested exist
in government agencies. But the movement to press for their use will
come from elsewhere. The suggestions for action made here have therefore been addressed to organisations of workers, and have been critical
of the current organisation of the labour movement while recognising its
present and potential organisations to be the main resource for mounting
attacks on the long-term and multiple causes of racial discrimination
in employment.

Anti-racist organisations in the labour movement and such legal
instruments as have so far been created to combat racial discrimination
are the product of a number of different policy lines. Most of them
have little to do with employment as such. They include the welfare
and educational provision for a plurality of needs or interests. They
also include various strands of anti-fascist politics. Both the pluralist and anti-fascist lines are prominent in the labour movement. Outside it, and apart also from other organisations pursuing these two
lines, pressure has come along the line of black resistance, fluctuating
in organisational size and separateness, but referring to a black
community in one way or another.

Together, these add up to the prominence of racism as an object of attack and to black or ethnic groups as the social and political entities primarily concerned. Particular practices contributing to racism and racialist effects are assumed under racism or racial discrimination. Into the concentrated focus of this perspective come whichever employment practices can be shown to be racialist. In this way a new alignment of forces is directed at practices that have been unchallenged or have only been diffusely and ineffectually challenged. In drawing attention to the extent of racialist effects in employment and to the marginality of the current operation of legal instruments, the CRE, and labour movement anti-racist activities in reducing these effects, I am also trying to draw the focus of anti-racist and black political attention to practices which have far wider repercussions than the effects registered as 'racism'. Any action seeking to end the isolation of secondary jobs in which black workers are concentrated will also address practices affecting other workers in secondary jobs. It will therefore also involve agencies other than those organised to combat racism and racial discrimination. Agencies such as the Low Pay Unit and, more to the point, any separately organised sections of the low-paid and low-graded in a union are necessarily included. The focus on racism, or the focus on equal pay and sexual discrimination, can be the means of forging cross-union alliances of the low-graded initially among black and women workers. To combat racial and sexual discrimination will mean taking on from another angle what the low-paid, and all who appeal to them as a constituency, face in current union practices - preserving differentials, protecting access to training and possession of acquired knowledge.

Related to these practices, the specific possibilities raised in this article are that all those in low grades where black workers are concentrated, take up TUC and individual union commitments to fight racism and establish equal opportunities in order to demand support for:

(1) job evaluation, and the full participation of the workers concerned
    in carrying it out;
(2) reorganisation of work conditions, so that training opportunities
    in the firm or industry are attached to their jobs.

For longer-term effect, these demands would have eventually to include or lead to:

(3) reorganisation of work, so that the jobs themselves are more varied,
    less destructive of personal initiative, and with more opportunities
    for transfer and promotion; and
(4) at the national level, increasing comparability as a means of
    settling pay in the direction of a wage structure in which there
    is the same pay for the same occupation, whatever the industry.
    This would not reduce pay differentials between occupations, but
    it would bring up the pay and reduce the isolation of the worst-
    paid pockets of 'unskilled' occupations.

How to organise, and in what forums - Trades Councils, regional TUCs, individual union meetings, the workplace, clubs, and cultural or recreational centres - to mobilise forces and support for these demands and other anti-racist activities must be for the workers concerned to decide. I have only suggested some means by which they can be promoted and the discrimination effects they are aimed at reducing can be discovered.

The model Equal Opportunity Clause and any TUC adoption of, and addition to, the CRE's Code of employment practice should include a TUC, Trades Council and union undertaking to do more than just review the state of disproportionate concentrations of black workers in low occupations. It should include a commitment to investigate the work organisation of a firm or section of industry where such concentrations occur.

In order to bring these concentrations to light, the CRE Code's section on monitoring should be stressed. Workers' organisations could by means of its adoption acquire the right to inspect or be given facilities to make records of the proportions of black workers, and for that matter women workers, in a firm or workplace. The unions could back this with an undertaking to keep records for the occupations and sections of industry in which they are concerned. Local Trades Councils and Community Relations Councils could compile records to monitor local labour markets and concentrations of black and women workers within them. Use could be made of volunteers from local colleges and universities in the work of monitoring and investigation. The monitoring should use the category 'black', not any information on birthplace nor any identification of individuals in counting the proportions.

Such investigations, together with those carried out by the CRE, and other government and semi-academic bodies like the Policy Studies Institute, can be used in tribunals to demonstrate the probability of an employer's practice being discriminatory. They can also be used to put pressure on governments to use powers of contract, licensing and purchase to insist on employers' monitoring and making changes in discriminatory practices. The CRE and the Equal Opportunities Commission should be linked with government departments having these powers by means of an interdepartmental inspectorate.

Action in tribunals and courts takes its place as a point of pressure and development of the means and organisations for more widespread and longer-term action. Cases, especially group cases, serve the purpose of bringing to light employers' conditions and requirements which have discriminatory effects, even though the means for deterring employers from using them are at the moment little more than the cost and time of mounting a defence. But in order to make tribunals serve even this function, the force of inference of racial discrimination would have to be increased and the ease by which employers can prove plausible alternative intentions much decreased.

To enhance discovery of patterns of employment conditions and requirements, and to increase the deterrent value of awards by tribunals in successful cases, something more like 'class actions' will be necessary, allowing applicants the initiative in mounting collective cases. Otherwise, the RRA 76 in tribunals will remain as marginally effective as it is, little more than the chance of costly solace for a few individuals.

NOTES

* On some practical points of detail I have been assisted by Ian Macdonald's briefing on the Race Relations Act 1976, both written (IDS Brief, Supplement 23, May 1979) and spoken for more up-to-date information. Many thanks to him. Thanks also to Ann Gibson of the TUC Women's Advisory Committee for sending documents in a very busy week.

1   For example, pages 15-21 of Michael Malone, *A Practical Guide to
    Discrimination Law*, Grant McIntyre, 1981, is devoted to 'indirect
    discrimination'. Unfortunately it makes it appear that indirect
    discrimination must still be shown to be intended to discriminate
    racially.

2   Such disadvantage as occurs in employment has been described as the
    result of 'a knot of bad employment practices' in David Smith,
    Racial Disadvantage in Britain, Penguin, 1977, p.144. The research
    by Political and Economic Planning (PEP) which this book summarises
    was the 'major touchstone against which deficiencies in the previous
    legislation were measured', as Ben-Tovin et al pointed out in
    Politics & Power 3, p.159. I might say here that this article
    differs from their article, but not in advocating use of the present
    race relations machinery, local and central. It differs in attempt-
    ing to state more definitely and in a particular field the different
    limits of its use and in discussing objectives: what and how much
    more must be done if racialism in employment is to be overcome.

3   In their account of the enactment of earlier Race Relations Acts
    Lester and Bindman have drawn attention to the obstacles thrown up
    by Common Law and the way of social policy enforcement (A. Lester
    and G. Bindman, *Race and Law*, Penguin, 1972). They hoped that the
    passing of the 1968 Race Relations Act would have reduced these
    obstacles by creating a clear public policy, and insisted that the
    law be concerned with eliminating patterns of racial discrimination,
    not just with individual grievances. But in their approach they
    themselves set limits: (1) on positive action they limited them-
    selves to provision of special educational needs; and (2) for
    eliminating the effects of past discrimination and disproportionate
    disadvantage, they relied on 'the economic and social environment'
    entirely (p.88). My argument is that the law could be much more
    incisive in identifying practices which continue past disadvantages
    and in stimulating positive changes in these practices, not relying
    on the effect of education and welfare.

4   'Occupational Ghettoes' - unpublished as yet. Copies available from
    me at The City University, Northampton Square, London EC1, for the
    cost of xeroxing.

5   Ann Barber, 'Ethnic origin and the labour force', *Employment Gazette*,
    August 1980, p.844. She is summarising a National Dwelling and
    Housing Survey (NDHS), conducted for the Department of the Environ-
    ment in 1977-78 on a sample of households in England and comparing
    them with the results of previous surveys.

6   *ibid.*

7   David J. Smith, 'Unemployment and racial minority groups',
    Employment Gazette, June 1980, pp.604 and 606. This summarises the
    full report (*Unemployment and Racial Minorities*) by the Policy
    Studies Institute (formerly PEP) of their survey sampling 18
    employment areas in England, in March 1979.

8   *Half a Chance?*, CRE, 1980, pp.18-19.

9   The proportion of ethnic minority workers among the unemployed is
    steadily increasing according to figures of the Department of
    Employment, published in *Employment Gazette*, March 1981.

10 Geoffrey Bindman, 'The law, equal opportunities and affirmative
    action', *New Community* VIII:3, 1980.

11 '... the greatest gains in the 1960s occurred for college-educated
   blacks. The relative gains for blacks in the lower schooling categories, where most blacks are still situated, ranged from much more
   modest to nonexistant. This pattern, together with occupational
   evidence cited earlier in the chapter, suggests that a black professional and managerial stratum expanded significantly in recent
   years, but that the majority of blacks were left behind.' Michael
   Reich, *Racial Inequality*, Princeton University Press, 1981, p.60.
   He deploys a number of econometric indices in support of this
   conclusion.
12 Reported by Mandy Snell, 'The Equal Pay and Sex Discrimination Acts:
   their impact in the workplace', *Feminist Review* 1, 1979, pp.44-45.
13 *ibid.*, p.46.
14 CRE, *Equal Opportunity in Employment: Why positive action?*, June
   1980.
15 Christopher McCrudden, 'A strategic use of the law: a paper for
   discussion', in *A Review of the Race Relations Act 1976*, Runnymede
   Trust, June 1979, p.88.
16 *ibid.*, p.83.
17 *Code of Practice for the Elimination of Racial Discrimination and
   the Promotion of Equality of Opportunity in Employment, Consultative
   Draft*, CRE, February 1980, p.16.
18 Geoffrey Bindman, 'Proving discrimination: is the burden too heavy?'
   Law Guardian Gazette, 17 December 1980.
19 Laurence Lustgarten, *Legal Control of Racial Discrimination*,
   Macmillan, 1980, p.226.
20 *ibid.*, pp.34-36.
21 *ibid.*, p.226.
22 *ibid.*, p.231.
23 William Gould, *Black Workers in White Unions*, Cornell University
   Press, 1977, pp.427-29.

COLLET'S LONDON BOOKSHOP
64-66 Charing Cross Road London WC2

Radical Book Bargains

Western Marxism:
a critical reader
reduced from £8.50 to **£3.50**
+ 85p p&p

Aesthetics and Politics
reduced from £8 to **£3.50**
+ 50p p&p

Red Bologna
Jaggi Müller and Schmid
reduced from £5.50 to **£2.50**
+ 50p p&p

Pig Earth
John Berger
reduced from £4.95 to **£2.75**
+ 60p p&p

Art and Revolution
John Berger
reduced from £5.95 to **£2.50**
+ 50p p&p

Success and Failure of Picasso
John Berger
reduced from £7.95 to **£2.50**
+ 55p p&p

Shop open;
Mon, Tues, Wed & Sat 10am-6pm
Thurs 10am-7pm
Fri 10.30am-7pm
Send cheques, postal orders or book tokens to
above address

Telephone 01-836 6306

Richard Hyman
Green Means Danger? Trade Union Immunities and the Tory Attack

The Government's Green Paper *Trade Union Immunities*, published in
January 1981, has the stated aim 'to prompt a wide and informed debate
on the law concerning industrial action and on the role in modern life
of trade unions and employers and their duties and obligations.[1] At
£5.30 for 111 pages, it is arguable how wide an audience this Paper will
actually attract to such a debate. And a reader expecting any discussion
whatsoever of the 'duties and obligations' of employers will be sadly
disappointed. This is in actuality a survey of the spectrum of familiar
proposals for legal restrictions on trade union organisation and action,
though notable in three respects. Firstly, it spells out in detail some
of the practical difficulties of implementing many of the favourite Tory
panaceas; secondly, it canvasses the idea of a 'system of positive rights'
which would constitute a major innovation in British labour law; and
thirdly, it gives no explicit indication of the government's own preferred strategy.

In this article I begin by outlining the historical background to
labour law in Britain, since this is necessary for an understanding of
its virtually unique character: most notably, the fact that the right
to organise collectively and to take industrial action derives whatever
legal basis it has not from positive guarantees but from a system of
negative 'immunities' from civil or criminal liability. The factors
leading to the industrial relations legislation of the past decade are
then discussed. Finally the alternatives contained in the Green Paper
are examined and their significance assessed in the context of the
current political and economic climate.

TRADE UNIONS AND THE LAW: THE HISTORICAL BACKGROUND

British trade unions were the earliest in the world to establish stable
organisation covering substantial numbers of workers, and to achieve a
significant influence in defending or advancing their members' conditions
of employment. This was attained in the face of a structure of law profoundly hostile to collective action by workers, and phases of acute
state repression. The struggle for reforms which would render labour

law, if not favourable then relatively neutral towards trade unionism, is
deeply embedded in the movement's historical consciousness.

The struggle against illegality has involved, in part, opposition to
specific statutory prohibitions - from the Combination Acts of 1799 and
1800 to the Industrial Relations Act of 1971. A more fundamental and
persistent obstacle to trade unionism, however, has derived from the
very basis of a legal system founded on the archaisms of the common law:
a system vesting in the judges a power, in effect, to act as surrogate
legislators. The principles of the common law, and the prejudices of
the judiciary, embody an overriding commitment to the rights of property
and the sanctity of the individual contract between employer and employee;
there is thus an irredeemable antagonism to collective worker resistance
to capital. In the familiar language of the 19th century, there is a
presumption that trade unions, strikes, and all other manifestations of
workers' efforts to impose collective controls over their employment
conditions, are illegal conspiracies 'in restraint of trade'.

Accordingly, the fight for legality primarily involved the attempt to
exclude normal trade union activities from the jurisdiction of the courts.
The concept of 'immunity' from the taint of common law illegality was
established in two vital pieces of mid-Victorian legislation, the Trade
Union Act 1871 and the Conspiracy and Protection of Property Act 1875.
But these initial definitions of immunity required extension as the
judiciary, towards the end of the century, invented new civil liabilities
which frustrated the intentions of the legislators. Among the most notable of the products of judges' ingenuity were the discovery of the tort
of 'civil conspiracy', and the ruling that trade unions as such could be
sued for damages - made famous by the Taff Vale judgment of 1901. The
remedy eventually pursued by the unions, and embodied in the Trade Union
Disputes Act of 1906, made trade unions exempt from civil action; excluded the new doctrine of civil conspiracy from actions 'in contemplation
or furtherance of a trade dispute'; and removed some of the restrictions
on picketing which judges had recently imposed.

'The Act of 1906 remained the legal bedrock of trade union freedoms
for over half a century';[2] and the specific and explicit content of this
legislation reflected equally enduring underlying principles.

> In strict juridical terms, there does not exist in Britain any
> 'right' to organise or any 'right' to strike. The law still
> provides no more than a 'liberty' to associate in trade unions
> and certain 'liberties' of action by which trade unions can carry
> on industrial struggle.[3]

Through the definition of an area of negative immunity, then, 'the statute
provides liberties or rights which the common law would deny to unions.
the "immunity" is mere form.'[4]

It has long been commonplace for writers on British industrial relations[5] to stress the strength of a tradition of 'abstention' by state
and law from the determination of employment relations, and to attribute
this to a philosophy of 'voluntarism' which holds that industrial stability is best attained when employers and unions are able to reach agreements (and if necessary pursue conflicts) with the minimum of external
interference. It is clearly in line with this tradition that what in
many countries are statutorily defined positive rights to organise and
to strike have their equivalents in Britain in the exclusion of the
courts from what are deemed to be the private concerns of workers, unions
and employers.

The development of a system of legal abstentionism - and its specific
reflection in the provision of trade union immunities - must however be
seen in its material context. It is important to note, first, that
'voluntarism' has never been absolute. In both world wars, a variety of
state controls were imposed. In the aftermath of the General Strike,
the Trade Disputes and Trade Unions Act of 1927 (repealed in 1946)
imposed an array of vindictive restrictions on trade unionism. And the
Emergency Powers Act of 1920 provides the state with draconian rights
to intervene in major industrial disputes. These qualifications to the
idea of state abstention help indicate the *conditional* basis of its
historical emergence. The lack of positive statutory control of industrial relations rested - as with the more general ideology of *laisser
faire* to which it was obviously linked - on an essentially practical
basis: that the state recognised no need to intervene directly in the
sphere of production, and that capital recognised no need to call on
state support in its day-to-day handling of labour. 'This meant in turn
that trade unions should lack either the power or the will to interfere
excessively with managerial objectives.'[6]
Historically there has often been a neat coincidence between the
health of British capital, the strength and combativity of trade unions,
and the development of labour law. The framework of mid-Victorian
legislation was set when capital was confident of its world dominance,
and when unions covered only a small minority of workers and embraced
respectable and collaborative policies. The judicial offensive of the
1890s reflected bourgeois alarm at the seeming radicalism of the 'new
unionism', and ran in parallel with an attack by major employers who
blamed their declining role in world markets on trade union militancy
and 'restrictive practices'. The 1906 Act was passed in a phase of low
strike activity, when the creation of national collective bargaining
machinery in major industries seemed to promise the orderly 'voluntary'
containment of labour disputes. Finally, the phase when judges proved
least antagonistic to unions covered the era of interwar unemployment -
when 'middle class opinion had little to fear from a weak and conciliat-
ory labour movement'[7] - and the years of war when unions represented a
force for discipline and restraint.

FROM POST-WAR CONSENSUS TO THE INDUSTRIAL RELATIONS ACT

The trade union movement emerged from the 1939-45 war with a new social
and political status: having collaborated closely with government and
employers in the organisation and control of wartime labour, it assumed
a continuing pivotal role in post-war reconstruction.[8] While union
representatives participated in a vast array of (quasi-) governmental
consultative and administrative machinery - a relationship viewed by
some authors as 'corporatist'[9] - the principle of union-employer autonomy in the routine of industrial relations was firmly underwritten.

> The priority of collective bargaining over legal enactment was,
> during the 1940s and 1950s, finally elevated to an ideological
> belief common to both sides of industry.[10]

The repeal of the 1927 Act by the Attlee government confirmed the abstentionist doctrine inherent in the previous statutes; a situation which
the Tories, concerned to maintain an accommodation with organised labour,
did not seek to challenge.[11]

By the 1960s the context was clearly changing radically. Relatively
full employment had altered the balance of class relations at the point
of production. In many industries - notably engineering - this involved
the consolidation of workplace union organisation, the negotiation of
earnings increases well above the level of national settlements, the
achievement of areas of job control: all sustained by the ability to
impose collective sanctions without excessive regard for the constraints
imposed by official procedures. One outcome was the growth of an intensive ideological campaign, fuelled by the media and right-wing politicians,
predicated on a hostile though not altogether consistent image of trade
unions as simultaneously too weak and too strong. Too weak in that the
discipline of 'responsible' leaders was, it was argued, systematically
flouted by 'unofficial militants'; the structure of multiple overlapping
unions with limited central control was often contrasted with the more
streamlined and authoritarian systems in Sweden and Germany. Too strong
in that the balance of power was said to have shifted unduly in favour
of the unions, which damaged or inconvenienced 'the public' with strikes
(often on trivial issues), tyrannised over individual workers, forced
employers to concede unreasonable wage demands, while at the same time
fettering production with outdated 'restrictive practices'.
   Three themes dominated this ideological offensive; they may be termed
respectively managerialist, individualist and legalistic. The first
involved the charge that union power, by encroaching on managerial prerogatives, obstructed industrial efficiency; the unions were thus made
the scapegoat for the dismal international performance of British
capital. The second presented the individual employee (and specifically
the non-unionist) as a victim or pawn of monolithic organisational controls; though employees' vulnerability to the growing concentration of
the power of monopoly capital (to which workers' collective organisation
offered a limited countervailing force) evoked little sympathy from such
critics. The third denounced the absence of a comprehensive and restrictive legal framework in industrial relations, presenting the traditional
structure of negative immunities as a recipe for anarchy which placed
unions 'above the law'.
   Such arguments struck a particular chord among lawyers. In 1958 a
group of Tory barristers published a call for new curbs on unions and
strikes; their basic perspective was indicated by their title, *A Giant's
Strength*. The judges were quick to take the cue; a series of decisions
restricted the protections contained in the 1906 Act, created new liabilities to inhibit industrial action, and granted injunctions wholesale
to employers faced by threatened strikes. Politically, toughness towards
the unions became defined as an electoral advantage. The Labour government which took office in 1964, anxious to be seen to be tackling the
'trade union problem' but reluctant to antagonise a movement whose
support was vital to the success of its strategy for wage restraint,
adopted the solution of appointing a Royal Commission under Lord
Donovan.[12] To the chagrin of several cabinet ministers, Donovan eventually reported against drastic changes in labour law. The central
'problems' of British industrial relations, the Commission argued,
derived from a lack of articulation between bargaining arrangements at
national and workplace level. The solution was to be found in institutional reforms initiated by managements and carried through with union
cooperation. More stringent laws against stikes would be inoperable,
would be ignored by most employers (who were normally unwilling to

utilise the legal sanctions already available to them), and would sour
the relationships on which voluntary reform depended.

The response of the Wilson government was equivocal. Its White
Paper[13] largely followed the Donovan recommendations, but added a handful of 'penal clauses' which provoked a bitter union resistance. In
June 1969 attempts to push through parliament a bill restricting strike
action foundered in the face of a back-bench revolt.[14] Twelve months
later, the Heath government was elected on a programme which placed
major emphasis on a transformation in labour law.[15] After a derisory
exercise in 'consultation', an Industrial Relations Bill was introduced
as the government's first major item of legislation; it became law in
August 1971.

The Industrial Relations Act was a hastily drafted measure which drew
heavily on some of the worst elements of American anti-union laws. It
contained 170 clauses and 9 schedules, in marked contrast to the 1906
Act with a mere five clauses. Firstly, the Act introduced a massive
dose of rigid legalism to British industrial relations. A new National
Industrial Relations Court (NIRC), headed by a judge, was given extensive jurisdiction, with power to impose unlimited damages and to issue
orders (non-compliance would constitute contempt). All collective agreements were to be legally binding unless the contrary was expressly stated;
and there was provision for the NIRC to impose legally binding procedure
agreements. Secondly, wide-ranging controls (detailed in no less than
30 pages) applied to the internal affairs of trade unions. Those
'organisations of workers' which did not register as unions, or whose
rules or activities failed to satisfy the new Registrar, remained subject to some of the controls and suffered a number of new liabilities.
Thirdly, and most crucially, there was a varied catalogue of restrictions
on trade union activities covered by the traditional system of immunities.
It became illegal for anyone but the authorised agent of a registered
union to organise a strike, or any other form of industrial action, in
breach of contract - in practice exposing almost every instance of
industrial struggle to an injunction or claim for damages. A wide range
of other 'unfair industrial practices' was specified, including most
forms of blacking and sympathy action, and the enforcement of 100 per
cent union membership. Finally, the government obtained powers to
require a ballot and impose other delaying devices in the case of major
disputes.

The fate of this experiment is now part of the folk history of the
movement - or more precisely, part of its mythology. Four points deserve
emphasis. The first is that the draconian strategy of the Heath government did not match the perspectives of important sectors of British
capital, whose aim was to enlist the 'voluntary' cooperation of union
representatives in imposing greater shop-floor discipline (a factor considered further below). Secondly, the legislation itself was contradictory; as Wedderburn argued at the time,

> Behind the dominant theme of the 1971 Act there are really two
> different, similar but not wholly compatible philosophies; as
> it were, two different phantom draftsmen who work together but
> who represent different aspects of middle-class opinion.[16]

While certain sections reflected a managerialist concern for greater
order and stability in workplace industrial relations, this aim was
overlaid by an individualist and legalistic bias reflected, for example,
in the attack on the closed shop and the attempts to make arguments

legally enforceable. It was precisely because this bias interfered with
managerialist objectives that most large employers colluded with unions
in evading key provisions in the Act. Thirdly, the indiscriminate character of the offensive, and the provocative consequences of the legislation
(the railwaymen's ballot, the gaoling of the five dockers, the fines
imposed on the AUEW) ensured a sustained and unified opposition from the
trade union movement. But finally, the nature of this resistance should
not be exaggerated. Some important union leaders sought compromise
('fight the clauses, not the Bill'), and the TUC was reluctant to impose
a firm line which might alienate influential affiliates. Only a sustained campaign from the shop floor, particularly within the AUEW, resulted in the decision (by a small majority) at the 1971 Congress to
instruct members unions not to cooperate with the institutions of the
Act. This policy was itself subsequently diluted, and but for Heath's
narrow defeat at the polls in 1974 it is difficult to believe that it
would have been maintained.

FROM SOCIAL CONTRACT TO THATCHER

One support for the TUC in its resistance to the 1971 Act was the explicit commitment to its repeal given by the leadership of the Labour Party:
a pledge representing one product of the close formal liaison between
the two bodies initiated in early 1972. The agreements on social and
economic policy reached within the new Liaison Committee were to become
known as the 'social contract', and formed the basis for Labour's programme in the 1974 elections.[17]
    The optimism which surrounded the initial formulation of the social
contract was of course quickly dissipated. Policies which might have
shaken the 'confidence' of British or overseas capital, or seriously
challenged Treasury orthodoxy, were rapidly shelved; the reality of cuts
and unemployment replaced the aspirations for enhanced equality and improved social welfare. Wage restraint - not explicitly mentioned in the
original social contract, despite an understanding that unions would
act 'responsibly' - was imposed with TUC cooperation in August 1975.
The main reciprocal gain - apart from a *formal* enhancement of union
status through close consultative relations with government and an expansion of 'quango' appointments - was in the field of labour law: vit-
ally important for the union movement, virtually costless for the government.
    The repeal of the Industrial Relations Act could not be accomplished
'at a stroke', for that Act had itself repealed almost the entire previous structure of labour legislation. Should the earlier statutes be
simply re-enacted, abandoning the whole experience of more interventionist labour law; or should the opportunity be taken to move from the
traditional system in directions favourable to union aspirations? In
its evidence to Donovan the TUC had articulated labour's deep-rooted
suspicion of positive legislation, even if well-intentioned. 'No state,
however benevolent, can perform the functions of trade unions in enabling workpeople themselves to decide how their interests can best be
safeguarded.'[18] Yet a minority of organisations - in the main recruiting
in the 'white-collar' sector, in the face of employers resistant to
unionisation - had advocated a different approach, calling in particular
for statutory support for union recognition and protection against unfair

dismissal. The 1971 Act had included provisions - albeit inadequate - on both issues; and the dominant view was now that these should be strengthened, not abolished. Virtually without debate, then, the TUC was converted to the desirability of positive legislation, and largely defined the content of the new Labour government's initiatives in this area: the Trade Union and Labour Relations Act (TULRA) of 1974, with amendments in 1976, and the Employment Protection Act (EPA) of 1975.[19]

In the first place, this new legislation restored the traditional system of negative immunities, seeking in the process to deal with some of the new liabilities recently invented by the judiciary. Secondly, a new set of institutions became established: the Advisory, Conciliation and Arbitration Service (ACAS),[20] Central Arbitration Committee (CAC), and Employment Appeal Tribunal. (Cynics may point to the parallels between the functions of these bodies and those, tainted in union eyes by the 1971 Act, which they replaced: the Commission on Industrial Relations; the Industrial Arbitration Board; and the NIRC.) Thirdly, the Acts defined various rights for individual employees, extending a process initiated in the 1960s;[21] the provisions on unfair dismissal in the 1971 Act were enlarged, 'guarantee payments' in case of temporary lay-offs were introduced, itemised pay statements were made compulsory, and a statutory system of maternity leave and maternity pay was introduced. In addition, the Sex Discrimination Act of 1975 and the Race Relations Act of 1976 created machinery for individuals to appeal to an Industrial Tribunal against discrimination in employment, and established statutory agencies with powers of investigation. Finally, the legislation introduced a range of collective rights: seeking to protect trade union members against victimisation; providing for complaints to ACAS by unions refused recognition; requiring consultation with recognised unions in advance of redundancies, disclosure of information for collective bargaining purposes, and time off for representatives; and permitting access to the CAC for awards against firms failing to observe the 'general level' of conditions for their type of employment. In addition, the Health and Safety at Work Act of 1974 provided for union representation in the new structure of safety committees and safety representatives.[22]

While the Industrial Relations Act was a focus of contention throughout the life of the Heath government, the new array of legislation stimulated remarkably little discussion within the labour movement. Only when the practical inadequacies of the new 'rights' became obvious - most notably as a result of the Grunwick dispute, which showed how easily a recalcitrant employer could dismiss unionists and defy the statutory recognition procedure - did significant debate ensue: mainly on whether unions should press for stronger legislation, or conclude that reliance on statutory support was futile. On the one hand it was clear that both individual and collective rights were narrowly defined, and the remedies for their breach derisory; on the other, that dependence on legal support opened the way for undesirable statutory controls, and that in any event the courts displayed a ready ability to find loopholes in even the most tightly drafted legislation. Hence disenchantment with the effects of TULRA and EPA created 'an element almost of schizophrenia in the British trade union movement'.[23]

Critics of the idea of further legislation cited not only the judges' traditional anti-unionism but also the lesson of American experience: where the Wagner Act of 1935, while assisting the unionisation drive,

created a climate of legalism in industrial relations which facilitated
the anti-union Taft-Hartley Act of 1947. Certainly the British version
of Taft-Hartley was not slow in coming. Despite the inadequacies of
Labour's legislation, employers, judges and Tory politicians were at one
in arguing that the balance had been tipped unwarrantably in favour of
the unions and should be swiftly reversed. More generally it was argued
that the superficial influence of the TUC on government policy - a trend
reflecting increasingly direct *state* intervention in the traditionally
'autonomous' arena of industrial relations much more than union assert-
iveness - was evidence of intolerable political power. Thus, despite
the signal *lack* of TUC success in its pressure for budgetary expansion,
egalitarian fiscal strategy, strengthened planning machinery and controls
over foreign trade and capital movements (demands which were central to
each of the annual *Economic Reviews*, the myth was sustained that the
trade unions were somehow 'running the country'.[24] To the three earlier
arguments for anti-union legislation - managerialist, individualistic
and legalistic - was accordingly added a fourth which may be termed
constitutionalist: the thesis that unions must be radically weakened
in order to curtain their political impact.

These arguments intensified in the period leading to the Tory election
victory of 1979, and doubtless contributed significantly to Thatcher's
success. Yet, while the commitment to 'reform' trade union law was even
stronger than a decade earlier, this time the Tories came to office without a comprehensive legislative blueprint. The fiasco of the 1971 Act
had clearly created doubts - at least among those with direct knowledge
of industrial relations - about the efficacy of any attempt at overnight
transformation in the traditional principles of labour law. In July 1979
the Department of Employment issued 'working papers' under three head-
ings: the closed shop, support from public funds for union ballots, and
picketing.[25] Simultaneously, some of the recently enacted individual
protections were weakened by ministerial order. In September three
further working papers proposed additional reductions in statutory
rights, including those dealing with union recognition, unfair dismissal,
maternity leave and low pay; yet another appeared the following month,
dealing with union boycotts of work produced in non-union establishments.

These proposals formed the basis for the Employment Bill which was
published in December 1979 and became law the following summer.[26] In
conjunction with the series of restrictions created by judicial invent-
iveness in the 1970s, the 1980 Act constitutes a serious and wide-ranging
attack on trade unionism. Most importantly, the ability to take effective industrial action within the law is further confined; a new basis
is created for judicial interference in internal union affairs; and a
variety of real if inadequate defences for the worst organised and most
vulnerable sections of the workforce are further diluted or removed
altogether.[27] However, these changes have been generally effected by
means of specific and at first sight narrow adjustments to existing law
rather than through patently radical innovations: a strategy made possible by the whole status of trade union law as a system of statutory
immunities against the common law presumption of illegality.[28] But
since it is far from obvious to the unsophisticated that detailed piecemeal alterations can entail substantial practical consequences, the
Employment Act was widely criticised from the Tory back benches and in
the right-wing press as insufficiently rigorous. It is in the context
of such arguments that the government's new document has appeared.

THE GREEN PAPER

The Green Paper commences with a brief introduction which clearly identifies its view of the nature of industrial relations 'problems': strikes,
'restrictive practices', 'overmanning', the 'enormous disruptive power'
possessed by 'small groups on the shopfloor' within a technologically
advanced and interdependent economic system. The debate which the document is intended to inform is explicitly linked to 'a widespread public
feeling' that unions 'have too few obligations and too much power', and
doubts whether they are 'fully representative of their members'. The
following section presents what, in the context of the Paper as a whole,
is a relatively balanced account of the historical development of the
system of labour law founded on negative immunities. Then come the two
crucial chapters: a lengthy survey of possible additional limitations
on the rights of union action; and a short discussion of the possible
replacement of the whole present system by a structure of 'positive
rights'. Finally there is a brief and highly tendentious account of
labour law in five overseas countries.

The central chapter examines eight separate areas of possible legal
attack, considering arguments for and against. The first issue is the
comprehensive immunity for trade union funds, conferred by the 1906 Act
and restored by TULRA: an immunity reflecting the recognition that the
judges, with their evident hostility to unionism, would soon erode any
lesser protection and thus expose trade unions to constant and costly
litigation. The Paper considers how far the immunity might be restricted, and to what extent unions might be made liable for the 'unofficial'
actions of their members. The main area of doubt which is indicated is
whether such changes would strengthen or weaken the disciplinary powers
of national leaders. (While much concerned that unions should be 'fully
democratic', the government is of course also anxious to achieve 'greater
internal discipline'.)

The next two issues have already been substantially covered in the
1980 Act: 'secondary' industrial action and picketing. Some ingenuity
is required to devise significant further restrictions on the now extremely narrow rights remaining to trade unionists, and these questions
receive very little discussion. More space is devoted to the legal
definition of a 'trade dispute', the pivot of the whole mechanism of
immunity in the case of industrial action, and one already attacked by
the judiciary. The main options outlined would withdraw immunity from
disputes adjudged predominantly 'political', from forms of solidarity
action, and in particular from international actions. The question of
making ballots (already encouraged by the Employment Act) compulsory
before strike action is also raised; the Green Paper recognises that
there would be many practical difficulties in this.

The three remaining items all figured prominently in the Industrial
Relations Act. The 1980 Act imposes restrictions on the operation of
closed shop agreements; but this applies only to *new* agreements, provides
merely for individual actions for unfair dismissal, and makes the
employer rather than the union the defendant.[29] Additional measures
which are discussed include outlawing the closed shop altogether, requiring regular ballots on its continuance, and making illegal various
indirect methods of enforcing 100 per cent unionism. In the light of
experience under the 1971 Act - when closed shop agreements, though
illegal, actually increased in incidence - the Paper recognises that

such provisions might be hard to enforce. The same conclusion is suggested in the case of proposals that collective agreements might be made
legally binding. Finally, attention is given to the possibility of
special restrictions on strikes in 'essential services' or those which
involve 'national emergencies'. The paper suggests that this is 'a
sensitive and difficult area'; more specifically, the farcical effects
of the one attempt to apply the relevant clauses in the Industrial
Relations Act indicate that the use of such powers 'may be counterproductive for the government'.

The whole chapter has many of the qualities of a *Guardian* editorial:
cautious and equivocal, conscious of the difficulties involved in any
course of action, reluctant to reach firm conclusions. On one reading,
indeed, it can be viewed as Prior's attempt to persuade the more hard-
line employers, Tory MPs and press commentators that little more can
readily be done to toughen the Employment Act. Yet in setting out so
exhaustively an agenda for further repressive legislation, the Green
Paper offers a programme for reactionaries whose capacity for nuanced
judgment has not proved overwhelming in the past. And for all its
qualifications, the discussion massively reinforces the view that
industrial relations 'problems' are essentially definable in terms of
excessive trade union power and irresponsible strike action: the
'holding the country to ransome' syndrome. It would be fatuous to
expect from such a source an analysis of capital-labour relations and
of the natural tendency of capitalist production to generate collective
worker resistance. Nevertheless, it is noteworthy that a document which
pontificates so readily about trade union power should so totally ignore
the power of capital and the specific role of employers in provoking
conflict.[30] Across the major span of managerial policy, trade unions
are unable - and do not normally even attempt - to exert significant
influence. The spectacular growth, in the past two or three decades,
of multi-plant enterprises has substantially strengthened the power of
capital in industrial relations; and it may be noted that one reason
for the growing prominence of picketing during strikes is the ability
of such firms to switch production between establishments. The rise of
transnational enterprises, to which the labour movement has as yet proposed no plausible strategy, shifts the balance of power even further.
No such considerations trouble the authors of the Green Paper, for whom
industry is seemingly a well-engineered machine disrupted only by the
actions of a minority of organised workers.

This perspective continues in the remaining chapter, which briefly
outlines the option of replacing negative immunities by 'positive rights'.
The case for such a change is plausible: most legal systems do prescribe
explicit rights of union organisation and action, while the British
tradition of immunities against common law liabilities is a recipe for
both complexity and obscurity (compounded, though the Paper does not say
this, by the 1980 Act itself). The objections to such a change are twofold. Firstly, no structure of positive employment law could be isolated
from the broader legal system; on the contrary, it would offer novel
scope for judges to define overriding common law liabilities in the
manner in which they have long proved remarkably adept. Secondly, it
is inconceivable that an *absolute* right to strike would be enacted;
conditions for its application would be prescribed. In Germany, for
example, the law protects only those strikes which are 'socially adequate': a formula which in practice imposes severe restrictions.

Significantly, the CBI itself suggested a year ago that trade union immunities might be replaced 'by a positive right to strike, subject to reasonable limitations'.[31] The Green Paper makes very clear that such 'reasonable limitations' would comprehensively reaffirm, and could well extend and reinforce, the restrictions which are inherent in existing labour law; and that in consequence the gains in clarity and simplicity would be negligible.

It is remarkable that a discussion headed 'an alternative system of positive rights' is in fact concerned *only* with defining more sharply the law on strikes. As is candidly stated, 'it is not primarily concerned with other rights, such as the right to associate and to join a trade union which are common features of other systems, except insofar as they may be considered an essential adjunct to a positive right to strike'. What makes this exclusion so breathtaking is that the uniqueness of British labour law lies *not* in its treatment of strikes, which through a distinctive method achieves a substantive result in line with that in many other countries; it is in the lack of any legal guarantees of the right to organise and bargain collectively. Were British unions to consider a system of positive rights desirable - and recent experience suggests, on the contrary, that a move to greater legalism would bring only limited benefits but entail serious dangers - then it is *these* basic preconditions of unionisation which would be of paramount importance. Their exclusion from the Green Paper merely confirms that, as far as the government is concerned, a system of 'positive rights' would in no way enhance the position of trade unions but would offer the pretext for additional restrictions on union action.

A decade ago, Wedderburn commented that the Industrial Relations Act, 'this comprehensive new code to set right industrial ills included no "emergency powers" to deal with mass lay-offs, plant closures or dismissals by which unemployment of a scale amounting to a national emergency has already been created'.[32] The point is of even greater cogency today. While the specific conclusions of the Green Paper are circumspect, the unquestioned framework of argument presents trade unionists as the scapegoats for a crisis created by the anarchy of world capitalism and exacerbated by the policies of the government itself.

SIGNIFICANCE AND STRATEGY

What is to be done? Given the obvious parallels between Thatcherism and the (initial) programme of the Heath government, and in particular the common commitment to legal curbs on trade unionism, it is important to recognise the contrasts which make most simple 'lessons' drawn from the struggle against the Industrial Relations Act unhelpful. Firstly, that struggle was sustained on a rising tide of industrial militancy, with strike figures reaching record levels; to an important extent, it was mass action and mass defiance which overcame Heath's abrasive industrial relations strategy. Today, the impact of six years of unabated mass unemployment (compounded for much of this period by union acquiescence in the 'social contract' wage controls) has blunted confidence and combativity.[33] The task of mobilisation against any further statutory offensive is thus immensely greater.

Equally significantly, the position of employers has altered markedly. As has been noted already, the 1971 Act was less the expression of a

coherent strategy for British capital than the product of the 'active,
conceptive ideologists'[34] of the ruling class. For most major employers
in the 1960s, the key 'problem' of industrial relations was the prevalence of small, sectional, 'unofficial' stoppages which forced piecemeal
concessions and obstructed managerial control of the labour process.
For the most part, their preferred solutions involved harnessing the
potential disciplinary powers of trade union organisation in the joint
construction of more orderly and predictable industrial relations arrangements. While some sectors of capital desired a more extensive framework
of legislation ('Donovan with teeth'), their aim was at one and the same
time to consolidate the status of unionism and to oblige its leaders to
enforce restraint and 'responsibility' on the subordinate membership: a
strategy which may be accurately termed corporatist. Insofar as the
dominant aim of the Industrial Relations Act was to weaken unionism at
all levels, it contradicted the primary objectives of leading employers;
hence their readiness to collude in evading many of its provisions.
    Today this contradiction has been largely transcended. Economic
crisis and intensified international competition are engendering a major
restructuring of production involving plant closures or reductions in
employment levels; new forms of technology and subdivision of labour; a
systematic attack on workers' traditional shop-floor job controls; and
a flexible and compliant labour force. If analogous objectives underlay
the 'productivity bargaining' offensive of the late 1960s, at least the
material context allowed significant 'packages' of improvements in pay
and hours to smooth the process. Today union negotiators are pressed
to make far greater concessions for far less in return; and compliance
is all the more difficult because workplace representatives (as part of
the process of 'post-Donoval reform') have become firmly integrated
within official collective bargaining machinery. The changed environment
of management-union relations helps explain the trend to larger, longer,
official strikes as well as the greater salience of determined picketing.
Far more than a decade ago, major employers recognised that their economic objectives necessarily imply serious confrontation with the unions.
Within British capital there are, of course, still important variations
in material position and strategic perspective; nevertheless, as the
policy stances of the major employers' organisations demonstrate, the
balance has shifted significantly towards favouring a tough and legalistic
treatment. There is thus far greater scope for convergence between the
managerialist and the more exclusively ideological Tory approaches to
industrial relations legislation.[35]
    One implication of this new alignment is that polite participation
in the 'debate' proposed by the Green Paper will yield few dividends.
The growing accommodation, in this area at least, between Tory policy
and employer interests offers little space for the insertion of 'rational'
argument. Rather, the ideological struggle must be waged outside the
confines of the formulation of 'public policy'; more specifically, it
must be conducted within the trade union movement itself. In 1970-71,
an impressive programme of strikes (largely 'unofficial') and demonstrations was directed against the Industrial Relations Bill, generating the
momentum which ensured official union resistance. But much of the mass
support was of a reflex character. Shop stewards who had won their
members' respect and confidence through years of successful workplace
bargaining were able to win their backing for token stoppages against
the Bill; the slogan 'Hands off the Unions' was often a sufficient
rationale.

After a decade in which the achievements of shop-floor trade unionism
have been far less impressive, such widespread and largely automatic
support cannot realistically be expected. On the contrary, recent experience at British Leyland is evidence enough that even on questions of
direct and fundamental relevance for wages and working conditions, the
lead of the shop steward organisation can be decisively rejected. It is
obvious that this reflects much broader ideological developments within
the working class, mirroring the general shift to the right in British
politics. Thatcher's electoral success depended upon a substantial proportion of working-class votes, a significant minority coming from trade
union members. For some years, opinion polls have regularly suggested
that three-quarters of the population, including the majority of trade
unionists, agree that trade unions are 'too powerful' (only some five
per cent suggesting that they are not powerful enough); and while facile
responses to pollsters' superficial questions provide little guide to
predicting concrete action, at the very least such results reveal the
weakness of most trade unionists' commitment to their movement and offer
encouragement to those who demand statutory curbs on union action. Unless trade union reactions to the Green Paper are addressed primarily to
the consciousness of their own members, the prospects of successful
resistance to further attacks must be bleak.

Why are trade union members susceptible to anti-union ideology? Two
key reasons can be suggested. Firstly, attitudes to strikes suggest the
readiness of workers and their families to view themselves as *victims* of
other workers' struggles. This readiness is certainly cultivated by the
media and by politicians. Nevertheless, it has a material basis in the
divisive sectionalism which so often characterises union demands and collective militancy; the *class* significance of industrial conflicts is
rarely explicit.[36] Hence the seemingly widespread belief among trade
unionists that all strikes are bad - except their own. To challenge
this ideology and its material basis requires, in effect, to restore
meaning to the slogan of a trade union *movement*: to pursue a programme
and a strategy which can unify rather than divide. In particular, this
points to the vital necessity of informing the often parochial perspectives of grassroots union struggle with a vision of the interests of the
class as a whole.

The second factor concerns the power relationship between trade union
organisation and workers as individuals: a relationship presented most
starkly, and most tendentiously, in debates over the closed shop. Trade
unionism *presupposes* a world-view founded upon the reality of collective
rather than individual interests, whereby the need for collective cohesion
and solidarity in the face of capital is taken for granted. (Naturally,
the Tory enthusiasm for secret ballots reflects a desire to subvert the
power of collective identity.) Since the participation of each is essential for the welfare of all, trade unionists have a common interest in
ensuring that no individual evades the obligations of collective discipline. Union discipline is thus, in principle, the expression of workers'
collective interests. Yet for many (perhaps most) trade unionists, 'The
Union' is a distant bureaucratic machine rather than part of their own
living identity. Officials and lay activists alike - who together run
the official machinery of trade unionism - seem increasingly unsuccessful in persuading the majority of members that they themselves are the
union; arguably indeed, their practices sometimes encourage a view of
'The Union' as an alien, unsympathetic and perhaps even hostile power.

Thus, paradoxically, the cultivation of discreet and cordial bargaining
relationships with management, on the part of full-time officials *or*
workplace leaders, can cause the organic link with the rank and file to
atrophy; so that when it is necessary to mobilise *against* management
(let alone the state) their collective identification and commitment
cannot be suddenly reconstituted. This must represent at least part of
the explanation of the British Leyland disaster, which in turn symbolises
far more general developments within British trade unionism. The whole
question of union democracy - of devising practices and internal relations
which transform the 'apathetic' majority into more than passive and
easily alienated dues-payers - is thus crucial for any effective
strategy to resist further encroachments by the state.[37]

It is therefore impossible to regard the debate on trade union law
as an isolated issue, and would be futile to rely on a low-key defensive
response to the convergent attacks from judiciary and legislature. The
ideological assault on trade unionism, far more than a decade ago, rests
on powerful material forces, and derives important additional strength
from contradictions inherent in British trade unionism itself. To mobilise an adequate countervailing force thus demands a sustained ideological
struggle within the ranks of trade union membership, and reciprocating
changes within trade union practice. What is at issue is *both* trade
union education - in its broadest sense - *and* trade union objectives and
strategy. To overcome a potentially fatal disenchantment among their
own members, unions need to be able to demonstrate - on the basis of
persuasive evidence in their own programmes and actions - that trade
unions today are too weak rather than too strong, that all workers would
gain from enhanced union strength, and that to achieve this demands their
own active commitment. Such a campaign would involve, above all else,
the cultivation of a 'subversive' world-view in which the power of capital
and its antagonism to workers' interests are unequivocally exposed; and
would be impossible without a radicalisation of trade unions' material
goals and methods. To expect such a response would perhaps be utopian;
but in a hostile climate, nothing less is likely to succeed.

NOTES

1 Cmnd. 8128, HMSO, 1981, p.9.
2 Roy Lewis, 'The Historical Development of Labour Law', *British Journal
   of Industrial Relations*, 1976, p.5.
3 K.W. Wedderburn, 'Industrial Relations and the Courts', *Industrial
   Law Journal*, 1980, p.69.
4 K.W. Wedderburn, *The Worker and the Law* (2nd edition), Penguin, 1971,
   p.314.
5 For example O, Kahn-Freund, 'Legal Framework' in A. Flanders and
   H.A. Clegg, *The System of Industrial Relations in Great Britain*,
   Blackwell, 1954; A. Flanders, 'The Tradition of Voluntarism', *British
   Journal of Industrial Relations*, 1974.
6 Richard Hyman, *Industrial Relations: a Marxist Introduction*,
   Macmillan, 1975, p.135.
7 K.W. Wedderburn, 'The New Structure of Labour Law in Britain', *Israel
   Law Review*, 1978, p.438.
8 For an early account of the developing union-state relations see
   V.L. Allen, *Trade Unions and the Government*, Longmans, 1960. More

recent discussions include Colin Crouch, *Class Conflict and the Industrial Relations Crisis*, Heinemann, 1977 and *The Politics of Industrial Relations*, Fontana, 1979; Ross M. Martin, *TUC: the Growth of a Pressure Group*, OUP, 1980; Keith Middlemass, *Politics in Industrial Society*, Deutsch, 1979; Leo Panitch, 'Trade Unions and the Capitalist State', *New Left Review* 125, 1981.

9   In my view - though this is not the place to develop the argument - the notion of corporatism fails adequately to explicate the changing relationship between unions, employers and the state: it cannot satisfactorily comprehend the contradictory nature of this relationship, stemming from the divergent perspectives and strategies of each party, their complex internal politics, and the shifting material context of their interaction.

10 Lewis, 'Historical Development', p.9.

11 It was specifically under the first post-war Tory government that the Ministry of Labour consolidated its image as a 'neutral' mediator between unions, employers and the state. The Minister, Monckton, was popular with union leaders and sought to distance himself from the general policies of the government and the Tory party.

12 Royal Commission on Trade Unions and Employers' Associations, 1965-68. The reference to employers' associations was a purely formal concession to the unions; given the concentrated power of capital wielded by employers even in the absence of mutual combination, their organisations are in no way analogous in function or status to those of workers. The Commission's report appeared in June 1968 (Cmnd. 3623).

13 *In Place of Strife*, Cmnd. 3888, January 1969.

14 For one account see Peter Jenkins, *The Battle of Downing Street*, Knight, 1970.

15 Its proposals were outlined in a document satirically entitled *Fair Deal at Work* and published in April 1968 (two months before the Donovan Report).

16 K.W. Wedderburn, 'Labour Law and Labour Relations in Britain', *British Journal of Industrial Relations*, 1972, p.282.

17 For a relatively balanced account of the genesis of the 'social contract' see John Elliott, *Conflict or Cooperation?*, Kogan Page, 1978.

18 TUC, *Trade Unionism*. 1966, pp.68-69.

19 The body of individual rights contained in TULRA and EPA, as well as some earlier statutes, was brought together with minor amendments in the Employment Protection (Consolidation) Act 1978.

20 ACAS was founded, though not on a statutory basis, in September 1974; it took over the traditional conciliation functions of the Department of Employment. The subordination of these functions to the pay policy of the Heath government had provoked considerable trade union criticism and had inspired the proposal of an 'independent' agency.

21 For example, the Contracts of Employment Act 1963 and the Redundancy Payments Act 1965.

22 For an account and assessment of the new structure of employment law see Jeremy McMullen, *Rights at Work*, Pluto, 1978.

23 K.W. Wedderburn, 'New Structure of Labour Law', p.456. Wedderburn, himself one of the architects of Labour's employment legislation, adds that 'its consequences ... were not perhaps fully thought out at the time of enactment. One consequence of the introduction of a

system of statutory employment 'rights' which *had* been anticipated
by some of its advocates (thus explaining why some of the first moves
in this direction in the 1960s were initiated by Tory governments)
has rarely been confronted in debates within the labour movement.
This is the tendency inherent in the law to *individualise* and
commoditise social relations. In place of collective resistance
to employer attacks, the law offers the solution of individual
resort to a judicial tribunal which judges 'fairness' largely by
the criteria of capitalist economic rationality; thus the power of
workers' solidarity, grounded at least implicitly in very different
norms of political economy, may be eroded. And the law does not
offer genuine protection against job loss or discriminatory treatment, but merely establishes the principle of (usually token) financial compensation for the worker who 'wins' his/her case; the right
to work, and on acceptable conditions, becomes a commodity to be
bought and sold (or rather, subject to compulsory purchase). Both
processes are manifest in the redundancy payments legislation, which
- as was in part the purpose - has made a united fight against job
loss much more difficult.

24 'On the level of unemployment, public spending cuts, import controls,
government intervention through planning agreements, the TUC gained
virtually nothing after 1975. It was, however, during this very
period that the unions conceded most...' (Colin Crouch, *The Politics
of Industrial Relations*, Fontana, 1979, p.130). As David Coates
insists (*Labour in Power?*, Longman, 1980, p.130), 'the visibility
of trade union leaders in the process of policy-making was less an
index of their power than of their subordination'.

25 These proposals were incisively analysed by Roy Lewis, Paul Davies
and Bill Wedderburn, *Industrial Relations Law and the Conservative
Government*, NCCL, 1979.

26 Following the reluctant decision by the law Lords reversing attempts
by the egregious Lord Denning to declare 'secondary' strike action
illegal, a further working paper was issued on this topic in February
1980 and the proposed restrictions were subsequently incorporated in
the Bill.

27 The Employment Act and associated changes are analysed in detail in
Jeremy McMullen, *Employment Law Under the Tories*, Pluto, 1981; and
Roy Lewis and Robert Simpson, *Striking a Balance?*, Martin Robertson,
1981.

28 One government minister, significantly, presented the Employment
Bill in the Commons as 'restoring to employers ... their common law
rights that statute has taken away'; see Wedderburn, 'Industrial
Relations and the Courts', p.93.

29 While employers are indeed entitled to 'join' a union as co-defend-
ant, it seems unlikely that this option will be widely used.

30 To be scrupulously accurate, the Green Paper *does* state (p.7) that
'employers share the responsibility for the present state of our
industrial relations'. But there are only two specific criticisms:
employers have been too tolerant of union pressure and union prefer-
ence for voluntary and informal procedures; and they have been too
slow in introducing systems of 'employee involvement' (which might
bypass union representation?). After these introductory remarks,
employers disappear from sight.

31 CBI, *Trade Unions in a Changing World*, 1980, p.22.

32   'Labour Law and Labour Relations', p.275.
33   The number of recorded strikes has fallen sharply; though because
     many that do occur are large and protracted, the aggregate level of
     strike-days remains high.
34   'The division of labour, which we already saw ... as one of the chief
     forces of history up till now, manifests itself also in the ruling
     class as the division of mental and material labour, so that inside
     this class one part appears as the thinkers of the class (its active,
     conceptive ideologists, who make the formation of the illusions of
     the class about itself their chief source of livelihood), while the
     others' attitude to these ideas and illusions is more passive and
     receptive, because they are in reality the active members of this
     class and have less time to make up illusions and ideas about them-
     selves. Within this class this cleavage can even develop into a
     certain opposition and hostility between the two parts...' (Karl
     Marx and Frederick Engels, 'The German Ideology', *Collected Works*
     5, Lawrence & Wishart, 1976, pp.59-60). For a useful analysis of
     divergent perspectives on industrial relations within British capital
     and the ruling class more generally see Dominic Strinati, 'Capitalism,
     the State and Industrial Relations' in Colin Crouch (ed.), *State and
     Economy in Contemporary Capitalism*, Croom Helm, 1979.
35   The most important reason why many employers today are likely to
     prove doubtful about further legislative initiatives is that new
     laws impose significant expense: in administrative procedure,
     training, legal advice and so on. In this respect, 'enlightened'
     employers would probably prefer some form of bi-partisan compromise
     (to which they and the TUC could at least tacitly agree) to a major
     alteration of employment law with each change of government.
36   This is not necessarily to argue (as does Eric Hobsbawm, 'The Forward
     March of Labour Halted?', *Marxism Today*, September 1978) that trade
     union action has become *more* sectional in recent years. Rather, the
     growing interdependence of production units - reinforced often by
     deliberate employer strategy - has meant that localised strikes can
     quickly result in large-scale lay-offs; while the spread of unionism
     and militancy in the 'public service' sector has involved strikes
     with a far more visible and immediate impact on the 'general public'
     than in the case of manufacturing industry.
37   I have tried to confront some of the issues which this problem
     involves in 'The Politics of Workplace Trade Unionism', *Capital and
     Class*, 8, 1979.

Women, Power, and Politics

MARGARET STACEY AND MARION PRICE

Tavistock Women's Studies

'How can it possibly be that when women have only had the vote for fifty years that so many of them have become involved in politics?' This is the surprising question that the authors felt compelled to ask after examining the evidence. They explore this question cross-culturally, historically, and in the context of contemporary social and political arrangements.

224 pages
Hardback 0 422 76140 0 £8.95
Paperback 0 422 76150 8 £3.95

METHUEN

Athar Hussain
Sexual Discrimination in Personal Taxation

It is a commonplace now that the system of personal taxation in Britain
is in need of a radical reform. Its discriminatory treatment of men and
women, in particular, has come in for criticism from all quarters. Both
the major political parties have committed themselves to the overhaul of
the system. The Green Paper *The Taxation of Husband and Wife*,[1] issued
by the present Conservative government in December 1980, was first promised by the last Labour government in 1978. It is a consultative document designed to solicit opinions on the ways in which the present system can be reformed. The criticisms of the system of personal taxation
are not new: women's groups and organisations like the Equal Opportunities Commission have since long pointed to the discriminatory and
regressive aspects of the system.[2]

Though there is a near unanimity about the need for a radical reform,
the detailed criticisms of the present system and the grounds on which
they are made vary widely. The same is true for the proposals of the
reform.[3] Given this, the principal purpose of the paper is not so much
to put forward a specific blue-print for reform, as to disentangle the
issues which are involved and to indicate the possible directions of
reforms.

At the outset it is worth emphasising that, though it is the discrimination against women embedded in the system of personal taxation which
has been the principal target of attacks on it, that alone cannot indicate the direction of reform. For, first, the discrimination between
men and women is just one of the web of objectionable discriminations
embedded in the present system. Secondly, the unfair discrimination
between men and women can be ended in a wide variety of ways, which are
not equivalent from the general point of view of social welfare. And
finally, sexual discrimination, though pertinent, is not the sole
criterion for assessing the system of personal taxation.

THE PRESENT SYSTEM OF PERSONAL TAXATION

A notable feature of the British tax system is that most individuals pay
taxes without understanding it. This ignorance - which is a barrier to
a reasoned popular discussion of the tax system - is perpetuated by the
PAYE system of the deduction of taxes before individuals lay hands on
their income, and the confusing medley of personal allowances and deductions. The objectionable features of the system are not immediately
obvious to everyone. Therefore, it is as well to start by outlining
the existing system.

    Though individuals pay a wide variety of taxes, this article restricts
itself to incomes from employment - earned income in the parlance of the
Inland Revenue - or from the possession of property. A significant
feature of the existing tax system is that it only recognises those
individuals who are in receipt of taxable income. Non-tax payers:
housewives and disabled persons, are relevant to the tax system only
if they happen to be dependent on a tax payer. However, if such persons
are not linked to a tax payer either through marriage or relations of
blood, then they become charges of the system of social security, and
are of no direct concern to the tax system. At this stage of the argument, this point may seem to be formalistic; it is, however, of significance. For the restricted recognition of persons by the tax system
is a corollary of a system of social security which is distinct - distinct in terms of the definitions it employs and the criteria it employs
when assessing needs - from the system of personal taxation. The co-
existence of these two parallel systems is, as has been well documented,
the principal source of inequities and arbitrariness in the joint
effects of the two systems on individuals and families.[4] Moreover, the
reform of the system of personal taxation brings into question the
present division of labour between the tax and the social security
systems.

    The system of personal taxation is constituted of the following
ingredients:
(1) personal allowances,
(2) deductions (tax relief on mortgage interest repayments and life
    insurance contributions),
(3) the schedule of tax rates and
(4) the distinction between earned and investment incomes.

    Tax payers are not treated alike. They are differentiated according
to the composition of their household, their age (above or below the
retirement age), the sources of their income (property or employment)
and the composition of their expenditure (mortgage repayments, life
insurance and pension contributions and occupation-related expenditure).
It is these differentiations which are ultimately responsible for the
objectionable features of the system. An important feature of the
British tax system is that all the specific circumstances of the individual tax payer are taken into account through personal allowances and
the deduction of permitted expenditures from the taxable income. The
schedule of tax rates is the same for all tax payers. It does, however,
vary for different types of incomes: investment income beyond a certain
level is taxed at a higher rate than earned income, and capital gains
are taxed at a flat rate.

    One has to turn to the system of personal allowances in order to
bring to light the web of discriminations which are embodied in the

system of personal taxation, and it is these which form the subject of
the Green Paper which is misleadingly entitled *The Taxation of Husband
and Wife*.

The system of personal allowances is not structured around the distinction between men and women, in that as individual tax payers they
are treated alike. Rather, the basic distinction is between individuals
and households built around marriage and blood relations. The three
principal components of the system of personal allowances are:
(1) the single person's allowance,
(2) the married person's allowance and
(3) the age allowance.
The first two set the norm for other personal allowances like the wife's
earned income allowance, and the additional personal allowance for
single parent families. The size of different types of allowance - not
the same as the cash value to their recipients - is as follows:

Table 1

Category	Amount	
1 Single Person's Allowance	1,375	
2 Husband's Allowance	2,145	
3 Wife's Earned Income Allowance	1,375	
4 Pensioner's Allowance		
(a) Single	1,820	
(b) Married Couple	2,895	
5 Additional Personal Allowance (given to single parent families)	770	(equal to the difference between the single and the husband's allowance)
6 Widow's Allowance (limited to the year of husband's death)	770	

These are 1980-81 figures. These allowances are meant to be linked
to the retail price index, but the Chancellor in his budget of March
1981, rather than raising the basic rate of income tax from 30% to 32%,
opted for the regressive measure of not raising the allowances at all
during the year 1981-82. It is only since 1978 - as a result of the
Rooker-Wise Amendment - that personal allowances have been linked to
the retail price index; till then the raising of allowances depended on
the whims and fancies of successive Chancellors. Furthermore, the ratio
of single to married allowances has varied a great deal during the post-
war period. As the Green Paper itself points out, up to the early 1960s
the married allowance ranged from 1.5 times to 1.8 times the single
allowance. In the subsequent decade the gap narrowed quite markedly:
in the early 1970s the married allowance was only 1.3 times the single
allowance. The present ratio of 1.6 is almost the same as the ratio of
social security benefits to single persons and married couples. What
these variations point out is that, though personal allowances are meant
to perform a social welfare function, they have not been based on a
consistent welfare criterion.

Leaving aside the pensioners' allowance, what the table makes clear
is that the first two set the norms for the rest. The purpose of the
last two allowances is to render the allowances received by the heads
of single parent families and by recently widowed women equal to the
husband's allowance. Moreover, the ratio of single to married allowance
for pensioners is almost the same as that ratio for non-pensioners.

The important feature of the allowances - personal as well as expenditure related allowances - is that they affect the income of individuals by reducing their tax liability: they are deducted from income
before it is assessed for tax. In contrast cash benefits raise the
pre-tax income of the recipients. In the British system they are not
taxed. Two features follow from this general characteristic of allowances. First, tax allowances are worth nothing to those individuals
and families who do not have a taxable income, housewifes and those in
receipt of social security and unemployment benefits. The second point
is that the cash value of an allowance, which is equal to the extra tax
that would have been paid in the absence of the allowance, depends on
the tax rate which the recipient pays on the last pound of his income.
Therefore to the tax payer paying the basic rate the cash value of the
allowances is equal to 30% of the amount of the allowance. It is higher
for high tax payers. This has some crucial implications for the social
welfare significance of the allowances, which will be pointed out later.
    The listing of all the personal allowances together masks the point
that they are not all on a par with each other. Leaving aside the
pensioners' allowances which raise different issues, the single person's
allowance and the working wife's allowance - which are essentially the
same allowances - are different from the rest. The first two would
exist under any system of progressive taxation. The rest form that
part of the social welfare system which is provided through taxes,
termed 'fiscal welfare' by Titmuss.[5] The husband's allowance would not
exist under a unified system of social security were housewives were
paid a cash benefit on the model of the present child benefit. The
welfare aspect of the present husband's allowance is brought into
relief by saying that a working husband receives a single allowance in
his capacity as the recipient of a taxable income, and in addition to
that he receives 56% of the single allowance as the representative of
his wife. The latter in keeping with the notion of 'fiscal welfare'
should be treated as welfare tax allowance to the wife. Qua welfare
payment, the peculiar feature of the allowance is that it is not granted
to the supposed beneficiary, even when she has an income of her own to
offset against the allowance, but to her husband. There are two points
which need to be made about this peculiar method of providing for wives.
The first is that it leads to an inequitable treatment of husbands and
wives as tax payers. And the second is that this method of welfare provision for wives is also inequitable, and that it has to be assessed in
relation to the alternative methods of welfare provision, a cash benefit
which is directly paid to the wives, for instance. However, before we
turn to a detailed discussion of these points, it is necessary to un-
earth the web of discriminations embedded in the tax allowances. The
essential point about these discriminations is that they concern both
the households and the husband and wives as tax payers.

DISCRIMINATION BETWEEN DIFFERENT TYPES OF HOUSEHOLDS

If we leave aside children and dependent relatives, then the tax system
only recognises the households built around marriage, and does not
recognise the household built around co-habitation. However, it is
necessary to take into account the allocation of allowances to co-
habitees for a variety of other reasons. A large number of households

in the Britain of today are based on co-habitation. Moreover, co-habitation is the relevant category from the point of view of social security regulations and of the family law. As is well known through the stories of snooping on the recipients of social security benefits, co-habitation can lead to a reduction in benefits. Moreover, co-habitation is recognised in the law concerning the division of family property on separation. If the husband's allowance leads to a discrimination between co-habitees and married couples, then the working wife's allowance, which does not affect the husband's allowance, leads to a yet further discrimination, between different types of married households. The resulting network of discriminations is best brought out by the following table, which gives the total allowance received by the household as multiples of the single person's allowance.

Table 2

Types of couples	*Total personal allowances*
BOTH WORKING	
(1) Co-habitees	2 (two single allowances)
(2) Married couple, but have opted for separate taxation	2 (treated same as category 1)
(3) Married couple	2.6 (1 married + 1 working wife's allowance)
ONE WORKING	
(4) Co-habitees	1
(5) Husband working	1.6 (just the married allowance)
(6) Wife working	2.6 (as in category 3)

NB This table, which only applies to income from employment, is drawn on the assumption that a working person's income is not less than a single person's allowance. The allowance for persons earning less than that - almost certain to be part-time workers - is equal to their income.

This table divides couples according to the extent of their participation in the labour market. The alternative to this is the division married/non-married couples. The choice of the scheme of classification crucially depends on what one regards as justifiable or unjustifiable discrimination. If we accept for the moment that it is the work-pattern of the couple which is essential, then what the table makes clear is that similar couples: couples in each of the two principal categories, get different tax allowances. Since allowances affect tax liability, the immediate implication of this differential allocation is that couples with the same pre-tax income would pay different amounts in taxes. To start with we concentrate on discrimination between couples with identical work-patterns.

A general point about discriminations. The tax system rewards marriage in that tax liability of a married couple is never greater than the tax liability of a co-habiting couple. In general the former always pay less taxes than the equivalent co-habiting couple: couple with the same pre-tax income and with the same work-pattern. The only exception is the married couple which has, in official terminology, elected to be taxed singly, which amounts to the same thing as being treated as a co-habiting couple. However, at the present rates of

taxation, election for separate taxation is only advantageous if the
joint income of the couple exceeds £17,000 p.a. - an income which is
well in excess of the average income of married couples in Britain.
The fact that the separate taxation election is disadvantageous for the
vast majority of married working couples is borne out by the Inland
Revenue statistics.[6] In the year 1977/78, the last year for which the
figures are available, only 135,000 married working couples out of a
total of just over 7 million (around 2%) elected for separate taxation.
Since there is no reason to believe that this proportion has changed
appreciably since then, it becomes clear that for almost all couples
who do not have a large investment income, marriage is at least a
fiscally rewarding experience, if not otherwise.

A closer examination of discriminations within each of the two major
categories brings out some interesting features. Under the present set-
up the co-habitees suffer on two counts. They are for obvious reasons
not entitled to the husband's allowance. In addition to that the unemployed co-habitee may be disqualified from social security payments
because the Department of Social Security and Health (DHSS) takes into
account the total income of the couple - whether married or just co-
habiting - when assessing need. As for the discriminations between the
married couples, the couple where only the husband works is treated
less favourably than the couple where the wife alone works. This is
due to the fact that the breadwinner wife is treated by the tax system
as a working husband as well as a working wife. The reason behind the
favourable treatment of the breadwinner wife is a noble one: women on
average earn less than men and therefore the families of breadwinner
wives are likely to be low income families.

The tax system does indeed reward marriage, but does it really uphold
the traditional family precept that a woman's proper place is in the
home, as the critics of the present structure of personal allowance -
the Equal Opportunities Commission - allege? In fact it has an ambiguous and contradictory relation to that precept. It does uphold it in
that it grants a married man an extra 56% of the single person's allowance. That extra has always been justified - including in the Green
Paper - on the grounds that a married man's income not only supports
him but also his wife, who, if the justification is to hold, is presumed
to be unemployed. However, the tax system also encourages married
women to go out to work in that they qualify for a single person's
allowance in addition to the married allowance which their husbands
receive. There are two ways of looking at the working wife's allowance.
It could be looked on as something which favours working wives or as a
measure which penalises the families where the wife does not go out to
work. However, whichever way it is looked at it is contrary to the
precept. In fact it goes further than that. Among the couples where
one partner alone works, the couple most favoured by the tax system is
the one where the husband stays at home and the wife goes out to work.
That is the only case where one earner receives 2.6 times the single
person's allowance. What this implies is that if one of a married
couple has to give up work to look after children or to acquire further
training in order to improve income prospects, then from the point of
view of the reduction of the tax liabilities of the family it is always
better for the husband to do so. Therefore it could be said that the
tax system implicitly favours the reversal of sexual roles, but less
unexpectedly it also favours the acquisition of further skill by the
husband rather than by the wife.

These strange implications of the pattern of allocation of personal allowances are obviously not intended. The existing pattern has resulted from the piecemeal changes which have been introduced since the end of the First World War. Each of those piecemeal changes is based on noble intentions, which are in their own terms perfectly justifiable. The point, however, is that the intended consequences do not exhaust the implications of the pattern of allocation of personal allowances. For instance, the favourable treatment of breadwinner wives rests on the desire to increase the post-tax income of poor families to which they normally belong. But that measure can also be used by a family which is not poor and imbued with economic rationality. Further, certain of the discriminations appear anomalous because social conditions have changed. To take one of the important changes which has taken place in the post-war period, the proportion of married women who work has more than doubled.[7] Now almost half of married women go out to work; this proportion might well be higher but for the present difficulty of finding employment. These changes cut the ground from underneath the argument that a husband deserves an extra allowance because his income goes to support his wife.

The answer to the question 'which of the discriminations between different types of couples is objectionable, and what could be done to remove it?' crucially depends on which of the two criteria for assessing the discriminations one adopts. One could divide the couples according to both working/one working, as is done here, and then argue that the tax system should not discriminate between the couples within these categories. One may term this the work-oriented criterion. The alternative to this is the marriage-oriented criterion, which divides couples according to married/co-habiting and then argues that there should not be any discrimination among married couples.

If the work-oriented criterion is adopted, then it is the discrimination between married couples/co-habitees within each category (either both-working or one-working) which has to be eliminated. This can be done in two distinct ways. Either by re-naming the husband's allowance as the principal breadwinner's allowance and making it available to married couples or co-habitees alike. This raises two problems. First, for this scheme to operate satisfactorily co-habitation will have to be an easily ascertainable category, which at present it is not. Secondly, since this scheme would make none of the married couples worse off and co-habitees better off, it would lead to a shortfall in the total tax revenue. Therefore, for this scheme to be viable it has to be indicated how this shortfall is to be made up. Generally speaking, this scheme ends the discrimination between the married and the co-habitees by treating the latter as the former. The alternative is to do away with the husband's allowance altogether to end the discrimination by treating the married like the co-habitees. This alternative, which is favoured by the Equal Opportunities Commission and other groups, would lead to an increase in tax revenue, and would increase the tax burden for all married couples, except those who have elected for separate taxation. The latter, as we shall point out later, has important implications for the acceptability of reform to the married couples who account for just over half of tax-payers in Britain.

The alternative is the marriage-oriented criterion, according to which it is the discrimination between the different types of married couples which ought to be the target of reforms. Though the criterion

goes against the grain of the reform proposals put forward by groups
like the Equal Opportunities Commission, nonetheless it does underly
some of the objections against the present system of personal taxation.
For instance the 1954 Radcliffe Commission on Taxation, which was firmly
in favour of treating a married couple as a single tax unit, regarded
the allowance to two-earner married couples as excessive. It, therefore, recommended a reduction in the working wife's allowance from a
single allowance to the difference between the husband's allowance and
twice the single allowance: .4 of the single allowance, according to
the present scale of personal allowances. Such a measure, if implemented now, will mean a reduction in the working wife's allowance from
£1,375 p.a. to £605 p.a. That change would, however, further accentu-
ate the discrimination within a two-earner couple - a discrimination
which so many people find objectionable, and to which we now turn.

DISCRIMINATION BETWEEN WORKING WIVES AND THEIR WORKING HUSBANDS

It is this discrimination which has attracted most of the recent criticisms, which straddle the two different aspects of the taxation of the
family: the aggregation of incomes and the allocation of allowances
granted to the family between the working wife and her working husband.
    The aggregation of income is a necessary consequence of taking the
married couple as the single unit of taxation; therefore it cannot be
removed without a radical alteration in the definition of units of
taxation. The principal criticism against aggregation as such, which
should be distinguished from the specific form with the aggregation of
incomes takes under the British tax system, is that it involves a loss
of privacy. This, at present, takes the asymmetric form of a wife
having to reveal her financial affairs to her husband, but not *vice
versa*. However, so long as the family is retained as a unit of taxation
a certain degree of loss of financial privacy is a necessary consequence.
    The peculiarity of the British tax system is that it aggregates the
income of a married couple by treating a wife's income as her husband's.
As if, to paraphrase Blackstone's memorable phrase,[8] in marriage husband
and wife are one tax unit, and that tax unit is the husband. The
aggregation has a number of consequences, some of which are offensive
to working wives. The first of these is that it is the husband who
fills up the tax form for the family, and it is he who is liable for
the payment of taxes. Until recently the working wife was not recognised by the Inland Revenue; the reply to the letters that she wrote to
her tax office was addressed not to her but to her husband. However,
since 1978 the Inland Revenue has started to treat a working wife as a
person worthy of receiving back the excessive amount which may have
been deducted as taxes from her salary, and as a person to be communi-
cated with directly. As for the liability of the husband to pay the
taxes of the family, it is not as onerous as it may sound. For under
the British tax system tax on earned income is by and large collected
at source, and therefore in such cases the liability is purely formal
in the sense that individuals do not have the option of withholding
their taxes. The liability is further diluted by the provision that the
Inland Revenue can collect the tax directly from the wife rather than
from her husband. In all, the important point is that many of the
features of aggregation which are offensive to working wives either

have been removed or can be eliminated by a formal change in the tax system. Formal in the sense that the change would simply involve a change in procedures of tax collection rather than an alteration in tax burdens. The implication then is that what is often singled out as the most offensive feature of the tax system does not furnish the ground for any radical alteration in the system of personal taxation.

Now we turn to the distribution of the tax burden between a working wife and her husband. The basic problem in this connection is that, due to the pattern of allocation of allowances granted to the two-earner family, a working wife often - though not always - pays a higher proportion of her income in taxes than her husband. By way of an example take the case of a two-earner married couple whose joint income does not take them beyond the band of the standard rate (30%), and where both the husband and the wife have the same earned income. In that case the take-home pay of the husband will be higher than his wife's. The reason is that the husband gets the married allowance: £2,145 p.a., to offset against his income, while the wife only gets a single allowance: £1,375 p.a., to offset against her income. This inequitable treatment of working wives and working husbands arises out of the rule that the married allowance is always allocated to the husband, except in the case where he has no income of his own and his wife earns. As pointed out earlier, in this case the working wife counts as both a husband and a working wife, and she as a result gets 2.6 times the single allowance. This inequitable treatment of working wives and their husbands taken in isolation can be solved by dividing the personal allowances granted to a married couple equally between the husband and the wife.

However, this is not the only dimension of discrimination which is relevant. Since in focusing on the distribution of tax burden between working wives and their husbands one is interested in the treatment of individual tax-payers regardless of their marital status, it is relevant to compare the respective tax burdens of their single counterparts. In terms of the allocation of personal allowances a working wife whose husband also works is treated the same as a single working woman. The breadwinner wives are, however, treated much more favourably, because they get 2.6 rather than only one single allowance. In contrast a married man, who has not elected for single taxation, is treated more favourably than a single man. There is a question of equity involved here too: why should a married man receive a higher allowance than a single person when his working wife is in no sense dependent on him? This inequity, one may note, can only be removed by doing away with the married allowance altogether. However, that would also affect the single earner family adversely, but that is best left for discussion later.

The married allowance is not the only cause of the inequitable distribution of tax burdens between working wives and their husbands. It is also affected by the pattern of allocation of other allowances deductions due to the family, of which the tax relief on mortgage interest is the most significant, and the method of collection of taxes levied at rates higher than the standard rate under the PAYE system. The essential feature in this connection is that all allowances and tax relief granted to the family are allocated to the husband. What this means is that, even when the wife pays a part of the family mortgage, the tax relief on her part of the payment does not accrue to her but to

her husband. In other words mortgage payment by a wife implies an increase in the post-tax income of her husband. However, married couples
can opt for what is termed 'separate assessment' under which, for
example, tax relief on mortgage payments is divided in proportion to
the income of husband and wife. Since women on average earn less than
men, such a division would generally imply a smaller share of the allowances and tax reliefs due to the family for a working wife than for her
husband. However, the Green Paper does come down in favour of an equal
split of such allowances and tax reliefs between a working wife and her
husband. Moreover, the problem with the present system of separate
assessment is that it is difficult for a married couple to obtain.

Now as for the payment of tax rates higher than the standard rate,
the problem only concerns a minority of two-earner couples whose joint
income takes them beyond the threshold of the standard rate. This becomes a source of inequitable distribution of tax burdens only because
of the way in which taxes are collected in Britain: the PAYE system.
Since under the PAYE system tax is deducted at source, it has to be
decided which partner of the two-earner couple is liable for higher
than the standard rate on that part of the family's joint income which
is beyond the standard rate threshold. Until 1979 it was the wife
rather than the husband who bore the brunt of rates higher than the
standard rate. This used to lead to what in the context of single
persons would be regarded as a highly inequitable situation where a
working wife who normally would have earned less than her husband was
paying a higher tax at the margin than her husband. The situation, however, has changed since 1979: it is now left to the couple to choose the
partner who would be paying higher than the standard rate.

In all, the discussion of the treatment of working wives and their
working husbands brings into relief a whole series of discriminations,
most of which are tilted against working wives. Moreover, the incidence
of these discriminations is not restricted to well-paid working women,
as is sometimes suggested.[9] It may also be the case that the majority
of two-earner couples do not have any particular objection to the present arrangement, as the Green Paper remarks. However, the problem is
not simply one of the distribution of dissatisfaction with the present
system; rather, one of whether the tax system should rely on discrimination which it itself rules out as unjustifiable and inequitable in the
case of single persons. Nearly all the features of the tax system which
we have pointed to in this section would fall under this category. Some
may argue that if the family is to remain a unit of taxation then discrimination within the family is inevitable, and, therefore, one cannot
object to it if one wishes to retain the family as the unit of taxation.

The choice, however, is not simply between individuals and families.
One may argue for a continued relevance of the family for certain,
though not all, tax purposes; yet one may also without any inconsistency
argue that individuals should not be assumed to be completely identified
with the family of which they are a part. The implication is that the
tax system should pay the question of equitable treatment of husband
and wife exactly the same attention as it does to the question of equity
between individual tax payers. The most straightforward way of ensuring this, which also happens to be easiest from the point of view of
implementation, is to change over to the system of mandatory single
taxation - a system favoured by the Equal Opportunities Commission.
Commendable though this system is, it raises a number of issues which

deserve further discussion. However, before we do that it is as well to consider the problems associated with the taxation of investment income.

TAXATION OF INVESTMENT INCOME

At present the option to married couples to be taxed singly does not extend to investment income, which is always aggregated and treated as husband's income. If the system of taxation of earned income encourages marriage, then the system of taxation of investment income provides an incentive to couples with a large investment income not to get married. The best professional advice to a married couple with a large investment income is that they should divide their income-yielding assets and get divorced forthwith. In general the implication is that the system of taxation of investment income is implicitly biased in favour of co-habiting couples.

But the important question is not one of discrimination between different types of couples, but rather, why should investment income be treated differently from earned income? Broadly speaking the reason does not concern the relative income levels of the recipient of earned and investment income, but the specific property of the sources of investment income. The essential point is that the sources of investment income: cash, shares, financial assets and tangible property, are easily transferable between individuals either through inheritance or through gifts. While the same, generally speaking, is not true for the sources of earned income, which by and large tend to be specific to the individual.

The family is of particular relevance from the point of view of transferability of property because to the extent that the family is a unit of consumption the intra-family transfers of wealth may not entail any sacrifice on the part of the donor. Such transfers between spouses are, for obvious reasons, of special importance from the point of view of the taxation of investment income. Then the basic justification for aggregating investment income is that married couples should not be provided with an opportunity to avoid tax payments by redistributing income-yielding assets between themselves. This justification acquires an additional force since the transfer of property from one spouse to another is not subject to tax; while other forms of inter-personal transfers of property are subject to the Capital Transfer Tax, albeit a rather mild and in some ways an ineffective tax.

It is, however, an open question as to how much inter-spouse transfer of property would indeed take place following an extension of single taxation to investment income. When answering this question one has to take into account the fact that couples may well be interested in minimising their tax liabilities, but married partners do not so easily part with their worldly goods. The latter acquires some force if we take into account the fact that the rate of divorce has almost doubled during the last welve years and the UK has the highest rate of divorce among the European Common Market countries.

The general point, however, is that so long as the family remains exempt from the Capital Transfer Tax, aggregation is a necessity from the point of view of the consistency of the tax system. Now there are very good arguments against a blanket exemption of the married couple

from the Capital Transfer Tax. In fact what is needed is a clear and
comprehensive family property law which lays down the criteria for distinguishing between what is to be regarded as the family property and
what is to be regarded as individual property of members of the family.
Such a law at present does not exist, and it is needed also for the
purposes other than the reform of the taxation of investment income.
For a litigation-free division of property on separation or divorce,
for example.

Investment income raises a number of complex issues because its
recipients form a heterogeneous category. There is a popular miscon-
ception about investment income. To start with it is worth pointing
out that in most cases the recipients of investment income are not the
idle rich living it up on inherited wealth. A rough index of this is
the fact that building society interest constitutes the largest single
source of investment income in Britain, most of which accrues to low
and average income families.[10] The rich armed with the advice of professional tax consultants can do better than putting their wealth into
building societies. Moreover, the distribution of investment income
is, as one would expect, highly biased in favour of the pensioners,
whose average income is lower than the average national income. For
the purposes of this article this is not directly relevant; instead
what is pertinent for the argument here is the ways in which the taxation of investment income discriminates against women.

First, while a married man can offset the married allowance against
his income, a married woman gets no allowance whatsoever to offset
against her income, which counts as not her income but as her husband's.
This means two things, both of which are highly objectionable to a large
number of women. First of all it requires a married woman to disclose
all her savings to her husband, including those from her earned income.
Secondly, a married woman's investment income, no matter how paltry
that may be, is taxed at the same rate which her husband pays on the
last pound of his income (ranging from 3o% to 60%). It is also
instructive to look at the tax which the married woman in receipt of
investment income would have paid had she been single. In that case
she should have been able to offset a single allowance against her investment income, which, unless she is fairly rich, would have implied
no tax on this income.

The pattern of their paid employment gives a special significance
to investment income among women. As the Green Paper in one of its
statistical appendices points out,[11] the majority of women in the age
group 16-24 go out to work, while the reverse is true for women aged
25-34. Thereafter, the pattern changes once again, a large majority
of women aged 35-60 going out to work. Therefore, what this points to
is the following typical pattern of work among women. They go out to
work till they have children, and then they stay at home or take up a
part-time employment in order to look after their children. Once
their children have grown up they go out to work full-time again. To
the extent that working women, like their male counterparts, save a
part of their income from employment, income from their accumulated
saving is their only source of independent income when they are out of
the labour market bringing up children. It is precisely during this
period that the aggregation of investment income comes to bear heavily
on them; for it is then that they end up paying a higher proportion of
their income in taxes than they did when they were working. Since, as

we have emphasised here, the recipients of investment income form a heterogeneous category, the specific place assigned to investment income here and the way in which the aggregation of investment income comes to bear on it may well be valid for a proportion of married women only. This, however, does not detract from the point of the argument: once one takes into account the life time pattern of working among women, the aggregation of investment income and the higher rate of tax implicit in it leads to a highly inequitable result.

The argument in favour of granting a single allowance to married women to offset against their investment income is a strong one. According to the Green Paper such a measure would cost £300 million[12] p.a. in lost revenue - a shortfall which can be easily made up if the married allowance in the present form is abolished. Further, though the Green Paper discusses them as if they are inseparable, the grant of a single allowance to be offset against investment income to married women does not rule out the aggregation of investment income over and above that allowance. It is true that such a grant would furnish couples in receipt of a large investment income with a perfectly legal possibility of reducing their tax liability by a cosmetic redistribution of property between them. However, the extent to which this can be done is limited by aggregating the investment income over and above the single allowance, and attributing that income to the better-off partner. This is already done in Sweden.

MANDATORY SINGLE TAXATION

This system, which is favoured by the Equal Opportunities Commission and a large number of other groups and individuals, is the only one which would with one stroke remove all the unjustifiable discriminations between different types of couples, and between married women and their husbands. Mandatory single taxation would mean a radical transformation in the system of personal taxation, though the Green Paper seems to be disparaging about this particular direction of reform. The essential feature of mandatory single taxation is that the family, as a tax unit, at least in its present form, would disappear, leaving only the individuals as tax units.

The changeover to this system of taxation raises a number of distinct issues, each of which deserves a separate consideration. These issues are as follows:
(1) the effect of the change on the tax burden on families
(2) the alternative methods of provision for housewives and other financially dependent adults
(3) the problem of investment income
(4) the arguments in favour of mandatory single taxation.
In its starkest form mandatory single taxation would consist of the following:
(1) the abolition of the married allowance altogether - a measure which according to the Equal Opportunities Commission is favoured by a large number of diverse groups;
(2) the replacement of the wife's earned income allowance by the single allowance available for offset against both income from employment and investment income.

The abolition of the married allowance will mean an increase in tax
burden for all married couples, except those who have chosen to be taxed
singly. The second measure would benefit married couples with an investment income. Overall, the two changes together would increase tax burden for most married couples. To analyse this change we first take the
implication of mandatory single taxation for allowances received by
different types of couples to offset against their earned income. This
is best done by adding another column to Table 2 showing the situation
after the changeover. One can then go on to analyse the effect of the
change on the tax paid by married working women and their husbands
separately, and the effect of the grant of a single allowance to a
married women to offset against her investment income.

Table 3

Types of couples	*Total personal allowances (in single allowances)*		
	at present	after the change	net effect
BOTH WORKING			
(1) Co-habitees	2	2	0
(2) Married couple, who are taxed singly	2	2	0
(3) Married couple	2.6	2	0.6
ONE WORKING			
(4) Co-habitees	1	1	0
(5) Husband working	1.6	1	0.6
(6) Wife working	2.6	1	1.6

What the table makes clear is that the change, which will lead to
the treatment of married couples as co-habitees, will increase the tax
burden for three out of the four types of married couples distinguished
under the present tax system. Since the change does not make any type
of couple better off, it will raise the total tax revenue, estimated to
be £2,600 million p.a. This estimate would be reduced by £300 million[13]
p.a., if one takes into account the revenue lost by allowing wives to
offset a single allowance against their investment income. The remaining sum - £2,300 million p.a. - is still a sizeable sum which can be
used to compensate the families adversely affected by the change. Whatever may be the merits of mandatory single taxation, the extent of
departure from the present system which it entails also makes it clear
that the married allowance cannot be abolished at one stroke. The
Green Paper and various groups have suggested a gradual reduction in
the gap between the married and the single allowance.[14] This can be
done very easily under the present system, under which all personal
allowances are meant to follow the retail price index, unless the
Chancellor decides to the contrary. All that needs to be done then is
not to raise the married allowance by the same amount as the single
allowance. However, the phasing out of the married allowance raises
two problems.

The first of these is that the allowance given to the single parent
families and to the recently widowed women are equal to the difference
between the married and the single allowance. These allowances will

have to be fixed independently, following the introduction of the mandatory single taxation, which does not pose any special problems.

Then there is the problem of the married allowance for pensioners,
which is higher than the married allowances for non-pensioners. At
present a married couple gets a pensioners' married allowance when at
least one of the partners is over the retirement age. Here the basic
problem is that the extension of mandatory single taxation of pensioners
is closely bound up with the scale of pensions. At present the pension
to married couples is less than twice the pension to single persons.
So long as that remains the case the married allowance to pensioners,
which is tied to the pension for married couples, cannot be eliminated.
Though the taxation of pensioners raises separate issues, the extension
of mandatory single taxation of investment income would necessitate
some adjustment in the scale of allowances for pensioners.

As for the consequences of mandatory single taxation for tax burden
on married women and their husbands as individual tax payers, the tax
position of married working women, with the exception of breadwinner
wives, would remain unaltered. But married women in receipt of investment income would, for the reasons stated earlier, gain. Nearly all
married men and breadwinner wives - who are also treated as working
husbands - would lose from the change. In all, the change would put an
end to the unequal treatment of married men and women as individual tax
payers. However, a completely symmetric treatment of working women and
their husbands would also necessitate an equal split of allowances due
to the family: tax relief on mortgage repayments.

The elimination of the married allowance does raise the problem of
financial provision for housewives, who furnish the justification for
the present married allowance. It is as well to start by considering
why the tax system or alternatively the social security system should
provide financial support to wives either in the form of an allowance
or cash benefit. The point which needs most emphasis is that housewives form a large and a heterogeneous category; they differ in terms
of the financial position and composition of their families. As a result any case for financial provision for housewives is likely to be
valid for only a section of housewives. The grounds for a financial
provision for all housewives regardless of their specific situation are
indeed very weak. In contrast, there are very strong arguments in favour
of financial provision for mothers with young children. Given the paucity of adequate creche and nursery facilities they are constrained to
accept only a few types of jobs. If this is accepted, then what is
required is neither an allowance nor a cash benefit to all housewives,
but instead a cash benefit paid to mothers with young children. There
are strong arguments for paying such a cash benefit to all mothers with
young children, whether or not they work. For if housewives with young
children incur the cost of bringing up children by foregoing income,
then working women with young children bear the cost in the form of payment to baby minders and creches and nurseries. Since such a cash
benefit could be paid with the present child benefit, it would amount
to child benefit on a sliding scale, higher for younger than for older
children.

In general there are very good arguments for using the extra revenue
raised by phasing out the married allowance to increase child benefits,
for younger as well as older children. For child benefits at present
are paltry, they are nowhere near the cost incurred in bringing up

children. To give an idea of the difference which this extra revenue
could make to child benefit, it is estimated that it would be sufficient
to increase child benefit from £4.75 per week to £9.25 per week.

As for the extension of mandatory single taxation to investment income, its scope will have to be limited for the reasons stated earlier.
A partial single taxation of investment income would take the form of
the grant of a single allowance to married women which they can use to
offset against either their employment or investment income. In addition, it would also entail the aggregation of the part of investment
income not covered by the allowance.

Obviously mandatory single taxation is just one of a large number of
schemes; moreover, it can take a variety of forms. But rather than
listing the other possible schemes it is best to end with a brief
review of the general issues.

GENERAL ISSUES

Broadly speaking the discussion in this article has been centred around
two issues. The first concerns the rights and the treatment of married
men and women as individual tax payers. And the second concerns the
propriety of maintaining the family as a unit of taxation in the present form.

One way of approaching what is wrong with the present system of
personal taxation is to start by taking into account the rights of
individual citizens, and the considerations of equity which supposedly
underly the tax system. Until recently the system of personal taxation
in its operation, by not acknowledging their existence, violated the
elementary rights which married women have or should have as citizens.
The tax system thus far has proceeded on the assumption that women by
entering wedlock partially forfeit their rights as individual tax
payers. In addition to that, in the case of married women the system
of personal taxation violates the very maxim which it upholds in the
case of individual tax payers: deductions and special allowances apart,
individuals with the same income should be entitled to the same allowances and the same rates of tax. However, the discrimination against
married women as individual tax payers is not a necessary corollary of
taking the family as the unit of taxation. It is perfectly possible to
design a system of personal taxation within the parameters of existing
personal allowances which treats married men and women symmetrically as
tax payers. Nonetheless, it must be pointed out that so long as the
family remains the unit of taxation - and there are very good reasons
for it to remain so in the case of investment income - married men and
women cannot have the same right of financial privacy as single tax
payers. It must, however, be said that most of the crass and unnecessary discriminations against married women have been removed in recent
years.

The second issue concerns the question of the propriety of maintaining the family as the unit of taxation for income. The married allowance is the foundation of the treatment of the family as the unit of
taxation. The increase in the participation of married women in the
labour market has cut the ground from underneath the traditional justification for the married allowance. In particular it is difficult to
find any convincing justification for granting a married allowance to

the husband whose wife goes out to work. *Mutatis mutandis*, the same is true for not granting a single allowance to married women to offset against their investment income. There are indeed good grounds for providing financial support to mothers with young children. But, as explained earlier, that does not constitute an argument for an allowance to the husbands of all housewives. From the point of view of welfare it would be preferable to give a cash benefit to all mothers of young children. There is yet another reason for doing away with the family as the unit of taxation of income. The rate of divorce and rate of second marriages has increased very rapidly during the last decade; something like a third of marriages end in divorce.[16] What this means is that, though most men and women marry, for a large number of them marriage is a transitory state. This alone is a powerful argument for not tethering the taxation of income to a state which is neither permanent nor stable.

Yet this is not an argument for rendering the family completely irrelevant for the purposes of taxation. It is important to avoid posing the problem in terms of the simple binary choice between the individual and the family. For certain purposes (the taxation of investment income and the transfer of wealth, and social security benefit) the family is and ought to remain pertinent. What is, therefore, needed is a varied approach. In each case one has to examine the merits and demerits of keeping the family - which need not be built around marriage - as the appropriate unit.

NOTES

1 *The Taxation of Husband and Wife*, HMSO, Cmnd 8093, December 1980.
2 Equal Opportunities Commission (EOC), 1977, *Income Tax and Sex Discrimination*. See also the response of the commission to the Green Paper. EOC, 1979: *With All My Worldly Goods I Thee Endow ... Except My Tax Allowances*.
   Fran Bennet, Rosa Heys and Rosalind Coward, 'The Limits to "Financial and Legal Independence": A Socialist Feminist Perspective on Taxation and Social Security', *Politics & Power* 1, 1980.
   Ruth Lister, 'Taxation, Women and the Family', in *Taxation and Social Policy*, ed. Sandford, Pond and Walker, Heinemann, 1980.
3 See EOC 1979.
4 David Piachaud, 'Taxation and Social Security', in *Taxation and Social Policy*, *op.cit.*, 1980.
5 R.M. Titmuss, 'The Social Division of Welfare', in *Essays on 'the Welfare State'*, Allen and Unwin, 1976.
   Chris Pond, 'Tax Expenditure and Fiscal Welfare', in *Taxation and Social Policy*, *op.cit.*, 1980.
6 Inland Revenue Statistics, 1980, Table 1.7, p.12, HMSO.
7 The Green Paper, Appendix 5, pp.65-66.
8 EOC 1979, p.29.
9 See for instance C. Morris and N. Warren, 'Taxation of the Family', *Fiscal Studies*, Vol.2, No.1, March 1981, pp.25-46.
10 Inland Revenue Statistics, 1980, Table 2.11, p.46.
11 The Green Paper, Appendix 5.
12 The estimates vary; Morris and Warren (1981) put the estimate at £500 million p.a.

13   See footnote 12.

Diana Adlam and Nikolas Rose
The Politics of Psychiatry*

It has been estimated that one woman in six and one man in nine will spend some time as an in-patient in a mental hospital during their life-time. In 1976, despite dramatic reductions in lengths of stay in mental hospitals, and in the number of resident patients at any one time, there were an average 105,000 residents in such hospitals on any one day in Britain. A further 58,000 people on average were resident in hospitals for the mentally handicapped. That is to say, over 40% of patients in NHS hospitals are there for psychiatric reasons. The number of in-patients has been contracting and continues to do so; this contraction has been about 20% in the period 1970-76. But it has been coupled with a rapid expansion of the availability and use of psychiatric outpatient and day patient centres - by almost 100% over the same period. Some 240,000 *new* outpatients used these services in 1976 and 44,000 *new* day patients - over one and a quarter million people receiving treatment in all.[1]

The extent of medical contact with problems diagnosed as psychiatric far outruns these specialised services. On average a general practi-tioner in the NHS will see 70% of the women and 62% of the men on their list in any one year. Although patients often complain of somatic symp-toms alone, or of a combination of somatic and psychological symptoms, almost a quarter will be considered by their doctors to by psychiatric-ally ill. Surveys suggest the prevalence of psychiatric disorders in the population is about 2%, and that most patients diagnosed as having marked psychiatric disorders and the majority of those with mild dis-orders, consult their doctors for assistance.[2]

Let us not prolong the statistics unnecessarily - three points will surely be conceded. Firstly, in our society many people suffer distress which they and/or others designate as psychiatric. Secondly, a vast amount of the time, work and resources of the NHS concerns cases which are considered to be psychiatric in nature. And thirdly, that the field of mental distress in Britain today is pre-eminently that of medicine. It is largely in medical terms that individuals conceive of and relate to their own psychical distress. It is medical agents, trained and qual-ified through medical channels, who are deemed competent to pronounce judgment on these questions. And the social practices and resources

organised around these problems are those of medicine - the clinic and
the hospital. Around these medical services swarm a variety of petty-
doctors of the psyche - psychologists, psychotherapists, educational
welfare officers, lawyers and pundits on child rearing depend for their
relationship with mental distress upon the psychiatric institutions and
practices of medicine. And psychiatric modes of thought, the medicalisation of mental distress, are widely diffused in our culture, beyond
specialist institutions into the schools, the courts, the mass media,
and individual and familial beliefs and practices.
    But if psychiatry is clearly a 'social' question, is it a 'political'
question; is there a distinctively feminist, socialist, progressive politics in the field of psychiatry? Are there distinctive explanations
and criticisms of the growth, nature and social consequences of psychiatry? And do feminists and socialists have any alternative principles
and objectives for the social treatment of mental distress? A number
of recent texts answer these questions in the affirmative.[3] They organise their criticisms and alternatives around a common theme - the inappropriateness of the medical conceptions, practices and treatments
now hegemonising the field of mental distress and the centrality for
socialist and feminist political strategies of contesting and displacing
this monopolisation of madness by medicine. In this article we examine
and contest the terms in which this critique is conducted, and argue
that it misunderstands in important ways the conditions, nature and consequences of the relations between medicine and madness. In doing so it
places severe obstacles in the path of constructing progressive political
strategies in relation to psychiatry, and inhibits the development of
alternative principles and objectives. Having thus cleared some ground,
in a further article to be published in a future issue of *Politics &
Power* we consider alternative policies, objectives, organisation and
administration with regard to mental distress. We shall however touch
upon questions of alternative therapies, particularly feminist therapy,
in the last part of this article.

THE CATEGORY OF 'MENTAL ILLNESS'

Before proceeding to the main arguments, it is necessary to make one
point clearly. Today a range of behaviours and forms of conduct, thought
and speech are unified in the category 'mental illness'. These include
behaviour disorders in children, a variety of forms of conduct designated
'neurotic', pathologies in the elderly, together with the behaviours
classified in the major classes of psychotic disorder - the schizophrenias and the affective psychoses. But this does not imply that
there is anything essentially the same about the form and causes of
the different constituents of 'mental illness'. Anxiety neuroses,
phobias, hyperactivity, degeneration of faculties concomitant upon
aging, depression, delusions, disorders of thought and speech are all
considered part of the field of mental illness and this sometimes leads
writers to regard them as unified at the level of their causation - in
malfunctioning biochemical systems in the brain, in familial pathology,
in social oppression. There are no good reasons to suppose that any
such unification amongst the various conditions designated as 'forms'
of mental illness exists at all - they concern radically different forms
of disturbance of emotional states, behaviour, speech and thought and

there is no reason to assume that the mechanisms which produce them have
any basic similarities. It should also be pointed out that
disturbances of thought, speech, behaviour and affect may be produced
as a consequence of very different processes - a similarity of outcome
does not mean a uniformity of mechanism.

This does not imply that the unity of mental illness is a myth, but
it is important to be clear about what sort of reality it is. Its unity
and reality must be ascribed not to any ontological identity between the
different elements that make it up, but rather to the modes of social
functioning of the complex of theories, practices and procedures of
psychiatry. The unification conferred upon the behaviours and beliefs
in question is thus a social and historical, rather than a biological
or psychical fact. This is not recognised by many commentators on
psychiatry, including those of radical persuasion and many psychiatrists
themselves, who treat the category of mental illness as if it were
essentially uniform. To complicate matters, different commentators
privilege particular conditions as exemplifications of the nature of
mental illness (for 'anti-psychiatry', for instance, mental illness means
almost exclusively schizophrenia). We shall take these problems into
account in our discussions, but to some extent we are forced to conform
terminologically with the way in which the arguments we are about to
consider utilise the general category 'mental illness' or one of its
substitutes. We take up the implications of these problems later in
the article.

THE POLITICISATION OF PSYCHIATRY

What are the forms of left politics in relation to psychiatry, mental
illness and mental health? The traditional left has given these questions low priority, and has approached them, if at all, within the terms
of social welfare - those of resources, rights and conditions. That is
to say, the problem has been concevied as one of inadequate funding of
a particular area of the health service giving rise to inadequacies and
inequalities of treatment which underprivilege the working class and
public sector and provide lucrative pickings and privileged treatment
in the private sector for those with money to pay. Inadequate resources
plus poor organisation and regulation, low status and poor training of
staff produce conditions in mental hospitals such that those designated
mentally ill are treated in inhumane and degrading ways. The periodic
scandals of the hospitals are witness to this. This denial of access
to adequate treatment and human rights forms the elements of one strand
of left politics of mental health - increase funding, provision, training
and status and safeguard patients' rights.[4]

A second strand, closely related to the first, is a utilisation in
the field of mental illness of a predominant left critique of medicine
in general - its concentration on acute, curative medicine rather than
preventative medicine which takes as its field of operation not simply
the sick body but the environment which produces illness. This is often
coupled with a critique of the institution of the mental hospital - that
the institutionalisation and segregation of the mad is a hangover from
olden times when the mad were seen as less than human, to be shut away
beyond the view of society at large - out of sight, out of mind. The
proper and human place for the treatment of the mentally ill in such a

view is, as far as possible, their families and their communities, who must learn the tolerance and skill necessary to cope with the mentally disturbed. This view is often supported by three other arguments. First, that psychoactive drugs provide the conditions under which such 'decarceration' is possible, through the extent to which they can control the more florid symptoms of mental illness. Secondly, the belief that, far from controlling and reducing pathology, institutions amplify it through crowding the insane together and through the deleterious effects of the hospital itself ('institutionalisation'). Finally, the view that the proper place for the treatment, usually short-term, of those for whom hospitalisation is unavoidable, is within the general hospital itself - a reabsorption of mental illness into the general domain of clinical medicine.[5]

However, such a strategy can be advocated as much by those of the right as by the left, it underpinned the policies of the National Health Service set in motion by Enoch Powell as Minister of Health in the early 1960s, and continued by Keith Joseph in the early 1970s.[6] Left critics who nonetheless support the strategy argue that such a decarceration was merely a response to a fiscal crisis and an attempt at financial economy, that the community mental health policy which was to replace the institution existed in name and as gesture only and was never adequately funded. This meant that the closure of the institutions (which did not proceed as rapidly in the UK as in the USA) merely devolved the burden of coping with the mentally distressed back onto the family, especially onto women, and that this further discriminated against the poor and working class.[7]

A left variant of the de-institutionalisation strategy, and one which features as both example and critique in recent writings, is the reorganisation of the mental health services in Trieste under the auspices of Franco Basaglia.[8] In British discussions, such a left strategy of de-institutionalisation is often linked to a critique which traces many of the problems of contemporary general medicine and psychiatry to the domination of all centres of decision making within the field of health and illness by a medical profession which seeks not so much to eliminate illness as to define and manage it to its own professional and financial advantage. The strategy advocated here is one of democratisation, of devolving power and decision-making back onto the community 'where it belongs', of displacing the domination of the doctors and bureaucrats in decision-making bodies and so on. This position is clear in much feminist writing on medicine, and feminists often develop the argument in their advocation of 'self-help' groups in both general and psychiatric medicine.[9]

Over the past few years such a strategy, perhaps because of its apparent radicalism, has tended to be accepted virtually without qualification as defining the space within which any progressive politics of psychiatry can be thought. Its power of conviction has been increased through the development of a conceptual rationale which integrates and extends that most potent and publicised critique of psychiatry, so fashionable in the wake of the events of 1968 - 'anti-psychiatry'. Anti-psychiatry was a diverse but relatively coherent amalgam underpinned by the work of three authors - Ronald Laing, Thomas Szasz and Erving Goffman. Let us briefly and crudely summarise what in their views is pertinent for the present debate.

For Laing, psychiatry makes a fundamental mistake in conceptualising and treating mental illness as analogous with physical illness. Its error is demonstrated in the way it treats the behaviour and speech of the patient as merely indications of an underlying organic malfunction. What for traditional psychiatry are simply symptoms, devoid of any intrinsic significance, merely indicators of the presence of a condition of illness (analogous to a high temperature or a sore throat) are, for Laing, *meaningful*. What we call mental illness (Laing is particularly concerned with schizophrenia) is a meaningful and intelligible response to particular social and familial situations. Those who become ill are alienated, their experience constantly invalidated by those around them, authentic responses made impossible through the presence of contradictory demands and expectations. Hence they withdraw and construct a set of defensive tactics in the form of apparently bizarre speech and actions. These can be understood by therapists if they are relocated beyond the individual, in the context of a pathological family relationship. Whilst Laing asserts that familial pathology is related, in some sense, to general social pathology (a sick and insane society) the precise form and nature of this connection and its mechanisms are never specified. It is within the family and in particular within the systems of communication of the family, that the attributes and behaviours of the mentally ill are constructed. Whilst individuals may manifest pathology, it is the family itself that is sick. Indeed, since Laing is unable to find any way of differentiating forms of communication in families which contain mentally ill individuals from those that do not, this account of the familial genesis of mental illness can, and easily does, generalise into a critique of the family as an institution which is always potentially pathogenic. It is not madness which should be our concern so much as that which passes, in our society, for normality. The 'mad' become those who see this charade for what it is, and mental illness can be a pathway to the discovery of the truth of oneself, if guided and learned from, rather than invalidated and reduced to mere pathology to be treated with drugs or electro-convulsive therapy.[10]

Laing produces a critique of psychiatry not by denying the existence of mental distress, its disabling consequences or the need for therapeutic intervention, but by denying its congruence with physical illness, asserting its social genesis and its intelligibility. For Szasz, the form of the critique is different. Szasz also argues that any notion of mental *illness*, analogous with physical illness, is nonsensical. But he denounces the pseudo-scientificity of psychiatric theory and practice by counterposing a notion of 'mental illness' to his notion of 'physical illness'. Physical medicine, apparently, deals with real entities like physiological disorders and organic mal-functionings, and is thus totally scientific, value-neutral, above society. Psychiatry deals with signs, meanings, communications from which it makes invalid inferences of organic roots. Mental illness is a metaphor parading as reality, psychiatry deals with objects that are purely imaginary, which it has placed on a par with those of physical medicine in order to capture some of the professional status, power and prestige attributed to doctors. And this illusion has a social funcion; it firstly gains power, prestige and handsome remuneration for psychiatrists, but, more important, psychiatry itself is a social product, a means of legitimating the scapegoating and oppression by 'the State' of deviant minorities, a way of confirming the values of normality, the contemporary equivalent of the witch hunts of the middle ages. Thus for Szasz it is not so much that 'mental illness' should be made intelligible, but that it is a myth, a social invention serving social ends.

Szasz does not deny that people currently termed mentally ill have problems; he denies that the problems are illnesses. To call them such is not only to perpetuate a myth, not only to support a form of social control, but also to avoid those individuals taking onto themselves the responsibility for their difficulties and their solution. For Szasz's critique, in the alternatives it proposes, is one from the radical right rather than the radical left - psychiatry is a 'disabling profession', the frontiers of the state must be rolled back, people will then take responsibility for their own 'problems of living' through the private contact which they enter with their therapist. Good is on the side of individual freedom, personal choice, private practice; evil on the side of state funding, regulation, organisation. Confusions, delusions, obsessions and hallucinations notwithstanding, in the absence of Institutional Psychiatry, rational actors in a free market will seek and find voluntarily the assistance they require. If they do not, and their actions harm others or infringe their rights, they should be dealt with by the sanctions of the criminal law.[11]

Whilst Szasz might appear a peculiar ally for socialists and progressives, his work was crucial in the anti-psychiatric amalgam which formed in the 1970s. Mental illness was a myth, psychiatry a means of social control, psychiatrists the contemporary equivalent of the inquisition. Society itself was sick and the mad were at one and the same time the victims of this sickness and the most authentic in their expression of it in explicit form. To this was added a third element, the argument of 'labelling theory' associated in particular, in the field of mental illness, with the writings of Erving Goffman and Thomas Scheff. Whilst both Laing and Szasz recognise the existence of mental distress, for labelling theory its initial elements are little more than non-conforming behaviour, itself neutral. It is social expectations and beliefs which force and constraint the deviant individual into adopting the role of the mental patient. By putting individuals through the degrading ritual of a psychiatric interview, by *labelling* them as 'sick' and treating them with drugs in psychiatric hospitals, psychiatrists engage in a process of 'deviance amplification' and thus actively *produce* what we designate full-fledged mental illness. Being mentally ill is not a product of biological, psychical or environmental causes, but the outcome of a moral career, which constructs and constrains the role of the mental patient.[12]

The contemporary successors to this heritage seek a 'critical psychiatry', they call for psychiatry to critically examine itself and its social role and functioning, and in doing so to become critical not just of psychiatry, but of society itself.[13] In these writings can be found echoes of anti-psychiatry but there have been changes of emphasis, the shading out of some ideas, the stressing of others and the introduction of some new themes. Critical psychiatry is less willing to privilege the authenticity of madness as a code of experience and to regard madness as a form of social protest or the made as a proto-revolutionary force. Thus David Ingleby writes: 'the real point, surely, is not that psychiatric symptoms lack political significance, but that they are not *effective* forms of social action'.[14] Madness is now seen, in the misery it leads to, the impotence it induces, as a criticism of, and endemic to, a contradictory and oppressive capitalist society. Not to recognise this is an index of political failure. Thus Treacher and Baruch, in the course of a virulent attack on the Labour Party's mental health policy earlier this century, write 'mental illness became merely a "social problem" which could be ameliorated; no longer was it construed as an endemic feature of a class society, which only a socialist reconstruction of society could attempt to eradicate in any fundamental way.'[15] But its account of the relation between madness and mode of production is no less gestural than that of anti-psychiatry - the force of its criticism is directed not so much at capitalism as at medicine. Where anti-psychiatry selected the family as the site of production of madness and the mother as the principle agent, critical psychiatry focuses upon the clinic and the doctor. Perhaps this has something to do with the general acceptance, by many who are critical of orthodox psychiatry and by much psychiatry itself, of some elements of familial and experiential explanation of mental distress. Indeed critical psychiatry's call for the recognition of the role of non-familial social factors fails to recognise the extent to which such factors are already stressed by some psychiatrists and many in social welfare. But perhaps more important in the demise of the family as the supposed source of mental disturbance is the response of feminism to the idea of a 'schizophrenogenic' mother. Mothers, it is said, are blamed for everything and now they are being blamed for driving their children crazy. The schizoprehnogenic mother is merely the medieval witch in modern dress - both are male fantasies. The general sexist bias in psychiatry - in respect of mothers as causes and women as patients - has been well-documented, though the explanations of this phenomenon are less satisfactory.[16] Feminism has its own ideas about the aetiology of mental suffering and has also been in the forefront of the development of alternative forms of therapy. To these we shall return.

What, then, does the argument of contemporary critical psychiatry consist in? We can isolate five components. First, it develops a critique of the 'medical model' of mental illness which argues that medical theories and concepts are not utilisable in the understanding of madness. Second, it provides an analysis which purports to demonstrate the deleterious consequences of this medicalisation of madness, objectifying, dehumanising, incarcerating or chemically subjugating the mad, rendering them passive and dependent upon medical 'experts'. Third, it constructs an account of how, given this inappropriateness of medicine to madness, it has come about historically that medicine does exercise its jurisdiction over madness to the virtual exclusion of other concepts and theories. Fourth, it deploys an argument as to the social functions of this hegemonisation both in terms of its specific benefits to 'medical men' and its general social function of control of deviant minorities and reinforcement of oppressive norms of behaviour. Fifth, it makes a suggestion, often inexplicit and scarcely ever articulated, that under socialism things would be very different, not simply with respect to the elimination of those social conditions which produce madness, but also in the forms of social organisation of practices and the accepted and utilised theories of mental distress. Let us turn to examine these contentions.

THE 'MEDICAL MODEL'

The characterisation by critical psychiatry of the rationale of modern clinical medicine is inadequate and the attack which it mounts upon the 'medical model' which is supposed to characterise psychiatric theory and practice is misleading. Numerous conceptions of the nature, role and significance of aetiology, diagnosis and treatment exist in psychiatric as in general medicine, and in the relations between such conceptions and psychiatric practice are complex and variable. To simplify our discussion here, we will consider the views of psychiatry's critics in relation to two of the most accessible recent discussions of psychiatric theory and practice by psychiatrists. Both John Wing, in *Reasoning About Madness*, and Anthony Clare, in *Psychiatry in Dissent*, defend the appropriateness of medical approaches to madness, but they do so in different terms and with different implications.[17]

Wing argues for the application of what we term a 'disease model' to mental disorders. This model consists of two elements - a particular way of characterising what is specific about modern medical thought, and an argument that this mode of conceptualisation is appropriate to some or all of the forms of behaviour which make up madness.

Thus Wing puts down the progress of medicine to 'the recognition of disease syndromes of increasing specificity: beginning with general concepts such as pallor or fever and progressing, *by means of a growing understanding of the underlying biological mechanisms*, to precisely delineated clusters of symptoms which allow the specific diagnosis such as iron-deficiency anaemia or meninginococcal meningitis'.[18] Typical of a disease theory is that it is specific and delimited to the symptoms to which it is appropriate, and that it links these symptoms, through a recognition of the biological mechanisms which cause them, to organic dysfunction in some form. Diseases, then, are abnormalities of the body with a proximate physical source. They manifest themselves in signs (high temperature, spots, swellings etc.) and in symptoms (stiffness, pain). The underlying and causative malfunction can be (in principle, although not yet for all diseases due to the imperfect state of our knowledge) precisely identified by medical technology, as enshrined in the pathology laboratory or the radiology department of the modern general hospital. The manifest syndrome allows the doctor to make an informed guess as to the underlying pathology - that is, a diagnosis - and this, when confirmed or rectified by the objective results provided by medical technology, dictates the appropriate treatment.

Having characterised the form of rationality which has underpinned the progress and the discoveries of modern medicine, Wing goes on to argue for an approach to madness which adopts, in principle, the same strategy. These theories must distance themselves from unscientific and commonsense notions about their object ('mad', 'crazy' etc.) and develop restricted theories based on the identification of specific syndromes linked together through hypotheses as to the particular organic mechanisms which produce them, hypotheses which can be subjected to rigorous evaluation. Where such disease theories can be formulated for forms of mental distress, then medical treatment, itself to be subject to testing and evaluation, is appropriate. If psychiatry proceeds thus, argues Wing, it can place itself on the same basis as physical medicine and expect the same progress and results.[19]

When critical psychiatry attacks the 'medical model', it is such a disease theory of mental distress to which it objects. It does not question or deal in detail with the first element of such a model - the characterisation of physical medicine - but denies the second - that such a model is appropriate to mental disturbances. What, it asks, are the signs and symptoms of mental disturbances, the psychological equivalent of swellings, palpitations, fever or pain? These are beliefs, habits, behaviours and speech, but the mental doctor, unlike his physical equivalent, is exercising a subjective judgment when he treats these, not as intelligible and valid forms of behaviour by an equal human subject, but as instances of 'delusion', 'thought insertion', 'anxiety states' or 'depression'. This denies the uniqueness and validity of each individual's experience, falsely generalising and seeing only an instance of the occurrence of a psychiatric syndrome. No such identifiable syndromes exist in mental disturbances, and the application of a diagnostic label, such as 'schizophrenia' or 'endogenous depression' is thus not the equivalent of a diagnosis in physical disturbances, where a clear and objective norm of bodily functioning is determinable. On the contrary, the diagnosis in cases of mental disturbance is principally a legitimation of the control exercised over madness and the mad by doctors, and the application of a label is the start of a profoundly damaging career for the subject concerned. The search for organic causes is futile and illusory, hence its lack of success. The pathology laboratory *can* have no equivalent in the mental hospital because mental distress occupies an entirely different sphere of reality to physical distress and calls for an entirely different set of explanatory principles and forms of intervention.

Let us investigate this critique, obviously dependent on anti-psychiatry, in a little more detail, using David Ingleby's 'Understanding "mental illness"' as our example.[20] First, he argues that, unlike conceptualisations of the physical world, descriptions of human activities and states of mind are always 'subjective interpretations', dependent upon social and cultural criteria. Thus psychiatric diagnoses can never aspire to objectivity in the natural-scientific sense, and to claim that they can is merely to conceal the tacit rules, conventions and biases which necessarily govern their application.[21] Further, Ingleby argues, there is no reliable evidence that supports the 'organic view' that mental illnesses have a direct physical cause.[22] The studies which are used as evidence for genetic transmission of mental illness suffer from methodological weaknesses so great that their conclusions can only be regarded as demonstrated through an act of faith not scientific judgment. The demonstrations of physical correlates of mental states are themselves unreliable and do not demonstrate that any correlates found are causes rather than effects of the mental disturbance or of a common third factor. And evidence on the supposed efficacy of physical treatments (drugs, ECT, psychosurgery) cannot be relied upon either. Firstly, they depend upon subjective judgments as to what is effective. And secondly, since a phenomenon can arise in many different ways, even if the treatment did have real and positive effects, it only demonstrates that the problem *could* have had a physical cause; not that it did.

For Ingleby there is a further and more fundamental reason why arguments as to organic causation of mental distress must fail. It is not simply because of the familiar statistical problem of the distinction between correlations and causes, but rather becuase, for Ingleby, the

very notion of 'cause' is inappropriate here. This argument is made on
philosophical and epistemological grounds - the use of the disease model
of mental disturbance is a specific case of the application of 'positivist' philosophical principles. Positivism maintains that the natural
and the human worlds may be investigated and explained in exactly the
same way, using similar principles and techniques. Positivism thus, for
Ingleby, is guilty of 'reification', of 'treating people like things'.
This, he asserts, is a philosophical mistake - it is not just that
different laws govern the functioning of the natural and human worlds,
but crucially that the human world cannot be explained in terms of laws
and causes at all. Rather, in that it involves actions and intentions,
it is to be 'understood' as the product of the definitions and meanings
of the subjects who make it up. Physical disease belongs in the natural
world; mental disturbance in the human world. Hence psychiatry is
guilty of a 'category mistake', a fundamental philosophical error with
deleterious social and political consequences.

Thus we can see that the *political* dispute between psychiatry and
these critics takes place, at least partially, on *epistemological* and
philosophical grounds. For Wing, positivist Popperian that he indeed
is, any doubts about existing hypotheses concerning organic mechanisms
in mental illness will be resolved given the development of research and
the testing of hypotheses through the collection of findings. Existing
hypotheses might well be found wanting and rejected, but the rationality
of the mode of explanation in which they partake is the condition for
advance. For Ingleby (neo-ethnomethodologist that he is), however many
findings are accumulated, however strong the correlations turn out to
be, *nothing* significant would be demonstrated. Thus he can argue 'one
cherised illusion which must be lost before we can hope to understand
"mental illness" is the myth that helps to keep orthodox psychiatry on
the move: the belief that what we need is simply more "findings"'.[23]
Whilst he offers no account of what the implications of any such 'findings' might be, one thing'is certain - they *could not* support the hypothesis of biological mechanisms underlying mental distress, because
such an hypothesis can be demonstrated to be inappropriate on philosophical grounds alone. What are we to make of this dispute?

At the outset it must be pointed out that argument by epistemological
fiat is neither necessary nor particularly helpful for making a critical
assessment of evidence from genetics, physiology and/or biochemistry.
There is no need for a complex philosophical argument in order to
demonstrate the many problems with the ways in which writers such as
Wing collect and interpret evidence as to organic correlations of mental
disturbance. We can demonstrate this with regard to just two of the
arguments attacked by Ingleby. Firstly, the question of genetic transmission of, in particular, schizophrenia. One does not have to deny
the evidence of studies demonstrating an hereditary element in some
mental disturbances to question an interpretation of this as evidence
for genetic causes. The correlational evidence is quite strong, yet
Ingleby simply dismisses it with generalities which would convince no-
one with even a slight acquaintance with the literature.[24] However,
even when such correlations have been found, what do they prove? Not
that every child of a schizoprenic parent will develop schizophrenia -
in fact the proportion is very low. Nor that every schizophrenic has
a schizophrenic relative - again the proportion of schizophrenics that
have such - family history is extremely low. And certainly not that

genetic factors *cause* schizophrenia; at the most they may provide some
of the conditions, neither necessary nor sufficient, for the development
of those heterogenous disturbances lumped together in the diagnostic
category of schizophrenia. The idea that to acknowledge this is in some
way intrinsically reactionary is simply absurd. The processes of inheritance are complex, involving many genes and their interaction, and
certainly requiring the presence of many other conditions - social,
familial, sexual etc. - if mental disturbance is to be manifested. The
supposed intractability of genetic material and its location in the
apparent origin of life itself - the chromosomal structure - does not
imply that it has the status of first cause. The same points can be
made with regard to our second example, the question of physiological
and biochemical correlates of mental disturbances. Even if such correlations could be demonstrated, and at the moment the evidence is circum-
stantial and weak, to accord to these factors the status of cause is
not only to deny that many other conditions are *equally* or *more* necessary
for the development of disturbances, but also to ignore the interaction
between social and environmental factors and physiological processes.
The physiology of the body is not an irreducible and primary datum, it
is subject to the influences of many and varied non-biological conditions.
     No complex epistemological arguments concerning the inappropriateness
of conceptions of cause to the sphere of human behaviour are necessary
to make the above points. Arguments such as Ingleby's are unable to say
anything about the status of the genetic and physiological correlations
that have been demonstrated, except that they are either false, or irrelevant or both. Rather than convicting those producing such evidence at
the court of philosophy, it is surely more productive to consider in
detail the specific mechanisms which might be involved in the production
of different mental disorders and the place and weight of biological,
social, psychical and familial conditions in relation to such mechanisms.
To our critical psychiatrists, this no doubt is 'eclecticism', but this
criticism can only be made if *philosophy* is allowed to dictate the forms
of possible processes which could be involved in the production of mental
distress, and to outlaw certain modes of explanation by fiat. 'The
human' is not a single ontological sphere with its own mode of being
which dictates what and how it can be known.
     Not only is critical psychiatry's excursion into philosophy dogmatic
and unnecessary, it is also positively misleading in the implications
which are drawn from it. It will be recalled that the 'medical model'
is constructed and denounced in terms of its 'positivism'. Put crudely,
the argument runs - positivism explains the human world in the same
terms as the natural world. It thus treats people as things. Modern
psychiatry is positivistic. Treating people like things happens not
only theoretically but practically, and treating people like things is
wrong. The argument is also posed historically. Thus Treacher and
Baruch assert 'as medicine became more scientific, more concerned with
measurement and classification and the theory of pathological processes,
it became less humanistic and tended to treat the patient as an object'.[25]
Thus the critique is at one and the same time envisaged as a criticism
of theory and an uncovering of the determinants of psychiatric practice.
But, of course, current psychiatric practice is no more a realization
of positivist epistemology than is an alternative mode of organising
therapeutic practice derivable from the alternative epistemology espoused
by psychiatry's critics. As Michel Foucault has demonstrated,[26] the

the formation of the set of theories, practices, procedures and agents
of modern clinical medicine was made possible by a complex set of
political, social, technical and theoretical shifts at the beginning of
the 19th century. Amongst these were the emergence of the hospital as
a result of increasing industrialisation and urbanisation, and a change
in the laws of assistance, making institutionalisation a condition of
medical treatment for those in receipt of relief; a change in relations
between doctor and patient, such that doctors may now observe a whole
series of instances of any particular condition, making possible the
tabulation and statisticalisation of diseases and the development of
classifications and diagnoses based on the link between symptoms and
prognosis, between symptoms at different levels, between individuals,
between successive events; a change in the methods of transmitting
medical knowledge whereby the hospital becomes a pedagogic apparatus in
which the poor, benefitting from the care they receive for free, compensate through the medical lesson they provide. It is shifts such as
these which produce the clinical conception of the case - the unique
intersection between a body and a life history - as the proper object
for medical knowledge and the practice of the cure. The formation of
the notion of the case is certainly conditioned by social and institutional changes, certainly 'political', but nothing can be said of its
conditions or consequences through an epistemological critique of
'scientism' or 'positivism'.
   Nor does the positivist refusal of the epistemological distinction
between the natural and social worlds imply that psychiatrists holding
a 'disease' model of mental distress are bound to treat their patients
as 'objects' in any pejorative moral or interpersonal sense. To take
the usual example, diagnostic interviews, whether or not they are helpful, can be carried out more or less sympathetically. It is quite
possible for a doctor (or anyone else) to be attentive to the meaning
and significance of what a person is saying and at the same time find
evidence of what psychiatry calls delusions, hallucinations and so forth.
Some psychiatrists are brisk, cold and impersonal to the point of cruelty,
others are genuinely concerned at the suffering and distress which their
patients as individuals undergo. A whole range of modes of relating can
and do occur within the confines of the same disease theory of mental
illness. Obviously those who care for the mentally distressed require
a range of personal qualities like patience, sensitivity and tolerance,
not to mention resilience and toughness. Medical training does not
select for this, and probably pays insufficient attention to it. In
addition the organisation, funding and authority structures of psychiatry
constrain the possibilities of devoting the necessary individual care and
attention to patients in a number of significant ways. These are problems which socialists must address; we return to discuss them in detail
in the sequel to this article. But to assert that these problems can
be understood or resolved through the ritual combat of philosophical
dogmatisms is quite simply ridiculous, and also serves to subvert any
possibility of conceptualising the difficulties and objectives involved.
   It should be noted that Ingleby's criticisms are not reserved for
those who hold to an *organic* theory of causation of mental illness; they
are extended to *any* theory of causation, including environmental and
social theories and concomitant forms of intervention. All such
theories are considered damned on the grounds of their positivism.
Thus work like that of George Brown and his colleagues who identified

such correlates of depression in women as poverty and isolation, using
standard sociological research methods is criticised in exactly the same
terms as disease theories: 'in claiming that a state of mind is *determined*
by a particular environment they are in fact making a subtle claim about
the nature of that mental state: for they imply that the person who has
it is not a rational agent'.[27] Ingleby then proceeds to get himself into
a terrible tangle in trying to decide whether social conditions such as
poverty and isolation are 'causes' and hence illegitimate, or 'grounds'
or 'reasons' which render intelligible and meaningful certain kinds of
experiences. No productive consequences flow from this debate, except
the assurance, again on epistemological grounds, that the correct basis
for work on mental disturbance is 'depth hermeneutics' which he identifies with certain variants of psychoanalysis. Indeed, he tries to argue
that epistemological paradigms can be assigned to different political
interest groups such that positivism represents reaction and interpretat-
ive paradigms are intrinsic to a socialist world view. It should be
clear that the effects of this rationalist form of argument are to place
most crucial questions of politics and practice far beyond one's grasp.

MADNESS AND THE CLINIC

Both anti-psychiatry and much of orthodox psychiatry have a particular
epistemological conception of physical medicine. The dispute between
them concerns whether mental disturbance ought to be assimilated to this
model or differentiated from it. However, as has been argued elsewhere,
orthodox psychiatry, anti-psychiatry and now critical psychiatry have a
very primitive view of the theory and practice of physical medicine.[28]
To illustrate this, let us turn to examine some of the arguments put
forward by Anthony Clare.[29] Clare's book has been dismissed as 'very
appealing to those who wallow in the various forms of empiricist anti-
intellectualism which dominate thinking in the area of mental health'
and 'little more than a smokescreen for exerting the hegemony of the
psychiatric profession'.[30] On the contrary, Clare's book is pertinent
to socialists precisely because it goes some way towards avoiding the
epistemologisation of argument which hegemonises much left debate and is
not underpinned by the naive utopianism which believes that a socialist
reconstruction of society will eradicate the problem of madness. It
thus enables socialists seriously concerned with the development of
political struggles and the formation of political objectives to pose
seriously certain technological and organisational questions in the
field of madness. We make no apology for having utilised Clare's book
to this end; we will be concerned not so much by his own positions as
with the uses to which his arguments can be put.
    In the first chapter of his book, Clare develops an uncompromising
assault on the way in which such criticisms of the medical model of
mental illness are set up. Firstly, he argues, diagnosis of physical
illness is as complex an act of cultural judgment as the diagnosis of
mental illness. Secondly, he shows that physical and psychological
symptoms are intermingled in all 'physical' and 'mental' illnesses.
And thirdly he demonstrates that definitions of health and illness in
each case are *social*. That is to say, all medicine, physical no less
than mental, involves the application of culturally determined norms
concerning definition of sickness and levels of health to particular

individuals. Norms concerning 'healthy' modes of functioning of organs
and bodies are just as much socially and historically determined as are
norms concerning beliefs and behaviours. And the application of these
norms in any specific instance always involves an act of judgment on the
part of the doctor, a judgment that may be 'subjective' but is by no
means an individual matter. Judgments of doctors are conditioned by
prevalent social attitudes and beliefs and constrained by the criteria
and practices of clinical medicine. They are constructed through a long
apprenticeship at the bed-side whose objective is the production of a
highly trained subjectivity and a regularised and standardised mode of
judgment.[31] The problem for psychiatry, as we shall see in a moment,
is not so much that its judgments are 'subjective' and socially relative,
for how could they be otherwise? It is rather, Clare argues, that the
norms in question are specified in imprecise and contradictory ways,
the conditions of their applications to particular cases are indetermin-
ate and hence the levels of standardisation of medical subjectivity
attained in respect to physical illness are rarely matched in psychiatry.

The mode of conceptualisation of illness that Clare develops is rather
different from the 'disease theory' version of the medical model. It is
what we shall term a 'clinical approach' version.[32] It is not the
identification of biological mechanisms underpinning symptoms which is
the justification for the medicalisation of madness, but the conditions
for the organisation of a clinical practice in relation to disturbances
of the body or the mind. It should be stressed that the elaboration of
this clinical model and the argument that it can apply equally to cases
of physical and mental disturbance does not imply that either physical
disturbances as a group or mental disturbances as a group or both
groups of disturbances taken together form any kind of ontological
unity. This is not to deny that Clare on occasion dabbles in ontological questions, but this is not integral to his elaboration of the
clinical approach to mental disturbance.

There is, however, a problem which we should make clear at the outset. The conception of the clinical approach in psychiatric practice
does not characterise the actual mode of operation of psychiatry today.
Clare proceeds by defending psychiatry from its critics through the
construction of an idealised model, and only then criticising the present state of psychiatric practice when it fails to live up to this ideal.
This enables him to sidestep certain crucial problems, to which we shall
return, but despite this (or perhaps because of it) he advances debate
considerably beyond the epistemologisation of an Ingleby or a Wing.

Clare argues for a clinical approach to mental disturbances because
of its utility for the organisation of therapeutic practices. This
clinical approach involves the use of techniques of interviewing, the
elicitation and recording of biographical and social information, the
investigation and classification of symptomatology, and the application
of a diagnostic category. The diagnosis is not the first step, as for
Wing, in identifying an organic mechanism underlying a syndrome, but
rather is 'phenomenological': it is based on the manifest presentation
of the patient and related not to a theory of mental illness but to a
theory of clinical practice, of the organisation of treatment, of the
investigation, comparison and communication of the effects of distinct
forms of treatment, of the making of prognoses for particular syndromes
and of the organisation of hypotheses as to aetiology.

Indeed, Clare points out that such a clinical approach implies no commitment to a theory of organic aetiology in mental disturbances. The identification of syndromes is one thing; hypotheses regarding causes are another. Thus both predominantly physical and predominantly mental syndromes could have biological, psychological or social causes (or any combination of the three). This clinical approach therefore neither implies a disease model or mental illness nor physical modes of treatment. And conversely, physical modes of treatment could quite consistently be prescribed by those who believe that the nature and causes of a person's distress are wholly psychological or social. This clinical approach thus breaks up and disperses the elements that are presumed necessarily to hold together in a disease model.

Let us investigate some of these questions a little further by discussing in some detail one particular feature of the clinical approach - the possibility and utility of identifying psychiatric syndromes. This question is crucial. For Clare the identification of syndromes is the condition for the organisation and treatment of mental disturbances in terms of a clinical practice, whilst critics of psychiatry assert the impossibility and inappropriateness of the identification of syndromes in cases of mental distress *tout court*.

A syndrome, in medical terms, is a set of signs and symptoms that occur together in a more or less regular fashion. Syndromes are never invarient or fixed, but they do exhibit some patterning. It follows that a crucial part of medical training lies in the recognition of such patterns. The first criticism which critical psychiatry levels at the notion of *psychiatric* syndromes is that doctors are unable to make such recognitions at all reliably. Research has shown that, presented with a set of cases, two psychiatrists will disagree on diagnosis more frequently than they will agree. Critical psychiatry takes this as evidence for its 'subjectivist' reproach. More recently, research undertaken internationally has shown that using a standardised form of psychiatric interview a very high level of agreement between large numbers of psychiatrists can be achieved. Indeed Clare cites evidence which shows that, given appropriate forms of training, levels of agreement in psychiatric diagnosis can be made as reliable as those in diagnoses within physical medicine.[33]

Of course a number of different conclusions can be drawn from this research. Wing, for example, concludes that these high levels of agreement imply that the diagnoses which are made are in some sense 'true', and further assumes that in many cases the identification of the underlying organic mechanisms has either already been achieved or cannot be long in coming. Critical psychiatry would rejoin that Wing conflates agreement and accuracy (the venerable problem of reliability and validity). It would continue to assert that the syndromes identified with such reliability were nonetheless the product of subjective judgment and hence little more than convenient fictions. But, as we have already shown, all categorisation of behaviour involves reference to social norms and definite forms of clinical training, so this accusation of 'subjectivity' is entirely beside the point.

The clinical approach of Clare is less interested in the 'truth value' of diagnoses and more concerned with what they permit one to do in the way of treatment and administration. If the utility of the diagnostic method could be demonstrated, then the fact of their dependence upon social norms would be no criticism. And the utilisation of

diagnostic categories is, in clinical psychiatry as much as any other
branch of clinical medicine, a necessary condition for the organisation
and evaluation of data, for the specification of links between symptomatology, aetiology and prognosis and the organisation of evidence as to
the efficacy of differential forms of treatment. The fluidity of diagnosis in contemporary psychiatric practice does not constitute an argument for its abandonment, but rather for the increase in the rigour of
psychiatric training, an increase in diagnostic specificity, a closer
specification of behavioural norms of functioning and clearer guidance
as to the application of norms to cases. Rather than jettisoning diagnosis, the problem is to provide the conditions for their clearer differentiation, tighter definition and critical rectification, to increase
their precision and utility from the rather gross means of dividing up
categories of patients that they are today.[34]

Critical psychiatry opposes diagnosis in terms of syndromes on
another ground - that they are both unnecessary and involve distortion
of the uniqueness of each case in the attempt to force it into a standardised and fixed category. Clare however argues that *any* approach to
personal distress of whatever kind must involve forms of classification,
the application of analytic principles and the organisation on the part
of practitioners of the experiences that individuals bring to them.
This is as true of the various psychotherapies and of psychoanalysis as
it is of orthodox psychiatry, although of course the principles of
classification and organisation differ. It is, of course, also true
of religious, social work or even political approaches to personal distress. The point is that even the most client-centred therapies or the
most experience-oriented of the anti-psychiatry techniques must do this.
Their principles may remain implicit but this merely allows them to
remain unscrutinised, obstructs the communication of new information and
techniques, and hinders attempts to evaluate them. Critical psychiatry
is right to be concerned that diagnostic procedures can be superficial
and have extremely damaging consequences for the patient as a result.
The point is that such consequences are in no sense intrinsic to the
carrying out of diagnoses in terms of syndromes: their consequences
could equally well allow the application of accumulated clinical experience to individual cases in a way which affords substantial therapeutic
benefits.

However, there are a series of substantial problems with the way in
which Clare conducts his defence of the utility of diagnosis in terms
of syndromes. It will be recalled that the importance of such diagnosis
is argued in terms of its role in determination of aetiology, decisions
as to treatment and predictions as to prognosis. However, whatever may
be the case in Clare's ideal model, the evidence concerning the role and
functioning of diagnostic categories in contemporary psychiatric practice
is no advertisement for Clare's argument. To take simply the example of
treatment, it is clear that the treatments which are currently utilised
are far from specific to diagnostic categories. Whether patients are
diagnosed schizophrenic, manic, suffering from personality disorder or
even in some anxiety states, identical forms of drugs are administered
(most probably one of the phenothiazines). Whilst hypotheses abound as
to the mode of action of these drugs, this is hardly a case in which
differential diagnosis leads to specificity of treatment, and indeed the
actual rationale for the administration of such substances is in terms
of their general tranquilising effects, rather than any specific effects

they might have on symptomatology. Similarly, almost any condition which
involves depression tends to be treated by the administration of a different group of drugs (triciclates or mon-amine oxidase inhibitors). In
other words diagnosis in practice involves a simple dichotomous classification - the deranged versus the depressed.[35] This does not, of course,
mean that in principle Clare's clinical model is unrealizable; the problem
is that, given the way in which his argument is set up, there is no means
of analysing the determinants of the divergence between the real and the
ideal; his text is as much programmatic as it is descriptive.

For example, most psychiatrists working in the NHS probably hold a
relatively crude disease theory of mental illness. One consequence of
this is a peculiar ambivalence concerning syndromes where no even remotely
plausible organic aetiology has been proposed - such as the 'personality
disorders'. In such situations their position leads them to act as if
the condition, if not a straightforward case of malingering, is nevertheless under conscious control, and to organise treatment regimes
accordingly. For the practical consequence of a disease model are to
deny the possibility of locating causes of mental distress which occur
in a psychological space yet are governed by laws and mechanisms which
are not amenable to transformations by a simple act of will.

We have already suggested that a central problem for psychiatry, if
one takes Clare's argument seriously, concerns the looseness and indet-
erminacy of the specification of its diagnostic categories. This point
is made vigorously by Coulter who argues that it is absurd to place in
one category people who believe their neighbours are plotting against
them, those who use extremely metaphoric and cryptic language (so-called
'word salad'), those who think their thoughts are being broadcast and
those whose voices order them to jump out of windows.[36] All such
symptoms would be diagnostic of schizophrenia, as would a range of
others. In considering this example of schizophrenia, Clare, like many
others, notes its imprecision and the range of behaviours which it
encompasses. Yet Clare does not go on from this recognition to question
the diagnostic utility of the category of schizophrenia itself, as he
should do bearing in mind the fact that such a diagnosis does not predict either the content of the disorder or its prognosis, and neither
has any uniform aetiology been delineated. Indeed, given the way in
which diagnoses of schizophrenia are made in Britain it would be difficult to argue that it constitutes a syndrome at all.[37] Despite his
sophistication, Clare constantly confuses a defence of the clinical
approach with a defence of existing diagnostic categories within psychiatry. To argue the utility of a clinical approach to problems of mental
distress, as we do, does not imply an acceptance of existing psychiatric
diagnostic categories.

There is one sense, however, in which Clare addresses these questions.
He argues that the critics of diagnosis are failing to make a crucial
distinction - that between the *form* of the disorder and its *content*.
To give a crude example, whether one is convinced one is Chairman Mao,
persecuted by Fascists or singled out for special protection by the
angels, one is still deluded. Anti-psychiatry, says Clare, pays
attention to individual content and often has success in unravelling
its meaning. What is not explained is why the disorder took this particular *form*, and what typifies mental disturbance is disorder of the
form of perception, the *form* of thought and the *form* of affectivity.
Despite the serious problems with this form/content distinction, it may

be used to make an important point. Experiences such as hallucinations, delusions and the various forms of thought disorder have not been ex- plained satisfactorily by the critics of psychiatry. They cannot explain why one person responds to confusing family communications by rebellion and another by becoming hallucinated. The fact is that *all* currently available explanations and treatments for these especially malignant forms of mental disorder are more or less inadequate. People who live in glass houses should be rather more careful about throwing stones.

Let us briefly sum up our argument in this section. It may seem to some that in refusing to give primacy to ontological or philosophical questions concerning the nature of madness we have avoided the central issues at stake for socialists here - issues of theory, of philosophy, even of materialism. We have discussed Clare's position at such length because we believe it displaces these issues in a number of important ways. Firstly, the clinical approach which he develops takes as central not a commitment to a particular theory of mental illness but the con- ditions under which a clinical practice in respect of mental distress can be organised. Secondly, he shows that such a clinical practice must always involve the application of judgments in relation to social norms, and that demonstration of the fact of such a judgment hardly amounts to a critique. Thirdly, he suggests the necessity and utility of the appli- cation of diagnostic categories in response to the critique of the deleterious effects of 'labelling' mounted by psychiatry's critics. The consequences of applying a label may not be 'deviance amplification' but the organisation and direction of accumulated knowledge and special- ised resources to a distressed individual. Fourthly, clinical practice does not inevitably deny the singularities in individual biography and experience but merely seeks to place these within an explicit and systematic analytic framework. Finally, Clare's clinical approach is capable of admitting the diversity ahd heterogeneity of those conditions currently put together under the category 'mental illness'.

Clare's argument concerning the necessity and utility of a clinical approach to mental distress, and the need for its refinement is salut- ary for those who pin their hopes for reform in the displacement of medicine as the regulative instance in the field of madness. If the conditions of an effective practice in relation to at least some forms of mental disturbance is the development of a well regulated clinical approach, such a displacement might simply result in the substitution of even *less* competent agents for doctors, even more variability in the application of diagnostic criteria, even less utilisation of avail- able knowledge and techniques. There is at least no reason to assume that other social agents and agencies - lay therapists, social workers or what you will - will do better than doctors, though may do no worse.

It should be said that Clare himself does not develop this argument nor give any *principled* reasons for medical jurisdiction in the field of mental distress. He addresses this question in passing and pragmat- ically - for the time being, whatever the critics of medicine might have to say, it is to medically qualified agents and to medical institutions that mentally distressed individuals turn for help. This is not simply because medicine controls the relevant social resources, but more that it is in medical terms that individuals conceive of their mental dis- tress. Not surprising, one might add, given the lack of alternatives and their cost which prohibits them as options for most. Nor surprising

given the referral processes of other social agencies. But are there
any reasons in principle for the medicalisation of madness? It is to
this question that we now turn, for it is one that critical psychiatry
answers in the negative. Or rather, to the extent that reasons can be
adduced, they are considered to relate not to the appropriateness of
medicalisation but to an historic coup, staged by medicine, in which
doctors seized control of a new social locus of power, the institutions
and practices of the 'mad business'.

'MEDICAL MEN AS MORAL ENTREPRENEURS'

The argument that is rapidly becoming orthodox amongst psychiatry's
critics is as follows. In the mid-19th century, medicine without any
substantiable claim to knowledge or expertise, but acting in narrow self-
interest and with a view to extending its power and influence, seized
control of madness. In order to do so the medical profession not only
engaged in calculated and cynical political manoeuvring. It also invented spurious theories of the organic causes of madness, utilising the
prestige of medicine to convince public and politicians alike that madness was an illness analogous to physical illness, requiring medical
forms of treatment and hence legitimately controlled by medicine. Its
real motive was the desire to monopolise and control the lucrative
pickings and growing career opportunities of the mad business. In
taking over madness for its own, medicine displaced the humane and enlightened forms of moral treatment, introduced by such reformers as Tuke
and Pinel, which for the first time had treated the mad as human and
aided them with kindness and sensitivity. Moral treatment, despite its
therapeutic potential, was defeated because, unlike medicine, it was
unable to draw upon an established professional grouping or ideology for
its support.
  The medical coup had significance, it is argued, in wider social terms.
It coincided with a general trend in 'social control' practices in modern
societies: to rationalise and legitimise control over troublesome and
deviant elements by consigning them to the ministrations of 'experts'.
Medicine took control of existing asylums, and encouraged the building
of others. In turning the asylum into a medicalised space, incarceration
was legitimated, by the extension to it of the mystique and prestige
attached to the doctor's ability to cure. Acceptance of the existence
and legitimacy of the asylum had a utility for other social groups.
Parish officials, relatives and others could use the asylum as a dumping
ground for those who for various reasons they considered undesirable.
Incarceration rather than therapy was the true social function of the
asylum. Confinement served the purpose of locking deviants away, forcing
them to accept the sick role, dehumanising them and turning them into
mere 'cases', invalidating their protest against social conditions and
rendering them dependent upon professional expertise rather than having
their fate in their own hands. Thus a collusion between medicine and
society enabled it to contain and consolidate its monopoly control over
madness, a control which it has maintained and strengthened over the
last one hundred years, supported by politicians not only of the right
but also of the social democratic and reformist left. The attempts to
close the asylums and to re-absorb the mad within the operations of
general medicine are but the apotheosis of this tendency. Medical

theories of madness today, and the very category of mental illness, are
merely the modern counterparts of the ideological smokescreen of the 19th
century, continuously reinvented by the medical profession in order to
sustain and extend its illegitimate and damaging hegemony. It is this
hegemony which socialists must seek to destroy.[38]

Thus a rationale is provided for the theoretical and political critique of the medical model by means of a history, and history and theory
combine to dictate the principle of a socialist politics of madness - a
politics of demedicalisation. But the historical account with which
critical psychiatry equips itself is as partial, unsatisfactory and misleading as is its theoretical assault on the medical model. Without
going into excessive historical detail, it is worth making the following
points.

Firstly, there is nothing inherently absurd or 'ideological' about
the theories of madness developed by medicine in the 19th century.
Critical psychiatry mimics the worst history of ideas in adjudicating
upon the inadequacy of beliefs in the past on the basis of its own unquestioned widsom. In the late 18th and early 19th centuries there were
four main forms of medical treatment of insanity, each linked to a specific theory of the origin and mechanisms of madness, and practised
largely outside the asylum. First, the administration of various
noxious substances in an attempt to strengthen the spirits or fibres
supposedly weakened in madness. Second a range of techniques of purifi-
cation - blood transfusions, bleedings, purges - linked to a theory of
madness involving the clogging of the fibres of mind or viscera. Third,
the use of immersions - baths, showers - with the aim of restoring
suppleness to the fibres and the added advantages of cooling and shock
to bring sufferers to their senses. Fourth, regulation of movement to
bring it into accord with external, worldly, rather than internal time.
None of these techniques or theories was absurd or inhuman, each was
linked with theories of the operation of the body and mind, could make
a claim to truth in relation to existing medical theory, and showed as
much success as any other form of treatment.[39]

Conversely, the view of moral treatment as sensitive, enlightened,
humanitarian, also duplicates the account given by triumphalist histories of scientific progress. Moral treatment was neither motivated by
kindness, nor was it simply applied humanitarianism coupled with common
sense as is often suggested. It relied upon a specific theory and
practice whose object was the reconstruction of the mad through a work
performed upon the core of reason which remained within them, a work
whose object was socialisation, the reattachment of the mad subject to
the social order, the production of socially acceptable forms of conduct. To these ends the asylum was constructed as a domain of morality,
modelled upon the family with the mad in place of infant. The asylum
was to be a machine for the construction and maintenance of good health,
good habits and good order, through the detailed organisation of every
moment of daily life of the inmates, continuous observation and surveillance and a complete system of moral management using techniques somewhat similar to the rewards and punishments of modern behaviour therapy.
Thus the great English Quaker reformer William Tuke asserts that 'the
principle of fear, which is rarely decreased by insanity, is considered
of great importance in the management of patients'.[40] And it was, indeed,
moral treatment that made possible the uses of earlier medical techniques
- shock, immersion, bleeding - not in relation to their original and

specific rationales but as a response to moral transgressions with the hope that the link between undesirable behaviour and unpleasant consequence would be internalised by the mad. Thus the shift from earlier notions of madness as animality and incurable to 19th-century beliefs in the remediability of madness and the concomitant forms of treatment is rendered unintelligible by the repetition of the banal themes of humanitarianism and reaction, or the notion of some fundamental opposition between medical and moral treatment in the development of the asylum.

What one sees in the struggles around madness in the 19th century is not a coup by cynical and inhumane medicine staged at the expense of humanity and enlightenment, with the implication that a politics could organise its objectives around the reversal of this historic victory, and the re-elevation of the vanquished principles of humanitarianism. For the exponents of moral treatment were just as much a specific and interested group of agents as doctors, and just as involved in struggles for jurisdiction over madness. Critical psychiatry makes much of the fact that doctors entered the asylum as managers rather than as therapeutic agents. However, it should be pointed out that in doing so they filled a space first constructed within moral treatment - institutional psychiatry is more the successor of moral treatment than of the mad-doctors of the 18th century. If medicine was victor in the battle for the asylum, it certainly had something to do with the success of its claim to superiority in the non-medical aspects of asylum work, with its assertion of moral rectitude and administrative competence in respect to the running of socially funded institutions. There are no reasons to assume that such considerations were then, or are now, absurd - professional and academic training still today serves as qualification for areas of work far removed from its initial focus. Such procedures of selection are certainly open to question, but that does not render them patently ridiculous as the critics of psychiatry appear to assume.

That they were appointed for non-medical reasons does not imply that doctors cynically invented their medical theories of madness as ideological supports for this function. As we have already seen, there is nothing any more obviously absurd or 'ideological' about medical theories than about moral theories of madness. It was neither a case of a false theory generating an inhumane practice (as we have already shown in relation to Ingleby's argument about 'positivism'), nor of a false theory *legitimating* an already existing practice. If doctors won the struggle to define madness, to designate those mad and to control the social and institutional organisation of madness, it was not so much because of the falsity of their claims but because of the ability of those claims to define an effective realm in which doctors, politicians, relatives and the mad themselves operated, and which indeed entered into the construction of those very behaviours and emotions designated mad. No legitimacy is provided for the denunciation of the medicalisation of madness by an appeal to history, for the account we are given is constructed precisely in order to provide grounds for such a critique. The claim by 'critical history' to have demonstrated the charlatanism of medicine, then and now, and to assert that medical men are merely 'moral entrepreneurs' cannot be taken seriously.[41]

Thus the corollary, that socialist politics must have as its objective the displacement of this illegitimate and harmful hegemony must also be regarded as undemonstrated. A political analysis of the conditions and consequences of the current links between medicine and madness, and of the means of formation of political objectives in the field of mental health cannot be derived from the radical history and sociology of critical psychiatry.

NORMS, TRANSGRESSION AND SOCIAL CONTROL

The attempt to found an analysis of the political functioning of the medicalisation of madness on the concept of 'social control' proves equally hollow and equally disabling politically. Since this notion is becoming so fashionable in sociologies of welfare, social policy and medicine, as well as madness, it might be worth examining it in a little detail.[42] What is meant when these authors assert that the medicalisation of madness serves the function of social control? At root there is a claim that this historical process can be explained through an analysis of the functions it serves for the maintenance of social order - the function of suppressing actual or potential threats to existing social and political conditions. Deviant behaviours are behaviours which pose such threats, and to designate a particular social process with regard to such behaviours as one of social control is simultaneously to characterise that process, to explain its social genesis and function, and to criticise it.

This argument is predicated upon a particular view as to the nature and origins of those behaviours against which social control mechanisms are brought into play - 'deviance'. Deviance has a particular directionality, meaning and social genesis: it is both a result of and a protest against the conditions of life, beliefs and expectations of an imperfect social order. However its political *potential* is assessed, the *fact* of deviance represents an implicit critique of existing dominant forms of social relations. Whilst the precise forms of deviance might change, its content and meaning remain the same, and its control by society's agents both suppresses a source of social danger and simultaneously confirms and legitimates those norms, beliefs and values which deviance threatens. Social control is thus, essentially, a police matter, brought into operation when 'ideology', the other control mechanism for ensuring social content and stability despite conflicts of real interests, breaks down.[43]

There are two basic difficulties worth pointing out with regard to this argument. Firstly, there is the problem of the homogenisation of all 'social problems' under the general rubric of deviance. Whether it be witchcraft in the middle ages, insanity in the 19th century, mental illness today, all are essentially the same, the product of the same social mechanisms and having the same social significance. And they are identical too in their social origins and function, to other forms of deviant behaviour - criminality, homosexuality, drug taking and so forth - all are manifestations of the same essential phenomenon, all are caught up within the same social mechanisms of response. But madness is not the same as witchcraft, and neither of these are the same as homosexuality or drug taking. Not only does such an analysis stage a spectacular and empty sociological reduction, where the mechanisms through which 'primary deviance' is produced remain unanalysed, but it also fails to take account of the specificity of the terms and conditions under which 'social problems' are constructed.

Secondly, its supposed *critical* function is just as questionable. For the designation of a mechanism as one of social control is only a criticism of such a mechanism if it is assumed that any such 'control' is in and of itself unjust. This is however what these analyses set out to demonstrate, yet they must assume it from the outset. Is *any* form of construction and regulation of social norms unjust, immoral, a violation of the rights of the individual to define their own reality? If not, then either the demonstration of the fact of 'social control' is otiose, for it merely demonstrates what is already known - the nastiness of capitalist society and hence of all practices within it - or it is irrelevant, since what needs to be shown is the specific points of criticism of specific mechanisms and social processes. In any event, the tedious repetition of 'unmaskings' of the social control functions of psychiatry, medicine, social policy and the welfare state gets us no closer to an analysis of the real political and social problems at stake.

Despite the apparent radicalism of the sociology of social control, its proponents fail to consider seriously some central 'sociological' questions, satisfying themselves with the passion of their humanist denunciations of the state and all its works and the amazing versatility of their analyses - in which everything (and hence nothing) can count as an instance of social control. It is necessary, therefore, to re-establish one or two simple points about social relations, norms and their violation, which have some implications for how we are to think of problems of madness.

All forms of human social organisation require and construct certain norms of behaviour and conduct; such social construction of human attributes is the condition of organised social relations.[44] The social and historical variability of all personal qualities, whether they be such basic bodily movements as posture or walking, or the experience and expression of psychical states such as emotions, is ample demonstration of the fact that such qualities can never simply be *expressions* of invariant biological or psychical givens. Personal and social behaviour is constructed and regulated by practices such as those of family, education, language and law and by belief systems ranging from 'popular culture' to explicit and organised political or religious ideologies. These social practices work upon biological and psychical processes which have their own specific mechanisms and effects and hence can never simply reflect unproblematically the social conditions which act upon them. It is not therefore merely a matter of 'socialisation' but of the particular relations and dependencies which obtain amongst and between these many conditions of human social life.

The very complexity of the social existence and functioning of norms of personal attributes, and the fact that the norms and expectations which converge upon any individual human subject will not be necessarily congruent, and may well be contradictory, implies that such norms will on occasions be violated, and the existence of agencies whose occasion and object is at one and the same time the social construction of the 'normal' and the constraint and regulation of the 'pathological'. Neither normality nor pathology have any ontological or natural status. Societies consist in definite practices, agencies and ideologies which constrain and regulate, produce and administer normality and pathology in the field of the personal. A society without categories of pathology is as unthinkable as a society without norms. This is as true of socialist or communist societies as it is of medieval Europe, primitive

communist societies without organised state forms or industrial Britain.
Of course, although the existence of social norms is universal, the
nature, content and means of social construction of such norms will vary.
But the mere discovery of the existence of norms and of social processes
for their regulation cannot pass for analytic acuity, still less for
political criticism. To this extent, the proclamation of the discovery
of a practice of 'social control' as if it in itself were a condemnation
of such a practice or an exposure of its corrupt truth is surely a
little naive.

All literate societies which have yet been studied contain a category
of pathology designated (something like) madness.[45] From Ancient
Palestine to the present, from the Azande to the Americas, such a category exists and functions in the construction and regulation of human
attributes. What *counts* as madness, the social consequences of the
recognition of madness and the manner of its division from 'normality'
and other forms of pathology varies widely. Both modern psychiatry and
radical sociology may well conclude that there is something fundamentally similar about the witches hunted by the Inquisition and the mentally
ill today. For psychiatry, witches were undiagnosed mental patients;
medieval Europe would disagree. Not because it did not recognise madness
but because, according to the forms of its recognition, the condition of
being a witch was precisely that one had been found not mad. For sociology, witchcraft and mental illness are both threatening forms of social
protest whose categorisation and persecution serves the same function of
social control. But what is necessary is not a collapse of distinct
forms of pathology into such generalities, but the analysis of the
particular historical and social conditions under which specific categories of pathology are constructed and the modes of their social
functioning.

These socially constructed conceptions of madness, witchcraft, and
normality are not merely 'labels'. Labelling theory argues that there
is a natural diversity of human behaviours and societies differ in those
which they label deviant, the affixing of such a label having consequences
for the individual so designated. But what is involved here is by no
means simply a question of labels. The designation of forms of normality
and pathology are the consequence of definite sets of organised familial,
social, political and cultural forces and technologies. And these practices are not subsequent to the construction of the behaviours and attributes in question; they enter into the construction of these very
capacities themselves. Witches are only possible in societies where
the ideas and practices concerning witchcraft are an integral part of
their culture.[46] Similarly madness exists only in and through the
social categories and beliefs which construct and recognise it. To
take just one example, Koro, a form of behaviour in which male chinese
develop an acute fear that the penis is retracting into the abdomen, is
not a generalised form of behaviour merely 'labelled' as a psychiatric
disorder in China. It depends upon the existence of a developed folk-
lore, tradition and set of superstitions which construct this as a
possible form of behaviour, partially through their entry into certain
familial and child rearing practices and certain conceptions and beliefs
concerning sexuality.[47] The same may be said of hysteria and schizophrenia. The social organisation of categories and personal behaviours
designated madness and the forms of existence and experience of madness
do not exist as separate levels or orders of reality, and the character-

istics of pathology are as much socially constructed as those of normality. This is not to say that such categories and processes do not work
upon psychical material which has its own reality, mechanisms and laws
of operation; it is not a case of 'conditioning' or 'internalisation'.
It is to say that this psychic space is necessarily condemned to work
upon material, and in relation to practices and processes, which are
social, and which are socially and historically variable. The psyche
can never merely express itself, but neither can it merely reflect pre-
given social conditions.
    To try and unify the distinct and varied processes we have briefly
sketched, the varied ways in which categories of normality and pathology
have been socially constructed and regulated, under the repetitive signs
of 'deviance' and 'social control' is somewhat unhelpful. It obscures
precisely what it is important to examine; the modes of construction and
functioning of categories concerning the person, and the social and
political organisation and consequences of such categories. To think
that the disclosure of the *fact* of social organisation and regulation
of the personal field becomes, simply through its designation as 'social
control', a 'critique' of such organisation is a breathtaking piece of
sleight of hand - impressive at first sight but uninteresting once one
has seen through the trick. Yet it is only through such a trick that
critical psychiatry can hold up the illusion of an alternative conception
of madness, in a way which implies at one and the same time that it is
true, and necessarily and reciprocally that it is free from social,
political or economic incursions into that truth. Thus it can avoid
the central problem: that psychiatry, as a social and political practice,
is constructed through social and political norms and cannot avoid being
such, and that the same is true of any alternative conception of, and
practice towards madness. There is no way in which any such practice
could avoid being so implicated; indeed it is just this that makes
psychiatry of political importance and makes the problem of constructing
socialist and feminist principles and objectives in this field so crucial.
It is the question of what such objectives might be that we now wish to
address and we shall do so by considering current debates about the
nature and possibility of a specifically feminist therapy.

FEMINIST THERAPIES

Flicking through the classified pages of *Time Out*, any Londoner is bound
to notice the bewildering array of techniques and activities which offer
release from psychic suffering, new levels of personal awareness and
understanding and, above all, the possibilities of 'growth'. Bio-
energetics, psychodrama, encounter groups, gestalt techniques, dance
therapies and many others are on offer. These are what are usually
known as the 'alternative' therapies; but alternative to what? One
might think that they are alternative to what is available within the
NHS, but there are two reasons why this is not so. Firstly, there are
other forms of therapy - classical psychoanalysis being the obvious
case - which are not attached to the NHS but would not be classed as
'alternative'. So 'alternative' here clearly has connotations, of an
'alternative culture', of something that challenges the *status quo*.
Secondly, many of these techniques *are* used within the NHS today in
both out-patient and in-patient settings. Many NHS hospitals run ward

'groups' and also offer activities which approximate to the alternative
therapies - psychodrama, encounter techniques, art and dance therapy.
It is a mistake to think that treatment in NHS hospitals is limited to
drugs and ECT.   It is, however, the case that these techniques are often
introduced by the more innovative doctors or that they are the province
of psychologists or occupational therapists.   Further, the supposed
point of the technique is sometimes explained to patients in a way that
physical treatments are not; and the doctor, psychologist of occupational
therapist usually participates actively.   However, their use in NHS
hospitals is incredibly haphazard and they are often clearly introduced
as a way of simply relieving institutional tedium.   There is certainly
no attempt to match particular types of activity to particular types of
disturbance.   It is rather a matter of keeping everyone 'occupied' and
quite how they are kept occupied is largely left to the discretion and
initiative of the staff on any particular ward or unit.   Thus there are
no means of evaluating what use or effects they might have; their conditions of implementation are far removed from their original rationale
and they occupy a limited and subservient position within the range of
therapeutic options.
    Are there then grounds for arguing that such therapies contain ele-
ments, principles or techniques which are somehow progressive?   In the
light of what we have argued so far, it is not surprising that advocates
of alternative therapies most frequently conceive of them in relation to
a critique of orthodox psychiatry in terms of its medical domination.
In particular, feminist therapy by and large accepts that medical treatments of mental distress are inappropriate as forms of therapy, although
it is sometimes acknowledged that certain drugs may be useful in times
of crisis.   Thus it is to the alternative techniques that feminist
therapy turns in order to utilise and modify them to its own ends.
    It is not surprising that feminists have been somewhat suspicious of
the standard left objection that the political advocacy of alternative
therapies focuses attention on the 'personal' to the exclusion of the
'political'.   Feminist therapists argue that therapy can be a fully
political practice.   In the discussion that follows, we shall concentrate on the recent book by Sheila Ernst and Lucy Goodison - *In Our Own
Hands*.[48]   Ernst and Goodison argue that the various alternative therapies
as well as the theories (though not the techniques) of psychoanalysis
can be adapted and put to use in the context of self-help groups in
order to bring about psychical changes which simply 'discussing problems'
or the practice of consciousness-raising cannot achieve.   They certainly
do not deny that consciousness-raising did bring about dramatic psychological changes for many women, but they consider that the way in which
women's experiences are constructed in contemporary society often runs
so deep and has such damaging features (emerging as 'symptoms' like
depression or anxiety) that the sharing of *conscious* experience can
only bring about partial changes.   They therefore refer, drawing somewhat metaphorically on Freud, to 'unconsciousness raising'.
    That this therapy can be done in self-help groups is central to the
argument which is concerned, firstly, with *democratising* therapy in the
sense of breaking down the distinction between 'expert' therapist and
ignorant patient.   For it is argued that the alternative therapies too
have their 'experts' and their forms of 'mystification':[49]

    Too often these theories, and especially the techniques, are
    inaccessible within the confines of privileged professions or

expensive training programmes. Demystifying them and making
them available to whoever is interested seems an important
contribution to the process of taking charge of our own
mental health.
The book is devoted to just this 'demystification'. The authors do not
deny that such demystification can take place in one-to-one therapy but
they clearly consider self-help groups to have a better chance of being
fully democratic. The second element in this is that participants in
the group must refrain from making 'interpretations' of what others do;
rather them must support and encourage each other to find out *for themselves* what their deepest feelings are and why they respond as they do.
Making interpretations assumes that one person knows best why another
is behaving or reacting as she is and that, it is argued, is authoritarian.
     As well as democratising therapy the book seeks to rid it of its
sexist bias and to push it in a distinctively feminist direction. It
is argued and it would be hard to dispute, that most therapies implicitly or explicitly seek to cure disturbed women by resolving psychical
difficulties in such a way that they will be content to return to or
enter a family situation. The goal of feminist therapy would be to
expose the psychical contradictions to which women are submitted in a
patriarchal society and thus open up possibilities of choice in respect
to how one lives one's life. Ernst and Goodison do not think that all
women have identical experiences but their emphasis on single-sex,
self-help groups indicates that they believe all women to have a considerable amount in common and that, for the most part, only women can
understand other women. This links to another point. Some approaches
to feminist therapy[50] consider that a major part of the therapist's job
is to *validate* the experience of the client by showing that environmental
factors forced her to act and feel as she did. Orthodox psychiatry, by
seeing acts as signs of sickness, and traditional psychoanalysis, by
making interpretations (which might tell the person that she is feeling
exactly the opposite of what she claims or expresses) constantly invalid-
ate people's experiences, and particularly the experiences of women.
This is a sort of reduced version of Laing; reduced because the environmental circumstances invoked are a lot more straightforward than Laing's
communication networks. This form of feminist therapy assumes a fairly
direct correspondence between environmental circumstances (either temporary or long-term) and psychical states. Ernst and Goodison do not
assume this in any simple way but there are obvious traces of it in
their writing. They often describe contradictions (for instance, between
the expectation that one be sweet and childlike and the demand that one
be a nurturer) which they believe are typical for women and are *reproduced* in women's psyches, both consciously and unconsciously, in a
limited range of ways. In our discussion we shall concentrate upon the
two basic aims of the book - to democratise therapy and to develop a
specifically feminist therapy. We shall see that the way in which these
arguments are posed exemplifies some of the general problems we have
already addressed in the politicisation of psychiatry.
     The assumption behind the argument that therapy can be democratised,
can be 'in our own hands', is that the theories and techniques involved
are fully accessible to anyone who wants to learn and only seem to be
specialised knowledge requiring a long training because it is in the
interests of the 'experts' to make it seem that way. But reading the

book it rapidly becomes clear that the authors themselves have had long
experience and training in different forms of therapy and both are practising therapists. To that extent, they are themselves experts and
this would seem to be unavoidable. They do present the ideas and techniques in a very clear way, but does this make them immediately accessible to anyone who wants to learn; available directly to those in
mental distress?

   The authors write:[51]

   Many people will read (this book) because they are deeply
   unhappy, confused, frustrated, depressed; suffer physical
   symptoms such as migraine; observe recurrent self-destructive
   patterns they cannot change; feel unable to take active control
   over their lives; experience their emotions as overwhelming or
   fear they have no emotions. The ending of an important relationship, the loss of a job, a birth or a death, eviction,
   racist attack, rape or a striving for greater self-understand-
   ing may be among the reasons pushing you towards therapy.

But the authors give very limited indication as to how those suffering
in particular ways within this vast range of difficulties are to tell
which of the techniques included within the text might be best suited
to each of these very diverse psychical and social conditions. Surely
this can only be done on the basis of consultation and advice from those
with accumulated experience and knowledge concerning the relationship
between particular problems, specific modes of therapy and prognosis.
Thus, as we have argued, some form of diagnosis is necessary in order
to identify who is and who is not likely to benefit from any particular
forms of therapy. And diagnoses imply the collection and accumulation
of knowledge, and its use in consultation by particular individuals.

   Further, the issue of really serious mental disturbance is almost
entirely avoided. Yet the kind of self-help group described requires
certain skills (listening to others, not interrupting, turn taking)
which severe depression, the schizophrenias, certain phobias and so
forth would definitely block. Hence attempts to impose group therapy
in acute wards in mental hospitals often ends in either indifference or
complete farce. Again, the crucial problems here are those of differential diagnosis and differentiated forms of treatment. Of course it
may be objected that self-help is appropriate for all but a very small
number of people; this is highly questionable, but even so it does not
avoid the problem of differentiation and the development of distinct
forms of treatment. Especially if one is not simply to wash one's hands
of severely distressed people in the way in which much orthodox psychiatry has done. In our view, such disorders will only be treatable
by intensive individual therapy with a committed *specialist*. The problem is not specialism as such, but the lack of specialists around,
especially within the NHS.

   Specialism implies the passage through intensive forms of training,
the induction into definite bodies of knowledge, the application of
techniques whose specific modes of action and rationale are therefore
not directly accessible to the patient. In addition, the theoretical
basis of some forms of therapy requires not only a discrepancy between
therapist and patient but also the maintenance of a certain distance
between them, and certain rights of interpretation attached to one and
denied the other, which might seem the antithesis of democracy. Psychoanalysis, the most intensive form of therapy available, is heavily

criticised for being authoritarian, mystifying and so forth for exactly
these reasons. There is, of course, nothing to prevent prospective ana-
lysands reading up a vast amount of the published material before making
any decisions. However, it is central to psychoanalytic treatment that
both the analyst and the analytic situation be 'strange' to the person
being analysed because much depends on the fantasies and ideas which she
or he weaves around them. The processes of transference and resistance
will always make psychoanalysis open to the charge of authoritarianism
by libertarians. But the 'non-democratic' nature of psychoanalytic
therapy can too easily be over-politicised, and assimilated to a general
critique of social organisation which ignores the specific nature and
function of the therapist-patient relationship and its theoretical and
practical function. To derive a critique of possible forms of therapy
from the general political doctrine of democratisation is to avoid the
real questions and problems of evaluation of forms of treatment.

So Ernst and Goodison make the argument that specialism can easily
be dispensed with too rapidly. The psyche is, no doubt, as complex a
system as the cardio-vascular system, yet it would surely be acknowledged
that specialised training and expertise would be required for cardiac
surgery. There is at least an argument to be had about the necessity
for equivalent forms of specialised training and expertise in those who
would seek to intervene into the structures of psychic life. This is
neither to say that this state of affairs exists in orthodox psychiatry
today, nor that there is not considerable scope for the generalisation
of competences in this field. It is, however, to argue that the political and organisational questions involved cannot be resolved purely by
references to the advantages of democratisation or the disadvantages
of expertise.

The crucial questions to ask concern the implications of different
forms of social organisation, regulation and evaluation of distinct
forms of treatment and therapy. Evidently we are not arguing that people
should be prevented from forming self-help groups. But we are asking
what kind of contribution such groups can make to the development of
innovative forms of therapeutic practice on a wider social scale. A
related point arises when it is asserted that feminist therapy in its
more organised form (for instance as exists at the Women's Therapy
Centre in London) should be state funded but not state controlled. Of
course, social regulation, state control and public funding do not
entail one another. Psychoanalysis is certainly socially regulated but
by institutions outside those of the state. Orthodox psychiatry, while
mostly publicly funded, is state regulated to only a limited degree,
having its own independent forms of regulation. Democratising psychiatry, in the sense of making it more accountable, would probably entail
more state regulation. But critical psychiatry and alternative therapies, despite their political intentions, have not yet begun to grapple
with the complex questions involved in the social organisation of
effective services in relation to mental distress.

THE POLITICS OF FEMINIST THERAPY

In what, then, does the claim of feminist therapy to be a fully *political*
practice consist? It revolves around the argument that personal and
psychical processes are themselves political, the product of political

conditions, having political functions. As we have said, Ernst and
Goodison do not take a simple 'environmentalist' approach to questions
of the psyche. Yet their position seems to be that a feminist understanding of social relations as *patriarchal* can explain a great deal of
the psychical complexes which are claimed to characterise women's experience. They attempt to marry this with a clear indication that there
exist processes *internal* to the psyche itself. This is perhaps clearest
in their chapter on dream analysis and 'guided fantasy'. Yet despite
the evident intra-psychic orientation of this chapter readers are
advised always to remember that the structures and contents of fantasies
take place within and are thus conditioned by male-dominated society.
More straightforwardly, they devote a lot of space to the examination
of psychic structures which are laid down in childhood, 'repressed',
and whose effects are intractable to current demands (even demands that
one be a 'proper' feminist). The aim of therapy would then be to gain
knowledge of these processes and the social pressures which produced
them initially in order that they be amenable to change. At each point
(be it in the present, past or future) an understanding of the factors
acting on the individual's experience as bound into patriarchal society
would make feminist therapy more valid and more liberating for women
than non-feminist therapy. And it is, of course, this way of conceptualising therapy that enables it to be designated a *political* activity.

   In an article which pre-dates the publication of *In Our Own Hands*,
Susan Lipshitz takes a critical view of feminist therapy and enters a
defence of psychoanalysis.[52] She understands feminist therapy to consist in the validation of women's experience and as having the goal of
'empowering' women. The analysis of society as patriarchal obviously
claims to show that women are denied access to power and an understanding of psychical powerlessness is then part of the process of breaking
the bonds of patriarchy. To summarise and simplify, Lipshitz argues
that the 'environmentalism' underlying feminist therapy means that
radically insufficient attention is paid to internal psychical processes. The Freudian concept of *fantasy*, and particularly unconscious
fantasy, demonstrates that the relationships between real events in a
person's life history and the meaning they take up in that person's
psychology are exceedingly tenuous, complex and unpredictable. Whole
areas of psychic life may bear no demonstrable relation to 'real events'
at all. The process of unravelling psychic reality, and of writing out
the 'symptoms' that may be stitched into it can, according to Lipshitz,
only be done within the psychoanalytic *transference relationship*, that
is, the relation which develops between analyst and analysand and in
which the analysand repeats his or her complex and diverse ways of
thinking about and relating to fantasy objects, which objects the
analyst will come to represent. Lipshitz argues further that bringing
political criteria to bear on therapy, for instance giving it the
explicit objective of empowering women as women, interferes with the
transference insofar as it blocks, interrupts and puts constraints upon
the free-flowing exploration of internal psychic reality. She states:[53]
'Feminist therapeutic activities ... raise the problematic issue of the
link between a political and a therapeutic practice, *a link which to my
mind is neither obvious nor necessary*. This article provoked an angry
response from the London Women's Therapy Centre.[54] Their letter made
two main points. Firstly, it argued that Lipshitz had drawn a caricature of feminist therapy which, rather than being a simple mix of

experience validation and 'assertion training', was in fact fully conver-
sant with questions of psychical reality, with psychoanalytic ideas and
with the concept of transference. Secondly, the letter took strong
objection to what was seen as the strict division drawn between 'the
social' and 'the psychical' such that Lipshitz appeared to be arguing
that psychical events occurred 'in a political vacuum'.

Now, given that the authors of *In Our Own Hands* are connected with
the London Women's Therapy Centre, it is clear that Lipshitz did have a
limited notion of what feminist therapy might be. In their conception,
feminist therapy *is* concerned with internal psychical processes and
does not reduce everything to simple reflections of environmental events.
And yet the particular conceptualisation of social relations as answering to a principle of patriarchy does place constraints on how psychical
reality is understood. Psychological phenomena have very limited autonomy from social ones, the two can always be linked together relatively
easily. It is interesting in this regard that Ernst and Goodison's
rendition of Freud turns psychoanalysis into a theory of *power* relations. Whether Freudian theory is right or wrong, power is patently
not its central object of investigation. What psychoanalysis does
demonstrate very convincingly is the complexity and richness of psychical
reality and its irreducibility to sociological questions. Additionally,
the failure of all 'social' explanations thus far to account for severe
mental disturbance, rather than being evidence in favour of biologism,
could be taken to support the *principles* of psychoanalytic reasoning
although it certainly says nothing about the validity of Freud's detailed
metapsychological theories.

Does this mean that Lipshitz is correct to separate 'the social' from
'the psychical' as her adversaries suggest she does? In point of fact,
this is not an explicit argument in the article, which is rather concerned to separate the political from the therapeutic. But the two
'separations' are evidently linked and a number of difficult problems
are at stake here. One is the status of the concept of patriarchy - a
concept which has the effect of understanding all social relations as
governed by a single *political* principle. This is an issue of continuing debate within feminism and we cannot deal with it here.[55] It is
clear that the terms in which one conceptualises the 'social' will have
an effect on how relations between it and the 'psychical' are understood.
If society is conceived as structured by patriarchy and if the principle
of personal politics is turned to the question of therapy, then we find
a variant of the traditional slogan - 'the personality is political'.
To the extent that Lipshitz is arguing against this then she could be
supported from a number of different positions and on many different
grounds.

The point which we would want to bring out most clearly in the context of the present argument is that no *general* relation can be said to
exist between psychic and social reality, the mechanisms that link them
are not all of a piece. Thus in respect to mental disturbance it can
be argued that some psychical states are linked to social conditions in
fairly uncomplicated ways. The work of Brown on depression in certain
groups of women is a case in point.[56] Now it can always be objected
that because appalling social conditions do not produce depression in
everyone, there must be more to it than this. This argument must have
some substance, but it does not follow that deep-seated dynamic reasons
lie ultimately or at the root of all psychological states. The extra-

ordinary psychological relief felt by many women in the mutual identification of experiences in consciousness-raising also shows this. We can
agree that there must be more to it than simple circumstance but in
respect to some experiences that 'more' is not very important, it certainly cannot be called the 'truth'. At the other end of the spectrum,
we would say that psychoanalysis has shown that some experiences or
psychical states are tied to social conditions by the most slender of
slender threads. This is as true of some 'normal' as of some 'pathological' states, and to make any sense of them one requires a Freudian
notion of the unconscious.[57] Between these two extremes and merging
into them are other ways in which social and psychical reality connect.
We could not possibly delinate them here and anyway the area is as yet
ill-understood. Let us be clear about what we are not saying. It is
not a question of some people having more complicated psyches than others;
rather that different registers of psychical reality, with different
types of connection to social conditions and to each other, exist in all
of us. So the opposition between the Women's Therapy Centre and Susan
Lipshitz constitutes a wrongly posed dichotomy. We take this to be the
implication of the latter's own reply to the correspondence, although
her correct distinction between therapeutic and political practice was
not unreasonably read as an attempt to sever all connections between
psychical and social relations.

  What are the implications of all this for the claim that there can
be a feminist therapy which is political? There is no question that the
techniques and theoretical orientations which constitute feminist therapy
will bring about psychical changes in the way women think about themselves as women and that this can be political inasmuch as it alters
understanding and activity in respect to power relations, including
personal power relations. But it is also clear, at least to us, that a
great deal pf psychical material will prove refractory to feminist
therapy insofar as its practice reflects its theory. We would suggest
that this is likely to be particularly so for severe mental disturbance.
To the extent that we are right, its status as a generally applicable
'therapy' is put in doubt. Even a socially widespread feminist therapy
would always, as the authors themselves appear to recognise, have to co-
exist with other and very different forms of therapeutic intervention.

  It has been suggested[58] that the women's movement has produced a
psychical revolution in its participants by changing them from 'feminine'
to 'feminist'. This is exactly what cannot happen, for persons are not
totalities in that sense. We have contested the idea that 'the personality is political' as much because we object to the idea of personality
as such as to the implied connection with social conditions. If 'feminine' and 'feminist' are taken to be internally coherent (if 'contradictory' in the first case) subjective structures, then both are fictions.
We have argued that there are important aspects of psychical reality
which concern a purely psychical space. The character of these for any
person has a strong element of singularity. By referring most of psychical life to 'patriarchy', feminist therapy must minimise these individual differences by making them secondary to a general sexual division.
Some of the aspects of psychical life we have been discussing cannot be
articulated to politics without making that term so elastic as to render
it meaningless. Thus one cannot derive from the general principles of
socialism or feminism what a progressive psychiatry or therapy would be.
This does not mean that there are no criteria for choosing between

different forms, rather that those criteria are of a different order than
can be read off from general political ideologies.

CONCLUSION

We have demonstrated a number of problems which exist within contemporary
critiques of psychiatry and the alternatives which are proposed. The
current criticisms of medicalisation, specialisation and clinical approaches to mental distress cannot be sustained; theoretically, historically and in terms of the construction of alternative principles and
policies they act as obstacles rather than as aids. We have implied
that a progressive *politics* of mental illness and mental health does
not need to depend upon any single *theory* of mental distress as its
support. Indeed any general theory of mental distress is a hindrance
to the development of such a politics since, as we have argued, mental
distress is far from homogenous in its nature, and in the place and
function of psychical processes and social conditions in its genesis.

Hence criticisms of existing practices and the elaboration of alternatives cannot be derived from the radical critiques we have discussed.
The determinants of existing practices are multiple and need assessing
in their own right; the consequences of the existing configuration of
theories, practices, agents and institutions operating in the field of
mental illness require detailed and specific examination and criticism.

We have not discussed in detail the specific treatments which are
utilised within orthodox psychiatry - drugs, electro-convulsive therapy,
psychosurgery, milieu management, behaviour modification, psychotherapy
and so forth - nor the radical criticisms of them. Suffice it to say
that in our view no single form of treatment can be ruled out on simple
doctrinal grounds; treatments must be assessed in terms of their conditions of application, the risks and side effects involved and evidence
as to their therapeutic success. In these terms some of these treatments have a claim to utility for particular conditions (e.g. some
drugs, behaviour modification); the effects of others appear only to be
damaging (e.g. psychosurgery). We would argue that no single form of
therapy or set of therapeutic or exploratory principles will ever be
appropriate to the range of distress which individuals suffer. Given
the different weight of biological, psychological and social factors involved in the genesis and construction of mental distress, there is no
reason why some therapeutic intervention should not be entirely concentrated upon the suffering individual, others at the reconstruction of
social practices and social relations. The need is certainly for increasing the availability of more and different forms of treatment, but just
because of this, for the utilisation of clinical approaches in the
collection and evaluation of evidence as to the efficacy of different
modes of treatment for particular conditions.

Similarly, with regard to the questions of asylums and institutionalisation. One should not confuse criticisms of the internal organisation,
conditions, treatment and rights of patients within existing forms of
institutional provision with an argument against institutionalisation
per se. Given the levels of distress, disturbance and self destruction
involved, the variability of support available from friends and family,
and the intensity of surveillance required in cases of severe mental
distress, in our view some forms of residential provision with professional

and continuous staffing will continue to be a necessity. Any progressive strategy will require residential facilities to take their place within a range of provision from such in patient treatment, through day centres and sheltered housing, to home support.

It has not been our intention in this article to enter an unqualified defence of existing psychiatric practices or of the role and function of the medical profession in relation to mental distress. It has merely been our aim to show that things are not so simple as the critics of medicine and psychiatry would have us believe, and that critical evaluation must be carried out in other terms. It should be noted in this respect however that strategies which base their hope for therapeutic success upon a total reconstruction of social relations are misguided. Not only is any eventual prospect of such a reconstruction scant hope for individuals whose suffering is located firmly in the present, and who wish help now rather than in some distant future, but also such theories are predicated upon an illusion. Whilst the forms, nature, categorisation, expectations and social responses to personal distress are subject to social and political transformation, madness will not be eliminated under socialism. Hence a politics of psychiatry must address itself to the question of the evaluation and transformation of the social organisation of madness. Progressive politics has to begin from present conditions of social reality, evaluate them with regard to the efficacy of distinct social responses to madness, the notions of cure they display, the relations of power that exist within them, systems of control and accountability, rights of those involved to safeguards and appeal and so forth. Only through such an examination can we hope to develop a politics which will operate upon those conditions in order to transform them in a progressive direction.[59]

NOTES AND REFERENCES

* We would like to acknowledge the advice and help, and comments on a rough first draft, which we have received from Mark Cousins, Barry Hindess, Paul Hirst and Dan Smith.

1 Estimates derived from Department of Health and Social Security, *Health and Personal Social Services Statistics*, HMSO, 1980; Royal Commission on the National Health Service, Cmnd 7615, HMSO, 1979. Anthony Clare summarises much data in *Psychiatry in Dissent*, Tavistock, 1980, pp.392-413.
2 These surveys are summarised and discussed in David Goldberg and Peter Huxley, *Mental Illness in the Community*, Tavistock, 1980. There is considerable variation between studies, and the significance and implications of results are open to debate. In particular we do not wish, at this point, to imply any judgment on the nature and validity of diagnosis, or any direction of causality between psychological and somatic complaints.
3 We discuss in particular David Ingleby (ed.), *Critical Psychiatry*, Penguin, 1981, and Sheila Ernst and Lucy Goodison, *In Our Own Hands*, Women's Press, 1981. Other recent texts arguing related positions are Peter Conrad and Joseph Schneider, *Deviance: From Badness to Sickness*, St. Louis, Mosby, 1980; Peter Schrag and Diane Divoky, *The Myth of the Hyperactive Child*, Penguin, 1981; Geoff Baruch and Andy

Treacher, *Psychiatry Observed*, Routledge and Kegan Paul, 1978. We also consider aspects of the key 'historical' account for recent criticisms of psychiatry, Andrew Scull, *Museums of Madness*, Allen Lane, 1979.

4 This approach is exemplified in the work and publications of MIND, the National Association for Mental Health; see *MIND's Evidence to the Royal Commission on the NHS*, MIND, 1977. We discuss this strategy in our forthcoming article mentioned above. At this point we shall emphasise that in our view such a strategy is not wrong, only partial. We would not criticise the valuable work and lobbying which organisations such as MIND undertake.

5 See for example J. Hoenig and M.H. Hamilton, *The De-Segregation of the Mentally Ill*, Routledge and Kegan Paul, 1969.

6 See Kathleen James, *A History of the Mental Health Services*, Routledge and Kegan Paul, 1972, Chapters 13 and 14.

7 Andrew Scull, *Decarceration*, New Jersey, Prentice Hall, 1977; Roger Matthews, 'Decarceration and the fiscal crisis', in Bob Fine *et al* (ed.), *Capitalism and the Rule of Law*, Hutchinson, 1979.

8 Basaglia has a chapter in *Critical Psychiatry*, *op.cit.*, note 3; see also his article 'Problems of law and psychiatry: the Italian experience', *International Journal of Law and Psychiatry* 3, 1980.

9 See Lesley Doyal, *The Political Economy of Health*, Pluto, 1979; Joyce Leeson and Judith Grey, *Women and Medicine*, Tavistock, 1978.

10 See R.D. Laing, *The Divided Self*, Penguin, 1965; R.D. Laing and A. Esterson, *Sanity, Madness and the Family*, Penguin, 1964. Laing's position changed substantially after 1968; we do not discuss these changes here. The best criticisms of Laing are in Clare, *op cit* note 1; Peter Sedgwick, 'R.D. Laing: Self, symptom and society', in R. Boyers and R. Orrill (eds.), *Laing and Anti-Psychiatry*, Penguin, 1974; Paul Hirst and Penny Woolley, *Social Relations and Human Attributes*, Tavistock, 1981; Jeff Coulter, *Approaches to Insanity*, Martin Robertson, 1973.

11 Szazs's ideas are repeated in a vast number of texts; see for example *The Myth of Mental Illness*, Paladin, 1972; *The Manufacture of Madness*, Paladin, 1973; *Ideology and Insanity*, Penguin, 1974. Good criticisms can be found in Clare and Hirst and Woolley, referenced above, note 10; Peter Sedgwick, 'Illness - mental and otherwise', *The Hastings Centre*, 1, 3, 19-40.

12 See Erving Goodman, *Asylums*, Penguin, 1968; *Stigma*, Penguin, 1968' Thomas Scheff, *Being Mentally Ill*, Chicago, Aldine, 1966. For criticisms see Clare, and Hirst and Woolley, cited above, note 10.

13 See *Critical Psychiatry*, *op.cit.*, note 3.

14 *ibid.*, p.143.

15 *ibid.*, p.143.

16 Phyllis Chessler, *Women and Madness*, Allen Lane, 1974; Dorothy Smith and Sara David (eds.), *Women Look at Psychiatry*, Vancouver, Press Gang, 1975; Ernst and Goodison, *op.cit.*, note 3.

17 John Wing, *Reasoning about Madness*, Oxford University Press, 1978; Clare, *op.cit.*, note 1.

18 Wing, *op.cit.*, note 17, p.17, emphasis added.

19 It should be pointed out that Wing's position is more sophisticated than might appear from this brief account. He does not argue that every form of psychic distress is amenable to a disease theory, but thinks that most will be. Some depressions and anxieties are, others

are not and should be treated non-medically; schizophrenia can usefully be treated as a disease but hysteria cannot. He recognises
the role of social factors in production of mental distress, arguing
that the more important such factors are in any case, the less useful are disease theories and medical treatment. He differentiates
between illness as a social attribution and illness as the product
of an organic malfunction and recognises that frequently those categories are discrepant. And he considers many of the points concerning the clinical utility of diagnosis which we discuss later in
relation to Clare. *But* he maintains that diagnoses are only appropriate where a scientifically testable disease theory links particular and differentiable clusters of symptoms to specific underlying
biological abnormalities. He is thus highly critical of the medicalisation and pathologisation of all forms of distress and deviance,
as for instance in the use of psychiatry in the Soviet Union, and
argues that the best safeguard against such abuses is the limit
imposed by the use of disease theories as he had outlined them.
Not quite the crude and imperialistic medical entrepreneur of
critical psychiatry's dreams.

20 In Ingleby, *op.cit.*, note 3.
21 *ibid.*, p.33.
22 Not even critical psychiatry denies that *some* mental and behavioural
    disturbances do have identifiable physical causes - for example
    'General paralysis of the insane' - personality changes, uncontrol-
    lability, impulsiveness, grandiosity and serious mental deteriora-
    tion - is accepted as being caused by the syphilitic spirochaete.
    But, argues critical psychiatry, doctors used such specific and
    atypical cases as ammunication in their unwarranted attempt to argue
    that this was the case for all mental distress. However, as soon as
    this exception is admitted, the attempt to establish a basic onto-
    logical distinction between the natural and human realms must
    collapse.
23 *op.cit.*, p.23.
24 The argument deployed by Jeff Coulter, *op.cit.*, note 10, are better
    made but still unconvincing. Clare, *op.cit.*, note 1, has a good
    discussion of the arguments and evidence.
25 In Ingleby, *op.cit.*, note 3, p.137. Here they follow Illich's argu-
    ment in *Limits to Medicine*, Penguin, 1977, which now is virtually
    accepted wisdom in the new left - see, for example, the texts cited
    in note 9.
26 See Michel Foucault, *The Birth of the Clinic*, Tavistock, 1973. The
    arguments of left critics of medicine are discussed in more detail
    in an unpublished paper by one of us: Nikolas Rose, A note on demands
    for democratisation in the health services, March 1979.
27 *op.cit.*, p.40. Ingleby does not seem to realise the paradox pro-
    duced by his simple acceptance of the notion of rationality in this
    context - if he were to do so it could strike at the heart of the
    neo-ethnomethodological 'project' which he espouses.
28 See, for example, the references by Sedgwick and Hirst and Woolley
    cited in note 11.
29 *op.cit.*, note 1.
30 Treacher and Baruch, in Ingleby, *op.cit.*, note 3, p.122.
31 See Foucault, *op.cit.*, note 26.

32 This is our term rather than Clare's, and we use it to characterise the rationale which underpins the explicit arguments made concerning aetiology, diagnosis, treatment and organisation in psychiatry. Clare himself uses the notion of the medical model to designate any approach in which scientific methods of observation, description and differentiation are employed, first of all characterising and seeking to ameliorate symptoms, then attempting to identify aetiology and pathogenesis and developing rational and specific treatment. Biological, dynamic, social and behavioural orientation merely, for Clare, represent different emphasis *within* such a medical model. *op.cit.*, note 1, pp.69-71.

33 Clare cites the evidence on diagnostic agreement on pp.129ff.

34 This discussion raises two questions which we will not deal with here. One is the notion of symptom itself, as that entity upon which diagnosis depends, the means of its recognition and classification and its links with that which it supposedly is a symptom of. The second is the notion of 'cure', and the ways in which the effectiveness of treatments are assessed within different conceptions of the nature and causes of mental distress and the role of therapy.

35 Studies would suggest that the specific choice of drug (e.g. from within the group of phenothiazines) depends more on the doctor or hospital involved, and on changes in prescribing fashion, than on presenting symptoms.

36 Coulter, *op.cit.*, note 10, Chapter 1.

37 The usual practice in Britain is to diagnose schizophrenia given the presence of a *single* 'first rank' symptom: thought disorder, disturbance of volition and the self, delusions, hallucinations, emotional disturbance. These symptoms are very diverse and it would be misleading to regard first rank symptoms taken together as a syndrome. They do not regularly co-occur and any one of them might last a short time or for life.

38 The key text for this account is Scull, *op.cit.*, note 3. Cf. also Treacher and Baruch, *op.cit.*, note 30. Szasz's arguments, in the historical sections of the texts cited in note 11, are similar.

39 See Michel Foucault, *Madness and Civilisation* especially Chapter 6. The best account of the history of madness in England remains unpublished: Michael Donnolly, Perceptions of Lunacy in Early Nineteenth Century Britain, Ph.D. thesis, University of London, 1976. Hirst and Woolley, *op.cit.*, note 10, gives a clear account of Foucault's argument.

40 Quoted in Foucault, *ibid.*, p.245.

41 Cogent theoretical and methodological criticisms of Scull are made by Jeffrey Minson, *Sociological Review*, 28, 1, February 1980.

42 Conrad's contribution to Ingleby, *op.cit.*, note 3, is a good example, but almost all papers in the book use the concept, as do most radical texts on social questions.

43 The apotheosis of this tendency was the radical criminology of the early 1970s, e.g. Ian Taylor, Paul Walton and Jock Young, *The New Criminology*, Routledge and Kegan Paul, 1973. Whilst it is less prevalent in criminology today, its theoretical premises have not been challenged and it continues to function in radical writing on social welfare.

44 Many of the points which follow in this section are dependent on
    arguments put forward by Paul Hirst and Penny Woolley in their
    recent book, *op.cit.*, note 10.
45 See, for example, George Rosen, *Madness in Society*, University of
    Chicago Press, 1968.
46 This is not to deny that people claiming to be witches exist today,
    but the meaning of witchcraft and its social role and function have
    radically changed. For a useful discussion of some of these ques-
    tions, see the papers collected in Bryan R. Wilson (ed.), *Rationality*,
    Blackwell, 1970.
47 See, for example, W. Kiev, *Transcultural Psychiatry*
48 *op.cit.*, note 3.
49 *ibid.*, p.1.
50 See, for example, the papers by Alison Griffith, Rita MacDonald,
    and Sara David in Smith and David, *op.cit.*, note 16.
51 *op.cit.*, p.2.
52 Susan Lipshitz, 'The personal is political': the problem of feminist
    therapy, *m/f*, 2, 221-31, 1978, our emphasis.
53 *ibid.*, p.22.
54 See correspondence in *m/f*, 3, 1979.
55 It should be clear that we have strong reservations about the con-
    cept. See Mark Cousins, 'Material Arguments and Feminism, *m/f*, 2,
    62-70, 1978; Diana Adlam, 'The case against capitalist patriarchy',
    m/f, 3, 83-102.
56 G.W. Brown and T. Harris, *Social Origins of Depression*, Tavistock,
    1978.
57 Ernst and Goodison imply that all unconscious structures and
    fantasies can be made conscious, hence their stress on 'unconscious-
    ness raising'. This is in contradiction of psychoanalytic theory,
    where the means of knowing the unconscious are varied and where it
    is never a case of raising the unconscious through re-inserting its
    contents into consciousness, but rather of restructuring it.
58 See Eva Eberhart, Kerry Hamilton and Sheila McKechnie, 'Amen', *Red
    Rag*, August 1980, 7-11.
59 These cryptic remarks will be elaborated in our forthcoming article,
    which deals in detail with strategies to transform the social
    organisation of mental illness.

Diana Adlam, Paul Hirst, Phil Jones, Chris Nawrat
The SDP, Space for Radical Change?
An Interview with Sue Slipman

Q: *If we can start by saying that we don't regard the interview as an interrogation of the Social Democratic Party by the true socialists. We are going to leave on one side many of the arguments made by members of the Labour Party or the Communist Party against the SDP. What we are concerned with is what possibilities you see for continuing your own kind of politics and why you see the SDP as a vehicle for that kind of politics. Now if I can start with a general question. You caused some considerable surprise by leaving the Communist Party and joining the SDP. Many people, left, right and centre, would see this at the very least as an unusual move. Why did you leave the CP and then go on to join the SDP, and what do you think the SDP offers to your particular kind of politics?*

SS: Those two questions are quite closely related. First of all on leaving the CP. I left the CP because it refused to change its practice of politics to correspond to its theory of politics, and in three specific areas. First of all the concept of the broad democratic alliance which seemed to me to be the most important development within the British Road to Socialism and that involved a turning away from the idea of revolution as a seizure of power by force and a turning towards social change through alliances. Such alliances would be forged over major questions of democracy and democratic development. The second thing that was important about what the CP was developing was the idea of pluralism. Pluralism is part of the broad democratic alliance and implies, across the political spectrum, a respect for philosophies and human development. Such pluralism has been outside of the traditional remit of socialism. I regard those things not just as tokenism, necessary to be part of an alliance, which allows us both to learn from the other philosophies and politics and to change our own accordingly in response to them. This could get us over the problem that Communist parties have confronted elsewhere in Europe, and that is the historic compromise and historic blocks between political forces. Those I think are the two major areas of the Communist Party's policy and theory that I identified with and still do. The BDA was in complete contradiction with the then 'left alternative' strategies, and the idea of a broad

democratic alliance and pluralism is in complete opposition to the idea
of left unity and a left government, a strategy based on the left alone.
The contradiction that the CP could not come to terms with was between
its democratised theory and its still Stalinist practice. The CP like
many other left groups wants the trappings of democracy without the
real practice of democracy, and that is a very big problem. So I left
the CP for that reason.

I joined the SDP partly for that reason but for many other complicated reasons too. The SDP is a potential 'centre' to a potential future
broad democratic alliance. The bit that is missing in order to bring
together the broad democratic alliance is a coherent left. That coherent left does not exist at the moment, nor is it going to emerge over
the next few years. If it were capable of emerging the left would have
responded rather differently to the SDP. And so, whilst there are a
huge number of problems for the SDP there are a number of things that
it can achieve and that it certainly does offer. One is that in alliance with the Liberal Party it can present a coherent if not complete
alternative to the present mould of British politics. Within that proportional representation is probably the most important strand. But
what it can do is to open the possibility of putting into practice the
broad democratic alliance in an appropriate political form. I think
that does have to happen through proportional representation.

Q: *Normally CP dissidents who get alienated by Stalinist practice in the
CP end up in the Labour Party. I think it would be useful if you outline why you decided not to join the Labour Party and, given your commitment to things like proportional representation, you could equally have
decided to join the Liberal Party which has long supported proportional
representation. They also unlike the SDP already have a grass-roots
organisation and some commitment to community politics. Could you
comment on that and explain why you think the SDP is going to offer
something that neither Labour nor Liberals have offered.*

SS: First of all, why not join the Labour Party? The current battles
that are going on within the Labour Party are the result of historic
blocks between the left and the right inside the Labour Party. Much of
the politics of each of those blocks is a mirror image of its opponent.
That presents us with a very big problem because that particular battle
is no longer the sort of battle that needs to be fought. That battle
is predicated on a concept of 'the working class' - held by the Labour
left in particular - that is outdated and prefeminist and has very
little to offer. That is not just a problem of the Labour Party; it is
a problem for the entire labour movement. The left cannot confront its
total inability to be strategic about politics because of its own obsession with class blocks which are no longer relevant to the vast
majority of people. In one sense the battles that are going on inside
the Labour Party are an absurd version of some of the battles that were
going on inside the Communist Party and without the added advantages of
the strategic responses that the Communist Party was attempting in
some of its theoretical work. So I had no interest whatsoever in joining the Labour Party and because there is no strategic centre in the
Labour Party then it is not possible for people like me to be anything
other than contained inside the Labour Party. The reason for not joining the Liberal Party? It's certainly not disrespect for the real

achievements of the Liberal Party. David Steel represents many of the
strengths of 'Liberal' politics, but I do not think that he is totally
representative of the Liberal Party. If anything he is much closer
strategically to social democracy than he is to some traditional ideas
of Liberalism. The real reason for not joining the Liberal Party is
that the Liberal Party alone is not going to achieve the sort of
alliances that would be necessary to shift historic blocks politically.

Q: *You mentioned the Labour Party as being pre-feminist. One of the
other things dissident Communist women do is decide to leave the
Communist Party and devote all their energy to the Women's Movement.
You have made reference in your public statements about the relationship between feminism and the SDP. Could you explain that?*

SS: I have not said that there is a direct link between the SDP and
feminism; that makes it much too much of a conscious link. That is not
the case at all. There will be, as there is in every institution, a
large number of anti-feminists and some of that may well become embodied in structures. But there is in the SDP an opening of space for
feminists if not necessarily as members then at least in terms of the
policy discussions. One of the problems with the traditional labour
movement and labour movement organisation and their pre-feminist history
is that what they have managed to do over the past few years particularly with a very active feminist movement is to add women's demands to the
list of demands the working class have. In times of stress and crisis
those demands simply fall off the end of the list. In fact because
these demands are simply papered over others they cover up what essentially remains an anti-woman ethic within the institutional fabric of and
the politics of the labour movement. Now the SDP won't have that in
terms of its history and it will have to be committed to positive discrimination in favour of women within its structure and within its
institutions. That is not feminist, but that is certainly an opening
of space for women in a way that there hasn't been in political parties
before. Secondly, some of the areas that are going to have to be dealt
with by the SDP in policy terms, which the conservative (with a small
'c') blocks of the labour movement aren't capable of doing at this
stage, are areas of economic policy in response to technological change
and economic crisis which will involve considering some very radical
ideas that can only benefit women, things like part-time working, work
sharing. All these areas are about freeing men from full-time work,
making possible commitments to play a role within child care and thereby challenging men. Now that is going to happen despite the SDP and
also with quite a lot of opposition to the conscious politics of feminism, but it does seem to me that a space exists there for radical policies which will bring to women far more power over their own lives than
actually do exist through the more traditional political parties.

Q: *The kind of issues that you raised in your review of the Stacey &
Price book in the* Guardian *suggest that in order to gain those demands
there does seem to have to be some kind of relationship between the
political forces and among the unions. Isn't that a problem?*

SS: That is not a problem just for the SDP. It is a problem for everyone on the left. It is a problem for all feminists and it is a problem

for all socialists and it is certainly a problem for the SDP because of
course the established response of the unions to the SDP has been to
set themselves against it. Labour movement institutions are going to
find it difficult if this political force, this centre force, can come
to the fore and become a viable alternative. It is going to be very
difficult for unions to hold their own members *and* maintain the myths
they currently have. It is, for example, complete nonsense for the
unions to have the close relationship with the Labour Party they do.
Everyone in the unions knows that at least 40% of their membership
votes Tory and certainly did at the last election. Therefore to affili-
ate your entire membership to the Labour Party is a complete nonsense.
The demand for a new political form of pluralism, changes in democratic
thinking, and in popular attitudes means that the unions are going to
have to pay heed to new political conditions. What they ought to be
doing for their memberships is negotiating with government across the
political spectrum on behalf of their members and that means them coming
to terms with the fact that their memberships have changed and no
longer have the same political aspirations. Moreover, women now form
a considerable part of the trade union movement and the unions have got
to be put in a position where they seriously start talking about their
demands and recognising that means the ending of privilege amongst men
as workers. The SDP is not necessarily going to achieve that but
because of the space it can open up elsewhere it will actually strengthen the arguments that feminists are attempting to make about some of
those things.

Q: *One of the things that runs through everything you say is this catch-
word 'space'. When you talked about the Labour Party you said 'I could-
n't join the Labour Party because I knew I would be contained'. So in
a sense you are almost physically breaking the barriers getting out.
That immediately throws up the question 'why do you want any party at
all?'*

SS: We don't exist as a society of individuals. We do in fact have a
very firm institutional basis within the society and many of those institutions are absolutely essential and will remain so. To begin to
have an impact on those institutions and change them it is necessary to
be part of some coherent political force and in one sense that gets us
back to the old debate about the relationships between movement and
political autonomy and leadership and where you see the role for leadership within political change. Now I do see quite a strong role for
leadership, in a very non-Leninist sense, and leadership for me is
about facing people with political choices. You need a fairly coherent
political force to begin to effect and raise those choices for people.
That is why a political party is necessary. But my views on political
parties have changed. There is a crucial form of leadership that needs
to be developed, and that is leadership across the political spectrum.
Leadership for a broad democratic alliance needs to be a broad democratic leadership. It's not going to be one political party and that
means therefore that there are roles for people who are either involved
in single issue politics or movement politics such as the Women's
Movement and people who are involved in political parties. Leadership
is going to come from an interchange between those people but you cannot

discount or throw off political parties, because they are still very fundamental areas where power is exercised in our society.

Q: *Can you say something about the nature of your critique of left politics and how that led you into the SDP. How does your view differ from other criticisms of left political style, like Beyond the Fragments? Is there not a danger of a new form of elitism in your position?*

SS: Well, in fact, part of the problem with the left is precisely a brand of elitism. I'm going back to NUS debates, debates of the early '70s where I came in. We were debating our idea of democracy in the early '70s and what it meant. And we came up with the theory, largely as a result of the '68 mass participation, that democracy was democracy when people participated. It was not a stone's throw from there to get into a position which much of the left has adopted and particularly the labour movement left, which is that if people don't participate it is their fault and they have disenfranchised themselves. Now, the disastrous part of that politics is that if you go along that channel and you lose more and more popular support and become more and more embedded within your own strategies because they are not in a vibrant relationship with a mass movement, then you quickly become part of an elitist politics which really is contemptuous of the mass of people, which basically says that they have no political rights because they've thrown them away. Now it seems to me that that is basically where the left is now, and it is sectarian to the n'th degree. So the critique of the left is that the left has abdicated its possibility for being the catalyst which is in vibrant contact with vast numbers of people, and there is a problem about the left's idea of participatory democracy as well. I am now at the stage where I am more interested in out-reach work and engaging people, re-engaging them in political structures where that's possible to do so. You need to end first of all the historic block that we're in with politics to be able to do that. I don't really have the answers or even really many glimmerings of what they might be when you get beyond that, but there are things within our grasp about changing the constitutional fabric, about creating the idea of pluralist political leadership at more and more local levels, which will make it more meaningful for people to fight the struggle around their own demands at fairly local levels which are accessible to them. The problem and the contradiction at this stage of politics is that all of those who are political animals are trapped within elitism, the SDP and the Liberals and everyone else included within that. But by breaking that block, and that involves working through people who are still trapped within it, you will open up some of those problems, to something else that comes after that. I happen to believe that to effect the things that I want to effect, the left needs to be changed. That is going to be absolutely essential because the left is a very crucial part of that broad domestic alliance. It's not the major part, but it's an absolutely crucial part of it if the alliance is to span that political spectrum and if the alliance is to be capable of areas of radical thinking. I despair of that happening now. What we're seeing in the left is that when people have been confronted with a series of choices to make a radical break from their history, to do what they say is their life task, which is a revolutionary task of being able to relate and identify with political and social change, to be a fish amongst people, they resist and instead

they're a kind of whaling boat at the moment. I don't see how that's
going to change. One of the only ways it's going to change, in fact,
is by defeat being inflicted on the left from the outside. The left,
from its internal structures, is not going to rethink itself. That for
me was the crucial thing about the SDP. The left was doing its normal
bloody trick of pouring scorn upon a valid political development. Even
if you believe in the broad democratic alliance as the strategic way
forward, you've got to see the emergence of a coherent centre as a crucial and good part of that development. The left was not doing that, it
was doing its 'this is evil strike it down' business, and it seemed to
me to be very crucial that people who were identified with the left
managed to get that development taken seriously. No where that gets us
in terms of the left I don't know, I don't know how the left is going to
respond. But what will really shake the left up is if we are able to
win proportional representation and if the left then wants a popular
power base it is going to have to respond to people and changes within
its constituency. So that is what I am hoping will happen. I also know
that for that to happen there has to be a really coherent grouping of
people within that left in all the political parties grasping whatever
space can be created elsewhere. My criticism of some of the people I
identify with most closely politically in the left is that they run for
cover over the SDP, they haven't stuck their head over the trenches and
fought for the level of democratic politics that we have got to fight
for to make realignment on the left even a remote possibility. In other
words I'd accuse a lot of my political allies of incredible cowardice,
if not complete political blindness.

Beyond the Fragments? At the time it seemed to me that Beyond the
Fragments was a really very serious and quite humble attempt to grapple
with all of the problems that I felt so passionately and was so despair-
ing about on the left. The problem with Beyond the Fragments is that
what the left really do is a kind of Mia Culpa socialism is dead, long
live socialism, without recognising that if you are saying that then
you have to really begin to look at what we mean by socialism. We know
that socialism as a concept is a failure in every possible way. So are
we saying that we are still socialists or are we trying to say well let
us look at the social form that we think is going to be the forerunner
of the kind of democratic and vibrant political society we want to live
in. Beyond the Fragments has not been capable of throwing that off.
My other big criticism of Beyond the Fragments, having attended the
conference, was that it remained almost entirely within patriarchal concepts of socialism and was not capable of coming to terms with the fact
that women were saying socialism is dead precisely because it has not
confronted and been changed by feminism.

Q: *I can see the political advantages of a successful SDP in terms of
proportional representation opening up political space, breaking the
two-party system etc. but at the moment the SDP is conducting itself in
the way other political parties do. For example, its concentration on
the media and the ballot box. All the perspectives that you offer don't
seem to be actually included in the way the SDP is practising politics
at the moment. How would you answer that?*

SS: The SDP has a dynamic relationship to a consistuency which most
other political parties no longer have. Now that dynamic relationship

can develop in a number of ways. It will have the ability to create
policies which will address themselves to where people are, even in
terms of popular prejudices. Let's take an example, disarmament. We
are very rapidly seeing the development on the left of the idea that
unless you are pro-unilateralist you are not in favour of disarmament.
Now it seems to me that if the Soviet Union goes into Poland we are
going to see a massive damaging of the disarmament position and we are
going to see a strengthening of the nuclear warriors. Now what the SDP
can do in that particular context, partly because it's got a commitment
to NATO, is to situate a debate about disarmament in a practical political context. Actual disarmament demands a credible politics. Now there
is a possibility of doing that within the SDP because of the worlds it
begins to bridge politically. I'd far rather be in that debate that
still standing on the cliff-tops screaming at people about unilateral
disarmament or whatever and ignoring the strategic questions of real
politics and of major questions. So the sort of fight that I'll be
engaged in in the SDP is to take some of the positions which are based
largely on prejudice and to try and tie them up with openings for explorations of alternative politics.

Q: *Can we bring you back to something you said a little while ago,*
which is you said socialism as a concept is a failure. Now obviously
to a large number of people on the left that would count as an out-
rageous statement. To the editorial board and readers of Politics &
Power *it would be a statement that at least needs explaining, because*
one of the things Politics & Power *has committed itself to is rethinking*
the concept of socialism, but within a socialist commitment. I think
many of the readers would feel that yes in many ways socialism has
failed, not so much as a concept but as a political movement. But
social democracy has failed no less disastrously both as a concept and
as a political movement. I wonder if you could explain exactly what
you mean about socialism and why you think the banner of social demo-
cracy in a sense is a better starting point for that kind of rethinking.

SS: First of all I don't accept that social democracy has failed as a
practice as much as socialism has. You only have to ask yourself the
question, would you rather be living in Britain or the Soviet Union?
There is only one answer to that which is I'd rather be living in
Britain because whatever else it does it gives me and it gives everybody, or those of us who at least are privileged enough to have full
time jobs or whatever, a level of individual freedom and collective
freedoms and political freedoms which are never present in most of the
socialist societies. So social democracy has not been as great a failure partly because not so much was vested in it as we expected to gain
from socialism. The despair at the practice of socialism is very great
indeed. So I'm going to turn the question round really and say that if
you're trying to rethink socialism in a socialist framework what on
earth do you mean by socialist framework? Do you mean a socialist
economy? If so, what kind of model do you mean for that? And it seems
to me that where socialist practice is leading has led traditionally
and is certainly leading in all of the parties that call themselves
socialist is towards a centralism that has authoritarian overtones.
Now if you are talking about a greater and fairer sharing of and democratic planning of the distribution of resources, then that comes

somewhere between traditional socialism and traditional social democracy.
Socialism has failed as a concept partly because it's not capable of
looking at that fairer distribution of resources until it comes to
terms with feminism and that is a breaking point for some of the authoritarian ideas about planning. I'm not sure if you then call that socialism or social democracy. I don't think it matters what you call it, but
it is something that is other than both. The social form that it gives
rise to will not be characterised in the classic term socialism within
a classic socialist framework, but if social democracy is going to be at
all capable of grappling with the problems we face then it is going to
have to be an awful lot more radical than the social democracy that we
have seen in Britain and elsewhere. One of the reasons why social democracy offers something at this stage is because that polarisation of
class forces has been mitigated by a whole range of new developments in
the working class and elsewhere.

Q: *Can you expand on what you meant when you introduced feminism there?
The implication of the things that you said about feminism, what you
thought positive in Beyond the Fragments, was basically that the structures developed by the women's movement or the breaking down of authoritarian structures as developed by the women's movement. But there are
at the same time whole areas of policy in feminism that have been much
more advanced than the rest, interventions within law and social policy
for example. So could you elaborate on this.*

SS: Yes, one of the problems about traditional socialism is that it is
largely based on patriarchal policy forms, and there is a clear relationship between structures and policies. Policies about the sharing
and the distribution of resources at the point of production have very
little to do with the problem of reproduction and with experience of
people within that sphere, that is with women. You need to begin to
develop a political structure that is capable of addressing itself to
those problems and producing those policies. The women's movement has
not solved that problem either. There's an awful lot of problems of
sectarianism within the women's movement itself in relation to women
as a concept rather than feminism as a concept. Feminists, nevertheless,
have gone beyond traditional socialists in terms of policy developments
about the sharing out of resources. What feminism has posed is that
there are choices about where resources get distributed. What socialism
has traditionally done is work on the list system, that everyone will
have a share in wealth when it's created. The list system is simply,
socially and politically irresponsible. Feminism has got beyond that
to look at the fact that if you are going to share out resources you
have to look at compensating those who are disadvantaged and discriminated against. And you have to look at taking away the privileges of
those who have had those privileges up until this point in time. So
feminism has a much better chance of grappling with a real politics
than socialism, because socialist policies remain very abstract.

Q: *Well we might agree with that but what's it got to do with the
Social Democratic Party?*

SS: What it's got to do with the Social Democratic Party is that some
of those debates have to emerge into practical politics if there is to

be any alternative force that can resolve some of the economic problems
we have. For example, it is perfectly possible that the Social Democratic Party-Liberal alliance can begin to solve things like the problem of
low pay. This would be over a period of time and involve a redistribution of wealth which will tackle the question of equal pay. Such an
initiative would break the immobilism of the labour movement on this
issue. Now those forms of radical policies are going to involve radical
changes in the way that we organise work itself. The labour movement
and traditional Labour Parties are no more able to grapple with that.
They are conservative - with a small 'c' - and therefore increasingly
reactionary towards new and radical policies. There is a possibility of
some of the policies that feminists have developed and policies that will
be needed to restructure the world of work. And this is merely to
grapple with coming realities of new technology and developments within
our society that have dynamics of their own regardless of any political
process.

Q: *I think you are being a bit harsh on the labour movement. Haven't
some unions tried to tackle these issues?*

SS: The answer to that is no they haven't. What they have done has
been largely cosmetic. The unions are at this stage incapable of
grappling with those problems, and whilst they put those policies forward as a kind of ideological statement, when it comes down to it the
practice of trade unionism is a complete denial of those policies.
Unions are organised around defending that which is, not restructuring.
I mean that's not just about women, it's about, for example, the whole
response of trades unions to cuts in public expenditure - which has
been a simple 'no', leading to a defensive oppositionism. As a result
of which the delivery point of services has been hurt to such an extent
that people are now turning more and more to private services. Even
quite ordinary people do not have the commitment to public services
that they once had. We've lost that battle. Now my line would be that
you have to grapple with that, you have to be the people who implement
cuts and you have to do it in such a way that you are restructuring and
streamlining services. That is an essential part in building the
political force and alliance able to defeat the right and to defeat the
present Tory government. Now we have not done that, and because we are
forever in a defensive stance. One of the problems is that it's not
so much that unions have too much power, rather they don't have enough
of the right kind of power. Part of the reason for that is their relationship to the Labour Party, a relationship which leaves 'politics' up
to political parties and therefore leaves unions remaining defensive
and reactive on every issue. And when you've got that astrategic def-
ensiveness, it is not possible to change. It should be emphasised,
though, that the problems lie deep. The infrastructure of employment
is such that women are an imposition on it rather than part of it, when
you are in economic recession, and the inevitable starts to happen, then
women will fall by the wayside. And that infrastructure works whatever
the conscious political commitment of members in such a way that the
relegation of women's issues becomes inevitable.

Q: *Can we take up a point which relates to the strengths of social democracy, and it follows on from what you've said, which is that two of*

the strengths of social democracy traditionally have been its commit-
ment to full employment and its commitment to a welfare state based on
universally distributed benefits. Now both of these strengths have
depended on action of the central government. Traditionally in macro
economic policies of demand management for the maintenance of full
employment, and in the welfare state sector in attempting to provide a
uniform state-financed service. A lot of what you've said has concen-
trated on talking about individuals and groups making decisions about
resources. One of the problems that follows from this is that it is
very difficult for individuals and groups to make the macro economic
policy decisions; central government has to make them. Secondly, if
you let people make decisions about the allocation of resources in the
welfare sector you are likely to get unevenness, which undercuts one
of the fundamental strengths of social democracy, which is its commit-
ment to universalism. Now what would you say about that?

SS: The commitment to universalism is being challenged anyway by quite
dynamic processes elsewhere. Full employment, moreover, now begs a
whole range of other questions which are about what *kind* of employment
and that seems a much more exciting political question. Much more related to the way that people live their lives, who they are, and what
their identities are than employment in the world of production has
traditionally been. There are a whole range of very interesting things
that can happen, part time work and the role of new technology in society are very much part of that. So universalism *is* being undermined.
But the problem of what happens when you start giving people responsibility for their choices is of course a very difficult one and it's hopefully one that socialism will have to face if it's not to be a totally
centralised development. The role of government then is not to impose
but it is to encourage and advise, to fill in gaps. A positive measure
will be the development of local taxation and then there will be a
great deal more control over resources at local level. That is probably
the only way we will engage people in politics at the local level.
There is still obviously a role for the state in compensating for and
in attempting to maintain a more even level and standard of distribution
of resources. Now how you balance that one out is incredibly difficult
and there will therefore be a whole range of areas in which the state
plays a role which is an encouraging role. The state could have a very
large role to play in terms of enforcing quota systems for women as a
policy. If it looked at government contracts before they were given
out and made it part of that contract policy that no firm got a contract
unless it accepted a whole range of policies. The state could play a
big role in leadership and in defining frameworks and structures.
Within such frameworks you open up a lot for space for people to take
their own decisions. Now I suppose you then have to weight up what
the imbalances are and where they are. That's a process that I fore-
see as a problem, but as yet I have very little idea how and where
that's going to emerge.

Q: *Can we ask you to follow up the last question. A good example of*
the issue in question is the recent debate over the continued existence
of ILEA. It wasn't a central government issue but a Greater London
issue. What do you think about the way that debate was resolved,
because it was all about if you break up ILEA then you're going to
have unevenness of resources?

SS: Ah no I don't think that that's the case at all. I certainly don't
think that that debate has been resolved. The debate that was going on
inside the overall debate was that the Labour leaders in ILEA were saying
this is not a question of democracy it's a question of resources. Now
where the Tories got their strength, and particularly the Wandsworth
Tories, was precisely that people feel the ILEA is an obstructive decision-making body that does not involve them in any way and that does not
present them with a choice. Now, another area of that debate, and in
fact it came from a Tory originally on the working party that first
looked at the ILEA, was the suggestion that the ILEA should continue as
an organisation but that its decision-making structures be brought much
more to a local level. Direct elections to the ILEA were seen as part
of the process of opening it up. Now it seems that it is perfectly
possible to have collectivisation of resources plus access to more direct forms of democracy. Where I completely distrusted and completely
disagreed with the Labour leaders was that they didn't see democracy as
a problem. Of course they didn't because they had control over the ILEA.
In fact parents in London *did* see ILEA as a problem. We are increasingly
going to have big problems with congolmerates of power like that. The
GLC, given its current policies, is likely to create the issue of whether
or not people in London are prepared to accept its very existence. When
you've got areas that are collectivised for the sharing out of resources
you have to be scrupulous about democracy and you have to keep realign-
ing them to be closely in tune with what people want, because otherwise
people aren't prepared to support them. The whole thing about ILEA was
that we won that particular round, we might not win a next round. It
ought to have been the left that was leading the campaign for the democratisation of ILEA. Without such positive initiatives we simply end up
throwing people into the arms of the right time and time again. I accept
totally all of the things about the need to collectivise resources and
that means needing to look at things like regional planning forms to
determine how to share resources but yet still maintain democratic
control.

Q: *To move onto a set of questions about electoral politics. Earlier
when explaining why you joined the SDP you gave a variety of answers.
One you didn't give but was implied in what you said is that parties
are necessary because they are the institutions that organise mass democracy and they are inescapable in a mass democratic system. And so,
political success implies some degree of electoral success. This is
an area where there are some quite serious questions about the Social
Democratic Party. Now, the first question is based on the assumption
that the Social Democratic Party is going to be successful electorally.
If an SDP-Liberal Party electoral coalition was far more successful in
the next general election than the Liberals on their own have been it's
quite likely that no party will have a majority of votes. The question
then is what prospects do you think there are for coalition politics
and particularly how would you conceive the political process of
negotiating a coalition with the Labour Party?*

SS: This is all very complicated of course. That is one of the options
of what happens next time. There are of course two basic options depending on the strength of the SDP-Liberal vote and what happens to the
other two major parties. If it is with the Labour Party that there is

to be a coalition then it seems to me that the price of that, the minimum price, is a referendum on proportional representation. Now, you
would then obviously have problems negotiating policies with that particular brand of coalition. The most optimistic option would be an
alliance with a Labour Party to form a coalition government. Whether or
not the Labour Party as it will then be is capable of coming into a coalition is another matter; this depends on the nature of its manifesto,
the degree of mandation of that manifesto, what happens within the constituencies, and what happens also in the infighting within the left
and the battle between the left and right. The other option would then
be an alliance with the Conservatives. We are possibly going to have
to face the fact that maybe the best that can be achieved by the next
election is a Conservative government where monetarism has disappeared
and where the option of getting rid of Thatcher is a possibility. It
may well not be possible to do that either depending on the strength
that you have. None of that is going to depend on the SDP-Liberal
alliance alone. It will also depend on the processes that are going on
within the other major parties by that stage. It does seem that there
is a possibility within the next few years that Thatcherism will be
weakened within the Conservative Party. But that is all conjecture.
Those seem to be the options available and the SDP-Liberal alliance is
going to have to take on board the possibility of *either* one of those
options if it manages to successfully gain enough seats to hold sway
within a hung parliament.

Q: *Yet there is an alternative possibility as well isn't there, which
was sketched out by Peter Kellner amongst others in the* New Statesman.
*He argues that it's quite possible that what'll happen is not an SDP
alliance with the Labour Party or SDP alliance with the Conservative
Party following on fragmentation of the party system. What you'll get
instead is a process whereby a strengthened Labour Party is installed
into power as the leading party. The argument is a very simple one,
it's that most commentators have made the mistake in looking at the
SDP's political prospects in identifying its electoral prospects with
its ideological critique of the Labour Party and therefore they assume
that most of the votes it will get will be taken from the Labour Party.
That tends to ignore the regional distribution of votes and voting in
constituencies in this country, which has produced a fairly solid block
for the Labour Party across the north and in a number of inner city
areas and which has also produced another regional quirk, which is the
strength of the Liberal Party in the Highlands and Islands, the Borders
and the West Country. That explains how the Liberals are able to get
at least fourteen seats, despite having broad appeal across the
country. Now the SDP doesn't so far have that regional concentration
but if it's likely to get it it's likely to get it in the South East
and possibly in the number of marginal constituencies that the Labour
Party currently holds, but also in a number of marginal constituencies
that the Conservatives hold. That could therefore lead to a situation
where a Labour Party is installed into power with the opposition divided between the Conservatives and the Liberals and SDP. In which case
your analysis is right, that the left within the Labour Party is much
stronger, because of the role of activists within the Labour Party, and
the SDP is that much weaker because it has no place whatever for
activists. That means that what you are effectively doing with the*

formation of the SDP is creating a situation of what it would call a
left Labour dictatorship.

SS: God the tortuous logic of that is wonderful. You mean someone
other than the Labour Party will be responsible for the authoritarianism
within the Labour Party. I accept that that's a possibility, but it
seems to me to be the worst of all possible options. My fear of what
will happen in that particular instance is that the Labour left will
represent a fraction of the electorate, it will represent not enough
political support for the policies that would then be carried through.
It will represent a whole range of regional variations, quirks, and
people not being able to vote strategically for example. I don't
believe that will be a representation of what people actually want.
Now in that context you have a potential for disaster. It could end
up being very frightening because of the political forces that emerge
in response to leftish government, and where people feel driven in
a response to a left wing authoritarianism and that would be a very
dangerous possibility. In that case it is even more crucial that there
is a safety net, that there is an alternative before people turn to
right wing authoritarianism. And for that reason alone if for no other
then the SDP-Liberal alliance is much to be welcomed.

Q: *Can we ask another question which is related to your answer. You*
said that what you are concerned with doing is creating a safety net
between two hostile dangers, one's a danger of left authoritarianism
and one's a danger of right authoritarianism. Now taking the latter
first, do you think that is a really serious prospect or could you per-
haps be conflating the existence of authoritarian populist attitudes
amongst the population, which have been known to exist for a very long
time, with actual policy developments which con't seem to go along the
sale direction at all and which there seems to be little likelihood of
developing. Secondly, with left authoritarianism, isn't there a danger
that what you're doing is that in focusing on some of the aspirations
and attitudes struck by some of the Trotskyist elements in the Labour
Party that you are underestimating some of the anti-authoritarian trends
on the Labour left at the moment? Such as the concern with participat-
ory democracy that is part of the general debate in the Labour Party at
the moment, which also informs the debate about democratising the
Labour Party itself.

SS: Well the answer to that is yes. I think there is a problem of conflating those things. I have been more dramatic than I actually feel
about it to emphasise the point. But starting with right-wing authoritarianism, it does seem to me that the development of a peculiarly British
kind of neo-fascism is there. It's very diffuse but certainly it is
there in a very military working class outlook that is now completely
cynical about the options of both left and right. The fact that there
is not yet a political force that can coordinate that outlook and bring
it from its diffuseness into sharp political focus doesn't seem to me to
be the most important point right now. The fact is that it's there and
capable of mobilisation, and is going to grow as race conflict grows.
It's not necessarily going to be as dramatic as that, but racism does
seem to me to give a cutting edge to right-wing authoritarian populism.
In considering left authoritarianism, the problems with those debates

inside the Labour Party is that when participatory forms are being discussed participation is still trapped in where we were in 1972, as an
activist participation. And it seems to me that until it is recognised
that there are forms of participation which are populist and popular
then you can't overcome some of the historical blocks to change in our
society. I don't believe for one second that the majority of the left
and the Labour Party are consciously setting out to create authoritarian
forms, but they are trapped in historical contradictions and really the
only way to break out of those contradictions is to stop situating the
party as the only answer and begin situating the political party as part
of the process of achieving answers through some form of alliances.
Until that's done the danger of the authoritarianism that both wings,
left and right, contain cannot actually be removed.

Q: *A crucial question arises from your earlier remarks. If your statement socialism is a disaster is outrageous to our readership, equally
outrageous is the statement that you would be prepared for the SDP to
form an alliance with the Conservatives. So obviously you are prepared
to think the unthinkable, but how far are you prepared to go in the
unthinkable? You supposed that Thatcherism was weakened but would you
actually think it was possible that the SDP and the Liberal Party would
form an alliance with a Thatcherite Conservative Party? Even if the
SDP got its minimum price of a referendum on PR, you know full well that
then the Labour and Conservative Parties would campaign against you and
given their access to the media and the tradition of innate conservatism
with a small 'c' of the British public, as we saw over the EEC referendum,
you are likely to lose it.*

SS: For a start I don't think that one would be likely to get any form
of proportional representation from a Thatcherite Conservative government. It's a non-starter. So it would not be possible to have an
alliance with a Thatcherite government. The price of that would be containment and there is no possible way that that would happen. But it
is perfectly possible to have a form of alliance with a 'met' Tory
government, which would not be the same kind of alliance as would be
possible with the Liberals, but there would have to be a potential for
a minimum programme of economic reconstruction. It would be possible
to have a kind of alliance within a coalition with a Heath style government for example. The reason that people will feel shocked about that
is because there is an idea that somehow the left has a strategy which
will be brought on from the wings and is going to 'regenerate' the
economy of Britain. You have to work with what is, and grapple with
actual economic and social problems now to open up potential future
answers. If you disdain doing that then you're not very serious about
the process of economic 'regeneration'.

Q: *Nothing the 'wets' have produced, nothing the Liberal Party has produced, nothing the Social Democratic Party has produced has in any way
come to terms with the very hard economic decisions that have to be
made given the place of Britain in the international economy. We are
faced with the potential wholesale collapse of British industry as a
result of five years of Thatcher policies and that at the end of those
five years there will be no choice but to have some state-directed
'alternative economic strategy', whether it be Bennite, Healeyite or*

*whatever. The Labour Party is the only party which is capable of pur-
suing national macro economic policies of a kind that have any chance
of success. A number of aspects of the AES have been strongly criticised in the pages of our journal; nevertheless it seems to us to be
disastrously cavalier to dismiss a Labour-directed AES. There is
nothing else.*

SS: OK, and I don't dismiss some elements of the alternative economic
strategy, which any government is going to have to take some of them
on board. Where I dismiss the alternative economic strategy is that it
has now become a set of abstract principles which bear little relationship to its possibility as a popular political strategy and economic
strategy. Let's take an example. It seems perfectly possible that you
could win sections of the population for temporary import controls in
various sectors of industry, but there's no way of keeping those people
unless you can give them something as consumers which is a better
British product. You're not going to buy space for the British economy
unless that economy gets some of its real problems of production and
its products sorted out. The role of government within that programme
is twofold; it is not just to lay down the framework by imposition, it
is also to look at the infrastructure of relations in British industry
which inhibit the production of better British goods, and that means
taking up a whole range of other areas of policy. So, whilst I recognise the statements you made about the alternative economic strategy
being the one attempt really to grapple with macro economic politics,
there are so many things missing from it. The AES is based on an out-
moded world view, it isn't really based on a serious look at Britain's
decline as an economic power, nor is it based on a look at Britain in
terms of its relationship to both Europe and to the developing world.
Where the government has a big role to play is in beginning to create
that awareness and in beginning to smash erroneous ideas about growth
which are at the base of the alternative economic strategy. Such ideas
are inherent in the AES, on maintaining a high rate of growth, increasing standards of living. We must have a government that is prepared to
grapple with the problems, not just in terms of resolving the problems
of economic growth and reducing unemployment, but also with some of the
real areas of concern that have developed about technologies and alternative technologies, emphasised in the arguments of conservationists
about what *sort* of growth and what *sort* of economic development we are
going to have. Nowhere does the alternative economic strategy deal with
those questions. The AES is based on institutions as they exist and
existing economic aspirations, rather than escaping from the immobilism
of those institutions. That isn't to say I discount all of the 'strategy', it seems to me that nearly all of its elements have some point of
interest and some point of relevance to what a reforming government
might eventually do, but the way that they are packaged together is
wrong in every way. The AES also leads to a style of strategy that is
inherently anti-democratic.

Q: *The point in favour of some version of the AES is that in a few
years time we may be faced with such a severe balance of payments
crisis and such a weakened position of Britain as an international
bargainer that the criticisms you're putting forward about what kinds
of growth, alternative structures, the transformations on the supply*

side, etc., while perfectly reasonable in conditions where there is more
space for manoeuvre, are not going to be viable in an urgent and immedi-
ate crisis. At least in its Healeyite version, the alternative economic
strategy for managing an immediate and inescapable crisis in which what
can be done quickly with existing institutions will have to be done.
And that is a form of political realism that it seems to us the politi-
cal programme and practice of the Social Democratic Party has come
nowhere near to taking on board.

SS: It's not as if the AES has been put forward as a kind of seige
measure; it's actually been put forward as the saving of Britain. It's
been put forward as the left's great opening to a future transition of
our society. In a crunch then many of those things may well have to be
done and we will have to accept them as impositions maybe. However,
that is not going to get us one iota nearer to the kind of society I
want to live in. That seems to me to be the very real problem with the
AES; it is not a visionary strategy, it is a politically brutal strategy.
I am interested in the point before we get to that stage and if it is
possible to earn the space to manoeuvre for other kinds of policies that
create a safety net against having to take those measures then that's
what I am interested in doing now. It seems to me that the biggest
block against doing that is the left and its immobilism, and the labour
movement and its immobilism, because they seem to think that the strategy consists in a vision of the society of the future. It may in the
end come to implementing the AES, in which case the left will undoubtedly do an 'I told you so', but that would seem to me to be a complete
tragedy.

Q: *Can we round off this discussion of the AES by commenting that some*
of the left views on the AES as you characterise them, but that there
is an important strand in thinking on the AES represented by the Cambridge
Economic Policy group and by the 'new' Healey which do not have those
defects. Both make it quite clear that the AES is not the vision of
the new society; it's a holding operation.

SS: Yes, but like all the other holding operations the product of a
'crisis mentality'. It is just as important, and maybe even more important, not just to think about what we do in a crisis, but how the way
we tackle that crisis is going to link through to what we eventually
want to see. How we are going to implement an alternative economic
strategy in such a way that it leaves a space to manoeuvre afterwards
to get ourselves out of the worst excesses that it may well bring
politically. That point is the one that isn't being tackled and never
is.

Q: *A final question. At the beginning you said that when you took*
the step of joining the SDP some of those people you classified as your
allies on the left were hostile; not only were they unsympathetic but
they accused you of being a traitor. You accused them of being cowardly,
of keeping their heads down to avoid unpopularity. A series of ques-
tions - why do you think they were so hostile? Why do you think that
very few people have followed you and you got the reception you did,
that caused you at all to rethink the step that you took?

SS: I think the real reason that people were completely freaked out had
more to do with the symbolism of left identity than the reality of left
identity, because most of the people I know are in despair about the left
and have been through real emotional, not to say psychological, let alone
political problems about everything that's happened on the left.   I think
however and I felt it too than when you give up your public claim to that
left credibility you're doing a number of things.   One is that you are
cutting yourself loose from a whole range of moorings in institutions
which is fairly frightening, given what you may then have to confront
politically - and I think people feel that.   Secondly, people have used
the kinds of arguments about individual personalities in the SDP to criticise it, but in fact if you've been in the Communist Party you could
also swap long lists of individual personalities who actually horrify
you in terms of their politics, and that's true of just about any other
political party.   What people have been doing has been actually refusing
to face up to the debates that we have actually started through some of
those discussions about strategy in the left and to look at the implications of some of those debates.   I'm now getting a bit perturbed by
people continuing to refuse to grapple with those problems.   What I've
said to people is not that I expect them to join the SDP, because in
terms of my politics that's a nonsense, because I'm not saying the SDP
is a solution.   What I am saying to people is stay where you are and
grab whatever political space this development can give to you to implement the kind of politics you want to see and to stop yourself being
contained by the immobilism of the left.   What I genuinely hope will
happen is that people will begin to realign themselves on the left in
response to potential democratic changes elsewhere in a way that can
have an impact upon the left as a whole.   The fact that I don't think
that is going to happen is the reason that I joined the SDP.   I don't
think the left is capable in its structural institutional form of doing
that, and that's it really.

Q: *Did it make you think again, have you had any regrets?   Did the fact
that you got the hostile reception make you think again?*

SS: Well, like most other human beings I don't thrive on hostility and
I have not exactly enjoyed the past few months, but actually it's been
quite confirming really.   What is beginning to happen now is that I'm
getting phone calls from all kinds of people who say how much they want
to have a political discussion about things they think are really important.   That's happening even where people disagree with the conclusions
I've come to.   I don't mind people disagreeing with the conclusions I've
come to providing they're interested in the process of that debate.
And it seems to me that that is now what is happening and I think
that's made me quite glad that I've actually done it.

GAY LEFT

A Gay Socialist Journal

Number 10

Democracy, Socialism &

Sexual Politics

GAY LEFT RATES

Inland	£1.00 each
Overseas Airmail	£1.50 or $3 (Sterling, US or Canadian cheques only)

Back issues are also available

GAY LEFT BOOK

HOMOSEXUALITY
Power and Politics

Edited by
Gay Left Collective

CONTENTS

Allison and Busby

38 CHALCOT RD. LONDON NW1

Chantal Mouffe
Democracy and the New Right

'The tide is turning' declares Milton Friedman in the conclusion of his
new book *Free to Choose*, whose main themes were also presented in a
television series shown during ten weeks in Britain and in the USA.
The whole operation very clearly had the objective of contributing to
the transformation of public opinion, particularly in relation to the
welfare state, announced by Friedman. According to him, after several
decades of government intervention in all fields of social life and the
failure of Western governments to achieve their proclaimed objectives,
the people are beginning to recognize the dangers of an overgoverned
society and the threat to human freedom represented by the concentration
of power in the hands of the bureaucracy. This widespread reaction
against 'big government' is causing the defeat of social-democratic
parties and policies in many countries and is contributing to the
emergence of a new climate of opinion clearly at odds with the ideas of
Fabian socialism and New Deal liberalism which had been dominant for
the last fifty years.
   Very few people will deny today that the advanced capitalist countries
are in crisis. There is indeed a surprising agreement among marxists,
conservatives and liberals about the existence of such a crisis. The
diagnosis might be different but (except for the orthodox marxist who
always believes that we have at last arrived at the moment of the final
economic crisis of capitalism) the other analyses: crisis of the state
(Poulantzas), crisis of legitimation (Habermas), cultural crisis (Bell),
crisis of democracy (Huntington), are all pointing out, despite their
differences, a basic common feature: a lack of correspondence in advanced
capitalist societies between their political and their economic structures. That lack of fit is the result of an overload of demands that the
state cannot absorb without creating inflation and jeopardizing the
profitability of capitalist enterprises. The interventionist state of
the last decades is therefore faced today with a dilemma that Claus Offe
presents in the following way:

> The capitalist state suffers from an overload of demands and
> requirements which it cannot satisfy without destroying the
> capitalist nature of the economy nor ignore without undermining
> its own institutional set up and the regulation of class conflict
> provided by it.[1]

Politics & Power Four

It is that conflict between the twin imperatives of accumulation and
legitimation which according to James O'Connor[2] are the two basic and
often contradictory functions that the capitalist state must try to
fulfil, that are at the root of the 'ungovernability' of Western democracies today. This conflict, intensified by the impact of the economic
recession, is destroying the fragile basis of the dominant ideology of
liberal democracy through which the post-war consensus had been cemented.
In *The Life and Times of Liberal Democracy* C.B. Macpherson has analysed
the slow processes through which, since the early 19th century, the
articulation between liberalism and democracy took place, whose aim was
to reconcile the moral principles which constituted the attraction of
the democratic ideal with the realities of a class-divided bourgeois
society. That long and complicated transformation, whose motor was the
class struggle (the aspect not sufficiently stressed by Macpherson), by
which the liberal state is going to be democratized and democracy
liberalized, culminates in the 20th century with the 'equilibrium model'
first formulated in 1941 by Schumpeter in *Capitalism, Socialism and
Democracy* and later developed by Dahl and the pluralist school.

The many critiques of 'democratic elitism' have been quick to point
to the impoverishment that such a theory imposes on the notion of democracy by defining it as mere competition between elites.[3] But such a
conception of democracy, which postulated not the real participation of
the masses but their passivity, was necessary for the capitalist system
to work. And it did work during the subsequent decades in the context
of the post-war economic recovery while the state was intervening along
Keynesian lines to maintain full employment and to ensure economic
growth. Indeed, in 1960 Daniel Bell ventured to announce 'The End of
Ideology' and the beginning of a new era in which pragmatism will dominate in the field of social reforms and no space would be left for the
rhetorics of revolution.

Nevertheless, the book had only just been published when the civil
rights movement in the USA and a bit later the student revolt worldwide
completely contradicted those hasty predictions. Since then the development and multiplication of the new antagonisms created by the growing
intervention of the state at all levels of social reproduction in conjunction with the economic recession have led to that overload of
demands which has provoked 'the crisis of democracy' diagnosed by the
experts of the Trilateral Commission. For them the present crises
renders manifest the dangers inherent to the functioning of the democratic system itself, in which political parties tend to promise too
much in order to win votes, and they declare that the only solution is
a reduction in the level of expectations and in the political participation of the masses.

We are in fact witnessing today a crisis of liberal-democracy which
puts into question the profoundly contradictory character of an ideology
which has tried to articulate two opposite principles. We agree with
Alan Wolfe when, after defining 'liberalism' as an ideology designed to
create, protect and promote the market system and all that goes along
with it and 'democracy' as a political ideal which combines the principle
of social equality with political participation, he concludes: 'The
predicament of liberal democracy is that liberalism denies the logic of
democracy and democracy denies the logic of liberalism, but neither can
exist without the other.'[4] In a period of expansion such a contradiction could be more or less managed and the potential antagonisms

neutralized, but the time has come when it has become necessary to dissociate the ideal of liberalism from the dangers of democracy. Huntington in his report for the Trilateral Commission is quite open about that need and specifies that in order to protect the achievements of American liberalism it is today necessary for the liberals to turn to conservatism. It is indeed in the arsenal of conservative thought that liberalism will find the arms that it needs to get rid of, or at least to neutralize, its cumbersome partner by undermining the two pillars on which lay the ideal of democracy: social equality and political participation.

FROM LIBERAL DEMOCRACY TO LIBERAL CONSERVATISM

What is at stake is a reorganisation of the dominant ideology whose objective is to transform the ideological parameters of advanced capitalist societies in order to adapt them to the new social and political strategy called for by the crisis and to create a new common sense among the masses better suited for the hard times that await them. That reorganisation is taking place through a redefinition of the existing elements of the dominant discourse and through an articulation of the fundamental themes of liberalism with especially selected conservative themes so as to form a new ensemble that we can call 'Liberal Conservatism'. In the process of emergence and elaboration of that new ideology we can distinguish three main ideological sources: the neo-liberals, the neo-conservatives and the new right. The labels are rather imprecise and not always accepted by the individuals involved, but are useful to differentiate three movements whose theses and orientations are in many respects specific and even sometimes opposed, but which provide the dominant themes which are being articulated in a new problematic.

The neo-liberals

The first exigency is to redefine *liberalism* which, because of its association with democracy, has acquired several dangerous radical connotations. Here the main inspiration is provided by the neo-liberal school of the social market theory. That group was created in the 1940s as a reaction to the rise of communism and fascism, and its international membership has been organized around the journal *Ordo* and the Mont Pélerin Society.[5]
    One of its most influential figures is Friedrich Hayek, whose work has been particularly important in restating the principles of liberal political economy. According to Hayek, Liberalism is the doctrine which insists on the need to reduce to the minimum the coercive powers of the state in order to maximize the highest political end: liberty. By 'liberty' or 'freedom' (he uses the words interchangeably) Hayek understands 'the condition of men in which coercion of some by others is reduced as much as possible in society',[6] or more specifically as the condition 'in which a man is not subject to coercion by the arbitrary will of another or others'.[7] That is for him the real meaning of the term freedom and he calls it 'individual freedom' in order to distinguish it from the other definitions of the term. Two other meanings are indeed more frequent: freedom as 'the power to satisfy our wishes, or the choice of alternatives open to us' ('freedom as

power'), according to which poverty, lack of education, unemployment are
deprivations of freedom because they restrict the alternatives offered
to individuals. Another important meaning is freedom as 'the participation of men in the choice of their government, in the process of legislation, and in the control of administration' ('political freedom').
But Hayek declares that 'political freedom' is not a necessary component
of 'individual freedom' and needs to be distinguished from it, and that
'freedom as power' is a very dangerous conception that ought to be
resisted because it could lead to the justification of the unlimited
intervention of the state and therefore to the destruction of 'individual
freedom'. Now, this is precisely what liberalism is trying to avoid and
for that reason it is necessary to protect individual freedom from the
constraints of the state through the delimitation of a sphere completely
free from government interference.

Defined in that way, liberty refers of course in the first place to
economic liberty, i.e. a system of free enterprise regulated by the
market and in which government intervention should be strictly limited
to handling those matters 'which cannot be handed through the market at
all, or can be handled only at so great a cost that the use of political
channels may be preferable'.[8] Such a conception, which is at the core
of the social market economy, implies that the government should abandon
almost all its welfare and regulatory functions and limit itself to
secure stable money by controlling the money supply, and guarantee free
competition and the security of property and contract. In Keith Joseph's
words:

> Governments can help hold the ring, provide an infrastructure,
> maintain a stable currency, a framework of law, implementation
> of law and order, provision of a safety net, defence of property
> rights and all other rights involved in the economic process.[9]

According to the neo-liberals a free market economy is the necessary
(and, as it turns out, sufficient) condition to guarantee 'individual
freedom'. Their argument is that, as liberty is indivisible, it is not
possible 'to have political and spiritual liberty without also choosing
liberty in the economic field and rejecting the unfree collectivist
order'.[10]

In *Capitalism and Freedom* Milton Friedman has attempted to demonstrate
that a 'free private enterprise exchange economy' provides for a developed society the only form of social organisation that respected the
principle of individual liberty because it was the only kind of economic
system which was able to coordinate the economic activities of large
numbers of people without coercion. His argument consists of showing
that in a model of simple exchange between direct producers, exchange
only takes place when the two parties benefit from it, and is therefore
achieved without coercion. He thus moves on to the more complex model
of competitive capitalism and declares that:

> As in the (simple) model, so in the complex enterprise and
> money-exchange economy, co-operation is strictly individual and
> voluntary, provided: (a) that enterprises are private, so that
> the ultimate contracting parties are individuals and (b) that
> individuals are effectively free to enter or not enter into any
> particular exchange, so that every transaction is strictly
> voluntary.[11]

In a devastating critique of Friedman's argument Macpherson has proved
how his demonstration rests on an elementary conceptual error because he

does not take into account what distinguishes capitalist economy from
the simple exchange model: the existence of a group of individuals
without capital who are obliged to sell their labour power in the market
in order to survive. In consequence, argues Macpherson, Friedman's
attempted demonstration fails, because in the case of capitalism 'the
proviso that is required to make every transaction strictly voluntary
is *not* freedom not to enter into any *particular* exchange, but freedom
not to enter into any exchange *at all*'.[12]

In Hayek, the defence of free market capitalism results much more
from a critique of the consequences of state intervention than from an
apology for the positive effects of the 'invisible hand'. The protection
of individual freedom requires according to him a very strict limitation
of the coercive powers of the state which need to be grounded on the
'rule of Law'. By that Hayek does not mean 'a rule of Law, but a rule
concerning what the law ought to be'.[13] It is in fact a meta-legal
doctrine concerned with the attributes which laws should possess to be
'true' laws and which does not apply to all the functions of government
but only to the limitation of its coercive activities. He establishes
a sharp distinction between law and bureaucracy, and argues that the
state must be forced to respect a series of laws, and that the power of
the bureaucracy must be severely restricted so as to prevent it from
using the law to increase its power. This is because, once this
threshold has been crossed, there is no way to stop the attribution of
discretionary powers to the government, and the society enters on 'The
Road to Serfdom'. A collectivist system (by that he means any kind of
interventionist state including the New Deal and the welfare state), is
therefore always the first step towards totalitarianism and the destruction of individual freedom. There lies the fundamental reason for his
opposition to any kind of planning and his defence of the market as the
regulatory principle.

With respect to democracy, neither Hayek nor Friedman are opposed to
its existence in principle, but they are far from being committed to
its defence. As we have already indicated, political freedom is for
Hayek not a necessary component of individual freedom, and democracy
ought not to be considered as an end in itself because it should only
be considered as 'a means, a utilitarian device for safeguarding
internal peace and individual freedom'.[14] If it comes to the stage
where democracy is putting individual freedom in danger there is no
doubt that it is the latter that must be defended. And Friedman, who
establishes a distinction between authoritarian regimes (with economic
liberty but without democracy) and totalitarian regimes (without
economic liberty or democracy), declares bluntly that the first type
could be acceptable to a liberal in certain circumstances, while the
second type would never be.[15]

The neo-conservatives

Once liberalism has been restated in terms of the defence of free
enterprise and individual freedom, the next step is to redefine *democracy* in such a way as to neutralize its potential antagonism with the
existence of a capitalist order. That transformation is taking place
via a critique of the two main tenets of the democratic ideal as it is
formulated today: social equality and political participation.

Here the principal role is played by the theorists of the group that
is called in the USA the neo-conservatives. The intellectual origins of
this group are very different from those of the neo-liberals. It is
mainly composed of intellectuals and professors in prestigious universities who have moved from a left-liberal position towards a conservative
critique of American society. They are in general not hostile to the
welfare state, but they are very critical of the project of the 'great
society' which led in the 1960s to placing too much emphasis on welfare
and resulted in overloading the state and thus causing a crisis of
authority which is now threatening social stability. The neo-conservatives believe that it is the democratic system which is to a large extent
responsible for that overload of the state. The 1975 Trilateral
Commission *Report on the Governability of Democracies*, which expresses
many themes of neo-conservative thought, declares in its conclusion that

Quite apart from the substantive policy issues confronting
democratic governments, many specific problems have arisen
which seem to be an intrinsic part of the functioning of
democracy itself.[16]

Constant demands for increased social equality are singled out as one
of the main factors in the present crisis, because they have led American
society to the verge of the 'egalitarian precipice'.

What has happened since the 1960s is a double shift in the meaning of
equality: (1) a shift from equality of opportunity to equality of results;
(2) a shift from equality between individuals to equality between groups.
That 'new egalitarianism' threatens, according to Daniel Bell, the true
ideal of equality whose objective is not an 'equality of results' but a
'just meritocracy'.[17] As for Irving Kristol, he considers that an
egalitarian conception of equality goes against the natural order of
things because 'human talents and abilities ... distribute themselves
along a bell-shaped curve, with most people clustered around the middle,
and with much smaller percentages at the lower and higher ends', and he
affirms that American society is exemplary because both the distribution
of income and the distribution of political power follows that bell-
shaped curve.[18] We can see here very clearly how, behind the pretext
of re-stating the 'true' ideal of equality against the distortions of
egalitarianism, what is really at stake is the acceptance and justification of existing inequalities.

It is not enough, according to the neo-conservatives, to defuse the
subversive potential of the notion of equality; it is also necessary to
narrow the field of political participation. Zbigniew Brzezinski, when
he was the director of the Trilateral Commission, proposed to 'increasingly separate the political system from society and to begin to conceive of the two as separate entities'. The idea is to withdraw more
and more decisions from political control and to make them the exclusive
responsibility of the experts. Such a measure aims to depoliticicize
the more fundamental decisions not only in the economic field but also
in the social and political ones. This argument is based on the contention that government and democracy stand in opposition to each other
and that if complex industrial societies are going to function they
need, as Huntington puts it, 'a greater degree of moderation in democracy'.[19] For Brzezinski, such a society would be democratic 'in a
libertarian sense; democratic not in terms of exercising fundamental
choices concerning policy-making but in the sense of maintaining certain
areas of autonomy for individual self-expression'.[20] As Peter

Steinfelds has pointed out in an excellent study on the neo-conservatives:
> For the neo-conservative, democracy does not seem to mean much
> more than the Founding Fathers meant by a republic: a government
> deriving its powers ultimately from the consent of the people
> but exercising them through delegated representation operating
> within a constitutional framework that preserves the kind of
> liberties enumerated in the Bill of Rights.[21]

On this aspect neo-conservative thought meets one of the central themes of the neo-liberals, who have a profound distrust of politicians and political institutions, which they consider to be unable to secure the management of public affairs with the necessary competence and independence. They insist on the need to remove from democratic control the functions of government and to hand them to apolitical agencies. Such measures, in conjunction with the ones aimed to limit the field of intervention of government and to reinstate the regulatory role of the market, should relieve the state from the overload of demands from which it is suffering. By releasing its responsibility for major social questions, they would also help to undermine the dangerous conception which has become dominant with the growth of the welfare state, according to which the state is seen as the principal agent of social and economic progress with a direct responsibility for the realisation of social equality.

Both the neo-liberals and the neo-conservatives are critical of the notion of distributive justice, the former because it implies a conception of equality that they question, the latter because it would justify the attribution to the state of a series of coercive powers that they wish to reject. Besides, says Hayek, such a notion is absolutely unintelligible because we do not have any objective criteria to determine the moral merit of an individual and the material reward that should correspond to it. In consequence all decisions concerning the 'proper' reward are bound to be determined by the arbitrary will of a given government.[22] The opposition of the neo-conservatives to the notion of distributive justice explains their violent criticisms of the work of John Rawls, whom they consider to be one of the theorists of the 'new egalitarianism'. According to Frankel we find in *A Theory of Justice* the fundamental premise of this position when Rawls asserts that the character of a man 'depends in large part upon fortunate family and social circumstances for which he can claim no credit'. And he argues that such a conception has to be rejected because
> A theory of justice which treats the individual as not an active
> participant in the determination of his fate, and which is guided
> by the model of life as a lottery, is unlikely to strengthen
> people's sense of personal responsibility.[23]

Friedman declares that 'fair shares for all' is the modern slogan that has replaced Karl Marx's 'To each according to his needs, from each according to his ability'.[24]

The New Right

The same attack on the idea of equality takes place on the other side of the Atlantic in the writings of the group which in France is called 'La nouvelle droite'. The movement is organized around a centre of the study of European civilization (G.R.E.C.E.), two journals, *Eléments* and

La Nouvelle Ecole, and a publishing house, 'Les Editions Copernic'.   It
has close contacts with the Club de l'Horloge, a grouping of higher
French civil servants and technocrats, and since 1977 has won an audience
of half a million readers with the emergence of *Le Figaro* magazine under
the editorship of Louis Pauwels, one of their open supporters, who
brought with him the leading theoretician of the group, Alain de Benoist.
    The French New Right is much more radical than the neo-conservatives
in their critique of the 'egalitarian utopia' which they see as causing
the death of Western civilization by destroying every type of diversity
in society.   Reproducing one of the main themes of 1968, they proclaim
the 'right to the difference' and assert that difference = inequality =
liberty, while equality = identity = totalitarianism.   Alain de Benoist
declares:

> I call *on the right* the attitude which consists in considering
> the *diversity* of the world and, therefore, the relative inequal-
> ities which are its necessary product, as good, and the increasing
> homogenization of the world defended and realized by the discourse
> of the egalitarian ideology, as evil.[25]

The New Right, which has perfectly assimilated Gramsci's conception
of hegemony (considered as a fundamental contribution by de Benoist) has
decided to fight for intellectual supremacy and has waged a 'cultural
war' whose slogan is 'Against totalitarianism, against egalitarianism,
against racism.   For a new culture'.
    It might seem a bit surprising that a right-wing movement will present
itself explicitly as anti-racist and it is very interesting to analyze
the roots of this position.   Our cultural warriors are preaching that
men ought to recognize that they are different from one another and that
they must accept the importance of heredity and the revelations of
psychometrics and sociogiology (they believe that biology should be in
the future as important in politics as economics has been until now).
It is this respect for human differences that allows them to present
their views as anti-racist.   But once that respect for the differences
is located in its anti-egalitarian context, as Jean-Francois Kahn has
pointed out:

> What the spokesmen of GRECE really mean is, for example, that
> a six-year-old child who has been singled out through tests as
> being especially gifted should in no way belong to the same
> class and receive the same type of education as a child of the
> same age who is not as gifted; it is that the elites must be
> selected very early and radically differentiated from the non-
> elites; it is that inherited cultures should not be mixed because
> it would pervert them; it is finally that all types of differences
> ought to be carefully preserved and defended, inclusively against
> any tendency to integration.   Now that is done very efficiently
> in South Africa and it is called 'apartheid'.[26]

Their crusade against equality leads the ideologues of the New Right
to challenge the whole Christian European tradition.   Indeed for them
at the root of the egalitarian utopia we find Christianity, called by
Alain de Benoist the 'Bolshevism of Antiquity'.   Quoting Nietzsche's
assertion that 'Christianity has robbed us of the fruits of ancient
civilization', he proceeds to argue that the cult of weakness and
humility spread by the Christians caused the downfall of the Roman
Empire and is at the root of the myth of equality which has proved so
destructive.[27]   For Robert de Herte

According to the classical process of development and degradation
of cycles, the egalitarian theme has moved from the stage of myth
(equality in front of God) to the stage of ideology (equality in
front of men) and then to the stage of scientific pretension
(affirmation of the 'egalitarian fact') - to be precise: from
Christianity to democracy and later to socialism and marxism.[28]

As we can see, it is not only the ideal of equality which is in question, it is also democracy which is directly challenged. Indeed the
French Revolution is presented as a landmark in the process of deterior-
ation of Western culture, and de Benoist proclaims that it is against
the spirit of the Declaration of Human Rights of 1789 that we ought to
revolt. For the ideal of democracy, with the determinant role attributed
to universal suffrage, puts all the individuals on the same level without
recognizing the very important differences between them. It results in
a uniformity and massification of the citizens upon whom a single norm
is imposed, hence the totalitarian character of democracy. To respect
human differences, declares Louis Pauwels, society should be organized
in the following way: 'To the brains ought to correspond the function
of sovereignty; to the muscles the function of defence; to the mouth the
function of production'.[29]

Ideas so openly and radically hostile to equality and democracy might
still (for how long?) be seen as too extreme to become the dominant ideology, but they certainly play an important role in the transformation of
the ideological parameters prevailing in advanced capitalist societies
and in the emergence of the new ideology of Liberal-Conservatism. As
we have seen, through the redefinition of a series of fundamental notions
like liberty, equality and democracy, and their rearticulation in a discourse whose central principle is the affirmation of 'individual freedom'
as 'the ultimate goal in judging social arrangements',[30] liberal-democratic ideology is being severed of its links with the defence of
democracy and social justice and is being turned into a 'New Individualism' spreading the old gospel of self-help, thrift and individual responsibility. The aim of that ideological offensive is to transform the
existing common sense articulated around social-democratic values so as
to reduce the expectations of the people, to destroy their sense of
solidarity and responsibility towards the underprivileged and to prepare
them for the more authoritarian type of society which is already being
installed in many places. That process is beginning to bear its fruits
and a new definition of reality has emerged according to which ideas
considered as unacceptable ten years ago seem today almost taken for
granted.[31] Such a shift in attitudes has certainly played an important
part in the rise to power of a new brand of conservatism in Britain and
in the United States.

RIGHT WING POPULISM

In 1970, in an article in *The Public Interest*, Irving Kristol drew
attention to the fact that the liberal-conservative ideal of a 'free
society' was completely divorced from the ideal of a 'just society'
and he argued that in consequence such an ideal could never appeal to
the masses in modern society.[32] Ten years later, the victory of
Margaret Thatcher in Britain and Ronald Reagan in the USA (on the basis
of programmes strongly influenced by the theories of the social market

economy) seem in glaring contradiction to that prediction. Do we therefore need to conclude that the masses have been converted to the virtues
of the market by the abstract thinking of the neo-liberals? Obviously
the phenomenon is much more complex and deserves careful attention.

First, as we have already indicated, since the end of the 1960s the
social-democratic common sense in which the notion of 'social justice'
played an important role has been consistently undermined by the shift
in the dominant ideology from Liberal-Democracy towards Liberal-Conservatism providing a new ideological terrain more favourable to the success
of right-wing movements. On the other side, the crisis of the welfare
state and the popular frustration which accompanied it have been at the
origin of an outburst of anti-state reactions and feelings which the
radical right has been able to translate in the terms of the neo-liberal
critique. The arrival in power of right-wing populism is far from being
the result of an accident. It has been prepared since the mid-1960s by
the development, both in Britain and the USA, of a series of right-wing
pressure groups and organisations tending to organise popular reaction
against the 'counter-culture', the 'permissive society' and the 'collectivist state'.[33] The results began to be felt around 1974/early 1975
with the arrival of Margaret Thatcher to the leadership of the Conservative Party, and in the first popular backlash against the campaign of the
1960s in Boston with the riots for the preservation of the racially
segregated schools. Since then the power of the radical right has
steadily been growing, especially through its capacity to link into a
national network a series of groups organized around single issues,
culminating in their victory in the elections in both countries.

Several analyses of 'Thatcherism' have shown how its growth had been
facilitated by the genuine popular discontent with the bureaucratic and
corporatist way in which the welfare state had been implemented in
Britain. In his path-breaking article 'The Great Moving Right Show',
Stuart Hall writes:

> The state is inbreasingly encountered and experienced by ordinary
> working people as indeed not a beneficiary but a powerful bureau-
> cratic imposition. And this 'experience' is not misguided since,
> in its effective operations with respect to the popular classes,
> the state is less and less present as a welfare institution and
> more and more present as the state of 'monopoly capital'.[34]

The close identification of the welfare state with social-democracy has
obviously been a powerful trump in the hands of the new conservatives,
but they needed to know how to play it and one must recognize that they
have been especially successful in articulating to the right a very wide
spectrum of popular responses so as to create a polarization in which
'Labour is undividedly "with" the state and the power bloc - and Mrs.
Thatcher is undividedly out there "with the people"'.[35] It is therefore
by a deliberate attempt to colonize for the right the very real antagonisms which have emerged as a result of the development of late capitalism, utilizing for that end the rich repertoire of anti-statist and
anti-egalitarian themes provided by the various trends of neo-conservative ideologies, that Thatcherism has become a popular force.

The characteristics of the radical right in the United States are
remarkably similar to the British case, and behind the most obvious
differences due to the specific conditions in each country we can recognize a common attempt to organize a new conservative majority through
right-wing populism. The battle is launched on two main fronts, the

attack on 'big government' is combined with a forceful reassertion of the traditional values concerning the family, role of women, abortion, homosexuality and other social questions. Indeed one of the most striking characteristics of this movement is that it tries to unite people across party lines and class divisions on the basis of social and moral issues. If in their war against state intervention and their campaign for big tax reductions they draw their ammunition from the neo-liberals (especially the monetarism of Milton Friedman and the Californian school of Arthur Laffer, the theorist of Proposition 13), in their moral and cultural offensive they have found a very important source of inspiration in the work of neo-conservative scholars like Daniel Bell and Irving Kristol with their persistent attacks on the 'adversary culture' and their proclaimed need for religion.[36]

A very important element in the US brand of right-wing populism is their defence of the patriarchal order. In a seminal article, Linda Gordon and Allen Hunter have shown that a new element has recently been added to racism which used to have the central role in American right-wing politics:

Racism has not diminished as a political force, but has been joined - and the whole right thereby strengthened - by a series of conservative campaigns defending the family, a restrictive and hypocritical sexual morality, and male dominance.[37]

The recent years in the USA have witnessed an important backlash against the development of the women's and gay movements expressed in the multiplication of single-issue organisations campaigning against the Equal Right Amendment for women, against abortion and against the rights of homosexuals. The radical right has been able to articulate all those 'pro-family' operations (of which the most powerful is the Evangelical Church of the Rev. Jerry Falwell); the defence of traditional patriarchal forms and of the male-dominated system of heterosexuality has proved to be a powerful ideological cement for the regrouping of the 'moral majority' as the Reagan victory has testified.[38] In Britain a similar patriarchal component is present (even if less pronounced at the moment) in Thatcherism which, as Tricia Davis and Catherine Hall have argued,

is not simply an attack on the rights of women but a much bigger attempt to rework old ideologies into a new consensus about the role of women and the nature of femininity as one of the ideological lynchpins for the restructuring of society.[39]

Since Liberal-Democracy has historically constituted a specific articulation of private property, family and democracy, at the moment when the need is being felt to underplay the role of democracy it is not surprising to see a growing importance attributed to the family and I would venture to predict that defence of the patriarchal family is going to play an increasing role in the emerging ideology of Liberal Conservatism.

IN DEFENCE OF DEMOCRACY

The development of monopoly capitalism since the Second World War and the growing intervention of the state at all levels of social life have led to a profound transformation of Western society and to the rupture of the traditional conception of politics. Indeed in all the fields where the state intervenes: health, housing, education, energy,

etc., social contradictions have become political ones and new antagonisms have emerged in which the state is perceived as the oppressor. At
the same time already existing contradictions based on the sex/gender
system and on race have become more acute and the whole realm of civil
society, of what was traditionally considered as 'private', is now
recognised as a terrain for political struggle. But neither the old
forms of party politics nor the more recent forms of tripartist corporatism are able to cope with that 'democratic upsurge'. We have therefore the release of an enormous potential challenge to the existing
order which does not find institutional channels to express itself.
Hence the proliferation of the new movements and single-issue groups.
In themselves most of these contradictions do not have a specific class
content and can be articulated into many different discourses as the
recent success of right-wing populism has proved. On that terrain the
left is very far behind the right indeed, and is only beginning to
realize the crucial importance of that terrain of struggle.

It seems to me that the shortcomings of the socialist forces in this
field stem from two main sources: (1) their prevailing economism which
prevents them from taking seriously contradictions other than the class
ones, and from recognizing that ideological issues can provide a powerful factor in the constitution and unification of social and political
forces; (2) their statist conception of socialism and the fact that
they do not seem yet to have fully come to terms with the transformations of bourgeois politics which have accompanied the implementation
of Keynesian policies. They go on as before presenting the intervention
of the state as the remedy for all social evils, without realising that
the brougeoisie has robbed them of their flag. No wonder that the crisis
of Keynesianism found them absolutely unprepared to offer a real alternative, since their only strategy is one of left Keynesianism. That is
why in many countries the crisis of the welfare state has first been
capitalised by the right. Fortunately that swing to the right has not
yet been consolidated, and signs indicate that the situation may still
be reversed.[40] But in order to gain a real long-term victory, one that
would provide a left solution to the present crisis based on a thorough
democratisation of society, we need a radical rethinking of the socialist
ideal and strategy.

What is definitively on the agenda today is the elaboration of a
strategy that could unite around a socialist project all the 'fragments'
of the democratic movement. Such a project requires a profound transformation of the dominant conception of socialism. For, as long as it
is only conceived in terms of the socialisation of the means of production, it has very little to offer to satisfy the demands of the 'new
movements'. The struggle must be waged at a much deeper level than it
is usually conceived by the left, and the elaboration of a socialist
alternative must engage with all the contradictions existing in society
and not only those located in the field of the economy. To end contradictions located in the sex/gender system or based on race must be
considered as important in the building of socialism as to end the
contradiction between capital and labour.

The elaboration and implementation of such a strategy is far from
easy, and it is not my intention to underplay the major difficulties
that need to be solved. But I would like to suggest some elements of
this process. It is sometimes said that there is no basis for a unity
between the different parts of the democratic movement. Indeed at first

sight their demands seem so different and even particularistic that, without postulating a pre-given unity, based on a common source - the existence of the capitalist mode of production - it might appear very difficult to justify the assertion that unity can and should be built. Nevertheless one can recognize the presence of a common element because all those demands are in some way or other the expression of a struggle for equality and participation and against oppression and exclusion. They point towards the need for a real democratization of society at all levels and such a common objective could provide the principle of an alliance between the fragments. However, for that to become a real possibility we need a much wider conception of democracy than the one at our disposal at the moment. Our present concept of democracy is too limited and has suffered a lot from its articulation in the liberal-democratic discourse. In order to transform it into a tool appropri-ate for the framing of a new socialist project it is urgent to reformul-ate it in such a way as to allow us to use it to advocate not only a real participation of the people in all the decisions concerning the organisation of social life, but also for a real equality among human beings irrespective of their sex, race or sexual orientation. To the offensive of Liberal-Conservatism to redefine to the right the dominant ideological parameters, it is necessary to answer with a stronger ideo-logical and political offensive to reaffirm and extend democratic values. Because the problems that we face today are not due to an excess of democracy, as the neo-conservatives would have us believe, but to a lack of it, the problem will only be solved by more democracy.

NOTES

1   Claus Offe, 'Notes on the Future of European Socialism and the
    State', *Kapitalistate*, No.7, 1978, p.33.
2   James O'Connor, *The Fiscal Crisis of the State*, St Martin's Press,
    New York, 1973.
3   See for instance Henry S. Kariel (ed.), *Frontiers of Democratic
    Theory* (New York, 1970) and Peter Bachrach and Morton S. Baratz,
    Power and Poverty. Theory and Practice (New York, Oxford University
    Press, 1970).
4   Alan Wolfe, *The Limits of Legitimacy*, New York, Free Press, 1977,
    p.57.
5   The thought of the group, especially its German members, is analysed
    by C.J. Friedrich in 'The Political Thought of Neo-Liberalism',
    American Political Science Review, 1955, pp.509-25.
6   Friedrich Hayek, *The Constitution of Liberty*, Routledge and Kegan
    Paul, London, 1960, p.11.
7   *ibid.*
8   Milton Friedman, *Capitalism and Freedom*, University of Chicago Press,
    1962, p.25.
9   Keith Joseph, *Conditions for Fuller Employment*, CPS, 1978, p.20.
    Quoted by Andrew Gamble in a very useful article on the social
    market economy and its followers in Britain: 'The Free Economy and
    the Strong State', *The Socialist Register*, 1979.
10 Willem Röpke, *A Humane Economy*, quoted in Noël O'Sullivan,
    Conservatism, London, 1976, p.139.
11 Friedman, *op.cit.*, p.14.

12 C.B. Macpherson, *Democratic Theory*, Oxford University Press, 1973, p.146.
13 Hayek, *op.cit.*, p.206.
14 Hayek, *The Road to Serfdom*, Routledge and Kegan Paul, 1944, p.52.
15 Andrew Gamble in the article referred to above (note 9) has shown the intellectual dishonesty of Friedman, who classified Nazi Germany as totalitarian despite the fact that the regime did not interfere with the economic freedom of private capital.
16 Michel Crozier, Samuel P. Huntington and Joji Watanuki, *The Crisis of Democracy: A Report on the Governability of Democracies to the Trilateral Commission*, New York University Press, 1975.
17 Daniel Bell, 'On Meritocracy and Equality', *The Public Interest*, Fall 1972.
18 Irving Kirstol, 'About Equality', *Commentary*, November 1972.
19 Samuel P. Huntington, 'The Democratic Distemper, *The Public Interest*, Bicentennial Edition, 1976.
20 Quoted by Pierre Dommergues, 'Les Etats-Unis à la recherche d'une nouvelle idéologie', *Le Monde Diplomatique*, August 1980.
21 Peter Steinfelds, *The Neoconservatives*, New York, 1979.
22 Hayek, *The Road to Serfdom*, pp.59-60; *Constitution of Liberty*, pp.231-33.
23 Charles Frankel, 'The new egalitarianism and the old', *Commentary*, September 1973.
24 Milton Friedman, *Free to Choose*, London, 1980, p.134.
25 Alain de Benoist, *Les idées à l'endroit*, Paris, 1979, p.81.
26 Jean-François Kahn, 'Ne pas se laisser prendre au piège des mots', *Les Louvelles littéraires*, 27 September 1979.
27 de Benoist, *op.cit.*, pp.167-84.
28 Robert de Herte, Collectif du G.R.E.C.E., *Dix ans de combat culturel pour une renaissance*, Paris, 1977.
29 Louis Pauwels, in *Maiastra, Renaissance de l'Occident*, Paris, 1979.
30 Friedman, *Capitalism and Freedom*, p.12.
31 It is interesting to note for instance that many themes of Reagan's campaign, considered as quite acceptable today, were felt as outrageous when formulated by Goldwater in 1964.
32 Irving Kristol, '"When virtue loses all her loveliness" - some reflection on capitalism and the "free society"', *The Public Interest*, No.21, Fall 1970.
33 For an analysis of that process in Britain see Stuart Hall *et al*, *Policing the Crisis*, London, 1978; in the United States, Bertram Gross, *Friendly Fascism*, New York, 1980, and Alan Crawford, *Thunder on the Right*, New York, 1980.
34 Stuart Hall, *Marxism Today*, January 1979, pp.17-18.
35 *ibid.*, p.18.
36 Especially in Daniel Bell, *The Cultural Contradictions of Capitalism*, New York, 1978, and Irving Kristol, *On the Democratic Idea in America*, New York, 1972.
37 Linda Gordon and Allen Hunter, 'Sex, Family and the New Right, *Radical America*, November 1977.
38 A very good analysis of the network of the New Right in America is provided by Alan Crawford, *op.cit.*
39 Tricia Davis and Catherine Hall, 'The Forward Face of Feminism', *Marxism Today*, October 1980, p.15.

40 The difficulties encountered by Mrs Thatcher in implementing monetarism and the growing popular reaction to her policies are leading to a
radicalization of the Labour Party that might create the conditions
for an emergence of a completely new type of socialist politics in
Britain. On the other side, the Mitterand victory in France is very
likely to provide an alternative model of solving the crisis that
will undermine the conservatives' claim that theirs is the only
solution, and act as a powerful ideological weapon against the rise
of the new right.

41 One should not restrict democracy to a formal mechanism of collective
decision-taking, as does Barry Hindess in his otherwise important
article in *Politics & Power* 1. As Bob Jessop has pointed out in his
critique of Hindess (*Politics & Power* 2), one must also engage in
struggle to interpellate 'democratic subjects'. But that requires
a new conception of democracy that is urgent to elaborate.

I&C

"Political analysis and criticism have in a large measure still to be invented."

(M. Foucault)

I&C (formerly titled Ideology & Consciousness) began in 1977 by taking stock of new intellectual currents available to left politics: radical critiques of social science, Marxist theories of ideology, and approaches via psychoanalysis, feminism and theories of language, signs and discourse to the 'subjective' dimension of power, domination and struggle.

Recent issues of I&C have moved towards a re-examination of the custodial-governmental functions of the 'human sciences' and the relations of power and knowledge they entail. As a journal, I&C sees its role less as building a manifesto of imperatives than as offering an exploratory space for questioning, reflection and research. For I&C political analysis entails a sceptical attitude to ready-made blocs of theoretical doctrine, but not the rejection of theory itself as a tool for grasping the real.

One of I&C's particular strengths is the presentation of work by new writers in other countries, mostly outside the established international of the new left, who pursue a more intellectually open and honest confrontation with their political present.

I&C 7 : TECHNOLOGIES OF THE HUMAN SCIENCES. Our latest issue includes: 'What is psychology?', an essay by the celebrated French historian of science George Canguilhem; a new introduction by Michel Foucault to Canguilhem's work, its political influence and originality; 'Psychiatry as a Political Science', a review article by Peter Miller; a study of the roots of criminology, science of 'social defence', by Pasquale Pasquino; Beverley Brown on the updated liberalism of the Williams report's proposals for law and pornography; Jenny Somerville's evaluation of Nicos Poulantzas's last major work to be published in English; State, Power, Socialism.

Some articles in previous issues: Nikolas Rose, 'The psychological complex: mental measurement and social administration' (I&C5); Jacques Donzelot, 'The Poverty of Political Culture' (I&C5);Diana Adlam and Angie Salfield, 'A Matter of Language', review of Language and Materialism by Rosalind Coward and John Ellis(I&C3);Michel Foucault, 'Politics and the study of discourse' (I&C3),'On governmentality' (I&C6); Colin Gordon,'Other Inquisitions', an introduction to Foucault (I&C6);Pasquale Pasquino, 'The genealogy of capital - police and the State of prosperity', Giovanna Procacci, 'Social economy and the government of poverty' (I&C4).

I&C is published twice yearly in spring and autumn by I&C Publications Ltd.

Bookshop distribution: Full Time/Southern Distribution.

Personal subscriptions (UK): £2.80 for two issues (students/claimants £2.25). Back issues (nos. 1-6) £2 each.

Address: I&C (SP), c/o G.Burchell, Westminster College, North Hinksey, Oxford OX2 9AT

Jim Tomlinson
Corporatism: A Further
Sociologisation of Marxism[1]

The concept of corporatism is enjoying a renaissance in both political
and social science arguments. (For general surveys see for example
Schmitter 1974, Panitch 1979a, Panitch 1980.) This renaissance has
been accompanied by an almost total confusion as to the meaning of the
term, a 'profound lack of agreement on what the concept actually refers
to' (Panitch, p.159). For the intending surveyor of this morass of
conceptual confusion there is a hard task to bring order and draw lines
of division. However, the purpose of this paper is not to engage with
the generality of the term 'corporatism' but to review the way it has
been used in one (albeit major) context - as a foundation for analysing
policies pursued by recent British (especially Labour) governments
largely in their relations with trade unions. My purpose is to argue
that the way in which Marxist writers have done this, taking on board
the notion of corporatism, has had serious regressive analytical
consequences.

My purpose is not to defend the purity of Marxism against the encroach-
ment of an 'alien' concept. Marxist itself is clearly in a confused and
chaotic state. But my thesis is that whatever the way out of this mess
for Marxism (if indeed there is one), it does *not* lie with embracing
notions of corporatism as a helpful category in understanding modern
capitalist economies and their politics.[2]

WHAT IS CORPORATISM?

The 'narrow' definition of corporatism that is at stake here is that
given (and preferred) by Panitch (1980, p.173). Corporatism is a
  political structure within advanced capitalism which integrates
  organised socio-economic producer groups through a system of
  representation and co-operative mutual interaction at the leadership level and mobilisation and social control at the mass level.
This is a structure which is combined with, and therefore not a replacement of, other political structures like parliament and 'pluralist'
activity.

This characterisation, albeit in a less formalised and in some cases
more equivocal form, has been used to analyse recent British developments
by *inter alia* Panitch (1971), Harris (1972, esp. Chapter 15), Hyman (1975,
esp. pp.142-45), Coates (1975), Panitch (1976, esp. pp.245-53), Panitch
(1979), Coates (1980, esp. pp.205-17) and Panitch (1980). The main
thrust of most of these writers has been that successive British governments, but especially Labour governments, and above all by the means of
incomes policies,[3] have attempted to incorporate trade unions as effectively agencies of the state, 'a means of integrating the working class
into capitalist society, thus serving as a mechanism of social control'
(Hyman, 1975, p.143).

By far the most theoretically sustained use of corporatism in this
sense has been by Panitch (1971, 1976, 1979, 1980), and in looking at
the bases of the arguments his work is concentrated upon, though the
other writers already referred to will also be mentioned where appropriate.

Corporatism is defined by Panitch as relating to the 'interest associations of business and labour, representing directly the central
actors in the balance of class forces in advanced capitalist societies'
(1980, p.173). But the main focus is on labour and trade unions rather
than capitalists and their organisations. The attempt to incorporate
labour is seen as part of a response by capitalism to the increased
strength of trade unionism brought about by post-1945 full employment.
But the Labour Party was particularly appropriate as the agency of this
attempt because of its dominant integrative ideology, which denied the
class struggle and stressed the need to subordinate 'sectional'(including working class) interests to national (Panitch 1971). Thus the dominant Labour ideology was functional for capitalism in post-war circumstances. (For a lengthy statement of this thesis see Coates (1980),
Chapters 6 and 7.)

However, this attempt to incorporate trade unionism has always run
up against clear limits, because of the inherently dual role in a
capitalist economy. On the one hand they have clearly a 'structural
connection' with capitalism - they primarily function to bargain over
the terms on which labour power is sold as a commodity. But on the
other hand trade unions

> are still predominantly working-class organisations which cannot
> deny what their members experience at the place of work - the
> divisions which still exist in modern capitalist society.
> (Panitch, 1971, p.196)

So Labour governments attempting to ignore the reality of class
struggle in pursuit of a 'national' image are constantly hitting
against the rock of the trade union's everyday experience precisely
because of that struggle. Trade union leaders in some cases may
personally favour 'incorporation' by incomes policies and the like,
but they are also aware of their ultimate dependence on their membership - and so many espouse voluntarism and free collective bargaining
as a positive response to this dependence.

Corporatism is then never likely to be successful because such
success is non-realisable whilst the underlying class struggle of
capitalism remains. Consequently corporatism is inherently unstable
for its full 'success' requires a class hegemony which ultimately can
only be attained by suppression, as in the classic corporatisms of
Fascist Italy and Nazi Germany (Panitch, 1980, p.175). Given general

opposition to such suppression, corporatism will remain an unstable and
only partial aspect of the British social formation.

INTERESTS AND CORPORATISM

The concern here is not with the political prognosis offered by corporatist analysis but its theoretical foundations. Central to these foundations is the concept of 'interest'. Interest as a concept in social
science argument has a variety of meanings, but two major ones are of
concern here.

The first one is that which conceives interests as inherent in a
particular set of social relations independent of any agency calculating
those interests. Because of their position in social relations certain
groups/classes have a common interest which exists as long as those
social relations exist and prior to and separate from any calculation
(by the interest concerned, or any others) as to what those interests
might be. This is the notion of interest which is operative in the
corporatist argument. Capitalist social formations are conceived of as
containing a variety of interests, but crucially construct two interests,
capital and labour. These interests, 'the central actors in the balance
of class forces in advanced capitalist societies' (Panitch, 1980, p.173)
are vital to corporatism because they are opposing, they are 'constituted
in terms of a contradictory relation to one another (ibid., p.176).
These major interests may be temporarily reconciled, but because their
contradiction is ontological, not for example the consequence of any
passing calculation by them or on their behalf, it is constantly reasserting itself in a variety of forms. Thus the instability of
corporatism, already referred to, unless it confronts and destroys
one of these interests.

The major alternative conception of interests is one which conceives
them as the product of a political argument. Thus for example the argument that the working class gained from British rearmament in the late
1930s can be sustained on grounds of rearmament being a necessary pre-
condition for the defeat of fascism. This is clearly a different kind
of argument from that given above because it involves a *problematic*
political calculation - e.g. that the weapons will be used to fight
fascism and not to suppress working-class discontent. Presumably few
would argue that high levels of armaments expenditure are inherently a
good thing for the working class (and only a relatively small number of
pacifists would argue that they are inherently bad) - their 'goodness'
or 'badness' is not inscribed in social relations, but a consequence of
particular political circumstance and calculations.

Clearly this latter example was chosen simply to make a specific
point, that different notions of interest are possible to that in the
corporatist argument. In practice in many arguments these separate
notions of interest are often conflated. Thus in relation to the
present Tory government in Britain it is commonly argued that it is
working 'in the interests of' capital and against working-class interests. Now clearly if by this it is meant that this government is working against what socialists conceive of as the interests of the working
class - strong trade unionism, high public expenditure, high employment
etc., and for the interests of what the Conservatives view as the
interests of capital - higher profits, weak trade unionism etc, this is

unexceptionable. But this argument also seems to imply that current policies are necessarily in the interests of capital and against those of
labour - that the consequences of these policies, if successfully pursued,
are given in advance because they merely reflect the play of these pre-
given interests. This latter is clearly problematic because it assumes
that somewhere there is in effect being made a calculation as to the best
interests of capital, and that this calculation is necessarily correct -
this agency always perfectly knows where the interests of capital lie
(see further below on the corporatist conception of the state).
      The pertinence to the corporatism argument of this distinction in the
conceptualisation of interests is clear. Panitch et al assume that the
working class has an interest as a consequence of its existence in the
exploitative social relations of capitalism - the suppression of those
social relations. This interest is not one calculated by the working
class - it would still be there even if every single member of that
class were violently hostile to socialism. In fact this interest *does*
manifest itself, certainly in Britain, albeit in 'distorted' forms.
This manifestation takes the form of strikes and other forms of industrial militancy. Thus Panitch writes:
      ... dissatisfaction with existing social relations is inherent
      in wage claims of 25, 30 or 40% ... in occupations of factories
      shut down in accordance with the law of profit ... in the large
      number of strikes challenging managerial prerogatives.
      (1976, p.253)
So particular instances of discontent function here merely as examples
of what is already known - that capitalism is against the interests of
the working class.
      The logic of the argument is thus two-stage. Workers have an inter-
est in the overthrow of capitalism (independently of any particular
political argument); this interest is expressed, albeit imperfectly, in
trade union militancy. Imperfectly because trade unions do not 'express
the corporate interests of the whole class on which they are based, much
less that they express the "true" interests of the whole class' (Panitch,
1980, p.177). Despite this imperfection, and particularly in the absence of the revolutionary party to give it more perfect expression
(Panitch, 1976, p.253; Coates, 1980, Chapter 7), trade union militancy
is a good thing *because* it represents the existence of this interest.
      By the same token, any attempt to limit this militancy, for example
by incomes policies, is clearly reactionary because it is a suppression
of the representation of the underlying interest. The consequences of
the conception of 'ontological' interests within the corporatism argument is thus made clear. It makes impossible any political calculation
of socialist/working-class interests which fall outside a scale running
from capitalism to socialism because it is at that level and only at that
level that interests are operative. Thus the calculation of possible
gains *within capitalism* is undercut - for example Panitch attacks (1980,
p.183) Crouch (e.g. Crouch, 1979, Chapter 8) for advocating a 'bargained
corporatism' in which trade unions secure gains and losses, but explicitly within a continuing capitalist framework. My purpose here is not to
defend Crouch's own arguments, but to make clear by this example how the
concept of interest operative in Panitch's work precludes assessing
Crouch's or similar arguments in their own terms. To do so would precisely preclude conceptualising interests ontologically at the level of
capitalism/socialism. Crouch's position is a political argument which

conceives (at least at this particular point in the book) interests as much more problematic than the corporatists would allow, because interests are not *a priori* but constructed out of a political argument, and those interests are not conceived as existing outside the particular political moment of the calculation.

POLITICAL CONSEQUENCES

Corporatism is then a process of compromising with inherently opposed interests, and therefore a subordination of labour's to those of capital, because whilst capitalism remains the interests of capital are by definition predominant. One cannot demonstrate (outside a naive positivism) that such ontological interests do or do not exist. All that can be pointed to is the consequences of conceiving interests in this way.

One of these consequences has already been pointed to - the circumscribing of political argument that it creates. Any particular political argument always 'slides off' into a general discourse on capitalism/ socialism. Incomes policies for example cannot be assessed in their particularity and (large) differences - they are all homogenised into a corporatism which is known to be 'bad' in advance of investigation. Thus the characteristic corporatist text (e.g. Panitch 1976) is one which uses particular instances not as a way of raising problems, but as examples of what is already known. The text is a labour of exemplification.

This absence of 'problem raising' in corporatist argument is not accidental. If interests are clear-cut and given, then political argument becomes a question of allocating any particular policy to one of two exhaustive categories - good or bad - serving the interests of labour or of capital. This comes over in their analysis of trade union organisation. As already noted, the corporatist argument depends on an unproblematic celebration of industrial militancy. This leads to a hostile attitude to any organisation which is seen as suppressing this militancy. This obviously includes the state (on which see below) but also to trade union organisations themselves - the TUC, trade union bureaucracies and even shop-steward organisations (see Hyman, 1979). All of these are seen as suppressing the inherent tendency of rank and file trade unionists to be militant. Clearly what such arguments have no room for is the linking of particular objectives to particular levels of organisation appropriate to those objectives. For example it can be argued that the TUC played a crucial role in the defeat of the 1971 Industrial Relations Act because of its policy of expulsion of unions which complied with the Act. Only the TUC could apply such a policy. Whilst in no way downgrading the importance of grass-roots opposition to the Act, the point is that without this central body and its role this militancy may well have been unsuccessful. This point is not considered at all by Hyman (1975), whose argument is simply that rank and file militancy propelled trade union leaders into greater resistance than they 'probably intended' (p.144). Equally Panitch (1976, p.251) considers the issue as simply an 'ideological' one, rather than one raising problems about levels of trade union organisation to achieve particular ends.

Another similar ambiguity in a simple endorsement of decentralised militancy is mentioned in passing by Panitch. Thus he argues (1980, pp.177-78):

> The development of corporatist structures *at the national level* in liberal democracies has entailed the integration of the central organisations of capital and labour and encouraged their further centralisation so as to be able to *overcome* sectoral divisions within each class in the application of state economic policy.

Now what this quote raises but also evades is the possibility that centralisation of trade unions may be a good thing from a trade union/ socialist position as well as from that of 'state economic policy'. For example, in Sweden centralised bargaining has been one element in making possible a 'solidarist' wages policy, i.e. the reduction of wage inequalities - something almost impossible to achieve with decentralised bargaining and decentralised trade unions. (cf. Panitch 1979a, where this centralisation is linked only to the question of suppressing rank and file militancy.) Now presumably most socialists would endorse such a policy - yet this kind of problem cannot even be discussed in the simple dichotomies of corporatism.

To sum up, we may say that the consequences of conceiving society as consisting essentially of two inherent interests is profoundly to limit the modes of political analysis available. In particular it makes it difficult or impossible (a) to analyse particular political questions in their own right - there is always a sliding off, and therefore a reductionism, to pre-given interest, (b) to recognise the problematic effects of many political movements and events - a recognition which can exist only if such movements and events are seen as other than simply emanations of interests constituted by capitalist social relations, (c) to recognise the problems of organisation in their own right - again only possible if organisations are not simply reduced to a sole representation of interest constituted elsewhere. Finally, political argument based on the notion of inherent interests will always tend towards consciousness-raising kinds of politics, because the political task of socialists is to make people *realise* where their interests lie. Such politics can provide no means for the reform of specific institutions and practices - this will happen 'naturally' once people know their true interests.

CORPORATISM AND NATIONAL INTEREST

Linked to but separable from the notion of inherent interests given by social relations in general is the way in which the notion of *national interest* is deployed in corporatist arguments.

Panitch et al rightly point to the way notions of national interest have functioned as a plank in the argument for incomes policies. Panitch (1971) argues that this national interest argument is characteristic of the Labour Party which from its inception has accepted the notion of a national interest which should override sectional appeals. Thus he characterises the Labour Party's dominant ideology as integrative because its effect is to integrate the working class into the existing political arrangements by effectively suppressing the claims of that class as separate from and opposed to the 'national interest' which as long as capitalism survives is bound to be in fact the interests of capital.

There are a number of points that need to be made on this. Firstly it is clear that at the level of rhetoric incomes policies have certainly been presented as in furtherance of the national interest. However, there is no reason to suppose that this is either a necessary component of argument for incomes policies or why this rhetoric needs to be taken as correctly describing the effects of such policies. Arguments for incomes policies can be put forward which do not depend on the notion of national interest - for example they can be argued for on grounds of socialist/class objectives like a more egalitarian wage distribution. Equally because the political right claims that incomes policies are good for the national interest we have no reason to suppose they have the monopoly of 'correct' calculation of such policies' effects. Their arguments may not only be objectionable, it may also be *wrong* even from their own perspective (or at least problematic).

A more serious problem perhaps is the way in which the corporatist argument depends on a dichotomy of 'class' versus 'national interest', the assertion of the latter necessarily implying the suppression of the former. The problem with this is that it implies that ultimately any talk of national interest is merely a mask behind which lie the interests of capital (e.g. Coates, 1975, p.127). The result of such a view is that questions of explicitly national policy can be simply denounced as ideological obfuscation. Yet this clearly will not do.

Take for example the common argument that incomes policies are resorted to, especially in Britain, because capitalists are being ground down between wage militancy and international competition. Assume a successful socialist revolution in Britain. How far would the problem of international competition disappear? Leaving aside the prospect of a nightmarish state of self-sufficiency, Britain would presumably continue to trade at least on some scale in order to provide food, raw materials and the many manufactured products not produced in Britain. As long as the world was still divided into separate currency areas there would exist a balance of payments problem in the sense of a need to balance receipts and expenditures of sterling. If this were not done, and a deficit led to borrowing, this would mean a creditor calling the tune in the same way that the IMF has done to capitalist Britain.

However much one may invoke 'planned trade' as the solution to such problems, even a world of totally planned trade would mean that at least some minimum cost/quantity etc. conditions would have to be achieved in order to make those goods acceptable to the recipients. There would therefore have to be policies geared to making sure those minimum standards were met, and these policies would be national in character *not* because of the dominance of bourgeois ideologies of national interest but simply as a consequence of the existence of a separate national currency.

The argument then is that a socialist policy would have to involve national economic goals (assuming that socialists were interested in the population being fed, clothed etc.), there would be a 'national interest' even without capitalists. Of course there is no reason why national currencies should remain for ever - in the foreseeable future for example there might be a move to a European currency. There would then have to be a 'European goal' in order to maintain some sort of balance with other nations and continents. Even a world currency would not dissolve the problem, though it would take a different form, unless one imagines Britain living on tribute from other nations - continuing to import but not reciprocating with acceptable exports.

The crucial point here is that any attempt to demonstrate that the notion of 'national interest' at any one time functions to further the interests of a particular section of the nation should not be taken to imply that talk of national interests is simply and only a mask for other interests. Existing notions of such a national interest may need to be broken up and deconstructed but these notions do relate in some manner to something which will not just go away even for a socialist government - the organisation of the world into separate monetary areas. Abstract internationalism is not an adequate riposte to the rhetoric of national interest.

CORPORATISM AND THE STATE

The corporatist argument depends on a particular conception of the state. Bargaining with the state, and therefore making concessions to it, is clearly bad from the corporatist viewpoint and this reflects the conception of the state as acting in the interests of capital. (It is not clear why bargaining with such a state is in principle worse than bargaining and compromising with capital directly, as in everyday wage negotiations; but this is not a major point.)

This conception of the state is of course surrounded by all sorts of qualifications and equivocations. Thus Hyman (1975, p.131) argues that whilst it is true that 'some actions of the state are contrary to specific capitalist interests, or serve the interests of the working class'. But what is granted at one point is quickly taken away at another. The advance of working-class interests by the state follows from divisions within capital or exceptional political pressure by the working class. But all gains made in this way are 'recouped' e.g. the welfare state provides healthy workers

and in the rare cases in which no direct advantage accrues from
legislative encroachments on their prerogatives, capitalists
may still reassure themselves that this is part of the ransom
to be paid for forestalling serious working-class attacks on
their *general* rights and privileges (p.131).

This is a fairly commonplace piece of Marxist functionalism, not specific to the corporatist literature. It is known in advance that all state agencies *really* aid the bourgeoisie, and all the equivocations of 'relative autonomy' etc. (see Hirst, 1977) cannot escape this initial functionalist premise.

Consequently the great bulk of Marxist discussions of the state 'know in advance' what significance can be attached to changes in particular state practices. Everything from the Poor Law Reform Act to the Redundancy Payments Act can be read as, however 'mediated', furthering the interests of capital. Because this significance is pre-given two crucial problems are ignored. Firstly, even if the Redundancy Payments Act did help capitalists, how did capitalists enact this statute - what are the mechanisms of this representation? Secondly, granted the premise that the Poor Law Act did aid capital does this exhaust its significance - what for example of its effects on the relations between central and local government - was this not politically important?

   The particular way in which this functionalism is built into the incorporation thesis is that this functionally is not conceived of only as
the *result* of Labour Government strategies but as their clear *interest*.
Thus discussing some of the 1974-79 Labour Government reforms Panitch
(1979, p.59) writes:
   This is not just a matter of Labour governments introducing reforms
   which are specifically structured to integrate the working class
   in the existing social order, reforms which constitute real gains
   for the class - but are designed to close rather than open room
   for further struggle.
The significance of such statements is twofold. First they have the
advantage over some Marxist functionalist positions of specifying the
'mechanism' whereby state intervention favours capital. The 'mechanism'
is the intention of the policies' begetters - the Labour Government
explicitly calculated the best way to defeat socialism and the incorporation strategy was the consequence. This surely is an extraordinary
conception of politics - it makes the ideology of politicians merely a
mask behind which their real intentions are hidden, as if, as Marx
argued specifically against, we believed all priests are atheists who
are also liars. The crucial point here is to distinguish between two
modes of assessment of political outcomes. For Panitch et al, policy
outcomes would seem to follow as night follows day from the intentions
of the policies' authors - at least if those authors represent capital.
Intentions and outcomes are entirely symmetrical. Now it is perfectly
possible to argue that incomes policies favour 'capital' without recourse
to such a dubious argument. Such a favouring can be read simply as a
consequence without any implication as to whether this consequence was
foreseen or engineered by capital - the consequence resulted instead
from an interplay of diverse and heterogeneous forces. Such an argument
would evade the reductionist conceptions of ideology and omnipotence of
capital which pervade the corporatist position. But this argument
cannot be accepted by corporatists precisely because it makes assessment
of the effects of state actions not pre-given but a political *problem*.
   The second, less generally important, point about the Panitch position,
which follows from the first, is the conception that the consequences of
a policy can be read off from the intentions of the policies' supporters.
Somehow these supporters have a kind of ownership relation to the policy
- they thought of it so they will determine what its effects are. But
why should this be so? Political history is strewn with unintended consequences, indeed one might go so far as to say that most politics is
about dealing witn unintended consequences of other policies. (Here
Panitch is out of line with much Marxist discussion, in which of course
class struggle is invoked as the mechanism whereby intentions may not
be realised.) Certainly there is no reason why the intentions of the
authors of a policy should exhaust its consequences. This links to a
previous point - there is no reason why because incomes policies are
commonly discussed under the rubric of 'national interest' that such
rhetoric should govern the consequences of such policies. As always it
is important not to confuse the rhetoric with the substance.

CONCLUSION

The general theme of this paper has been that the taking on board of
the notion of corporation by Marxist writers has extremely unfruitful
analytical consequences. Such an uncritical borrowing of concepts
from political sociology may reflect Marxism's own thinness in political
philosophy, but that is a poor reason for adoption of a concept whose
consequences are so negative.

Panitch chides Crouch for using a 'general model of class domination
in authority terms that owes more to Weber than to Marx' (1980, p.182).
But the very notion of domination which the corporatist case employs
itself cannot be transformed simply by separating it from Weberian
sociology, by arguing that it relates to exploitation and class struggle
rather than 'authority'. Of course domination *can* be assimilated to
Marxism in this way but the poverty of the term remains. Political
argument reduced to analysis of domination by one class or another is
itself productive of many of the problems of corporatism noted above -
the conception of politics as the play of pre-given interests, with the
means of representation of these interests reduced to being of no
account, with outcomes determined in advance by the class which is
'dominant' overall. Polemically one might stress that one more reason
for challenging the usefulness of the orthodox Marxist notion of
societies as structured totalities (Cutler et al, 1977) is precisely
the assimilation of dubious sociological concepts this facilitates.

Lest this seem a rather harsh assessment of the corporatist literature, let us give one final concrete example of the consequences of
their argument for the kind of political analysis it encourages.
Panitch is concerned to stress, against other discussions of corporatism, that he does not see it as an exhaustive characterisation of
political structures - it accompanies but does not displace parliamentary, bureaucratic and other forms. Now this point opens the way for
an analysis of the ways in which incomes policy forums as a means of
representing working-class interests might differ from parliament, how
these different forums might interrelate, what advantages representation
through 'corporatist' means might have over parliamentary representation.
The latter would seem particularly relevant given the long-standing
Marxist critique of parliament as a way of representing working-class
interests. Yet none of this is done - everything is lost in the swamp
of the generalities of corporatism and domination. The paradoxical
consequence of this is that the corporatism argument effectively serves
as a defence of parliamentary politics, because one of the most plausible
attempts to escape the confines of parliamentarism is precisely the object of corporatist criticism. In this context the corporatist argument
is much less perceptive of the political consequences of incomes policy
than those on the political right, who have precisely opposed such
policies because of their consequence of strengthening the political
position of trade unions (see Brittan, 1979; Lomax, 1977).

NOTES

1 I am very grateful to Stuart Burchell for helpful comments.
2 For a critique of more general notions of corporatism from a Marxist
   position see Westergaard (1977). For a later attempt to construct a
   Marxist theory of corporatism see Jessop (1979).

3 Similar arguments have been used against policies such as industrial
  democracy by means of workers on the board. Much of the analytical
  foundation for the argument is similar (though not exactly the same)
  same as) that used in relation to incomes policies.

REFERENCES

Brittan, S. (1979), 'The Futility of British Incomes Policy', *Challenge*,
  May-June
Coates, D. (1975), *The Labour Party and the Struggle for Socialism*,
  Cambridge University Press
Coates, D. (1980), *Labour in Power?*, Longman
Cutler, A. et al. (1977), *Marx's Capital and Capitalism Today*, Routledge
  and Kegan Paul
Harris, N. (1972), *Competition and the Corporate Society*, Methuen
Hirst, P. (1977), 'Economic Classes and Politics' in A. Hunt (ed.),
  Class and Class Structure, Lawrence & Wishart
Hyman, R. (1975), *Industrial Relations: A Marxist Introduction*,
  Macmillan
Jessop, B. (1979), 'Corporatism, Parliamentarism and Social Democracy'
  in P.C. Schmitter and G. Lehmbruch, *Trends Towards Corporatist
  Intermediation*, Sage
Lomax, D. (1977), 'Labour Power in the Modern Economy', *The Banker*,
  No.611, January
Panitch, L. (1971), 'Ideology and Integration: The Case of the British
  Labour Party', *Political Studies* XIX, 2, June
Panitch, L. (1976), *Social Democracy and Industrial Militancy*, Cambridge
  University Press
Panitch, L. (1979), 'Socialists and the Labour Party: A Reappraisal' in
  R. Miliband and J. Saville (eds.), *The Socialist Register*
Panitch, L. (1979a), 'The Development of Corporatism in Liberal
  Democracies' in Schmitter and Lehmbruch, *op.cit.*
Panitch, L. (1980), 'Recent Theorisations of Corporatism', *British
  Journal of Sociology*, XXXI, 2, June
Schmitter, P. (1977), 'Still the Century of Corporatism', *Review of
  Politics*, 36, January
Westergaard, J. (1977), 'Class, Inequality and Corporatism' in A. Hunt
  (ed.), *Class and Class Structure*, Lawrence & Wishart

politics of sexuality

DOUBLE ISSUE   no 5 & 6   1981

A Feminist Interest in Pornography
                         Beverley Brown

The Assertion of Homosexuality
                         Jeff Minson

Rape - Sexuality in the Law
                         Delia Dumaresq

Women and Shi'ism in Iran
                         Mina Modares

Psychoanalysis and Social Relations
                         Paul Hirst

Mary Kelly's Post-Partum Document

Introduction to Post-Partum Document
                         Elizabeth Cowie

Translation of Julia Kristeva On Motherhood

Introduction to Julia Kristeva
                         Claire Pajaczkowska

Translation of Moutafa Safouan on the universality

of the Oedipus Complex

Review of Foucault's History of Sexuality
                         Athar Hussain

m/f

£2.95

22 Chepstow Crescent
London W11

Conference of Socialist Economists 'Money Group'
A Note on the Wilson Committee and the Left

A committee headed by Harold Wilson which reports against an extension
of nationalisation can be easily dismissed by the left as one more
example of only-to-be-expected defeats. But this review argues that
the outcome of the Wilson Committee's activities reflects the left's
own weaknesses as well as the strengths of the right. These weaknesses
can be separated broadly into two: those concerning the left's approach
to Royal Commissions, and those concerning the focussing of the left's
attention on nationalisation.[1]

As is well known, the setting up of the Wilson Committee resulted
from an attempt by the Callaghan government to defuse the conflict which
arose from the 1976 Labour Party Conference decision to support the
nationalisation of the banks as proposed by the NEC (as embodied in
Labour Party (1976)), a decision publicly denounced by Callaghan. The
ploy of setting up a Royal Commission or Committee to evade making an
immediate decision is of course a well established one (Cartwright,
1975, Chapter 6). But for socialists this Committee was clearly different in that for the first time since the Sankey Committee on the Coal
Industry (1919) consideration of nationalisation was written in to the
terms of reference of a major government enquiry. The lineage claimed
by the Report (paragraph 1) is that of previous committees on the
financial system (Macmillan 1931 and Radcliffe 1959), neither of which
gave any substantial attention to nationalisation. Now this lineage
appears a legitimate one for Wilson to claim, precisely because its
deliberations, despite the immediate background to its setting up, were
dominated by concerns other than the question of nationalisation. The
final report in consequence reads more like a textbook on the financial
system than a deliberation on a contentious political question. The
nationalisation issue is dealt with in one chapter and appears rather
'tacked-on' to the main report.

THE FAILURE OF THE LEFT TO INTERVENE

This focussing of the report was no doubt partly a strategy of opponents
of nationalisation who both appointed and largely peopled the Committee.
But it also reflects the attitude of the left to such enquiries. Broadly
speaking the left does not see such enquiries as significant political
arenas, as arenas where the left may be able to make its case and,
because of the public nature of the enquiry, have some scope for getting
its case well known.

Now clearly such a point has to be qualified. Enthusiasts for such
commissions clearly overstate their role when they write

> Royal Commissions and Departmental Committees offer a unique
> mechanism for public participation in British government. At
> no other point in the political process is there a comparable
> opportunity for private individuals or interest groups to take
> part in the making of public policy.
> (Cartwright, p.6)

Nevertheless a recognition of the 'dispersion' of sites of decision
making (Hindess, 1980) within the government and state allows a greater
role for Royal Commissions and the like than would those fairly common
left analyses which see the state as a unitary force with all its parts
effectively subordinated to a central strategy.

The capacity to affect the activities of a Royal Commission is obviously partly a consequence of the make-up of the Committee and the
relation of that Committee to the evidence. A fairly sharp contrast
can be made here between the Wilson Committee and the Royal Commission
on Criminal Procedure (Report Cmnd 8092, 1981). In the latter case the
Commission was made up largely of legal experts, and they received
evidence mainly from two well-established interest groups - the police
and civil libertarians. Given the expertise of the Committee and both
the well-worn and offsetting nature of the evidence, the Committee was
largely able to write its own report. By contrast the Wilson Committee
was much more of a 'representative' rather than an 'expert' one; even
the academics were not all financial specialists.[2] This seems to have
meant that the Committee was much more affected by the evidence presented to it - there would seem more space for 'dissident' kinds of evidence
to have an impact with this kind of 'representative' committee than with
the 'expert' kind. Of course committees like this always have considerable scope for playing up or ignoring evidence, for example in whether
they call certain persons to give oral evidence, or whether evidence is
cited in the Report. However, in the case of the Wilson Committee a
major problem was that the left did not present very much in the way of
evidence. Of the 356 pieces of evidence presented (listed in Appendices
volume of the Report), only 8 came from persons or organisations that it
would seem at all possible to classify as part of the left or the labour
movement (TUC, Co-op, Fabian Society, the Labour Party NEC, the Post
Office Unions and the Society of Civil and Public Servants plus Francis
Cripps and Ron Thomas MP). Thus *one* Labour MP gave evidence, very few
trades unions and only one person identifiable as a leftish academic.
This thinness of evidence meant that when oral evidence was taken the
Committee could quite 'reasonably' restrict those called to a few
standard 'representative' groups, with only the TUC putting a position
for the Labour movement (see Second Stage Evidence, Vols.1-5). Of
course this is not to suggest that this was the only factor operative;

by any standards the failure to call the Labour Party NEC to give oral evidence was extraordinary.

Clearly this paucity of contribution marks a striking feature of the British left: for all the talk of this being the age of finance capital etc. the left generally appears to have singularly little to say on either the broad questions of the relations between the financial and other sectors of the economy or on the institutional arrangements which construct this relation. Most striking perhaps is the absence of any grouping of left academics able to formulate and argue through socialist positions in this area - contrast social policy for example, where the left has continuously made serious contributions (Titmuss, Townsend, Abel-Smith, Wootton etc.), or the law (Griffiths, Wedderburn, Zander).[3] Equally there is no institutional equivalent as a pressure group to the CPAG or LAG or the NCCL.[4] A grouping of academic economists (and others) such as the CSE has been singularly unproductive of either material on finance capital in general (the one excepting being Hussain 1976; see also Overbeek 1980) or on proposals for changing financial institutions in Britain.

These shortcomings are difficult to explain. They may in part be a function of the domination of Left economics by a particular kind of Marxism, which is nothing like so true for social policy or law. This Marxism has privileged on the one hand value theory and on the other very general analyses of 'the state', 'the labour process' etc., both of which have perhaps been inimical to analyses of the financial system. This is not of course all of the explanation - even within more specific discussions of modern capitalism, the stress of much British left writing has been on 'monopoly' as opposed to 'finance' capital (a position which hopefully will be at least partially remedied by the publication of Hilferding's *Finance Capital* in English for the first time in 1981).

These theoretical trends have been added to by the obstacles put in the way of *policy* discussion per se by the reformist/revolutionary dichotomy. This dichotomy has tended to make much CSE policy discussion extremely defensive because always likely to incur the charge of 'reformism' (a problem not of course peculiar to the CSE within the British left).

The weaknesses in the left's ability to mount a case for nationalisation of the banks is reflected not only in the lack of evidence putting such a case but also in the conduct of the Committee vis-à-vis other evidence. Thus the lengthy London Clearing Banks evidence on nationalisation (LCB 1977) passed more or less unchallenged before the Committee - and one of the main reasons was surely the shortage of ammunition for sympathetic members of the Committee to use to question this evidence. As far as arguments went, almost all the artillery was with the right. This position of weakness is also reflected in the fact that the Report of the Committee is so close to unanimity. There is only a short note of dissent concerning the provision of a new investment facility; on the rejection of nationalisation there is no dissent at all.

Committees like Wilson are almost bound to see a major part of their proceedings as consulting the 'relevant' interest groups. This means that the form of representation of interest groups is going to have a significant impact on such a committee's activities. Given that the *form* of representation of such interests partly constructs what is represented, these forms should themselves be seen as arenas of struggle for the left. In the case of Wilson a very important interest group

consulted was the small business lobby; so important was this that the
financing of small firms was the concern of one of the total of three
pieces of research commissioned by Wilson. Yet the small business lobby
has become in Britain the almost exclusive preserve of the right. This
is evident in the Bolton Committee and other arenas where small business
has been discussed. But there is nothing inherent about small business
that makes it clearly an ally of the right (see Tomlinson 1980), and
the political alignment of small business with City of London interests
might be considered perverse rather than natural. Few elements in
Britain are more powerful generators and supporters of large size and
monopoly than the City. If the left could at least contest the hegemonisation of such interests by the right then this, like an organised
caucus of socialist academics, would be a means of making a position
heard within public commissions and committees.

Such a contestation is all the more necessary because of the lack of
any already constituted interest on the left or in the trades unions to
which policies on the financial system could be linked. Whilst the TUC,
as in so many other areas, has shown a concern with broad issues of
policy atypical of most individual trade unions, this has led to general
support for changes rather than detailed policy proposals on the financial system. (No doubt this in part reflects the resources available to
the TUC.) The only individual trades unions much concerned with the
issues raised by Wilson were the unions organising workers in the financial sector, and not surprising they saw their main objective as safeguarding the interests of their members, especially where nationalisation
might lead to a 'rationalisation' of the banking system and a loss of
jobs. The evidence given to Wilson no doubt exaggerates the lack of
interest by trades unions, as they had a considerable input into the
discussions at the stage of the original formulation of the Labour Party's
proposals. Nevertheless it cannot be said that proponents of radical
change in the financial system have a clear trade union interest to work
with.

Clearly the possibilities offered by Royal Commissions, and other
public committees of enquiry, for interventions by the left should not
be exaggerated. If such interventions were mounted this would probably
lead to a response by the right. And of course, whatever a Royal
Commission may say, it is the government of the day which decides the
legislative programme, and commissions putting forward views not amenable
to governments have often been ignored. But of course the suggestion
being made here is not that taking seriously such channels as Royal
Commissions is a replacement for struggles elsewhere, but that the left's
position should be 'no avenue unexplored'. Royal Commissions and allied
enquiries are likely to be a more profitable avenue than others, partly
because of their 'public' nature. This makes it possible to at least
partially break out of the bounds of suffocating secrecy characteristic
of much British governments' policy discussion.

A WEAK CASE FOR NATIONALISATION

The first half of this review implied that the shortcoming of the left
in respect of Wilson was a failure to operate in a way to get a 'good
case' more widely publicised and debated. In this section we will
suggest that the case made by the left for nationalisation of the banks
is not in fact a very strong one.

Proposals to nationalise the banks have a long if intermittent history
on the British left. However, the justification for such proposals has
varied enormously, including

> redistributive justice and economic power ... efficiency, the
> maintenance of employment, the prevention of poverty, the control
> over foreign policy, the planning of industry, efficiency and low
> cost in banking, the prevention of fraud, the reduction in nepotism,
> the development of long-term investment....
> (Pollard, 1978, pp.184-85)

Clearly this history reflects the role of nationalisation as the traditional centrepiece of the economic objectives of British socialism. The
nationalisation proposals which led up to the Wilson Committee - the
Labour Party's *Banking and Finance* (1976) - at least used a clear line
of argument to justify its proposals.

The document takes off from the argument that Britain's economic
problems stem centrally from a low level of investment in manufacturing
activity.[5] Much of the blame for this lack of investment is said to
lie with the financial institutions, and therefore nationalisation of
the banks and insurance companies is the means to achieve higher levels
of investment and ultimately thereby to solve Britain's major economic
problems.

There are a number of criticisms which can be made of such an argument. First it is *not* the case, for most of the last couple of decades
during which this low level of industrial investment has been apparent,
that British industrial firms have generally been starved of investment
funds. For most of that period (until the current recession) industrial
firms have been net *lenders* to the rest of the economy. The reason for
this is that industrial firms, who are in no way constrained in their
investment outlets, have commonly found more profitable use for their
funds than investment in industrial assets. In particular they have
purchased government debt which has offered much higher rates of return
than most kinds of industrial investment.

Two major points are important in relation to this. On the one hand
it should not be taken to imply that the conditions under which credit
is granted to firms does not itself affect their assessment of investment opportunities. As Thompson (1977) has argued, the financial institutions by operating certain lending criteria *do* bias investment decisions towards those areas which yield a high short-term cash flow and
this in many cases acts as a bias against industrial investment which
typically has a long pay-off period.[6] But if the banks are to be criticised, one major strand of criticism should concern their lending
criteria and their effects on the *pattern* of investment, rather than a
stress on an *absolute* shortage of funds which is not supported by the
evidence.

A stress on lending criteria means bringing out the width of discretion that lending institutions have, as opposed to the passive 'inter-
mediary' role that is sometimes ascribed to them. Also the importance
of institutional features irreducible to any general theory of capitalist social relations is apparent when British financial institutions
are compared with those in other countries. Despite the clichéd nature
of the point, it remains true that much of the British financial system
is not organised to 'serve' industry - it does not have the personnel
and competence to deal with industrial matters. It is in this context
that *illustrative* international comparisons can be made with the

financial systems of West Germany and Japan. The point is not that the
practices of these countries can be simply transferred to Britain, but
that those practices serve to underline the particular biases and shortcomings of those of British banks.

The other implication of this 'net lender' position of industrial
firms is that it should bring out the importance of state financing to
the operation of the financial system, something entire absent from
Banking and Finance. The argument here is not, as many on the right
have alleged, that government borrowing 'crowds out' private investment.
The amount of credit is not a fixed 'cake' and indeed is increased by
certain forms of government borrowing which provide the reserve assets
to support expanded bank lending. The point that should be stressed
is rather that under current conditions of government financing (i.e.
mainly sales of financial assets to private institutions), this financing
has to be made 'attractive' to private financial institutions. This
means that it is also bound to attract lenders from the industrial
sector. The policy implication of this is the need to explore different
modes of state financing (including both taxation and borrowing) as a
way of severing the link between state borrowing and private financial
institutions.

Borrowing policies might aim at attempting to 'segment' the market,
i.e. offering different forms of debt to different markets. A good
example of this is the current government's expansion of the index-
linked 'granny bond' scheme, though of course the government's reason
for this is to increase the sale of debt outside the banking system as
part of a monetary policy. The left has been strikingly less imaginative
than the Tories in this regard. Such 'segmentation' could help both to
lessen the effects of debt sales in bidding up interest rates, and at
the same time reduce the leverage which private financial institutions
exercise over government policy through the terms on which they agree to
buy the debt.

A second major strand of criticism relating to the Labour Party proposals is the sparse attention given to building societies as financial
institutions, as opposed to their role vis-à-vis housing problems. As
the London Clearing Banks (1977) rightly point out, the Labour Party
document almost ignores the fact that building societies receive a
larger flow of funds than do the clearing banks, and in that sense are
more important to the economy than the banks. Perhaps some of this
skating over the role of the building societies relates to the fact
that they are not private, profit-making institutions, but mutual
societies. But here, as in other areas, the private/public distinction
between institutions does not give much of a guide to the desirability
of their practices (cf. Taylor, n.d.). In the case of the building
societies, there is a very good case for very large reforms relating
to their lending policies, their excessive branch proliferation etc.
More important, in relation to their financial influence, there is a
very strong case for removing the tax privileges given to house purchase
which in part is responsible for the large role played by building
societies. There seems little logic in encouraging spiralling house
prices by various tax exemptions and subsidies which serve to make house
purchase one of the most prifitable forms of investment rather than just
one item of consumption. If, as the Labour Party rightly says, the
banks' aid to property speculation is to be attacked, it makes little
sense at the same time to gloss over the fact that building societies

are also agencies for channelling funds into highly dubious uses. The
other side of such tax changes might be to give a specific tax subsidy
for lending to *industry*.

A great deal is made in the Labour Party document of international
comparisons which show a much larger public share in financial institutions in other Western European countries compared with Britain.
However, the mechanisms of the relation between this larger public
sector and the high levels of investment to which it is implied to be
linked are never spelt out. This really takes us to the heart of the
problem, for what the case for nationalisation has to establish is
that nationalisation is relevant to the criteria used by financial
institutions in their lending policies, as well as that these lending
policies are crucial for the level of investment by industrial firms.
The second proposition has already been suggested to be highly problematic, but the first seems equally so.

The Labour Party document in relation to the Bank of England accepts
that nationalisation per se may make little difference to the practices
of institutions: 'The Bank of England was nationalised 30 years ago.
It has yet to be socialised' (paragraph 48). Now rightly this is
stressed as implying increased accountability by the Bank, but also a
change in policies. Yet when the nationalisation of the clearing banks
is discussed there is no clear case made as to what these changes of
policy will be, except the idea that the banks will be less willing to
finance property speculation and other non-industrial uses of funds.
But then it is far from obvious why such a policy requires nationalisation. The Bank of England, by the Nationalisation Act of 1947 already
has the legal power to control bank lending. The fact that this power
has not been used, and that it is clearly subject to constraints, still
leaves a policy of Bank of England regulation a more likely effective,
and politically plausible, policy to follow than nationalisation.

Equally it could be argued that if the common problem is that
industrial firms have funds, but choose to spend them on non-industrial
assets, this may be an argument for, for example, legal constraints on
what they can invest in (similar to the Investment Reserve Fund Scheme
mentioned in the Labour Party document (paragraphs 41 and 52)). This
indeed would appear to be a policy more likely to change investment
levels than *any* change in the financial institutions.

A further criticism which can be easily made of the Labour Party
proposals is the complete absence of any discussion of the international
context in which the financial system operates. Given both the massive
international role of the City of London on the one hand, and the importance of international financial flows to the British balance of payments
on the other, this is really an extraordinary omission. In particular
the role of this international 'vulnerability' of the British economy
in raising the level of interest rates to domestic borrowers is surely
important (see Fishman, 1980). And for an explicitly *political* document
Banking and Finance seems hardly alive to the possible international
consequences of the measures proposed.

Nationalisation per se may not make much difference to the attractiveness or otherwise to foreigners of holding deposits in these banks (this
seems to have been true in the French case - Wilson, paragraph 1363).
But clearly in Britain where so much of the financial system is internationally oriented the *international* policies to be pursued by any new
institutions need to be spelt out. Would socialists for example have

objections to nationalised British banks continuing to bale out the Polish government, to take a typical example? Here again the thinness of the left's case is apparent.

ALTERNATIVES TO NATIONALISATION

These arguments are in no way intended as a defence of the status quo. Rather they are intended to highlight the way in which nationalisation as a policy for the financial sector singularly fails to come to grips with the 'problem', *even* where that problem is accepted to be one of low manufacturing investment.

A much better proposal, which is briefly included in the Labour Party document, is one which attempts to combine and greatly expand the existing public sector in banking, the National Giro and the National Savings Bank. This would have the merit not only of providing a competitive public bank against the domination of the clearers, but also it could be coupled with measures aimed at aiding a policy of financing public borrowing from within the public sector, thus undercutting the role of private institutions in determining government finance (as noted above). Another possible effect of such an expanded public banking sector would be to undercut the extremely conservative view that the clearers take of their role vis-à-vis industry. This of course would not be *guaranteed* by such public sector ganking, but could be encouraged by the possibilities this would offer for greater scrutiny of bank decisions. It is striking for example that in their evidence to Wilson, the clearing banks argue (London Clearing Banks, 1977, pp.215-16) that they see their role as 'responding to demand subject to credit worthiness'. No idea here of the banks seeking out 'demand' and encouraging investment in projects - and therefore no wonder that they have expanded their medium-term lending to industry *only* in response to aggressive American competition (*ibid.*, p.213). The existing clearing ganks are on the whole extremely ignorant of industry and do not have the means in many instances to act as *catalysts* for investment - but in the face of competition this also could be changed.

The proposal to merge the NSB and Giro was discussed and rejected by Wilson (Report, paragraphs 1368-1401) and perhaps if more attention had been focussed on this proposal it would have been less easy for it to be dismissed on the basis of very weak arguments.

Finally one may draw from the Wilson episode a lesson: the need for the left to broaden the arenas where they are willing to engage with the opposition. Also the lesson that in the particular area of finance there is an enormous amount of both theoretical and empirical work to be done to formulate plausible, workable policies.

NOTES

1 The Money Group itself is not exempt from these criticisms, especially those relating to the first aspect.
2 Excluding Harold Wilson who may be considered *sui generis* it consisted of 4 trades unionsts, 4 academics, 3 industrialists, 4 men from financial institutions (including the Chairman of the Co-operative Bank), one financial journalist and an accountant.

3 For a more extreme case one might imagine the scale of response from the left if there were to be a Royal Commission on History. (though there was remarkably little socialist interest in the recent Committee on the Preservation of Public Records, despite the clear political significance of those records, illustrated by the recent suppression of records relating to the Metropolitan Police).

4 There does exist the Labour Economic, Finance and Taxation Association which has produced some useful documents but not apparently attempted to act as a pressure group (see especially Taylor, n.d.).

5 This view is open to considerable dispute - see Caves and Krause, 1980.

6 The stock exchange may have a similar effect, not because it provides much of industrial investment funds, but because the secondary market in shares acts as a form of scrutiny of the financial performance of quoted companies.

REFERENCES

Cartwright, T. (1975) *Royal Commissions and Departmental Committees in Britain*

Caves, R. and Krause, L. (eds.) (1980), *Britain's Economic Performance*

Fishman, D. (1980) 'A Radical View of the European Monetary System', *Politics & Power* 1, pp.175-84

Hindess, B. (1980) 'Democracy and the Limits of Parliamentary Democracy in Britain', *Politics & Power* 1, pp.165-74

Hussain, A. (1976) 'Hilferding's "Finance Capital"', *Bulletin of the Conference of Socialist Economists*

Labour Party (1976) *Banking and Finance*

London Clearing Banks (1977) Evidence by the Committee of London Clearing Bankers to the Committee to Review the Functioning of Financial Institutions

Overbeek, H. (1980) 'Finance Capital and the Crisis in Britain', *Capital and Class* 11

Pollard, S. (1978) 'The Nationalisation of the Banks: The Chequered History of a Socialist Proposal', in D. Martin and D. Rubenstein (eds.), *Ideology and the Labour Movement*

Taylor, T. (n.d.) Nationalisation of Banking and Insurance: A Dissenting View, Labour Economic Finance and Taxation Association

Thompson, G. (1977) 'The Relationship between the Financial and Industrial Sector in the UK Economy', *Economy and Society* 6, 3

Tomlinson, J. (1980) 'Socialist Politics and the "Small Business"', *Politics & Power* 1

THE ECONOMISTS' BOOKSHOP

CLARE MARKET, PORTUGAL STREET, LONDON WC2A 2AB

* We have a stock of over 10,000 titles which
  include both classic and modern texts in
  economics, politics, economic and political
  history, statistics, industrial relations,
  management, sociology, anthropology and
  philosophy.

* We have an excellent secondhand bookshop
  'The Shop Across the Street' where you can
  buy bargain and out of print titles.

* We have a thriving mail order service

MON - FRI 9.30 - 6.00 p.m.
SAT (during term time)
10.00 - 1.00 p.m.

TEL : 01 405 5531

WE ARE THE SPECIALISTS, SO
WHY NOT PAY US A VISIT ?

Andrew Mack
The Soviet Threat: Reality or Myth?

INTRODUCTION

That Americans should be so deeply concerned by current trends in world
politics is wholly comprehensible. In the past three decades America's
hegemonic position in world politics has eroded dramatically while
Soviet military power has grown. In 1950 the US accounted for half
the world's military expenditure and held a de facto nuclear monopoly.
Half the world's financial reserves were in American hands and the US
economy accounted for two-thirds of world production. Yet by 1975 the
US share of world military expenditure had shrunk to a quarter, and its
share of world production to less than one third. By the end of the
decade less than 7% of world monetary reserves were held by the US.[1]
    In the same period the portion of national wealth allocated to
defence in the US had fallen from over 10% of GNP in the early 1950s
to just over 5% at the end of the 1970s. In the meantime, according
to the CIA, the Soviets have been increasing their defence expenditure
both absolutely and as a percentage of GNP. Many US strategic and
political analysts argue that the Soviet arms build-up, especially
during the 1970s, has created massive asymmetries in military power
which favour the USSR and pose a growing threat to Western security.
    The importance of the relative American decline and the Soviet build-
up becomes readily apparent, such strategists argue, in the context of
a Vietnam-induced paralysis of political will in Washington. Relatively
weakened US military strength and Washington's reluctance to pursue its
'global responsibilities' have severely eroded the containment policy
which successfully blocked Soviet expansionism during the first two
post-war decades. The Soviets' ideological commitment to world domination remains firm; US resolve to contain such expansionism has weakened.
US overall capability has declined relatively, that of the Soviet Union
has increased. The consequences are predictable and have been manifest
in the upsurge of Soviet expansionism in the Third World following the
American debacle in Vietnam. Hence the Soviet successes in Angola,
Ethiopia, South Yemen, Kampuchea and, of course, Afghanistan.
    America's growing incapacity, it is said, has been further underlined
by the collapse of the so-called Nixon Doctrine with the overthrow of

the Shah of Iran in 1979 in the strategically crucial Gulf region. The
Nixon doctrine had sought to use such powerful regional allies as the
Shah as US surrogates. These 'regional influentials' were to be armed
and trained by the US. Their armed forces were to fulfil essentially
the same counterrevolutionary role as US interventionary forces in the
1950s and 1960s but without the political odium or the huge economic
costs of Vietnam-type direct interventions.

Thus a weakened US is seen to confront an increasingly powerful,
increasingly aggressive Soviet Union, and can expect little help from
either its European allies, who have shown a marked reluctance to 'share
the burden' of US global responsibilities, or from its Third World allies
whose potential instability means, as Iran has shown, that they cannot
be relied on.

This picture of the decline in American power and parallel growth of
the Soviet threat will be familiar in one form or another to most
readers of the popular press. In the US it has been pushed with great
effectiveness by such neo-conservative organisations as the American
Security Council and the Committee for the Present Danger which have
consistently advocated the hard-line foreign policies now being adopted
by the Reagan administration.

In this paper I will argue that the neo-conservative argument is grossly
flawed, that it is based on analyses of Soviet capabilities, interests
and foreign policy behaviour which are extraordinarily one-sided and
hence misleading. Furthermore, the neo-conservative case ignores alternative interpretations of Soviet behaviour, or seeks, quite unwarrantedly,
to dismiss their proponents as appeasers. In the following sections of
this paper I shall examine neo-conservative claims that the nuclear and
conventional balances have tilted decisively in the Soviets' favour. I
shall also examine the argument that Soviet post-Vietnam 'successes' in
the Third World provide convincing evidence for the thesis that the
Soviet Union is an increasingly successful imperialist power. Finally
I shall suggest an alternative perspective on Soviet foreign policy to
balance that of the neo-conservatives.

The paper does not seek to provide a 'balanced' analysis in the sense
of giving equal space to all points of view. Rather it seeks to present
an alternative view, to redress the neo-conservative-determined *imbalance*.
It should hardly be necessary to point out that a critique of the neo-
conservative anti-Soviet position in no sense implies advocacy of a pro-
Soviet position.

THE STRATEGIC (NUCLEAR) BALANCE

> ... the United States has been standing still - even unilaterally
> disarming - in strategic forces for the past decade, while the
> Soviet Union has doggedly driven ahead.[2]

Thus the new conventional wisdom. The neo-conservative case can be
plausibly supported with the use of carefully selected statistics.
Hence we are told that the Soviet Union has more strategic delivery
systems (these include land-based missiles [ICBMs], submarine-launched
missiles [SLBMs] and intercontinental bombers) than the US - the numbers

are 2348 (USSR) versus 2050 (USA). The total explosive yield of the Soviet strategic attack force is 4,497 megatons versus 3,210 for the US.[3] In historical perspective the picture is apparently even more alarming. Since 1969, the Soviets have added nearly 1,000 delivery vehicles to their total while the US has actually reduced its delivery system total by some 200.[4] In 1965 the US had a 7:1 lead over the Soviet Union in total megatonnage. Today the Soviets have a 1:4-to-1 lead over the US.

Each of the above facts is true, yet presented in isolation (or with other equally selectively chosen facts) they create a grossly misleading impression of the overall strategic balance. At first glance the entire argument seems irrelevant. President Jimmy Carter pointed out to Americans in his 1979 State of the Union message that just one of America's relatively invulnerable Poseidon submarines - less than two per cent of the total US nuclear force - carries enough warheads to destroy every large and medium-sized city in the Soviet Union. The remaining 98% of warheads might then seem to be superfluous. The Soviet Union also has an enormous 'overkill' capability against US cities. However, Soviet cities are no longer the primary targets for US missiles - nor have they been for a long time. Current US strategic doctrine focusses on military targets - the USSR's land-based missile installations, air fields, command, control, and communication (C3) centres, submarine bases and so forth. Since there are many thousands of military targets - many of them heavily protected (missiles in heavy concrete silos for example) there is also, so it is argued, a corresponding need for many thousands of offensive weapons to destroy them. Military or 'counter-force' targetting, in sharp contrast to 'counter-value' city targetting, generates an inexhausitible demand for new weapons. Given wholly predictable Soviet reactions to new US weapons' programmes, 'counter-force' targetting is also a prescription for a permanent arms race. The increased American emphasis on targetting militarion installations was underlined by President Carter's Presidential Directive (PD-59) of 25 July 1980, which now excludes targetting the Soviet population per se - though economic and industrial centres in urban areas may still be targetted. Currently the US SIOP (Single Integrated Operational Plan) lists some 40,000 potential targets - compared with 25,000 in 1974.[5]

Since Soviet nuclear weapons totals are also grossly in excess of the needs of a 'city-busting', minimum-deterrence doctrine, and since the accuracy of Russian missiles, like those of the US, is far greater than required for such 'soft' targets as cities, there is no doubt that the Soviets, like their opponents, are also targetting military installations.

There are many reasons for the increased emphasis on military targetting in the US. In part it arose out of a belief that the old emphasis (at least in *official* policy) of Mutual Assured Destruction (MAD) was too inflexible. If, as the official declaratory policy implied, each side held the other's civilian population hostage to a nuclear attack; if each strike could still inflict devastating damage on the other even if the other struck first, then there was a sense in which nuclear forces were stalemated. It would never be rational for either side to use them. This, said the critics of MAD, meant that the city-busting MAD policy was no real deterrent at all. Confronting Soviet aggression in, say, Europe, the US would be confronted with the choice of suicide if it used its nuclear weapons against Soviet cities

(because the Soviets would respond in kind), or surrender if it did
not.

Targetting military installations offered the choice of a 'flexible
response'. The critics of MAD argued that it was important to be able
to fight a *limited* nuclear war with 'surgical' nuclear warning strikes
against carefully selected targets. Nuclear war was thus deliberately
made less unthinkable. Nuclear weapons were now to be seen as war-
fighting weapons rather than simply war-deterring weapons; their
increased use-value would also increase their deterrent capability.

The new nuclear war-fighting doctrine was heavily criticised when it
was first announced publicly by US Defence Secretary James Schlesinger
in 1974. Critics were quick to point out that making nuclear weapons
more useable made their actual use more probable. The new doctrine
increased the risk of nuclear war when there was no evidence that the
MAD deterrence doctrine had failed. Furthermore, given the Clausewitz-
ian strategic maxim of rapid escalation to maximum force levels in order
to secure victory - or (more importantly) to avoid defeat, what was to
prevent the 'limited' nuclear war rapidly escalating into unlimited
nuclear holocaust? This question was particularly pointed since, to
make strategic sense, the limited nuclear war doctrine depended on the
Soviets accepting the Pentagon's rules of the game. Clearly the US
doctrine would make no sense if an American 'warning' nuclear strike
against the USSR was to be met with a several thousand missile 'spasm'
counter-attack from the USSR. Yet, since 1974, the Soviets have
emphatically rejected the US concept of limited nuclear war.

Recognition of the 'difficulty' that limited nuclear wars may become
unlimited has also led to a stress on maximising 'damage limitation'
capacilities. If, for whatever reason a nuclear war does break out,
then it becomes of crucial importance to maximise damage to the opponent's offensive nuclear capability in order to minimise damage to oneself. As former US Defense Secretary Donald Rumsfeld noted in 1978,
'The most ambitious (damage limitation) strategy dictates a first strike
capability against the enemy's strategic offensive forces...'[6] A 'first
strike capability' means the ability to totally disarm the opponent's
land, sea and bomber-launched offensive nuclear forces in a single
massive pre-emptive strike.

The new public emphasis on nuclear war-fighting, damage-limiting,
strategies places a premium on maximising warhead numbers and the lethality, reliability and readiness of delivery systems, and on minimising
the vulnerability of those systems. In each of these areas the US has
a substantial advantage over the USSR.

I argued earlier that the fact that the Soviets had a larger number
of delivery systems than the US (2348 vs. 2050) with a greater total
explosive yield (4,497 MT vs. 3,210) was no true guide to the nuclear
strategic balance. There are two major reasons for this. First,
missile delivery systems are now simply launching platforms for 'multiple independently targettable re-entry vehicles' (MIRVs), and 'MIRVing'
has been the major technological development in missile warfare of the
1970s.

In contrast to the 1960s, when each missile launcher carried one
warhead, during the 1970s the MIRV revolution had massively increased
the US strike capability. Minutemen missiles (ICBMs) were fitted with
three warheads, the Poseidon C-3 missile has ten. The MIRV revolution
meant that, although the number of US delivery systems was less than

that of the USSR, and actually declined during the 1970s, the US *warhead*
total increased dramatically - from just over 4,000 in 1969 to 9,200
today.   The Soviets lag the US by some five years in MIRV technology and,
according to official US figures, *their* current warhead total is only
around 6,000.[7]   As Henry Kissinger once observed, one is hit by the warheads not the launchers.   In other words, it is warheads not delivery
system totals which provide the better measure of strike capability.
The US has maintained its warhead lead since the nuclear arms race began.

The use of total megatonnage (where the Soviets do lead the US) as a
'measure' of force efficacy is also misleading.   A far more appropriate
measure is *lethality* - the ability of a weapon to destroy a designated
target.   Lethality is a function of explosive yield and accuracy.   And
here we find that the much-vaunted Soviet lead in missile explosive
yields is more than offset by US advantages in missile accuracy.   Accuracy is in fact considerably more important in determining the lethality
of a weapons system against 'hardened' (i.e. blast-resistant) targets
such as missile silos than is explosive yield.   To put it simply, 'making the warhead twice as accurate has the same effect as making the
bomb eight times as powerful'.[9]   Accuracy improvements in US missile
guidance systems since 1970 have 'nearly tripled the ICBMs' effectiveness
against the hardest of Soviet targets...'[10]   Furthermore the US ICBM
improvements have been '... more than six times as cost effective as
Soviet improvements'.[11]

Two more important factors should be noted at this point - the reliability and readiness levels of the opposing sides' strategic missile
forces.   Reliability refers to the probability that missiles will
complete their mission when launched.   Here again the balance clearly
favours the US.   'The reliability of US missiles ranges from 75 to 80%.
Soviet reliability is somewhat lower at between 65 and 75%...   Readiness
denotes the number of missiles ready to launch at any given time ...
the readiness of US strategic forces is 95%, while the corresponding
Soviet readiness is only 75%.'[12]   The above quoted reliability and
readiness figures are for 1975.   Actual values may have changed since
then, the US *relative* advantage still continues however.)   To give some
idea of how these factors may affect the comparisons of the strategic
nuclear balance, consider the following example.   Both sides start off
with 1,000 missiles but, due to the readiness factor, the US can count
on 950 being ready for use at any time, the Soviets can count on only
750.   When the reliability index is factored in, 80% of the 950 ready
US missiles (at best) can be counted on to complete their mission.
The effective, reliable US operational missile total is thus 760 out
of the original 1,000 missiles.   The Soviets with (at best) 75% reliability for their 750 ready missiles can only count on 570 effective and
reliable missiles.   Our hypothetical example shows that even the Soviet
numerical advantage in delivery systems is more than offset by their
disadvantages in reliability and readiness.

Thus it can be seen that US superiority in MIRV and guidance system
technology, in reliability and missile force readiness have kept the
US well ahead in the strategic arms race and will continue to do so.
Table 1 shows how the US has constantly led its major rival in weapons
systems innovations.

Politics & Power Four

Table 1   Comparative Technological Innovation in Offensive Strategic Weapons [13]

Nature of innovation	United States	Soviet Union
Atomic (nuclear) explosion	1945	1949
Intercontinental bomber operational	1948	1955
Hydrogen (thermonuclear) explosion	1951	1953
Deliverable thermonuclear weapon	1954	1955
Nuclear-powered submarine	1954	1958
First test of intercontinental ballistic missile (ICBM)	1958	1957
Operational ICBM	1960	1959
Operational submarine-launched ballistic missile (SLBM	1960	1957
Solid propellant ICBM operational	1962	1968
Test of multiple re-entry vehicle (MRV) (US deployment: 1964)	1962	1968
Test of multiple independently targettable re-entry vehicle (MIRV)	1968	1973
ICBM with MIRVs operational	1970	1974/75
Test of modern long-range cruise missiles (ALCM, SLCM)	1976	1979(?)
High operational ICBM accuracy (CEP approximately .15 nautical mile)	1980	mid-1980s
Antisatellite weapons	mid-1980s	mid-1980s

THE QUESTION OF VULNERABILITY

I noted earlier that the vulnerability of delivery systems was of crucial strategic importance. Indeed the growing vulnerability of America's ICBM Minuteman force has become a highly controversial political issue in the US over the past few years. Neo-conservatives argue, quite correctly, that the US Minuteman force will become vulnerable to a Soviet ICBM attack in the early 1980s. Once Soviet missiles achieve a sufficiently high degree of accuracy no further 'hardening' of US missile silos will protect them.

Quite why this particular area of vulnerability should occasion so much concern in the US is not clear. First, as the Soviets are very well aware, the US always has the option of adopting a launch-on-warning response to a Soviet attack. In such an event Soviet missiles would hit empty American missile silos while the US missiles were en route to their Soviet targets.

Secondly, and more importantly, even if the Soviets were successful in knocking out all the US ICBMs (which is unlikely), this would still leave the US submarine ballistic missile fleet and bomber force completely intact. The US has only 21% of its strategic warheads deployed on land-based ICBMs compared with 54% on submarines and 25% on bombers.[14] The Soviets by contrast have 79% of their warheads deployed on land, none on bombers and the remaining 21% on submarines.[15]

Thirdly we must ask what conceivable interest could the Russians have in attacking US ICBMs while leaving 79% of the US nuclear strike force unscathed? The answer is surely none at all. Furthermore there

is not a shred of evidence from past Soviet behaviour to indicate that
Moscow would even contemplate such a totally irrational attack. Since
the Cuban missile crisis of 1963 the Soviets have gone out of their way
to avoid *any* direct military confrontation with the US.

With the exception of the current generation of ICBMs, America's
nuclear forces are well protected. As former US Defense Secretary
Harold Brown noted in his 1980 Fiscal Year report, the current generation
of US ballistic missile submarines is invulnerable for the foreseeable
future.[16] Soviet antisubmarine warfare technology lags a long way behind
that of the US. A 1978 US Congressional Research Service Report stated
that the 'Soviets apparently have no effective capability for open-
ocean ASW, regardless of the scenario envisaged'.[17] This last point is
of considerable importance since the new Trident I missile currently
being retrofitted to US Poseidon submarines has a range of some 4,000
nautical miles compared with the 2,500 nm range of the Poseidon missile.
The additional range '... expands the area of ocean from which our subs
can operate by a factor of 10 to 20'.[18] This of course will complicate
the Soviets' ASW task still further.

In contrast to ballistic missile submarines it might well be thought
that the lumbering, 20-year-old sub-sonic B52 bombers which carry a
fifth of the US warhead total would be highly vulnerable to the USSR's
increasingly sophisticated air defence systems, which will shortly
include look-down-shoot down interceptors. Indeed the potential vulnerability, as well as the cost, of manned penetrating bombers was one of
the factors leading President Carter to scrap the multi-billion dollar
B-1 programme - a decision condemned by neo-conservative critics as an
act of 'unilateral disarmament'.

However, the age of the B52s' airframe belies the up-to-date nature
of many of its avionic systems. The bomber's performance has actually
improved very considerably over time - and is likely to continue to do
so as a result of a planned avoinics modernisation programme in the
early 1980s.

In one sense the debate about penetrating bomber vulnerability is
becoming decreasingly relevant. In the 1980s manned bomber tactics
will de-emphasise the capability to penetrate Soviet air defences.
Under the terms of the SALT II agreement (which remains unratified but
is still being unofficially observed), the US will equip each of its
151 operational B52G bombers with twenty air-launched long-range cruise
missiles (ALCMs).[19] This will enable the bombers to 'stand-off' out
of range of Soviet air defences and launch their missiles at targets a
thousand miles inside the Soviet Union. The cruise missile with its
highly accurate 'map reading', computerised guidance system (TERCOM),
its ability to hug the terrain at very low altitudes, and its relatively
tiny radar cross-section (one thousandth of that of a B-52)[20] presents
an extraordinarily elusive target for the Soviet air defence system.
The highly accurate guidance system and the 150 kiloton warhead also
give the cruise missile an extraordinarily high degree of lethality.
It can destroy anything it is aimed at. The Soviets currently have no
long range modern cruise missile capability.

There is little doubt that, in time, the Soviets will develop new
means of detecting the cruise missile, such as look-down and over-the-
horizon radar, and new surface-to-air missile (SAM) systems to destroy
them. Long range interceptors may also be developed to attack the
cruise missile launching platforms (B52s) *before* the missiles are

launched. But such future Soviet developments would simply stimulate US counter measures, and the technological advantage lies squarely with the Americans.

In sum we can see that the United States' strategic weapons are more numerous, more accurate and hence more lethal, more reliable, more technologically advanced and less vulnerable than those of their Soviet adversaries.

THE STRANGE CASE OF SALT II

> To enter into a Treaty [SALT II] that favours the Soviet
> Union, as this one does, on the ground that we will be
> in a worse position without it, is ... appeasement in
> its purest form.[21]
> (US Senator, Henry Jackson)

The SALT II Treaty was signed in Vienna in June 1979, but has still not been ratified by the US Senate. Senate ratification was postponed indefinitely as a form of punishment directed against the Soviets for invading Afghanistan.

A major thrust of the neo-conservative critique of SALT II has been to claim, as the above quotation from Senator Jackson suggests, that the agreement concedes too much to the Russians and amounts in effect to a form of unilateral disarmament by the US. Yet any sober, impartial analysis of the treaty suggests that such claims are quite unfounded.

Neo-conservative critics have been extraordinarily selective in their choice of data to support their charges. For example, while protesting against the alleged Soviet 'advantage' derived from the current Russian lead in delivery system totals, they have failed to also point out that under the terms of SALT II this 'advantage' disappears completely, and that to achieve the agreed parity level of 2,250 the USSR will actually have to dismantle some of its delivery systems. The US on the other hand will be able to increase its overall total (adding in some areas, subtracting in others).

No current of planned major US weapons system procurement is prohibited by SALT, indeed this is one of the major criticisms of the treaty made by the few surviving arms control doves. Under the terms of SALT II the US can deploy the MX missile, the Trident submarine with its new missiles, and the long range air-launched cruise missile.

Much has been made by SALT II's conservative critics of the fact that the Treaty doesn't limit the 200 new Soviet Backfire (TU-22M) bombers which could, in theory at least, be used on one-way nuclear attack missions against the US. However, at the 1979 Carter/Brezhnev summit, the Soviets agreed to limit production to 30 Backfires a year *and* to avoid upgrading the planes' intercontinental capability.[22] None of the critics have explained how dumping SALT II would persuade the USSR to promise more than this. Indeed it is clear that without SALT II the Soviets would have no interest in maintaining the constraints on Backfire agreed at Vienna.

While it is true that SALT II does not deal officially with the Backfire issue, neither does it could in the strategic delivery system total: '... the 66 US FB-111 bombers that most assuredly *would* be used against the Soviet Union in a nuclear war; nor does it limit the 500 or so US aircraft in Europe that might be used to drop hundreds of nuclear weapons on the Soviet Union.'[23] On this issue the neo-conservative critics have been largely silent.

These so-called forward-based systems (FBS) have been a source of considerable and understandable concern to the Russians. 'Tactical' nuclear weapons (i.e. those mounted on short and medium-range delivery systems) are not counted in the strategic arms limitation talks at all despite the fact that their explosive yields are often many times greater than the Hiroshima bomb. These 'tactical' warheads, when mounted on US or other NATO fighter bombers, or intermediate range missiles (IRBMs) can be used to strike the Soviet Union.

Thus in the controversy about the new 'Eurostrategic' missiles, while it is quite true that the Soviets have already deployed their new mobile - SS-20 IRBM, it is also true that this missile cannot be used against the US itself. The American Pershing II missile, by contrast, with its 1,700 km range and the ground-launched cruise missile (2,500 km range),[24] which the US intends deploying in Europe by 1983, can both be used to strike deeply into the Soviet Union. Pershing II (which is nearly ten times as accurate as the SS-20) can reach Moscow from West Germany - the cruise missile can travel considerably further. Since the Pershing II flight time will only be 4-6 minutes (compared with 30 minutes for a US-launched ICBM), it will be an ideal first strike weapon. The Soviets have long held, and with good reason from their point of view, that US forward-based systems constitute a fourth arm of American strategic forces (the other three being the ICBM, bomber and submarine 'triad'). In addition to US forward-based systems the Soviets are also threatened by French, British and Chinese nuclear capabilities which are also ignored in SALT negotiations. The USSR's allies, of course, have no independent nuclear capability.

The Soviets have no forward bases from which to attack the US. When they attempted to obtain just one such base (for IRBMs), on Cuba in 1963, their action led to a highly dangerous nuclear confrontation with the United States. If the US were in a similar position to the Soviet Union there would be Soviet forward bases in Mexico and Canada from which several thousand 'tactical' nuclear weapons mounted on Soviet medium-range bombers and missiles could be used to strike at the US. Washington has consistently refused to include FBS systems in the SALT talks.

Perhaps the most important concession made by the Soviets in SALT II relates to the freeze on the number of warheads which can be deployed on each missile. Soviet missiles on average have a much greater pay load or 'throw weight' than do those of the US (the ratio is 11:7 approximately). This means that they can deploy either more powerful or more numerous warheads on each missile. The major Soviet ICBM, the SS18, currently carries eight warheads, but it could be modified to carry up to thirty.[25] Under the terms of the SALT II agreement the Soviets will be limited to a maximum of 308 SS-18 missiles, with a further maximum of ten MIRV warheads per missile[26] giving a total of 3,080 warheads for the SS-18 ICBM force. Without SALT II the 308 Soviet SS-18s alone could theoretically be modified to carry 9,240 warheads - more than the entire current US strategic warhead inventory. By contrast the US MX missile, which may be deployed by the late 1980s, is designed to carry ten warheads - 200 MX missiles are planned. The current generation of relatively low throw-weight Minuteman III carries three warheads and has been tested with seven.[27]

In signing the SALT II agreement the Soviets have voluntarily denied
themselves the ability to translate their throw-weight advantage over
the US (which was a major cause of neo-conservative criticism) into a
massive increase in independently targettable warheads having a counter-
force capability.

A US BID TO REGAIN NUCLEAR SUPERIORITY?

Why have the neo-conservatives been so hostile to SALT II if, as has
been argued, the Soviets have conceded more under the terms of the Vienna
agreement than has the US?

A possible reason is that some projections of warhead totals under
SALT II show the Soviets catching up or even surpassing the USA in the
mid 1980s. The projections have been contested, but what this would
mean in strategic terms is not at all clear - the US would still retain
lethality, invulnerability, reliability and readiness advantages, but in
any exchange which utilised the total available strategic forces on both
sides, the resulting destruction would be so appalling that any notion
of 'winning' becomes utterly meaningless for either side. This is true
even for the side which strikes pre-emptively. In a major nuclear war,
'... at a minimum, the United States would suffer 140 million fatalities
and the Soviet Union 113 million.'[29] A so-called counter-force war in
which military installations only were targetted, would leave anything
from 2 to 20 million Americans and 3.7 to 27.7 million Russians dead.[30]
And, as noted earlier, there is no guarantee that a limited war would
stay limited - a point strongly emphasised by former US Defense
Secretary Harold Brown, who stated in his 1979 report that 'it is difficult to visualise any nuclear exchange that could be kept from escalating to all out attacks on cities'.[31] Once certain thresholds have been
exceeded a few thousand more or less warheads has very little true
strategic significance. As Henry Kissinger pointed asked in 1974:

   ... what in the name of God is strategic superiority? What
   is the significance of it politically, militarily, operation-
   ally, at these levels of numbers? What do you do with it?[32]

If the strategic significance of numerical parity is of no great
import why the controversy? In part the answer lies in the fact that
the nuclear numbers game has acquired a political importance and significance largely divorced from any strategic meaning. The state of the
strategic arms race has come to symbolise relations between the super
powers. For the Soviets, SALT II means the attainment of the strategic
strike force numerical parity which they have long sought because parity
symbolises superpower equality. For American neo-conservatives parity
is equated with a US defeat. Hence it is hardly surprising that the
new Reagan administration should have signalled that it seeks a return
to American strategic 'superiority'. This of course is advocated in
part because, as new National Security Council Soviet expert Professor
Richard Pipes argues, 'Nuclear missiles ... have not only a military
utility; they are equally and perhaps even more useful as a means of
political and psychological suasion.'[33]

The Reagan victory represents the culmination of the steady rise in
influence of the neo-conservatives in the past five years. The new
administration has embarked on the largest and most expensive peace time
military build-up in American history. A five year expansion plan will

boost the defence budget from US$171 billion in fiscal year 1981 to $367.5 billion in 1986.[34] SALT II it seems has been rejected completely. The current US Defence Secretary, Caspar Weinberger, has denounced the Vienna agreement as permitting 'an enormous further increase in Soviet offensive capacity while presenting the danger of lulling us into a false sense of security'.[35]

Without SALT II the US will be able to engage the Soviet Union in a new nuclear arms race, capitalising on US technological superiority and Soviet economic weakness. For the neo-conservatives the point is not to halt the arms race but to win it. Soviet attempts to match US military build-ups will fail because the Soviet economy is in crisis - the US can 'spend the Soviets into the ground'.

US FIRST STRIKE CAPABILITY AND THE QUESTION OF SOVIET PERCEPTIONS

I have argued thus far that while 'winning' the nuclear arms race - restoring the American numerical ascendancy of the 1960s - may make sense in domestic political or symbolic terms, it has little strategic significance in the age of massive nuclear overkill. This is true as long as both sides retain their 'mutual assured destruction' (MAD) capability.

'Winning' the arms race does however make strategic sense if the objective is the achievement of a disarming 'first strike' capability. This implies the ability to knock out all of the opponents' offensive weapons in a single massive attack.

The new mood in Washington, the logic of 'damage limitation' strategies pushed to extremes (see former Defense Secretary Rumsefld's quote on this point in footnote 6), the very high lethality of the new US land- and sea-based strategic systems (the MX and Trident II [D-5] missiles), plus US advances in anti-submarine warfare technology, all lend credibility to charges that the US is seeking a disarming first strike capability against the Soviet Union.

Prudent strategists will always tend to argue that defence planning should be oriented towards the 'worst plausible case'. This means assuming the worst of an adversary's future intentions and the best of his future abilities in the area of weapons systems technology and production. The worst 'worst case' for any superpower defence planner is the prospect of an adversary gaining a disarming first strike capability. I have already discussed the considerable alarm generated in the US at the prospect of the Soviets gaining a first strike capability against the US ICBM force before 1985. Since such an attack would leave 79% of the US air- and sea-based strategic forces unscathed this hardly constitutes a *disarming* first strike in the normal sense of that term. Consider, by contrast, the propsect which confronts the Soviet 'worst case' planner. It will be remembered that approximately four-fifths of the Soviet strategic warhead total are mounted on some 1,400 land-based missiles. The new ten-warhead MX missile, some 200 of which are planned, is a first strike weapon par excellence - its warheads are not only 38 times more powerful than the Hiroshima bomb, but also twice as accurate as the current generation 3-warhead Minuteman III ICBM. (MX deployment is not expected until the mid-1980s and the basing mode is still undecided.) Two thousand MX warheads plus some 1,650 Minuteman warheads (the current total), all with a 'hard target' capability against Soviet

Soviet missile silos, would pose a grave threat to the 1,400 odd Soviet
ICBMs. As President Carter's arms control impact statement for Fiscal
Year 1980 pointed out:
> ... if the M-X were deployed in substantial numbers, the US
> would have acquired, through both the Minuteman and the M-X
> programmes, an apparent capability to destroy most of the
> Soviet silo-based ICBM force in a first strike.[36]

US 'first strike' capabilities against Soviet missile silos will be
still further enhanced at the end of the decade when the new D-5 Trident
missile enters service - thousands more 'hard target'-capable warheads
will be added to the US total. The D-5 is also a first-strike weapon
par excellence having the accuracy of modern land-based missiles but
without their vulnerability. The air-launched cruise missile, of which
some 3,000 plus are planned, also has a hard target capability, but the
missile's relative slowness renders it unsuitable as first strike
weapons.

A successful first strike capability against Soviet ICBMs would
threaten nearly 80% of the Soviet strike force (assuming current ratios
were maintained) but would leave Soviet submarines intact. A totally
disarming first strike would need to knock out all of the Soviet ballistic
missile submarine fleet as well as the ICBM force. Here the Soviets are
again at a disadvantage. While US submarines will remain invulnerable
to Soviet anti-submarine warfare for the foreseeable future, the reverse
is not the case. First, US ASW technology is considerably more advanced
than that of the Soviet Union. As the Stockholm Institute pointed out
in its 1979 report:
> The technological lead of the USA in both ASW detection and
> ASW weaponry creates an asymmetry which is enhanced by various
> geographical factors, in particular the severely restricted
> access of Soviet vessels to the open ocean.[37]

Current detection technologies - traditional sonar, fixed sea-bottom
sound surveillance systems (SOSUS), magnetic airborne detection, active
air-dropped sonobuoys, towed sonar arrays, the SEASAT oceanographic
satellites etc. - are becoming increasingly effective. More exotic
techniques - infra-red sensor detection or thermal anomalies (via aircraft or satellite), laser detection from space and detection of submarine hydrodynamic signatures by over-the-horizon radar or SEASAT -
are being developed.[38] A 1978 US Congressional Research Service Report
stated that, while the US did not have a first strike capability against
Soviet submarines at that time, 'research and development is leading in
this direction, and that Soviet decision-makers have grounds for fearing
such a capability'.[39] Since more than four-fifths of Soviet ballistic
missile submarines are normally in port (in unhardened pens), *their*
destruction in a surprise attack would be simple. The Soviets have
every reason to be deeply concerned about these developments. Worst
case analysis must lead the Soviets to suspect that the US is in fact
aiming to acquire a disarming first strike capability. Current US
developments in anti-satellite warfare technology and space-borne anti-
ballistic missile laser systems must heighten such suspicions still
further, as must the US refusal to disavow first strike strategies.
Defense Secretary Harold Brown stated in his 1980 Fiscal Year Report
that 'US and NATO strategy allows for a possible NATO first use of
nuclear weapons, if that should prove essential'.[40]

Is the US in fact aiming for a disarming first strike capability?
Certainly the characteristics of the next generation of US strategic
weapons systems and the political ascendancy of the superiority-seeking
neo-conservatives in Washington must strongly suggest this to the Russians.
And in determining the course of the arms race what people believe is
real may be more important than reality itself. There is little doubt
that there is in Washington today considerable nostalgia for an earlier
epoch in which the Soviet Union could be forced to back down in crises
because of US strategic preponderance. In the Cuban missile crisis, for
example, the US had a seven-to-one lead over the Soviets in ICBMs - plus
a strategic bomber force which the Soviets lacked. Underlying the
current thrust for strategic 'superiority' is the pervasive belief
exemplified above in the quotation from Richard Pipes - namely that
perhaps the most important role for nuclear weapons is as 'a means of
political and psychological suasion'.[41]

The consequences of all this for the strategic arms race are as predictable as they are tragic. The Soviets will move to offset the perceived threat to their strategic capability by building up their offensive and defensive forces. In Washington this in turn will be taken as
confirmation of the aggressive nature of Soviet strategic policy.
Extremist statements by hardliners in the US strategic community will
strengthen the hand of hardliners in Moscow - and vice versa. As
Alexander Dallin has noted of both Soviet and American hawks:

>The commitment of each to worst-case analysis requires the
>assistance of the other to provide support (at least in their
>own minds) for self-fulfilling policies of doom.[42]

SALT II had many drawbacks; it would have permitted a considerable
expansion and modernisation of the weapons' systems of both sides, but
it did impose certain limits on the arms race, and help to establish
the principle of strategic arms control. In abandoning SALT II, in
pushing aggressively for nuclear 'superiority' and in continuing the
emphasis on nuclear weapons as war-fighting rather than war-deterring
weapons, the new Reagan administration will not only ensure that the
arms race accelerates still more rapidly, but will also greatly increase
the risk of nuclear war.

THE CONVENTIONAL BALANCE

Charges that the conventional (non-nuclear) military balance has tilted
decisively in the USSR's favour have also become part of the neo-
conservative conventional wisdom. On closer inspection these charges
turn out to be as misleading as those relating to the nuclear balance.

It is of course true that the Soviet Union's military capability has
grown very considerably since the Second World War. Since the USSR
started from a low base in the immediate post-war years, since her
leaders have always been obsessed with security, and since the Soviet
economy is the second largest in the world, such growth is hardly surprising. Today the Soviets have a blue-water fleet and a proven ability
to project power to remote areas of the Third World (e.g. the air lifts
to Angola, Ethiopia). It is also true that the Russians have a quanti-
tative lead over the US in certain areas. There are, for example, some
3.6 million Soviet citizens under arms compared with 2.1 million for
the US.[43] The Soviet numerican advantage in combat ships, large and

small, is almost 5:1.[44]   The East/West theatre balance in Europe shows
a clear Soviet advantage in the numbers of divisions deployed and in
many key weapons' systems.   In North and Central Europe, for example,
the Warsaw Treaty Organisation (WTO) has 19,500 tanks to NATO's 7,000.
In artillery pieces (including rocket launchers) NATO has only 2,700
compared with the WTO's 10,000 plus.   In fighter interceptors NATO has
386 to the WTO's 2,050.[45]

Neo-conservative organisations such as the Committee for the Present
Danger and the American Security Council present statistics such as
these (which are accurate enough in themselves) in such a way as to
create a grossly misleading and inaccurate overall impression.

Consider each in turn.   In the case of the different manpower levels
between the US and the USSR the first thing to note is that, in contrast
to the US, a considerable fraction of Soviet forces are employed in
such activities as construction and internal security which are in no
sense threatning to the West.   Secondly, the US has a (relatively)
highly paid professional army, whereas the overwhelming majority of the
Soviet Union's forces is made up of very low paid, and often poorly
trained, conscripts.   The Soviets can, and do, use their military manpower in a profligate manner.   Furthermore, the East/West numerical
troop imbalance disappears completely if, instead of comparing superpower manpower levels on their own, one compares the balance between
NATO as a whole and the WTO; here the figures are 4.9 and 4.7 million
respectively.   In addition, the Soviets confront the 4.4 million[46]-strong
Chinese armed forces on the Eastern front.   Approximately *one quarter*
of Soviet forces are deployed along the USSR's eastern border.   Since
1965, as *Strategic Survey 1979* has pointed out, 'Much of the [Soviet]
numerical expansion [of divisions] had resulted from the military build-
up in the Far East...'[47]

Consider next the alleged Soviet 'advantage' in large and small
combat ships - the 5:1 ratio cited as so alarming by the American
Security Council - a claim which, incidentally, provides a typical
example of that organisation's misleading and irresponsible alarmism.
First, it is based on an absurd counting procedure which gives equal
weight to heavy and light combat vessels.   A more realistic (though
still misleading on its own) comparison would be between major combat
surface ships.   Here the figures are 173 for the US, and 289 for the
Soviet Union.[48]   If one takes gross tonnage rather than vessel numbers,
then we find that the US leads the USSR.   However, as with troop numbers, the full alliance comparisons should also be noted.   Here we
find that 'overall US and other NATO navies have twice the naval tonnage
and several times the firepower of the Soviet and other Warsaw Pact
navies'.[49]   Furthermore, the US Navy is superior to the Soviet in
'strike warfare, amphibious warfare, and anti-submarine warfare as
well as in readiness'.[50]   As former President Gerald Ford pointed out
in 1976, 'The fact is you don't compare navies by numbers.   You compare
total firepower, you compare tonnage and combat capability - and you
find we are on top.'[51]   The Soviet fleet is also hampered by the facts
of its geography and lack of overseas bases.   Soviet naval forces,
divided between four quite separate fleets, are so deployed that reinforcement of ships in one theatre by fleets from other theatres would
be extremely difficult.   Passage between theatres is constrained by
geographical bottlenecks which sould be subject to interdiction by US/
NATO naval operations in time of war.

When we turn to the figures relating to the central and northern European theatre balance we again find that the neo-conservatives present a 'misleadingly' one-sided picture. It is quite true that the WTO has more divisions in this theatre, but nearly half of the Pact's troops in Central Europe are drawn from East European states whose reliability can by no means be taken for granted. Soviet forces have never been deployed in anger against the West; they have, however, been used twice to invade Pact allies. Furthermore, many Soviet divisions have very low levels of readiness. Writing in 1978, US defence analyst Fred Kaplan claimed that '... of the 86 Warsaw Pact divisions in the Central Region of Europe, only 30 are as much as 75% ready'.[52]

When we look at the alleged weapons' systems advantages enjoyed by the Soviets we find that once again a misleading picture has been painted. The Soviet advantage in battle tanks is offset by US advantages in anti-tank guided weapons. NATO has more than 193,000 highly effective anti-tank missiles.[53] Soviet tanks are also, on balance, lighter, shorter-ranged, less reliable and less lethal than those of NATO. The Soviet numerical lead in artillery is offset by the US lead in precision-guided-munitions (PGM), fuel-air explosives, rocket-delivered mini-mines, etc. US target acquisition capability is also superior to that of the USSR and its allies.

The WTO numerical advantage in air defence interceptors poses no threat to NATO in itself and anyway is offset by the US lead in fighter/ground attack aircraft of 1,602 to 1,350 in the northern and central European theatres.[54] NATO air forces also have important qualitative advantages in aircrew capability, and in aircraft range, payload, all-weather capability, target acquisition performance, advanced air-delivered weapons, manoeuvrability, and command and control flexibility.

In fact, it is extremely difficult to assess the true balance between NATO and WTO forces; each side has certain advantages, and many of the more intangible factors (e.g. morale, leadership) simply cannot be measured and factored into the somewhat mind-numbing 'bean counting' exercises which dominate so much of the media discussion on 'the balance'. Two final points are, however, worth noting. First, it is frequently forgotten in discussions of the military implications of the balance that, all other things being equal, the defence has a decided strategic advantage in combat over the offence. This is not to suggest that the old military rule of thumb of a 3:1 advantage of the offence over the defence being necessary to ensure victory applies in Europe; it *is* to suggest that, even in the absence of NATO nuclear capabilities, the Soviets would need a decisive and clear conventional lead over NATO to make an invasion of Western Europe a rational act of policy. The USSR does not have such a lead.

It is also typical of the current debate that so much attention should focus on manpower, weapons systems and logistics and so little on intentions or interests. Yet intention and interest are crucial. If there is no Soviet interest in aggression against the West, if there is no Soviet intention to launch an armed assault against Western Europe, then we need be no more concerned about Soviet military power than we are about that of the United States. In fact no Soviet actions since the post-war division of Europe into Eastern and Western spheres of influence suggest any such aggressive intent. The brutal Hungarian and Czechoslovak invasions were launched in order to maintain the European status quo, not change it.

Currently the Soviets confront enormous problems in controlling their
increasingly restive East European satellites - as events in Poland
clearly demonstrate. So what conceivable Soviet interest would be served
by an invasion of Western Europe? The Reagan administration is now arguing that instead of a clear 'fire break' threshold between conventional
and nuclear weapons there should be a 'seamless web', i.e. nuclear
weapons ('mini-nukes', the enhanced radiation weapons and other 'tactical'
nuclear weapons) are now to be seen as usable, war-fighting battlefield
weapons. So the risks of any conventional attack meeting a nuclear response have grown still further. Given the logic of escalation and given
Soviet war-fighting doctrines, the risks of 'tactical' nuclear war
escalating into a holocaust are very grave. (This incidentally is one
'worst case' that American neo-conservative, nuclear war-fighting enthusiasts invariably discount.) What would the Soviets stand to gain from
a holocaust-risking attack on Western Europe? Currently unable effectively to control Eastern Europe, they would, in the wholly implausible
event of victory, have landed themselves with the incomparably greater
problems of occupying and controlling Western Europe. Having watched
the demise of European imperialism, and themselves been major actors in
the collapse of Napoleonic and Nazi imperialism, the Russians are well
aware that empires collapse when over-extended - why should they put
themselves in such a position? No neo-conservative writer has produced
a single convincing scenario for a deliberate Soviet assault on Western
Europe. To produce a credible 'Soviet threat' scenario it would be
necessary to demonstrate a sufficient Soviet military capability for a
successful invasion and occupation *and* to show how such an assault is
consonant with Soviet intentions, with Soviet interests and with past
Soviet behaviour in the region. It is impossible to present such a
case.

ARE THE SOVIETS REALLY OUTSPENDING THE WEST?

Another 'fact' frequently quoted to support the 'growing Soviet threat'
thesis is that the Soviet Union is outspending the US, both absolutely
and relatively (i.e. as a percentage of GNP). However, the statistics
on which such claims are made are computed by highly questionable procedures. Ascertaining what the Soviets really spend is extraordinarily
difficult. No Western analysts use official Soviet figures, which for
1978 were 17.2 million rubles. This figure compares with CIA estimates
of some 60 million rubles.[55] However, since the CIA estimate includes
expenditures which may not be counted by the Soviets, the figures are
not strictly comparable.
    The discrepancies in estimating the Soviet defence budget are con-
siderable. The CIA dollar estimate for the USSR in 1978 is US$148
billion, compared with a US expenditure of $108 billion.[56] The independ-
ent Stockholm International Peace Research Institute estimates Soviet
expenditure for 1978 as US$104 billion.[57] In other words, the CIA's
estimates show the Soviets spending nearly half as much again as the
US, while the Stockholm Institute suggests that they are actually spending slightly less than the US. Since dollars and rubles have no military capability in themselves, the importance of the expenditure debate
is primarily political. But clearly the political issue is important -
the CIA's figures seem far more alarming than those of the Stockholm

Institute, and it is the former's figures which are most widely
used.

The Stockholm Institute argues that the CIA's estimate of the cost
of the Soviet military effort is 'a wholly misleading figure for virtually any purpose'.[58] The CIA arrives at its total by noting the numbers
of troops in the Soviet armed forces and estimating the annual Soviet
output of weapons' systems etc. To get the dollar estimate of the
Soviet defence budget, CIA analysts then value these outputs by estimating what they would cost to produce in the US. Soviet troops' salaries
are also costed at US levels. Thus, each Soviet soldier is valued at
what it costs to pay and maintain a US soldier.[59] This accounting procedure has the somewhat bizarre consequence that increasing US service
pay increases the Soviet defence budget.

The problem with such an accounting procedure is that it ignores the
fact that mass conscription encourages the Soviets to use manpower in a
wasteful manner. For example, the Russians have approximately five
times as many men assigned to each strategic missile as the Americans.[60]
It is simply not legitimate to value Soviet manpower costs at US prices.
As the authors of the London-based *Military Balance* point out, '... faced
with the American price structure, the Soviet Union might opt for a
pattern of spending different from her present one. This particular
method *tends to overstate the Soviet defence effort relative to that of
the US.*'[61]

To give some idea of how hit-and-miss US estimates of Soviet defence
outlays can be, it is instructive to look at the CIA's record in 'guess-
timating' the percentage of GNP which the Soviets devote to defence.
Up to 1975, the figure was 6-8% of GNP, comparable with a US figure of
6.0%. After 1976, the CIA drastically revised its figures, claiming
that Soviet expenditure was 11-12% of GNP - or even higher. Some
commentators believed this meant that Soviet defence outlay had suddenly
increased; it hadn't of course. The CIA was simply stating that it had
grossly over-estimated the efficiency of the Soviet military procurement
sector.[62] The Stockholm Institute, which is by no means alone in its
criticism of CIA methodology,[63] also argues that claims that Soviet
defence expenditures have been increasing rapidly are dubious. The
Institute's own estimates suggest and the authors eschew any claims
for precision - a slight decline in the percentage of GDP allocated to
Soviet defence over the last 20 years.

The 'facts' of Soviet defence expenditure, which are asserted with
such confidence, and which provide such potent political ammunition in
current campaigns to boost Western defence budgets, turn out under
close scrutiny to be based on a highly controversial methodology which
considerably exaggerates Soviet defence outlays.

THE SOVIET UNION AND THE THIRD WORLD

Even those analysts who concede the high improbability of the USSR
resorting to armed aggression against the US or Western Europe still
point to Soviet behaviour in the Third World as evidence of an increasingly successful expansionist Soviet foreign policy. Soviet capabilities to project power into the Third World have increased dramatically,
and what Richard Pipes calls 'Soviet Grand Strategy' has been facilitated both by the decline in US capability and the malaise of the

'Vietnam Syndrome' - i.e. the US reluctance to confront the expansionist Soviets or their surrogates (Cubans, East Germans, etc.) in Third World crisis areas. Thus, in the first decisive post-Vietnam clash - the 1975 Angolan civil war - it was the US which backed down and the Soviets, with their Cuban 'Ghurkas', who triumphed. US assistance to the anti-MPLA factions was cut while Soviet aid to the Marxist MPLA was boosted massively.[64] Soviet successes in South Yemen, Vietnam and Angola were followed by further gains in Ethiopia, Kampuchea and, most recently, Afghanistan.

While there is no doubt that the USSR's capability to project power into the Third World has increased considerably while that of the US has declined relatively, the importance of these changes has, once again, been grossly overstated by the neo-conservatives. Compared with the US, Soviet capabilities in the Third World remain modest, while Soviet foreign policy 'successes' have been offset by many failures.

Take first the question of capabilities. The US 'now spends perhaps a quarter of its military budget on Third World intervention forces ... while the Soviet Union devotes less than ten per cent of its defence effort to the same mission'.[65] While the US has 184,000 marines - the key naval interventionary force - the Soviets have only 12,000.[66] The Soviet amphibious fleet has one third the US carrying capacity while Russian airlift forces have half the US capacity.[67] Of the Soviet Union's four aircraft carriers (one being built), none can operate modern combat aircraft. The US has fourteen aircraft carriers (one being built) on average twice the size of those of the USSR.[68] Furthermore, the USSR has very few naval bases compared with the US, which has forty-four. Four out of the six major Soviet bases in the USSR itself freeze up in winter. In sharp contrast to the claims about the Soviet Union's threatening new interventionary capability in the Third World, the authors of the 1979 *Strategic Survey* remind us that 'the existing balance of the Soviet Navy's tasks ... gives first priority to countering US naval power, and *puts the projection of power ashore ... well down the list.*'[69]

The usefulness of the Soviet airforce for operations in remote areas of the Third World is circumscribed by the USSR's lack of overseas air bases and the fact that few Soviet transport aircraft or tactical fighters are designed for inflight re-fuelling.[70]

SOVIET ARMS TRANSFERS TO THE THIRD WORLD

The massive transfers of Soviet military hardware to Third World trouble spots are, correctly, seen by critics as part of the Soviet Union's undeniable drive to expand its influence in the Third World. Yet once again we find that an oversimplified picture of the implications of Soviet arms transfers has been painted. According to the Stockholm Institute, out of a total value of some $61 billion worth of arms exported to the Third World between 1970 and 1979, the US exported $27.7 billion or 45%, and the Soviets $16.9 billion or 27.5%.[71] In other words, if we assume that 'selling guns buys influence', it is not at all clear that the Soviets have done better than their rivals. When British, French, Italian and German arms transfers are added to the total, the West's share rises to 65%.[72]

It can legitimately be objected that measuring Soviet arms transfers in dollars may be misleading - that we should look instead at the nature and quantity of the arms transferred instead. Examining the relevant data here we find that, while the Soviets lead in some arms export categories (e.g. tanks, surface-to-air missiles), the US leads in others (e.g. helicopters, surface combatant ships). Indeed:

> According to figures released by the [US] Arms Control and Disarmament Agency ... *the Soviets have delivered more than the United States worldwide in only five out of fourteen categories.*[73]

Changing patterns of Soviet arms sales are also a response to the Soviet Union's economic crisis and growing need for foreign currency. The gifts of military hardware and generous credit terms which marked Soviet arms transfer programmes in the past - and which could only be explained in terms of influence-seeking behaviour - are giving way in- creasingly to hard cash-on-delivery terms. (This pattern of decreasing aid and increasing hard currency sales is also evident in the US.) A recent CIA study indicated that in 1977 half of the USSR'e exports (in terms of value) to the Third World was made up of arms sales.[74] Three- quarters of the USSR's Third World customers now settle deals in hard currency.[75]

What this shift in the terms of Soviet arms sales suggests is not so much the influence-seeking drive of a confident imperialist power (though the influence-seeking of course remains), but rather the normal trading behaviour of a state which is facing a large and worrying foreign currency debt.[76] It is also worth noting that the Soviet Union lost US$5 billion in Egypt after 1972 and $3 billion following the debacle in Indonesia in 1965.[77] As these two cases and those of Somalia (1977) and Iran (since 1979) suggest, the supply of Soviet arms to a Third World state does not necessarily translate into Soviet control over that state. As Ian Clark has pointed out:

> There is strong evidence that in virtually every area in which an arms relationship might be expected to endow a supplier with political influence, the USSR has recently had disappointing experience.[78]

That this should be the case should occasion no surprise to students of American foreign policy - the US inability to influence the policies of such highly dependent allies as Israel or Thieu's South Vietnam has been notorious.

SOVIET NON-MILITARY CAPABILITIES

The debate about the Soviet ability to influence events in the Third World tends to focus primarily on military capabilities and arms trans- fers. But, as the Russians themselves insist, what really counts is the total 'correlation of forces' - not simply military instruments of suasion, but the ability to bring to bear economic, diplomatic and political pressures as well. Consider the economic 'correlation of forces':

> The annual Gross National Product of the Warsaw Pact countries for 1977-78 was estimated at $1 trillion; that of the United States at $2 trillion; that of Western Eruope at somewhat above $2 trillion; that of Japan somewhat under $1 trillion. By this

yardstock the present correlation of economic forces is 5:1 in
favour of the West...[79]
If we look at official economic aid - the most obvious non-military means
of political suasion - we find that the centrally planned economies as a
whole provided *less than 4%* of total global economic aid flows in 1980.[80]
Using other indicators we find that the USSR also has extremely low levels
of investment in, and trade with, the Third World compared with the US.

At the political level the Soviets' heavy-handed diplomacy has wasted
much of the political capital which the USSR gained in early post-war
decades as the champion of anti-colonialism. As US African specialist
Gerald Bender has noted of Soviet behaviour in Africa:

> The very style that earned US citizens the reputation of 'ugly
> Americans' in the 1950s and the 1960s appears to characterise
> the Soviets in the 1970s. Throughout the continent, Africans
> complain that the Soviets are clannish, impatient, and that
> they treat them like difficult children.[81]

Soviet standing in the Third World deteriorated still further as a consequence of the brutal invasion of Afghanistan in 1979.

SOVIET 'SUCCESSES' IN THE THIRD WORLD

So much attention has been focussed on the so-called Soviet 'successes'
in the Third World that we tend to forget, firstly, that the USSR has
also suffered some spectacular failures and, secondly, that Soviet influence in the Third World is neither large - nor growing. A recent
study undertaken by the American Center for Defense Information showed
that in 1958 Soviet-influenced countries accounted for some 31% of the
world's population and 9% of the world's GNP. But 'In 1979, the Soviets
were influencing only 6% of the world's population and 5% of the world's
GNP, exclusive of the Soviet Union.'[82]

In examining the list of past Soviet successes in the Third World it
is also instructive to note that many countries moved into the Soviet
camp only after being rebuffed by the West. Examples include China in
1950, Afghanistan in the mid-1950s, Egypt in 1955, Castro's Cuba following the US embargo, and, most recently, Vietnam, which pleaded for
Western aid and investment, which was rejected, and is now a member of
Comecon. These past and present Soviet 'successes' are more plausibly
explained as resulting from American 'rjectionism' rather than Soviet
'expansionism'.

The list of 'successes' so frequently intoned by the neo-conservatives
is also somewhat meaningness except in comparison with the parallel list
of Soviet failures. Table 2 gives a more balanced picture:

Table 2   Soviet Gains and Losses in the Third World post Second World War

Gains		*Losses*	
Afghanistan	Libya	Albania	India (?)
Angola	Mozambique	Algeria	Indonesia
Cambodia	Syria	Bangladesh	Iraq
Congo	Yemen (Aden)	China	North Korea
Cuba	Vietnam	Egypt	Mali
Ethiopia		Ghana	Somalia
Laos		Guinea	Yemen (Sana)
			Yugoslavia [83]

We may note that on the debit side the Soviet's have 'lost' the world's most populous nation - China; two of the key states in Africa - Algeria and Ghana, and the most populous state in East Asia - Indonesia. Sadat's expulsion of the 17,000 Soviet 'advisors' from Egypt was a massive blow to Soviet prestige in the Middle East, and the Westward shift of Iraq in 1979 leaves the Soviet Union with minimal influence (Syria and South Yemen) in the region. (Libya is hardly a Soviet surrogate.) In being forced out of Somalia in 1977, the Soviets lost their largest overseas naval facility at Berbera. In Latin America, the revolutionary movements and progressive governments of the late 1960s and early 1970s have been overthrown or crushed by anti-communist juntas. Only in Central America have anti-rightist forces made any headway.

Why should these Soviet successes in the Third World cause so much concern in the US? No radical pro-Soviet government in the Third World has ever refused to sell its raw materials to the West - on the contrary. Since the Soviet Union is largely self-sufficient in raw materials it does not provide an alternative market. Where economic links have been cut between new revolutionary governments and the West it has usually (Kampuchea is a notable exception) been the US which has done the cutting (China, Cuba, Vietnam, etc.).

Western corporations are increasingly realising that communist countries with their low levels of inflation, lack of industrial unrest, low wages and stable governments, offer excellent trading and investment opportunities. Radical governments such as those in Mozambique and Angola have demonstrated a thoroughly pragmatic approach to Western multinational corporate investments. In the Cabindan enclave of Angola, Cuban troops guard Gulf Oil's operations.

While neo-conservatives typically evaluate conflicts in the Third World in terms of the East/West balance, seeing indigenous radical movements as Soviet-funded and manipulated, a more sober and realistic approach states with a quite different set of assumptions.

Assumption: The fissiparous tendencies in the world communist movement manifest in the 1948 Yugoslavia defection from the USSR, the Sino-Soviet split and, most recently, the Vietnam/Kampuchean war, have served to reinforce the growing realisation that nationalism is a more potent force than communism.

Assumption: Threats to Third World regimes from radical movements arise out of indigenous socio-economic conditions which exist independently of Soviet foreign policy - but which may be exacerbated by both Soviet and American intervention. (The struggle in El Salvador and the Israel/Palestine conflict provide current examples.)

Assumption: Quite apart from any ethical considerations, US support for repressive regimes in the Third World is counterproductive in terms of America's own foreign policy goals. It provides an entree for the Soviets to whom radical oppositions will turn because there is no other source of aid or military supplies. US support for repressive regimes also increases the probability that, if and when such regimes collapse, the US will have gained the bitter enmity of the new government. The Iranian revolution provides a classic example of this process.

Assumption: A supportive, or at least agnostic, approach to progressive change would deny the Soviet Union many of the opportunities

it currently exploits and also avoid the political and economic costs of Vietnam/Iran-type debacles.

Assumption: The emergence of radical governments in the Third World has
not, and does not, alter the strategic East/West balance
significantly. And, as noted above, no major Western economic interests (trade, access to raw materials) are affected
by the emergence of radical/communist governments. The
burgeoning US trade and investment in East Europe and the
USSR, and the continuation of economic activities within
nations such as Angola suggests that the opposite may be
true.

Assumption: The creation by the Soviet Union of 'dependency' relationships with its Third World allies - e.g. Cuba/Vietnam - is
ultimately self-limiting. The drain on the Soviet economy
in propping up such allies is huge - and not affordable on
a large scale.

Given the political, diplomatic and economic costs of Afghanistan-
type actions, given the increasingly severe problems confronting the
Soviet economy, and given the doubtful ability of the Soviet Union to
translate foreign and military aid into political control on a permanent
basis (Egypt, Somalia, Indonesia, etc.), it is not at all clear how the
alleged benefits of an expanding empire can outweigh the massive costs
which the drive to expand necessarily incurs.

SOVIET FOREIGN POLICY: AN ALTERNATIVE PERSPECTIVE

That Soviet foreign policy is opportunistic, cynical and frequently
brutally repressive is not in question. But the neo-conservatives'
apocalyptic vision of a Soviet Grand Design ignores or misinterprets
other dimensions of Soviety foreign policy which make it appear in a
much less alarming - if still unattractive - light.

The alternative perspective stresses, first, the Soviet obsession
with security, and secondly the various capability constraints on Soviet
expansion. There are of course special difficulties in studying Soviet
foreign policy. Since the Politburo does not leak information as US
decision-making bodies do; since revealing and indiscreet memoirs by
Soviet foreign policy-makers do not surface in the public domain; since
there are no Soviet equivalents of the Pentagon Papers, or even access
to archival material; and since it is extraordinarily difficult to distinguish between fact and propaganda in public Soviet policy statements,
there is a very real sense in which the roots of Soviet foreign policy
are unknowable in a way that those of US policy are not.

Nevertheless, by focussing on the Soviet obsession with security and
on Soviet capability constraints, a very different image of the USSR
emerges to that of the neo-conservatives. This alternative perspective
on Soviet foreign policy may be crudely summarised as follows. First,
Soviet history, starting with the intervention by US, French and British
troops in the 1917-21 civil war against the Bolsheviks, provides ample
reason for the notorious Soviet obsession with security. In the Second
World War, 20 out of the 22 million Allied casualties were Soviet.
Secondly, in the late 1940s and 1950s, the US containment doctrine,
the creation of NATO, the anti-communist hysteria of McCarthyism, and
the ringing of the USSR by more than fifty US bases revived traditional
Soviet fears of encirclement.

In the 1970s, despite detente, the Soviets have witnessed the US rapprochement with China - the USSR's bitterest enemy, the growing political ascendancy of neo-conservatism with its anti-Soviet confrontationist policies, and the development in the US of first strike strategic weapons systems. By the end of the decade US policy-makers were explicitly discussing the so-called 'China Card' as a political weapon to be used against the USSR. And, as US political scientist Miles Kahler write recently, 'For Soviet leaders obsessed by Bismarck's *cauchemar des coalitions*, the China card is a nightmare which might drive them to extremes'.[84]

The Soviet obsession with security might seem irrational in the West, indeed it is clear that both worst-case prescriptive theory and military-industrial-complex pressures also play an important role in Soviet defence planning, nevertheless it is impossible to explain the Soviet invasions of Hungary in 1956, Czechoslovakia in 1968, or Afghanistan in 1976 in terms which ignore the security dimension. Each invasion is an example of 'defensive aggression' - clearly aggression *vis-à-vis* the invaded nation, but also defensive *vis-à-vis* the USSR's superpower rival. The potential geopolitical dangers which would have attended the 'loss' of any one of these countries were considerable - one only has to imagine the reaction in the US to - say - a communist government coming to power in Italy, to get some idea of how the Soviet 'worst case' planners would have viewed Dubcek's 'socialism with a human [i.e. non-Russian] face' succeeding. The real danger to Soviet security was, however, not so much the obvious physical threat posed by a gap in the band of East European buffer states, but the threat of ideological contagion.

The Soviet leadership endures a permanent, if suppressed, legitimacy crisis - most obviously with respect to the East European satellites but also one of increasing importance within the Soviet Union itself. The danger posed by Dubcek's 'socialism with a human face' was not that it was anti-socialist, but that it challenged Soviet ideological - and political - hegemony. Permitted to flourish it would have encouraged similar movements in other East European countries - the Kremlin's 'domino theory' makes sense. Ideological contagion would not stop at the Soviet Union's borders. If Hungarians and Poles were permitted to 'seize their freedom' this would surely generate pressures for major change in Latvia, Estonia, Georgia and the Ukraine, and among the rapidly growing Soviet Muslim population. Thus, loosening Soviet political control and allowing Soviet satellites to choose their own political destiny ultimately threatened the security of the leadership in the USSR itself. The US is not in a similar position - a communist Mexico would, in itself, be no more likely to undermine the political legitimacy of the US political system than a communist Cuba has done over more than 20 years.

This line of reasoning also renders the Soviet Union's decision to invade Afghanistan more comprehensible than neo-conservative arguments which stress expansionist Soviet drives to gain warm water ports and/or control over Gulf oil. Afghanistan had been under varying degrees of Soviet influence since the 1917 revolution. In the 1950s, after being rebuffed by the US, the Afghan government turned to the Soviets for military aid and training. Links with the USSR were greatly strengthened following the Taraki coup of 1978. The new Taraki government embarked immediately on a series of reforms. A 'revolution from above' was to be imposed on a backward, conservative rural sector,

traditionally hostile to central authority and bitterly opposed to 'god-
less communism'. Growing rural resistance to the reform programme, which
was in many cases ineptly and brutally implemented, led to increased
Soviet military aid and advice. In September 1979, Taraki was assassin-
ated by his former right hand man Hafizullah Amin.

At this point there is some disagreement. Did the Soviets intervene
in December that year, because, as Jacques Fauvet in *Le Monde* put it,
'Nobody denies that the Islamic rebellion ... was going to carry the
day'[85] or because they believed that Hafizullah Amin was becoming an
'Afghan Tito' - a socialist heretic?[86] Either eventuality posed the
very real risk of Afghanistan moving out of the Soviet sphere of influence, and of signals of Soviet lack of resolve being transmitted to the
restive East European opposition groups and to the increasingly assert-
ive Soviet Muslim population.[87]

From the above perspective the brutish Soviet invasion of Afghanistan,
like Hungary in 1956 and Czechoslovakia in 1968, is a clear case of
'defensive aggression' - unambiguous aggression against the Afghans but
explicable in terms of the USSR's security obsessions. These are
interventions designed to maintain the status quo, not to change it.
However, in the circumstances, it is hardly surprising that Soviet in-
security should appear somewhat menacing to countries like Pakistan
which now has Soviet combat troops on its border.

Clearly, 'defensive aggression' type explanations will not do for
Soviet interventions which take place well outside Soviet border areas
- Angola, Ethiopia, South Yemen etc. Yet the Grand Strategy thesis is
not particularly plausible in explaining these events either. The
latter would imply that the Soviets deliberately and purposefully create
their own opportunities according to a well thought out master plan,
whereas the evidence suggests that, by and large, they respond pragmat-
ically to opportunities created by others. As Stanley Hoffman has
argued, Soviet post-Vietnam successes have been tied by two threads:
low risks and opportunities provided by previous Western mistakes,
defeats of (as in Afghanistan) indifference'.[88] The 'opportunism'
thesis certainly explains the increase of Soviet influence in Afghanistan
in the 1950s (when Kabul was rebuffed by Washington), and in 1978 (when
aid was massively increased following the Taraki coup), but it is less
persuasive in explaining the 1979 invasion than the 'defensive aggression'
thesis.

From the Soviet perspective, detente represents what might be called
the politics of antagonistic collaboration. Limited cooperation between
the US and its major allies is absolutely essential to avoid the risk of
direct military confrontation which, if unchecked, can lead to the
nuclear holocaust in which all parties lose. Hence the Soviet Union's
quite genuine support for strategic arms control, hence also the great
caution with which the Soviets conduct their direct relations with the
US and Western Europe. But, as Hedley Bull wrote recently, 'As the
Soviet Union sees it, the rules of *detente* never embraced cessation of
the political and ideological struggle for national liberation in the
Third World...'.[89] In pursuit of its influence-expanding objectives in
the Third World the Soviet Union has given modest amounts of aid to
various liberation movements. Massive aid - military hardware transfers,
advisors, etc. - has generally only been offered to internationally
recognised *governments* and not insurgent groups. In other words Soviet
behaviour has been not dissimilar to that of the US - though on a far

more modest scale. Russian combat troops have, however, never been used
for direct military interventions outside the USSR's border areas, as
have US troops on numerous occasions from Korea to Vietnam.

Since the Soviets have never made any secret of their view that
'political and ideological struggle' would continue in the Third World,
it is disingenuous to say the least for neo-conservatives to depict
Soviet activities in Angola, Ethiopia, etc. as a 'betrayal of detente'.

In sum we can say that the USSR seeks to avoid confrontation with the
West in areas where Western, especially American, vital interests are at
stake. (The Persian Gulf is clearly one such area.) On the other hand,
as Roman Kolkowicz has argued:

> There is little doubt that the Soviets are committed to gradual,
> non-provocative but sustained exploration of the vulnerable
> regions of the Third World as targets of opportunity.[90]

Kolkowicz also notes that

> Such a policy is seen by many Soviets as one of low risks,
> low costs, and potential high payoffs; while a continued
> confrontation and arms race with the West is seen as one of
> high costs, high risks and low payoffs.[91]

I have already argued that the USSR's attempts to expand its influence
in the Third World may ultimately be self-limiting in terms of the
costs - political as well as economic - which they generate. Economic
cost constraints will become more salient in the 1980s given the Soviet
Union's current economic problems.

Soviet economic problems are increasingly serious. 'Overall economic
growth having peaked at 7.7% in the 1966-70 period, was down to around
3.9% in 1976-9, and rates of 2% or even less were expected to be seen
during the 1980s'.[92] If we look at national income growth we find that
the 1979 figure (1.9% according to official data)[93] was the lowest since
the Second World War. Some analysts believe that the Soviets could
achieve zero or even negative growth rates around or soon after mid-
decade. Addressing the Central Committee of the Party in November 1979,
President Brezhnev himself noted some of the problems - the growing
shortage of oil, the crisis in agriculture, chaos on the railways.[94]
These problems may well be exacerbated by constraints on Western technology transfers. The rate of growth of Soviet productivity is declining and likely to continue to do so, in part, because the less educated,
less skilled non-European (especially Muslim) population of the USSR
is growing while the European population is stagnating. The yield on
capital has also been falling as has the level of profitability.
However, the material problems of the Soviet economy though important
should perhaps not be overemphasised. As British economist Alec Nove
has noted, the basic cause of potential socio-political instability in
the Soviet Union '... is the increasing gap between *rising expectations*
and slowly changing reality'.[95] If, as the CIA claims, Soviet defence
spending is growing as a percentage of Soviet GNP, and if the economy
is slowing down, then the gap between rising expectations and reality
is likely to increase.

Among the strengths of the Soviet economy are the healthy current
balance of payments situation and the nation's decreasing foreign debt.
Maintaining these positive trends is, however, predicated on the continuation of Soviet hard currency oil sales to the West (and gold sales
to a lesser degree). Due to severe production problems in the Eastern
oil fields, Soviet oil production for export is expected to fall during

the 1980s.[96] This will pose some problems for the Soviet Union, but far
greater difficulties for the East European states which have run up huge
hard currency debts with the West. The current endemic economic problems
of East Europe (and Cuba) will be enormously exacerbated once the East
Europeans are forced to buy oil on the world market and pay for it in
hard currency. And of course in command economies an economic crisis
is, by definition, a political crisis.

All this suggests that, far from seeing the 1980s as a 'window of
opportunity' for massive expansion overseas, the cautious and conservative
Soviet leadership will be absorbed in attempting to control the increasingly severe and intractable economic and political problems both at
home and, with much greater difficulty, among its restive bloc allies.

One final point must be made here. In response to the sort of arguments made in this paper, neo-conservatives frequently invoke the Munich
analogy. In the 1930s, it is argued, appeasers refused to recognise the
reality of the Nazi threat. Today's appeasers similarly refuse to recognise the reality of the threat of Soviet aggression. The analogy is
however misplaced. In the 1930s war was still rational in the sense
that the fruits of victory could exceed the costs of achieving it. In
the nuclear age this is no longer the case. The threat of a nuclear
holocaust not only deters nuclear aggression but serves as the most
powerful deterrent against even the lowest level acts of conventional
military aggression. It is this factor which creates the commonality
of interest - i.e. that of avoiding mutually suicidal war - between the
USSR and the US. No such commonality of interest existed between the
Allies and the Nazis in the 1930s. What happened in the 1930s has very
little relevance for the 1980s.

CONCLUSION

This essay has attempted to provide an alternative perspective to what,
in the US at least, has become the dominant orthodoxy. Neo-conservative
policy prescriptions are now being implemented by the Reagan administration; as a consequence we confront the certainty of a massive accelera-
tion in the nuclear arms race. Defence expenditure will double between
now and 1986 despite the overwhelming evidence for, at minimum, strategic
parity, between the superpowers; and despite the complete lack of evidence of any Soviet intention to launch an armed assault against the US
or its European allies. With respect to the Third World the renewed
hardline stress on military intervention, together with the commitment
to support the most repressive and reactionary regimes in Asia, Africa
and Latin America, will provide new opportunities for a Soviet Union
whose political fortunes in the Third World had been on the wane. US
policy in other words may be self-defeating even in terms of its own
goals.

What makes neo-conservative policy particularly dangerous is the
pervasive believe that - boosted by a new Rapid Deployment Force and
the exorcising of the 'Vietnam Syndrome' - the US can somehow regain
its previous hegemonial status in world politics. However, as I
suggested at the beginning of this essay, this is no longer possible
- not because the Soviets have gained the dominance which the US has
lost, but because of the *relative* decline of the Americans' military,
political, economic and financial status in the world arena - a decline

which owes far more to the rise of Europe and Japan and OPEC, than to Soviet gains. Thus the US can no longer persuade or coerce its allies to 'share the burden' of acting as Third World counter-revolutionary policeman (contrast the situation in the Korean War). Neither can the US on its own afford the inflation/balance of payments costs which Vietnam-type conflicts generate. Moreover, despite the present bellicose trend in American public opinion, the real lesson of Vietnam is not likely to be quickly forgotten. No US administration can count on sustained domestic political support for long drawn out wars in the Third World, and the collapse of the Shah has signalled the effective end of US reliance on Third World surrogates.

The combination of aggressively interventionist US *intentions*, plus relatively weakened US intervention *capabilities*, increases the danger of a resort to limited nuclear war options in a crisis situation. The Reagan administration, obsessed with the lessons of Munich (1938), seems unconscious of the dangers of 1914. Major powers have frequently been drawn into wars they sought to avoid (as in 1914). Limited nuclear war options become 'thinkable' when crises escalate to the point where direct military confrontation is inevitable and backing down is politically impossible. This is not mere speculation. One of the world's most volatile and strategically vital areas of potential crisis is the Persian Gulf. Testifying before the Senate Armed Service Committee in March 1980, General R.H. Ellis, Commander of Strategic Air Command, revealed that so-called Limited and Regional Nuclear Options (LNOs and RNOs) could be used in response to Soviet *conventional* military activity in the region. As an example of a Selected Attack Option (SAO), General Ellis noted that there were contingency plans for nuclear strikes against Soviet military facilities near Iran in order to 'significantly degrade Soviet capabilities to project military power in the Middle East - Persian Gulf region for a period of at least thirty days'.[97]

For a superpower in a state of hegemonic decline, without supportive allies and without the ability to face down its rival (as the US could in the Cuban missile crisis), limited nuclear war options become a logical, if somewhat desperate, contingency strategy. In other words the neo-conservative analysis is not merely biased and misleading. Its prescriptions, if translated into policy, will constitute perhaps the single greatest threat to world peace in the 1980s.

NOTES

1   C.W. Maynes and R.H. Ullman, 'Ten Years of Foreign Policy', *Foreign Policy* (Fall, 1980).
2   L. Aspin, 'Judge Not by Numbers Alone', *Bulletin of Atomic Scientists* (June, 1980), p.28. Note Congressman Aspin is arguing *against* this position.
3   Data from Stockholm International Peace Research Institute, *World Armament and Disarmament Yearbook, 1980*, pp.xxvii and xxviii. The London-based International Institute of Strategic Studies gives slightly different figures, i.e. 2,048 for the US delivery system total, v. 2,426 for the USSR. See *The Military Balance 1980-1981*, International Institute for Strategic Studies, London, 1980, pp.90-91.

4   Aspin, *op.cit.*, p.28.
5   D. Ball, 'Counterforce Targetting: How New? How Viable?, *Arms Control Today*, February 1981, pp.6-7.
6   D. Rumsfeld, *Department of Defense Annual Report, Fiscal Year 1978*, p.76.
7   Current US and Soviet warhead totals in H. Brown, US Department of Defense, *Annual Report Fiscal Year, 1981*, p.77. The Stockholm Institute's SIPRI Yearbook for 1980 (see footnote 3) gives warhead totals for the US as 10,154 and the USSR as 7,078.
8   R. Aldridge, *The Counterforce Syndrome*, Institute for Policy Studies, Washington, 1978, p.23.
9   Aspin, *op.cit.*, p.30
10 *ibid.*
11 Data from B.R. Schneider and S. Leader, 'The United States - Soviet Arms Race, SALT and Nuclear Proliferation', *Congressional Record*, Senate Vol.212, No.87, June 5 1975, cited in Aldridge, *op.cit.*, pp.21-22.
12 Table taken from W.H. Kincade, 'Over the Technological Horizon', *Daedulus*, Winter 1981, p.124.
13 Percentages from *World Armament Yearbook, 1980, op.cit.*, Table 3, p.xxviii.
14 *ibid.*, Table 2, p.xxvii.
15 Quoted in Stockholm International Peace Research Institute, *World Armament and Disarmament Yearbook, 1979*, Taylor and Francis, London, 1978, p.428.
16 *ibid.*
17 Aspin, *op.cit.*, p.31. Operating at the same range as the Poseidon missile, Trident I is considerably more accurate, giving it a significant counterforce capability.
18 *World Armament Yearbook 1980, op.cit.*, p.230.
19 Aspin, *op.cit.*, p.30.
20 Quoted in 'Pentagon Rebuts Charges of US Military Weakness', *Defense Monitor*, Vol.IX, No.8, 1980, p.8.
21 *ibid.*, p.9.
22 'SALT II: One Small Step for Mankind', *Defense Monitor*, Vol.VIII, No.5, July 1979, emphasis in original.
23 *World Armament and Disarmament Yearbook, 1980, op.cit.*, p.xxv.
24 'The Defence Budget Controversy', interview with Rear Admiral Gene La Rocque (Retd.), *Challenge*, May/June 1980, p.41. Deborah Shapley of the Carnegie Endowment for International Peace says the SS.18 can be modified 'quickly' to carry 20 warheads but does not mention the 30 warhead figure. See D. Shapley, 'Shrugging Off SALT', *New Republic*, June 7 1980, p.11.
25 *World Armament Yearbook, 1980, op.cit.*, p.217.
26 *ibid.*
27 *ibid.*, p.239.
28 D.J. Ball, 'Developments in US Strategic Nuclear Policy Under the Carter Administration', *Working Paper No.17*, Strategic and Defence Studies Centre, Australian National University, Canberra, September 1979, p.11.
29 D.J. Ball, 'Counterforce Targetting: How New? How Viable?', *Arms Control Today*, Vol.11, No.2, February 1981, p.8.
30 Quoted in Ball, 'Developments in US Strategic Nuclear Policy...', *op.cit.*, p.6.

31 Quoted in 'War Without Winners', *Defense Monitor*, Vol.VIII, No.2, February 1979, p.6.
32 R. Pipes, 'Soviet Global Strategy', *Commentary*, April 1980, p.36.
33 'A Bonanza for Defense', *Time*, March 16 1981, p.24.
34 Quoted in *ibid.*, p.27.
35 Quoted in Aldridge, *op.cit.*, p.39.
36 *World Armament and Disarmament Yearbook, 1979*, p.427.
37 *ibid.*, Chapter 4, for details of these programmes.
38 *ibid.*, p.449 for reference.
39 Quoted in 'MX: The Missile We Don't Need', *Defense Monitor*, Vol. VIII, No.9, October 1979, p.5.
40 Pipes, *op.cit.* For a further discussion of the *political* function of nuclear weapons see E. Luttwak, 'The Problems of Extending Deterrence', in *The Future of Strategic Deterrence*, *Adelphi Papers*, No.160, International Institute of Strategic Studies, London, 1980.
41 A. Dallin, 'The United States in Soviet Perspective', in *Prospects of Soviet Power in the 1980s, Part I*, Adelphi Papers, No.151, 1979, p.21.
42 *The Military Balance 1980-1981*, International Institute for Strategic Studies, London, 1979, p.96.
43 'Pentagon Rebuts Charges of US Military Weakness', *Defense Monitor*, Vol.14, ·No.8, 1980, p.5.
44 *The Military Balance, 1980-1981*, *op.cit.*, pp.112-13.
45 *ibid.*, pp.96-97.
46 *Strategic Survey, 1979*, International Institute for Strategic Studies, London, 1980, p.39.
47 *The Military Balance 1980-1981*, *op.cit.*, pp.7 and 11.
48 'Pentagon Rebuts Charges ...', *op.cit.*, p.5. For a more extended discussion of the central naval balance see *World Armament and Disarmament Yearbook, 1979*, *op.cit.*, Chapter 6.
49 *ibid.*, p.5.
50 *ibid.*, p.12.
51 F. Kaplan, 'NATO and the Soviet Scare', *Nation Review*, August 11 1978, p.12.
52 'NATO, Nuclear Weapons, and the Death of Detente', *Defense Monitor*, Vol.IX, No.2, 1980, p.3.
53 *The Military Balance 1980-1981*, *op.cit.*, p.113.
54 *ibid.*, p.13.
55 *ibid.*, p.13.
56 *World Armament and Disarmament Yearbook, 1980*, *op.cit.*, p.20.
57 *World Armament and Disarmament Yearbook, 1979*, *op.cit.*, p.24.
58 *ibid.*, p.28.
59 *ibid.*, p.28.
60 *The Military Balance 1980-1981*, *op.cit.*, p.13, emphasis added.
61 *World Armament and Disarmament Yearbook, 1979*, p.30.
62 F.D. Holzman in his 'Are the Soviets Really Outspending the US on Defence?', *International Security*, Vol.4, No.4, Spring 1980, suggests that the CIA estimates may exaggerate Soviet defence spending by up to 40%. The Center for Defense Information describes the US dollar costing of Soviet expenditure as '... unsupported statistically and meaningless practically'. See *Defense Monitor*, Vol.VIII, No.7, June 1979, p.8. See also 'Soviet Military Expenditures' in *World Military Expenditures and Arms Transfers 1968-1977*, ACDA, Washington, 1979, and M.A. Cox,

'The CIA's Tragic Error', *New York Review of Books*, 6 November 1980.

63 US aid was cut by Congress against the wishes of the then administration.

64 B.R. Posen and S.W. Van Evera, 'Overarming and Underwhelming', *Foreign Policy*, Fall 1980, pp.104-05.

65 *ibid.*, p.105.

66 *ibid.*, p.105.

67 *The Military Balance 1980-1981*, *op.cit.*, pp.7 and 11.

68 *Strategic Survey, 1979*, *op.cit.*, p.22, emphasis added.

69 Posen and Van Evera, *op.cit.*, p.103.

70 *World Armament and Disarmament Yearbook, 1980*, p.65. The CIA and the US Arms Control and Disarmament Agency figures suggest that Soviet arms transfers are greater than those suggested by SIPRI.

71 *ibid.*, p.65.

72 'Soviet Weapons Exports', *Defense Monitor*, Vol.VIII, No.1, January 1979, p.7, emphasis in original.

73 *World Armament and Disarmament Yearbook, 1980*, *op.cit.*, p.72.

74 *ibid.*, p.2.

75 As a consequence of sharp rises in the world price of gold and oil and a growing market for gas - all major Soviet exports - Soviet hard currency indebtedness has shrunk considerably. At the end of 1979 Soviet hard currency debt was approximately US$10 billion - half that of Poland. See *Quartely Economic Review of USSR*, Economist Intelligence Unit, London, 1980, 3rd Quarter, 1980, p.14. The QER's 4th Quarter, 1980 issue refers to Moscow's '... apparent obsession with containing and reducing indebtedness...', p.14.

76 'Soviet Weapons Exports', *op.cit.*, p.2.

77 I. Clark, 'Recent Trends in Soviet Conventional Arms Export Policy', paper presented to Australasian Political Studies Association, Hobart, 1979, p.39.

78 R. Pipes, 'Soviet Global Strategy', *Commentary*, April, 1980, pp.36-67.

79 *World Development Report 1980*, World Bank, Washington, August 1980, p.29, Table 3:6.

80 Quoted in 'Soviet Weapons Exports', *op.cit.*, p.5.

81 'Soviet Geopolitical Momentum: Myth or Menace?', *Defense Monitor*, January 1980, pp.4-5.

82 *ibid.*, p.4.

83 Quoted in H. Brand, 'After Afghanistan', *Dissent*, Spring 1980, p.140.

84 Quoted in *Guardian/Le Monde*, English edition, 13-14 January 1980.

85 See S. Harrison, 'Did Moscow Fear an Afghanistan Tito?', *New York Times*, 13.1.80.

86 The Soviets faced a no-win situation on the Soviet Muslim issue. Savage repression of the Afghan Muslims could alienate their co-religionists and fellow ethnics across the border in the USSR. *Failure* to repress the Afghan uprising could encourage the spread of militant Islam to the Soviet Muslim population.

87 Quoted in M. Harrington, 'After Afghanistan', *Dissent*, Spring 1980, p.138.

88 H. Bull, 'Force in International Relations: The Experience of the 1970s, The Prospects for the 1980s', paper presented at the Australian National University, Conference on the Development of Strategic Thinking in the 1970s: Prospects for the 1980s', Canberra, 1980, p.6.

89 R. Kolkowicz, 'On Limited War: Soviet and American Doctrines', paper
    presented at the Australian National University, Conference on the
    Development of Strategic Thinking in the 1970s: Prospects for the
    1980s', Canberra, 1980, p.45.
90 *ibid.*, p.36.
91 *Strategic Survey 1979, op.cit.*, p.40.
92 *Quarterly Economic Review of USSR: 1st Quarter 1980*, Economist
    Intelligence Unit, London, 1980, p.1.
93 *Strategic Survey 1979, op.cit.*, p.40.
94 A. Nove, 'The Soviet Economy: Problem and Prospects', *New Left
    Review* 119, January/February 1980, p.17, emphasis in original.
95 The debate about the extent of the 'Soviet oil crisis' is extremely
    complicated. In brief it seems that CIA reports on Soviet oil pro-
    duction have been unduly pessimistic. The Agency's 1977 report
    suggested that the USSR, which is currently the world's largest
    producer and second largest exporter, would actually be *importing*
    oil by the mid-1980s. This estimate was revised in 1979. An
    Economist Intelligence Unit Special Report suggested that Soviet
    exports to Eastern Europe will fall steadily to 1990 by which time
    the East Europeans will be getting half their oil from the West.
    See *Soviet Oil and Gas to 1990*, Economist Intelligence Unit Special
    Report No.90, 1980, and M. Goldman, *The Enigma of Soviet Petroleum*,
    Allen and Unwin, London, 1980.
96 D. Ball, 'Counterforce Targetting...', *op.cit.*, p.7.

ECONOMY AND SOCIETY

VOLUME 10, PUBLISHED IN FEBRUARY, MAY, AUGUST AND NOVEMBER
INCLUDED :
1981

Pasquale Pasquino	Introduction to Lorenz von Stein
Karl-Hermann Kastner	From the social question to social state
Bruland / Smith	Economic historiography
Jim Tomlinson	Was economic policy ever Keynesian?
Geoffrey Wood	Empirical philosophies of mind
Reinhart Koselleck	Modernity and the planes of historicity
Barry Hindess	The politics of social mobility
Johnson / Rattansi	Social mobility without class
Andrew Levine	Althusser's Marxism
Ellen Hazelkorn	Marx, agriculture: the case of Ireland
Keith Tribe	Introduction to Neumann
Franz Neumann	Basic Laws in Weimar Constitution
Heiner Ganssmann	Steedman's economic metaphysics
Jean-Michel Servet	Primitive order and archaic trade
Paul Bew	Britain's modern Irish question

TEN YEAR INDEX FOR VOLUMES 1 - 10 INCLUDED IN SUBSCRIPTION

Annual subscription is £18.50.   Requests for subscriptions
should be sent to:

ROUTLEDGE JOURNALS
Broadway House
Newtown Road
Henley-on-Thames
Oxon. RG 9 1EN

David Cobham
Marxism and British Capitalism

BOOKS REVIEWED:

The Political Economy of British Capitalism: A Marxist Analysis, by
Sam Aaronovitch and Ron Smith, with Jean Gardiner and Roger Moore,
McGraw-Hill, 1981, 397pp.

Capitalism in the UK: A Perspective from Marxist Political Economy, by
Mike Campbell, Croom Helm, 1981, 204pp.

Both of these books set out to provide a coherent Marxist account of
British capitalism which can be used as a textbook in universities,
polytechnics and colleges and which will also be accessible to the
general reader, particularly the labour movement activist. There is
certainly a place for such a book - it is difficult to find material
that can be recommended to such an audience, and the attempt at synthesis
involved in writing such a book ought to be extremely fruitful.

Campbell's book is undoubtedly the weaker of the two. It starts with
'A Critique of Orthodox Economics' and an 'Introduction to Marxist
Political Economy', and proceeds via 'Big Business', 'Inequality',
'Economic Crises' and 'International Perspectives' to 'The State'.
There is no discussion of the Alternative Economic Strategy (AES) or
of any other strategy for transforming capitalism. The position taken
is generally well towards the fundamentalist end of the spectrum; other
socialist viewpoints are rarely discussed and orthodox viewpoints, with
a few notable exceptions such as consumer preferences, are treated
cursorily and often derisively.
  The book is shot through with reductionism: orthodox economics 'is
ideological, for it serves the class interests of the owners of capital'
(p.12), capital and the state are consistently treated as subjects,
'the chain of causation is predominantly from economic base to superstructure' (p.36), 'newspapers are capitalist enterprises and ... are
hardly likely to back labour against capital' (p.66), and the creation
of the EEC is regarded as the development of a political superstructure

corresponding to the internationalisation of capital at the base. The
theory of the state presented is essentially 'capital logic + class
struggle' and 'the superficial appearance of political democracy is a
facade' (p.171). Campbell manages to avoid any mention of problems in
and debates over the labour theory of value although much of his analysis
stands or falls with a fundamentalist interpretation of the theory. His
formulation of the tendency for the rate of profit to fall, which is
close to (though substantially less coherent than) the position of Fine
and Harris (*Rereading Capital*, Macmillan, 1979), similarly contains
little discussion of the critiques which have been made.

His applied economic analysis often weak - for example, he mentions
only one figure for the contribution of merger activity to the growth of
industrial concentration although a wide range of estimates can be found
in the literature; his discussion of the effect of inflation on UK export
competitiveness makes no mention of the exchange rate; and his presentation of figures for the UK's *visible* trade only is unjustified (and unjustifiable). The bibliography is substantially more catholic than the
text but contains, for example, no references to Gramsci, Steedman,
Hodgson, Poulantzas, Laclau, Warren, Prior or Purdy. The book also
suffers from some repetition (especially on the tendency for the rate
of profit to fall) and from excessive cross-referencing.

CAPITALISM IN THE UK

The book by Aaronovitch and Smith (henceforth A&S) is altogether a more
competent and solid piece of work. It is divided into five parts: Part
One (Background) includes introductory material of a theoretical nature
on the economic decline of the UK; Part Two deals with the state, Part
Three with international capitalism, Part Four with capital and Part Five
with labour; and the book ends with a chapter on 'Conclusions and Prospects' which includes a brief discussion of the Alternative Economic
Strategy.

A number of chapters or sections in the book are particularly good.
For example Chapter 17 contains a good discussion of trends in industrial concentration in the UK, while Chapter 16 includes an excellent
theoretical and empirical survey of the debate on the separation of
ownership and control in industry. Chapter 9 gives a concise but theoretically informed review of public expenditure and taxation in the UK,
of a kind which is surprisingly rare in the (orthodox or Marxist) literature, and Chapter 15 does the same for UK financial institutions (though
some attempt at international comparisons would have been helpful here).
There is much useful information and discussion on the development of
British trade unions and trade union militancy (Chapters 20 and 22).
And Chapter 18 contains an excellent survey of trends in the profitability of UK companies. On a broader level the book consistently emphasises
the importance of the strongly organised, but generally defensive in
orientation, British labour movement as a factor in explaining the
development of the British economy.

The book also makes a number of significant points at a more detailed
level. For example the explanation of the UK's low growth rate in terms
of the domestic and foreign elasticities of demand for UK imports and
exports is rejected as description rather than explanation. The Bacon
and Eltis thesis that UK growth has been constrained by a shortage of

labour to the marketed sector due to the expansion of the non-marketed
sector is decisively criticised in a number of places. The point is made
that class relations are not the only source of social conflict.   The
'new classical macro-economics' emphasis on *voluntary* unemployment is
trenchantly criticised in Chapter 21.   Chapter 9 mentions, though it
does not develop, the problem of identifying the incidence of taxation,
that is who actually bears the cost as opposed to who has to pay it to
the relevant authorities.   And Chapter 14 makes the point that the
balance of payments costs of UK investment overseas are relatively small.

SERIOUS WEAKNESSES

However, A&S's book also suffers from a number of weaknesses. One of
the most serious of these is that, despite numerous disclaimers, there
are frequent hints of reductionism in the analysis. The view of the
state put forward seems close to that of the Frankfurt group in the
German capital-logic debate - the state responds to the needs of capital
but is affected by (and affects) class struggle, and the state may well
not always respond in the most appropriate manner. Thus the 'state in
the UK is capitalist, in that the institutions developed in response to
the needs of capitalism and to maintain that system' (p.98), while the
'ultimate source of social control is, of course, military power' (p.142).
There is too much emphasis here on coercion rather than consent, and the
discussion of consent sometimes has manipulative overtones - e.g. the
identification of 'ideology' as one of three 'possible instruments' for
minimising threats to the system (p.133), or the discussion of education
(pp.137-39).
    A second major weakness relates to A&S's thesis that the international
orientation of UK capital has had a significant impact on UK economic
growth. There can be no doubt that there is much truth in this thesis,
but A&S's presentation of it is ultimately unconvincing because the
international orientation is itself not adequately explained, and appears
too often as exogenous to the system. An adequate explanation would
require on the one hand a detailed analysis of the development of the
ideology of various capitalist and other social groups - an area in which
A&S, like many other Marxists, are unwilling to get involved - and on
the other hand a serious attempt to construct microeconomic foundations
for the thesis at both the theoretical and the empirical level - an
area in which Marxist economic analysis is seriously lacking.
    A third serious weakness of the book is the failure to integrate
analysis of macroeconomic policy with that of structural developments
in the economy. For example the view presented of the UK's recurring
balance of payments problems is a thoroughly structuralist one, and the
analyses of both the collapse of the Bretton Woods system and the
declining trend of profitability in the UK would have benefitted from
more attention to macroeconomic, especially monetary and exchange rate,
policy. A related point is the apparent willingness to accept a
bankers' conspiracy theory of the 1976 sterling crisis (p.85). Furthermore, the discussion of orthodox macroeconomic theories is sometimes
superficial and uncomprehensive.
    There are many other problems in the analysis, some of them undoubt-
edly serious. The discussion of the history of economic thought rejects
the vulgar Marxist view of orthodox economics as mere apologetics but

has little of substance to put in its place, while throughout the book
there are a number of misplaced attacks on orthodox economics - e.g.
the argument that the latter regards domestic labour as 'not contributing
to social production' (p.299) (the basic point made here is made in
virtually every elementary orthodox economics textbook). The discussion
of value theory is orthodox Marxist, if not positively fundamentalist,
although there are references to Sraffa and Steedman (but not to Cutler,
Hindess, Hirst and Hussain). The credit multiplier analysis given on
page 234 is widely recognised by orthodox economists as inappropriate
for the UK. Chapter 10 repeats the traditional Marxist claim with
respect to the nationalised industries that there are 'some sectors of
industry that produce goods and services necessary for the reproduction
of the system that cannot be provided either effectively or profitably
by competitive private capital' (p.126): A&S apply this argument in a
dynamic context, where it can be sustained, but present it at a general
level without noting that it is impossible to substantiate it in a
static context. Unquestioning credence is given to the political
business cycle theory of macroeconomic policy (p.79), although its
applicability to the UK is extremely dubious. Finally the book contains
no references, even in the final chapter on the Alternative Economic
Strategy, to any work by Bill Warren, Mike Prior or David Purdy: to the
present reviewer this omission is unjustifiable and extremely disturbing.
    A reasonable generalisation on A&S's book would seem to be that it
is much more successful in areas where the authors have themselves
specialised and done original research, but in other areas and at the
broader theoretical level it suffers from serious deficiencies. The
main problem may well be simply that too little high level research has
so far been done by socialist economists for an adequate comprehensive
textbook to be written. Nevertheless on balance it seems to the present
reviewer that this book (unlike Campbell's) could be recommended to
students and activists in the labour movement, provided that they are
also pointed towards more orthodox literature and enjoined to take A&S's
further reading seriously.

Finally three wider reflections are provoked by these books. Firstly,
socialist economists would benefit significantly from a cross-fertilisa-
tion with other areas of thought in the Marxian tradition, especially
work of Gramscian inspiration on the state, on ideology and on the base/
superstructure distinction. Secondly, once the vulgar Marxist critique
of orthodox economics has been rejected, a far more serious (and explicit)
attempt should be made to draw and build on the orthodox tradition in
economics, which for all its faults has achieved in some areas a rigour
of analysis which many Marxists apparently do not even dream of; this
implies some rethinking of the simple counterposition of orthodox and
Marxist analyses implied by the subtitles of both these books. And
thirdly, now that socialist economists are no longer a small and beleag-
uered handful trying desperately to keep some sort of flag flying, it
is time that we turned our energies far more to original research and
right away from the kind of armchair theorising and casual empiricism
that is parasitical on the very orthodoxy it aspires to criticise.

Simon Watney
On Gay Liberation: A Response to David Fernbach

I am writing to you in reply to David Fernbach's article on 'Ten Years
of Gay Liberation' (*P&P* 2), which seems to me to be sadly indicative
of a tendency in the British gay movement at the present time to fall
back into the false security provided by the liberationalist politics
of the late 1960s. I should therefore like to take this opportunity to
reply to and criticise that position, as well as the extraordinary
moralism which runs throughout the whole piece.

The central shortcoming of all liberationist theories of sexual
politics lies in their necessary dependence upon a belief in irreducible sexual essences or instincts, which are held to be simply 'repressed' under capitalism. The more structural the repression, it is
argued, the more revolutionary the liberation. Unfortunately David's
article exemplifies the way in which all such liberationism is obliged
to employ the arbitrary and vitiating categories of masculinity and
femininity as if they themselves were unproblematical, thereby incor-
porating and reinforcing the most fundamental aspects of the overall
ideology of sexuality as we experience it. Hence, for example, his
call for a 'feminisation of Marxism' (p.184) which, however well
intended it may be, surely introduces even more problems than those
which it might seek to resolve.

David is right to note the radical effects of the introduction of
the term 'gay' into the discourse of homosexuality. But I am not at
all sure that one can employ such terms as 'proper men' and 'effeminacy'
without having already given too much ground to the rigid process of
gendering which we are supposedly attacking. The absence of the very
concept of gender in the early literature of the Gay Liberation Front
movement (henceforth GLF) is hardly surprising, implying as it does the
positive *production* of particular identities in relation to sexual
behaviour and desires. Indeed, the entire belief-system of GLF was
founded upon an incompatible repression/liberation model of sexuality
which was totally unable to theorise the actual range of experienced
homosexualities, or modes of being gay, which are not necessarily
homogeneous, let alone compatible. In other words, GLF posited the

existence of some fundamental shared essence within all gay people,
rather than a socially structured system of *sexuality* which organises
all human beings according to their sexual desires and practices. In
the liberationist model there is some thing, 'homosexuality', which is
simply in need of liberation. But since the theorisation of the oppressive forces involved was so vague, e.g. 'The Family', 'Capitalism', and
so on, the sites for potential political struggle were never made
entirely clear. David Fernbach's debt to this tradition of sexual politics is apparent in his casual use of the given categories of masculinity
and femininity without ever being able to reach, let alone criticise, the
underlying ideology of *sexuality* itself, which is still seemingly regarded
as some kind of natural force or energy, independent of its particular
historical forms.

It is also apparent in his use of the old GLF notion of 'self-oppres-
sion' which remains, as it always was, a hopelessly voluntaristic and
moralistic way of criticising most gays for failing to come up to true
revolutionary scratch. Gay society is neatly divided in a Manichean
split between the liberated (how? who? why?), and the miserable ranks
of the self-oppressed. For if, as early GLF often argued, homosexuality
is *innately* revolutionary, then any lesbian or gay man who was not GLF
identified could be viewed as somehow 'betraying' their sexuality (still,
of course, preserving intact a thoroughly traditional and unquestioned
notion of sexuality itself), whilst the liberated elect were left to
congratulate themselves and one another for their miraculous and inexplic-
able radical purity. It was from precisely this kind of politically in-
sensitive vanguardism, writing off most gays as if they didn't exist,
that GLF managed to alienate so many of the politically undefined people
who wandered in to meetings, only to be driven out by this kind of high-
minded moral elitism, albeit strenuously couched in the rhetoric of
liberationist theology.[1]

The same repression/liberation model lies behind David's evident faith
in the old chestnut belief that 'the violent hostility to male homosexuals
expressed in queer-bashing of all kinds notoriously derives from those
men who have substantial difficulty in repressing their own homosexuality'
(p.176). This is a neat but ultimately bizarre explanation of sexual
violence. Do heterosexual rapists suffer from a substantial difficulty
in repressing their desire to be raped? The problem with all such applications of Freud's theories of transference to 'explain' complex social
phenomena is that they are universally applicable and sidestep the central issue of *conscious* motivation. It is also surely a very strange
kind of consolation to argue that one's most aggressive opponents are in
some intrinsic sense the same as one's self!

It is also this same inability to regard homosexuality as other than
a simple unitary category which makes it possible for David to note that
'the degree of our deviance is by no means uniform' (p.177), whilst
almost in the same breath he advances the extraordinarily reductive
assertion that 'in the great majority of cases this orientation follows
from a continuing identification with our mothers', and so on. Now
where have we all heard *that* one before?! Static unitary categories can
always be explained away in terms of static unitary causes. Unfortunately
for the liberationist position, the actual plenitude of homosexual
identities and cultures deny the validity of any such attempt at either
categorisation or explanation. Since GLF tended to theorise homosexuality
exclusively in opposition to a highly abstracted and unitary notion of

heterosexuality, it was not possible to grasp the *systematic* organisation
of sexuality as a whole. This picture of two rival sexualities as it
were was encouraged by a particular relation to the radical feminist
wing of the Women's Movement (henceforth WM). Whilst I agree with David
that one cannot overestimate the impact of the WM on gay politics, I am
less than convinced that this was an altogether helpful experience. For
GLF tended to take from the WM only that which was soluble, as it were,
within liberationist theory. It was in this context that GLF developed
an analysis of gender which was heavily reliant on such ideas as 'sexism'
and 'stereotyping' which were as blind to the issue of class as traditional Marxism had been blind to the problem of sexuality. The resulting
analysis was to prove implacably hostile to any attempt to think the
relation of sexuality and capitalism in other than essentialist and patriarchy based arguments.[2]

This is why David draws back from any attempt to discuss the situation
of lesbians in relation to that of gay men, as if this *necessarily*
assumed some ontological correspondence. It is, after all, from a particular reading of radical feminism that David derives his dualistic methodology which regards masculinity and femininity as essences in gay men
which are supposed reflected as actual sexual roles. This is highly misleading, and was certainly not a position shared by many of the women who
were themselves involved in both movements. The various ways in which
GLF in Britain selectively raided feminist politics is a complex subject
which deserves serious attention, but at this point I would only like to
suggest that a certain 'born-again' element in GLF was understandably
attracted to parallel feminist tendencies. This involved a straightforward attempt to read off a specifically gay politics from a crude patriarchal analysis of sexual relations in capitalist societies which was
not necessarily socialist at all. In this respect the history of *Gay
Left* for example was something of an exception, with its insistent denial,
as Elizabeth Wilson put it, 'that by some well-meant effort of will we
can here and now transcend our society and miraculously have new and un-
alienated forms of sexual love relationships'.[3] The liberationist gay
movement has never been able to satisfactorily answer this type of criticism, and is constantly squeezed back, like Marcuse, to theories of
innate revolutionary subjectivity,[4] or to a reductive feminist influenced
analysis 'which seeks to explain sexuality in terms of the developing
needs of capitalism'.[5] It was thus unlikely to be open to the work of
sociologists like Gagnon and Simon or, a little later, of Michel Foucault.
Thus, having discovered the term 'gender' as if it answered all our problems, David is unable to understand its role within the larger construction of sexuality as a whole, whether this construction is defined
statistically, as for Gagnon or Simon, or through an analysis of power
which calls into question the entire repression/liberation hypothesis,
as in the work of Foucault.[6]

It is from the perspective of that hypothesis that David views the
history of GLF as 'a mass gay movement focussed behind a radical leadership' (p.179). Deeply embedded in his thought, here as elsewhere, is a
Great Leap Forward vision of revolutionary politics, and the problem is
always therefore finally one of masses and leadership.[7] What is really
at stake is the basic idea of what the gay movement actually *is*. For
the history of gay politics in Britain over the course of the last
decade or more provides an excellent example of socialist organisation
and action which is scarcely even comprehensible within the framework

of recent left party politics. Which, presumably, is why we have so
consistently been overlooked by them as anything other than a potential
recruitment tank. The point is that by their very nature gay politics
cannot be centralised in a vanguard party framework. Hence the irony
of David's employment of a Reformist-versus-Revolutionary terminology
which can do nothing but obscure the tremendous scope of contemporary
gay politics, with their emphasis on the relations between the public
and the private, and the insistence that 'the struggle for democratization requires more than the establishment of a "socialist state"'.[8]
This is why it is so extremely misleading of him to describe the work
of the Gay Left Collective (of which I was a member) over the last five
years as being 'chary of challenging established dogmas' (p.183). More
than any other publication *Gay Left* resisted, particularly in its last
five issues, precisely the kind of workerism-cum-liberationism which
David's article continues to paddle.

This is especially apparent in his closing remarks, which are based
on his stated desire to establish 'the *ethical goal* of communism as a
mobilising force that can rise above the tangled thicket of immediate
material interests' (p.184). Quite apart from the strongly Thatcherite
ring of this statement, contrasting 'material interests' to the
'quality of life', one has to ask on what grounds one can speak in the
first place of a Marxist ethics. As Bertell Ollman and others have
argued, the very idea of ethics is incompatible with Marx's attempts to
explain just that separation of 'facts' from 'values', which ethics
assume, as a symptom of our alienation in capitalist societies, with
ethics on the one side and political economy supposedly on the other.[9]
David states proudly that in GLF 'we had nothing but contempt for the
"straight-gay" scene' (p.185), meaning of course the lives of the vast
majority of lesbians and gay men, and he proceeds to maintain that
snobbish gayer-than-thou stance with truly breath-taking confidence.
Having criticised attempts to 'project the future course of our movement
in far too unilinear a fashion' (p.186), David proceeds to launch into
just such a unilinear picture of the Good Gay Life as he would have us
all live it. He attacks, for example, the 'numbing promiscuity' of
North American gays, with their emphasis on the 'butch, macho image'
which, he reassures us, is 'only an image, by which effeminate gay men
seek to mystify both themselves and prospective sexual partners' (p.186).
This entirely (and callously) disregards the real issues that ought to
be borne in mind whenever one is considering the construction of gay
subcultural identities - issues of class, physical safety on the streets,
ageing, the tyranny of gendering *as experienced and mediated by gays*,
and so on. In his condition of advanced individual liberation David is
clearly able to overlook these trivial matters. He also uses the term
'promiscuity' in a way which I find simply offensive, assuming as it
does an entire code of bourgeois heterosexual property relations,
advanced as a moral code for the whole of humanity.

He also criticises 'the spread of sadomasochism and other extreme
forms of role-playing, and ... the constant use of intoxicants such as
amyl nitrate to enhance an otherwise jaded sexual palat' (p.186). He
then carries on to note the same tendencies in Britain where, he argues,
'as always with such negative phenomena displayed by oppressed groups,
from the traditional miserliness of the Jews to the football hooliganism
of working-class kids today, it is the situation of oppression that must
be blamed, not something 'innate' about Jews, working-class youths, gays

or whatever' ('whatever'!). As always in liberationist thought, analysis
stops at the very moment at which it should begin, with an opening out of
the concepts of oppression and repression. But over and above this problem I take the strongest exception to David's wildly misleading and
politically dangerous grouping together of such disparate and totally
unconnected social phenomena, organised and evaluated solely by *his* social
relations to them, as examples of 'negative' behaviour which are used to
establish his own putative moral authority. Like all Moralists David
uses the tactic of employing completely spurious analogies in order to
establish the universality of his particular social and sexual prescriptions. What right has David Fernbach to preach to us about 'hooliganism'
for example, as if it had some autonomous existence of its own? As
Stanley Cohen pointed out long ago in a similar context, 'it is not
understood that adolescence is itself a creation of industrial society
and the attribution to it of problem status sometimes tells us more
about the society than the problem'.[10]
    I would also like to know exactly what David means by 'Sadomasochism'.
Is he referring to Freud's distinction between moral, feminine and ero-
togenic masochism? Does he mean one, or possibly none of these? Or is
he rather referring to the changing organisation and 'industrialisation'
of sex? If this is the case, then it seems to me fundamentally wrong to
'blame' gays for responding to changes in the objective social world
without so much as suggesting what those changes might mean, how they
have arisen, and why sexuality frames gender in such historically specific if highly mutable forms. It ill behoves a self-proclaimed gay
radical who professes a serious concern for the miseries endured by all
gay people in childhood to thunder out against sexual desires which are
not his own, especially when he is ostensibly championing a 'progressive
and democratic' socialism. We all form our sexual identities variously
and vicariously from the elements of our surrounding cultures. If our
erotic and emotional attractions are directed to our own sex, and that
sex is consistently portrayed as greedy, violent and selfish, then it is
hardly surprising that greed violence and selfishness will have to be
confronted in the bedroom as well as elsewhere in our lives. As Jeffrey
Weeks has argued, 'we live in a universe which privileges sexuality as
the core of our being, the *truth* about ourselves, and this is as true of
the "puritan" as of the "libertine"'.[11] True to his liberationist position, David is unable to appreciate the danger of collapsing 'the politics of desire'[12] into grand but empty talk about some ultimate 'path of
liberation' (p.186). For ultimately liberationism is only able to think
of sexuality as either an uncontrollable force or as a series of individual acts of self-transformation, and is therefore incapable of advancing
any kind of material social analysis from which a politics of *change*
might be developed.
    Why, after all, should it be the case that gay men are, according to
David, 'more prey than any other group' to the 'deforming effects' of
capitalism? All liberationist arguments require this kind of special
pleading since they are forced by their very insistence upon a mechanical
picture of sexual repression to reject any analysis which sees sexual
regulation and prohibition as part of a larger process of social and
ideological construction. Thus, while I agree with David that it is
wrong to see the paedophile issue as 'the cutting edge of the gay
struggle' (p.185), what is really at stake here is the idea of sexual
'rights'. For David's argument against paedophilia assumes yet again

that there is just a unitary 'thing', in relation to which one must hold
some fixed position. His universal observations about the 'particular
vulnerability of children' (p.188) and 'male supremacy' should on no
account tempt us to regard them as 'natural', and therefore unchangeable.
Nor should they be used, as by David, to avoid the absolutely central
issue of the relations between the historically constructed domains of
sexuality and of childhood, our understanding of which undoubtedly is
one of the most immediate 'cutting edges' of gay politics. David's pre-
varications on this point are particularly ironic at a time when the
State (yes, it is still there!) is acknowledging 'undesirable' shifts in
sexuality with an offensive in this area which has effectively *created*
the category of The Paedophile, just as a century ago it created the
modern Homosexual. Liberation theory cannot understand this process of
categorisation and regulation and therefore has to argue for the 'liberation' of paedophiles and children, or else to deny their 'rights'.

   It needs to be understood however that the widely-held popular association between male homosexuality and child molestation is not simply
an ideological distortion of some pre-given and essential 'truth' about
all gay men. Otherwise one runs the risk of implicitly regarding homosexuality as a natural rather than a historical (and therefore mutable)
category. For the association in question is demonstrably a fundamental
aspect of the category of homosexuality as it was constructed by early
sexologists around the turn of the century. Working within a crudely
behaviourist framework, they concluded that there are in fact two distinct types of male homosexual, equating these types with highly reductive notions of sexual performance imported from their equally reductive
picture of heterosexuality. Gay men were thus theorised or 'explained'
with reference to what were seen as the two basic sex-drives or instincts,
the principles of femininity and masculinity understood as if these were
simply 'facts of nature'. Thus on the one hand there was the invert,
the 'natural' (e.g. incurable!) homosexual, emotionally and/or sexually
attracted to his own sex. And on the other hand there was the 'passive'
and, it was generally assumed, basically heterosexual object of the
invert's desires. Homosexuality was thus theorised in its very conception as a *relation* between predatory seducers and 'innocent' victims.

   What is at stake here are the ways in which the invert/pervert hypothesis has been transmitted through the mass media of the 20th century,
the ways in which homosexuality has been regarded as 'newsworthy' and
hence given a particular public profile. It is this profile or silhou-
ette which constitutes the prevailing everyday 'common-sense' of the
whole subject, shared of course by most gays themselves. It is the
inability of many gay men on the left to think through the political
consequences of this latter point which so often leads them to reject
what they dismissively describe as the 'gay scene', thereby exiling
themselves into a curious kind of social and political limbo from which
they purport to speak 'for' all other gays. Certainly the historical
processes by which images of sexualities are socially fixed are inadequately understood, and much work needs to be done in this area. We
need, for example, to understand the practical consequences of growing
up in a society in which parents think the issue of homosexuality not
in terms of the comparative likelihood of their having a homosexual
child, but rather of the continual threat of sexual attacks on their
offspring. It is in this way that gays and lesbians have become the
folk-devils of our society, the 'Other', to be shunned and feared.

This situation presents particular problems for the project of gay politics, which must take as its starting point the actual range of gay lifestyles, desires, and political positions. The result is frequently a kind of 'double-focus' effect, given that we are constantly obliged in the short term to defend our hard-won civil rights in specific campaigns around individual cases of discrimination, whilst at the same time we work towards the eventual transformation of the conditions which define us all. This is why gay politics *have* to be concerned with the *totality* of sexual ideology and practice, which means that we have to be especially careful not to slip into a politically debilitating separation of forces between activism and theoretical work. It also means that we have to be equally careful not to stumble into a well-intentioned but poorly thought out liberationism which, in defending one apparent 'sexuality' against another, ends up by calling upon the very ideology which so impoverishes us all.

For, as Jane Caplan pointed out at the 1980 Gay Socialist conference in London, paraphrasing Marx, we do in a sense make our own sexuality, but not under circumstances chosen by ourselves. Hence the danger of merely re-writing all the old assumptions of liberationism under the new rubric of some kind of 'gender politics' as seemingly envisaged by David Fernbach and others.[13] For that tradition in gay politics has proved itself incapable of transcending the separatism and individualism in GLF from which it still so evidently takes its major inspiration. It also runs the serious risk of regarding a temporary resolution of the masculinity/femininity dichotomy as the answer to *all* our present difficulties. Not only does this avoid the question of how the class/sexuality matrix constructs individuals *and* self-conscious social groupings *across* the boundaries of sex, class, race and gender, it also posits an 'equality in difference' solution which the history of British feminism shows to be inadequate to deal with the basic inequalities within and between the sexes.[14] Pursuing Jane's text a little further, we might remember Marx's memorable description of the way in which 'the traditions of the dead sit like a nightmare on the brain of the living'.[15] The tradition of liberationist politics stems from a very particular moment in recent British history, a moment in which the 'personal' was excitingly and absolutely correctly reintroduced into the political arena. But as we now move into the 1980s it is crucially important to reject the GLF assumption that gays automatically, by the very nature of our sexuality, constitute a radical class just waiting for the call to revolution. It is also equally important not to allow our contemporary politics to remain defined in opposition to the shades of those on the left who blocked our way ten years ago.

In GLF there was a choice between a sexual politics of liberation, with all that that implied both for good and for ill, and the largely anti-feminist and anti-gay 'straight' left. That is *not* the choice today, save perhaps for those like David Fernbach who took the latter choice in the early 1970s and now re-emerge in the gay movement after an absence of many years like Rip Van Winkles, touting a brand of moralistic liberationism which is so embalmed in memories of the 1960s that it is totally resistant to the evidence of logic and of history. This explains, I think, something of the revivalist tone of his article, as well as his significant under-playing of the very real strengths and achievements of the gay movement today, a movement which clearly demonstrates in its very diversity the total inadequacy of *both* of the

alternative choices in GLF to our current situation. In this context I
can only conclude that David's 'path of liberation' to a 'new civilisation' (p.186) points us *not* to a future in which we might indeed be
able to transform the circumstances within which our lives are framed,
but back to the worn-out Durkheim-based moralism which can only bewail
the 'breakdown of social solidarity' (p.186). If this were all that
gay politics had to offer, not only will the left not listen, they will
be perfectly right not to listen. But why is David still so concerned
to have the left, which he has supposedly rejected, 'learn the language
of gay liberation' (p.186)? What matters is to build up the autonomous
gay movement which seems to me to be the living heir of what was best
in the GLF position. Otherwise we shall end up with a backward-looking
and increasingly self-satisfied puritanical gay movement which, as in
David's article, makes the smug pieties of the orthodox left all the
more chilling for being litanised in the dulcet tones of Beyond the
Fragments.

NOTES

1   For a more detailed account of these problems see my 'The Ideology
    of GLF', in *Homosexuality: Power and Politics*, Allison and Busby,
    1980.
2   See Michèle Barrett, *Women's Oppression Today*, Verso, 1980,
    Chapter 1.
3   Elizabeth Wilson, *Red Rag* No.10, p.9, quoted in 'Within these Walls',
    Collective Statement in *Gay Left* No.2.
4   See Jurgen Habermas's perceptive and moving obituary to Herbert
    Marcuse, 'Psychic Thermidor and the Rebirth of Rebellious Subject-
    ity', *Berkeley Journal of Sociology*, Vol.XXV, 1980.
5   Michèle Barrett, *Women's Oppression Today*, *op.cit.*, p.50.
6   See 'Power and Sex: an Interview with Michel Foucault', in *Telos*
    No.32, Summer 1977. See also Jeffrey Weeks, 'Michel Foucault and
    the Body Politic' in *Gay News* No.206, 1981.
7   See for example David Fernbach's *The Superpowers, the Threat of War
    and the British Working Class*, Second World Defence pamphlet No.1,
    1976. Here, as more recently, he calls for the reintroduction of
    national service, given 'further democratic reforms in the armed
    forces to make it politically acceptable' (p.23), to enable us to
    resist the threat of Soviet invasion which he regards as an immedi-
    ate risk. In *Marxist Strategy in Britain*, 1976, David sees 'two
    great leaps forward' in 'the history of working-class struggle in
    Britain' (p.36). These were the winning of suffrage and the estab-
    lishment of the Welfare State. But, he notes, 'there is no *political
    leadership* in Britain today that can channel working-class energy
    in the direction that really counts - towards further major changes
    in the basic framework of social relationships between the classes'
    (p.37). Hence his call for a 'British Workers' movement' (p.41) to
    combat the threat of the Communist Party of Great Britain and its
    Soviet allies.
8   'Democracy, Socialism and Sexual Politics', Collective Statement,
    Gay Left No.10.
9   See Bertell Ollman, *Alienation*, Cambridge, 1977, Chapter 4.

10 Stanley Cohen, 'Breaking Out, Smashing Up and the Social Context of Aspiration', *Working Papers in Cultural Studies* No.5, Spring 1974, p.69.
11 Jeffrey Weeks, 'The Rise and Fall of Permissiveness', *Spectator*, 17 March 1981.
12 Gilles Deleuze, 'Politics', *Semiotext(e)* Vol.3, No.2, 1978.
13 See Mario Mieli, *Homosexuality and Liberation*, Gay Men's Press, 1980. See also my review of Mieli in *Gay News* No.192, 1980.
14 See Elizabeth Wilson, 'Beyond the Ghetto', *Feminist Review* 4, 1980.
15 Karl Marx, *The Eighteenth Brumaire of Louis Napoleon*, various editions.

POLITICS & POWER

&

POWER

POLITICS & POWER 1   0 7100 0593 8   £4.95

About Politics & Power	Editorial Board
Nuclear Power	Mike Prior
Marxism and Energy	John Mathews
Defence and Conservatives	Dan Smith
Alternative Economic Strategy	Dave Purdy
Socialist Feminism	Diana Adlam
Parliamentary Democracy	Barry Hindess
Trade Union and Labour	Coates/Topham
The Marxist Inertia	Graham Taylor
Socialism and Small Business	Jim Tomlinson
European Monetary System	Dave Fishman
Socialist Feminism, Taxation	Bennet,Heys, and
and Social Security	Coward
The Gramsci Boom	Showstack Sassoon
Socialist Journalism	John Ellis
Out of the Ghetto	Doreen Massey

POLITICS & POWER 2   0 7100 0716 7   £5.75

Labour Politics	Interviews
Left Labour Government	Barry Hindess
Labour Governments 1945-51	Nina Fishman
Tripartism and Beyond	Don Sassoon
Communism and Labour	Nawrat/Roberts
Social Policy	Peter Townsend
Socialism and Social Policy	Nik Rose
The Thatcher Experiment	Phil Jones
Gay Liberation	Dave Fernbach
Workers' Plans	Mike Rustin
Multinationals & Third World	Sheila Smith
After Polaris	Dan Smith
Togliatti and Politics	Ernesto Laclau
The Limits of Hindess	Bob Jessop

POLITICS & POWER 3   0 7100 0830 9   £5.95

Sexual Politics, Feminism, and Socialism

ORDER FROM YOUR BOOKSELLER, or in case of difficulty use the Order Form below:

TO: ROUTLEDGE & KEGAN PAUL, Broadway House, Newtown Road, Henley-on-Thames, Oxon. RG9 1EN

Please supply ..... copy/ies POLITICS & POWER 1 @ £4.95 each + 10% post & packing

Please supply ..... copy/ies POLITICS & POWER 2 @ £5.75 each + 10% post & packing

I enclose my full remittance of £.............. (Cheques should be payable to ROUTLEDGE & KEGAN PAUL).

NAME ....

ADDRESS ....

Mike Prior
Letter of Resignation

I have only resigned from two other things in my life: as a school
prefect and from the Communist Party. Both acts were greeted with
particular kinds of incomprehensions; in the first, that it was not
possible, in the second as to why it had taken so long. I fear that
resigning from the Board of *Politics & Power* will also be met with in-
comprehension - at least on your part. Nevertheless, I feel I ought
to give some explanation.

The situation is, to say the least, bizarre. A year ago we agreed
to make the question of our support of socialist feminism a priority
issue. After meeting together throughout the year, the men on the
Board produced an editorial, unanimously accepted, which itemised the
crucial importance of the feminist movement, accepted key points of its
critique of socialist practice and made a specific commitment to
developing *Politics & Power* as an alliance between socialists and
feminists. And after meeting similarly for a year, five out of six
women on the Board have produced an accompanying editorial which says
that the whole enterprise has been a failure and that it is impossible
as feminists to work with us. All this is laid out in *Politics &
Power 3*.

So now we are a board of ten socialist men and one woman, committed
to supporting feminism but finding it difficult to find feminists who
support *us*. How *could* we have got ourselves into so ridiculous a
position? How could we have managed to encapsulate all the daftness
of the eternally dividing left into our position, which was almost
defined to be flexible and unsectarian?

I have heard two explanations offered by those who remain (clearly
the departing women have a rather different version). One is the conflict of personalities; that A couldn't stand B and C disliked D, both
to such an extent that someone had to go. The other is a kind of sub-
merged conspiracy; that the women, or at least some of them, knew all
along that it wasn't going to work, that they in some sense engineered
a split in order to prove a point. Their departure was inevitable
because they were too busy elsewhere, not prepared to do any work and
(above all) not prepared to be reasonable.

Such explanations would be self-evidently ludicrous if worked through but of course they never are. Rather they are half-submerged in the most common reaction, a barely concealed relief that at last we will get some peace and be allowed to carry on with our proper purpose of ...; well, of whatever our proper purpose is, as distinct from continually having to satisfy the unrequited moans of those women.

It is that reaction which causes me to resign, not the original prox-imate cause of the quarrel, an article which, although not particularly good, seemed within the normal limits of tolerance we ought to set our-selves. It is a reaction that, in the end, I find to be personally deeply insulting for it attempts to draw me in, by the use of veiled words and gestures, to the well-worn passages of male exclusivity. 'After all, they do, well they do *go on* a bit, if you know what I mean'. Well, yes; I do know what you mean. 'What is it, it is often asked, that women want which always seems to be in excess of what is offered?' (*Politics & Power 3*, Mens Editorial, hereafter quoted without reference).

At the beginning of 1980 I sat for a long Sunday afternoon writing the first draft of our editorial and wondered what nudged at my memory, what seemed familiar.

It was a simple emotion and very unpleasant to him - he was getting tired of Negroes and their rights. It was a miserable recognition and on many a count, for if he felt even a hint this way, then what immeasurable tides of rage must be loose in America itself.... Every time that [an] American turned in his thoughts to the sweetest object of contemplation in his mind's small town bower ... then *there* was the face of an accusing rioting Black in the middle of the dream - smack in the centre of the alley - and the obsession was hung on the hook of how to divide the built, how much to the white man, how much to the dark.... Not to know if one was partially innocent or very guilty had to establish an order of paralysis.[1]

It is of course quite unfair to quote Mailer - such an inappropriate man in the circumstances. Yet his arrogantly phrased, self-absorbed con-cerns seem to me to sum up much of the response of the *Politics & Power* Board just as it sums up a good deal of the current mood of the left.

It is at the bottom a uniquely sexist response, one that would not be applied in such a pure and open form to any other section of what may be loosely called 'our' movement. The eternal concern of trade unionists with their 'obsessions' about free collective bargaining and the next round of wage bargaining; the 'paranoia' of Labour Party members about details of party organisation; the niggly way in which black activists keep bringing up the issue of racism: none of this ever seems to provoke quite the response raised on the left towards women who keep on regarding their own perceived oppression as the dominant political area of their lives.

Of course, it very seldom happens that the obsessive interests of these other sections of the left ever intersect in quite the way that the interests of the women's movement have cut across our own in the past year. Indeed, it would be very difficult even to interest half a dozen union activists in the working of *Politics & Power*, let alone engage them for a year in our functioning. The issue of resignation, because we did not take trade-union affairs sufficiently seriously, cannot even be conceived. Our job, it is felt, is to woo *them*, convince *them* that we deserve to be taken seriously, build up a serious trade union and Labour Party readership who might be marginally influenced by our views.

When the women's movement accuses the left of not taking feminism seriously, part of what is at stake is a series of responses which purport to have assimilated the feminist challenge, but end up by leaving the business of left politics more or less unchanged. Overt adherence to the view that women's liberation is a marginal or petty bourgeois concern or can be deferred until 'after the revolution' is rare today,... But the various positions adopted within the main body of the labour movement and the organised left are only slightly more adequate.

To return to Mailer, to the issue of guilt, to the cries of 'Just what is it that we have done to them'.

The central point is that it is just this issue of personal guilt - in what degree am I specifically guilty of oppressing women; in what ways, to whom? - which is the critical evasion of our practice. We are meshed into a society which is, in its generality, a masculine one. The male roles which we act out in that society are not simply those that relate as individuals to individual women (though of course these are not negligible). They also act in all else, including and perhaps most important, how we act towards each other.

It is an obvious enough observation, but it tends to be lost sight of, that what glues a male-dominated society together is how men relate to men. What sustains power is how men form (largely) male hierarchies. The principal channels of authoritarianism at large run from men to men. They have to, for women are, by and large, excluded from these hierarchies, whether in business, trade unions or political parties.

The differential oppression which women suffer by such exclusion does not need elaboration. I am not putting forward a version of the idea that we are all equally oppressed by sexism. What I am suggesting is that the kernel of our proclaimed support for feminism does not lie in our personal nor, for that matter, our collective attitudes towards women but how we comport ourselves in the male society within which we largely move and, specifically, how we work between ourselves on this editorial board.

The reason the feminists left the board (here I make a personal assumption) was not, at the sticking point, any particular act of sexism towards them by any particular male. It is *you*, or at least some of you, who want to make it such in order to make their resignation a triviality rather than face up to the fact that they left because we worked as a board along lines structured by male society. And most feminists find it intolerable to work within such structures, or at least to do so under the guise of a project supportive of feminism. Let me illustrate this by returning to the bizarre side of our situation, the editorial which we prepared so carefully over nearly a year.

To initiate that editorial we had two meetings; amorphous, discursive, nervy meetings, but productive. We then prepared a draft based on the ideas thrown up in them and immediately the whole character of our meetings changed. Henceforth we were back into channels we knew and understood; the battle over a form of words on paper that we have all participated in over the years. Heads were counted, calculations made, ruses undertaken, manoeuvres undertaken. I did it myself, just as I know you did. I suggested that one of you prepared one of the revised drafts simply because I knew you could not resist the challenge to make

a particular set of ideas, badly phrased and lacking in structure, into
a polished piece. And that the act of doing that draft would thereafter
neutralise your ability to challenge these ideas, many of which you disagreed with. I could list half a dozen other ploys carried out by others,
all aimed at some form of blocking or amendment or expansion, *but none
connected with actually discussing the issues involved.*

Every one of the points raised in the final piece was introduced
within the initial draft with one exception, which is of itself revealing.
Two of you, dissatisfied with the fact that no mention had been made of
sexuality, wrote a large insert and presented it. Eventually after some
cuts and some reordering it was so included. But it was never discussed.
It became rather part of the paper shuffling, the manoeuvring which
characterised our work and epitomises the way in which male forms of
organisation enter into our practice.

One of you asked me when discussing this letter whether I am referring
to all forms of male political practice as corrupt and whether that was
not a rather pessimistic judgement. Yes, I suppose that within the
bounds of my own experience, I do think just that, for I have never
found any political grouping including those on the left, often in particular those on the left, not defined by precisely those patterns of
authority and domination which effectively distill out of those organisations all but the most formalised version of political activity.

One of the most pervasive forms of that distillation is the production
of paper statements, produced after long hours of committee negotiation,
full of fine sentiments which no one believes and no one is expected to
believe. I don't think the Mens Editorial falls exactly into this category. But it does demonstrate how, even into the most well-intentioned
of groups, there drift back the old processes, the same gap between
words and deeds, the same corruption.

And yes, that is a pessimistic judgement.

I will not pursue this further into yet more detail; it becomes dull,
repetitive, the real content of actions becomes elusive, a matter of
doubt and hesitation. I myself would freely admit that I understand
very little about what forces are at work. And certainly I colluded in
such practice. Yet,

> If politics involves power relations and efforts to maintain or
> transform them, it therefore includes the details of relations
> between individuals.... These relations are not natural,
> essential or eternal but socially and historically variable and
> are thus also possible objects of political transformation....
> This process of transformation cannot be pursued through more
> or less distant policies or political tactics; the process
> must begin at the times and in the field to which it is addressed
> - at the level of behaviour and personal life itself.

I would add as a footnote that one of the defining characteristics
of the women's movement is just such a concern with the details of its
working practice. Of course, 'The women's movement's practice is, no
doubt, a good deal less elevated than its ideology'. But I suspect
that such practical deficiency within the women's movement makes working
within a group such as ours more rather than less difficult for feminists.

This is as close as I can come to explaining why our practice is
corrupt, why most of the feminists resigned and why I find it necessary
to follow them. At least it tries to cope with the first two points for
I realise that the largest gap between you and me is why it matters to

me and yet, apparently, so little to you; that it should be such a clear
relief no longer to have these stroppy women around.

That, finally, I must try and explain. It is very easy to admire, to
want to admire a certain description of a feminist. The one who is tough
and independent; who is passionate and understanding in bed; who has
style and warmth and street cunning; who can talk about politics and
film and (even) structuralism; who has her own life and her own future
and who decides to spend some of the immediate future with me or you.

Like all stereotypes this one is not without its grounding in reality,
just like quiet, domestic, dutiful, man-respecting woman is solidly
grounded in reality. And it is also better than this last. However
loosely it fits reality, the feminist stereotype is a few degrees
further on. But it is still a male fantasy, still mother/lover/daughter/
virgin in a new guise.

Not that fantasy is necessarily bad if it can offer comfort, mutual
support, fun for women as much as for men. It is after all in part
their constructed image as much as ours even when we insert our own
interpretations. But it has to end; it has to come up against the
reality, which is that feminists are more complex and various and much
more difficult than that stereotype permits. And certainly the feminists were difficult on *Politics & Power*. But then what did you expect?

Let me put this at the wretchedly personal level at which I arrive
when groping for a way to explain. I walk in a world, a society which
seems to be a madhouse. It seems corrupt, violent, and desolate, in-
habited by people who barely restrain their disturbance and pain.

Yet at least when I walk these streets I do not fear violence, least
of all sexual humiliation. I am not assaulted by the implications of
the bra adverts or the posters for films consisting mainly of various
ways women can be sliced apart. I am not touched up in the tube nor
do I have cars slowing down beside me as I walk home. I am one hundred
and eighty pounds weight and a heterosexual male. As a final resort,
the stereotypes work for me and not against me. And I *do* use that
final resort more often than I care to admit. I can cope with the
stresses; even admit that I would find it difficult to live without
them. But it is as a man that I cope. I do not have to bother with
any pressure that my life slips outside the proper role; that I am
denying my proper biological response by not having children, that I
am emphasising/not emphasising my physical attractiveness too much, or
that I lack some necessary 'human' component. These are social circumstances which every woman internalises and adjusts accordingly her mode
of life, her patterns of activity. However, feminists consciously
externalise them, analyse the enforced patterns, try to reject them
and impose others on themselves. And that is a very particular stress
which you and I can only partially glimpse.

I am not, emphatically not, suggesting therefore that allowances
have to be made, that special areas of toleration have to be set aside
for 'difficult' feminists. Such an attitude is, in fact, at the root
of our male collective response to the feminist's resignation, that in
some sense the allowances had all been used up, that enough was enough.
What I am asserting is that feminism works within a political form
which is actually quite different from ours, is sustained by different
forces and meets with us only in various forms of negotiated alliance.
The terms of that alliance shift perpetually and can never rest easy,
at least not within our tactical timespan.

For the crux of the feminist argument is that for women there is
a particular consistency in the experience of the relations as
oppressive across the whole range of personal, social and political context, and this experience of oppression is a political
problem and an appropriate and possible object of political
struggle.

Much of this will provoke a sad shaking of the head. Such muddled
thinking, such misplaced categorisation, such ill-understood concepts.
And perhaps the bottom line is really this. I work in a political vein
that comes from my gut; it has very little cerebral content. I am quite
consciously an intellectual and have been educated in a high bourgeois
tradition, albeit one rather different from most of the board. I work
to use an intellectual facility in the service of what I call socialism.
Yet in the end I trust my gut rather than my brain, and in this instance
my gut says that I would rather go with those who resigned than stay.
I respect their fears because they are where I can see them. I do not
trust yours because they are half-concealed behind 'ambiguous and deft
formulations'.

Such expressions of solidarity are always likely to be ineffectual
and faintly ridiculous. But it's better than keeping your head down
and hoping that the shadow will pass. It won't. We have very little
idea of where we are travelling. Much of our political thought has
collapsed over the last decade; we have actively participated in the
demolition of a classical Marxism in whose ruins we now wander, somewhat bewildered. So be it.

But the difficult times have hardly begun yet. We have to attempt
the construction of something new in an external environment that is a
lot colder than it was. It matters in such times that we keep faith
with each other. And we haven't kept faith. Either you see it or
you do not.

NOTES

1 Norman Mailer, *Miami and the Siege of Chicago*, Penguin, 1968.

Dan Smith
Men and Feminism

This essay is an intervention into and a product of the debates and disputes in and around the Editorial Board of *Politics & Power* about the issue of socialist feminism and P&P's relation to them. As such it is neither an attempt to 'set the record straight', nor a statement on behalf of the Board.

As Mike Prior says in his resignation statement, P&P's situation is bizarre. Although we affirmed the importance of socialist feminism in the editorial statement in P&P 1, and although P&P 1 carried two important articles about issues raised by socialist feminism, it is clear that the first two issues were no advertisement for a socialist feminist commitment by the Board. A lengthy process of evaluating and articulating the meaning of a 'commitment to socialist feminism' was set under way in the early part of 1980 by the women on the Board, with neither unanimous support nor unanimous obstruction from the men. At the end of the year, P&P 3 was ready to go to press, containing several articles on themes raised by socialist feminism, a long editorial by the men which painstakingly constructs the arguments for a male engagement with the political issues of feminism, and an editorial by all but one of the women on the Board which indicts the men and announces their resignations.

   It is particularly striking that the indictment was issued just as movement in what seemed like the right direction was being registered. Whatever more one says, the precise timing of the indictment and resignations is remarkable, but there are two points to make about the movement registered by P&P 3. First, certainly one article, probably a few and perhaps most of them may fail to correspond to the kind of discussion that was being demanded of us. Second, to the extent that some movement has been registered, this concerns only the product, not the working practice of the Board. By the time of the resignations, the Board's working practice had not changed one jot. At the same time, it is not only those who resigned who have criticised the Board's practice. But there is another more important point about the practice.

   The women's editorial describes the experience of being a member of the P&P Board as excruciating. So say I, at least as far as the formal meetings were concerned. So say many if not all of those who are still

on the Board. The men who have stayed are almost certain to have experienced the excruciating-ness of the meetings in different ways from the
women who left, and we are probably better equipped to deal with
excurciating-ness and continue operating within it. But the point is
that, given the particular group of people and the particular project,
it was almost inevitable.

We keep telling each other and everybody else that we come from diverse political and intellectual backgrounds, with major disagreements
among ourselves, united by very little except for a critique of the left.
Within and on this diversity we have attempted to establish P&P as a
forum, with wide boundaries of what is 'acceptable', in which issues,
policies and strategic perspectives can be debated. We have talked in-
cessantly about diversity and forum, but we did not seem to grasp that
we then had a choice between two options: continuing conflicts if the
issues were argued out, or the paralysis of suppressed disagreement if
we did not want the conflict. Both options are excruciating, as is
swinging uneasily between them, which is what happened. In a sense,
what distinguishes some at least of the women who have left P&P from
some at least of the men who have stayed, is that the women tended to
choose conflict (in a particular area) while the men tended to choose
paralysis.

Does this mean, then, that political collaboration between women and
men around the issues of socialist feminism is impossible? Is the P&P
Board, as the women's editorial in P&P 3 implies, to be viewed as a
microcosm of male-female collaboration, its failure as a demonstration
in miniature that such collaboration is simply not on?

The answer to these questions is No.

The view of the Board's practices which I have outlined is clearly
influenced by the prioritisation of processes as political problems in
their own right, a prioritisation which has been accomplished within the
women's movement. But what I would flatly deny are those analyses from
within feminism which take the basic contradiction in any and every process to be the contradiction between men and women. Despite the views
of the women who resigned from the P&P Board, I think the experience of
P&P bears out my objection to the constant evocation of a single sex-
based contradiction. The division between the men and the women was not
uniform - neither 'side' was homogeneous in its views on anything; the
division was cross-cut by other issues, including ones concerning the
running of the journal (should all Board members read all articles?
what are the conditions of Board membership? what kind of commitment to
the project do we expect from each other? how long should the issues of
P&P be? how should we commission articles? and so on, and on) in which
agreement or disagreement with any particular proposition was divided
among both the women and the men; and all our work was informed/compli-
cated by our particular personal and political histories, including our
previous and developing personal and political relations with each
other. There was simply too much, too many separate but intertwining
factors, at work for it all to be reduced to a single consistent division between the women and men *as* women and men.

There is a further point. Many political groupings include a diversity as great as or greater than that in the P&P Board, and face similar
tensions between the poles of conflict and paralysis. The political
functioning of such groupings is often strengthened by that very diversity; the key is the unity which can be generated from diverse perspect-

ives around the political project which brings the group together. But
the production of a journal offering itself as a forum for the left on
the basis of a critique of the left is a project very different in nature from a political campaign. The polarity of conflict and paralysis
becomes more of a dilemma, for conflict is more of a burden on the
practical work and less of a direct input to the basic decisions, while
paralysis is more of a cop-out.

Accordingly, to view the experience of P&P as some kind of a test-
case for female-male collaboration and to draw political conclusions
appropriately is to overload the project of P&P quite massively. In a
sense, even though the initial challenge about the meaning of a commitment to socialist feminism was entirely justified, and even though
arguments were soon entered and still continue about the concept of a
forum, the demands which flowed from that challenge were effectively inappropriate to P&P as it had been initially conceived and as it continued to operate even while the challenge was being taken on board.

Now, it is always difficult to attempt to identify the 'real' reason
why others do as they do, and it is very likely to sound arrogant (which
is a warning that I am now going to do precisely that). In my view,
although the *reasons* which the women who resigned have given for doing
that were valid, and although they relate to real problems on the Board,
the *cause* of the breakdown which led to the resignations was *not only*
the problems on the Board *but also* the discrepancy between what P&P
could be and what some at least of the women who resigned were politically most interested in. Among the supporting evidence for this view
are several statements from the women's editorial in P&P 3.

This view is not advanced in order to underplay the real problems
on the Board, especially in relation to the question of socialist feminism, or to get the men off the hook. The point is that there is a different way of looking at what happened on P&P than the one advanced in
the women's editorial, and that there are therefore also different conclusions to be drawn from the experience. In my view, the conclusions
relate to the problems of attempting to operate a journal like P&P far
more than they relate to inherent problems of political collaboration
between men and women. However, at the moment I want to stick with the
arguments about collaboration between women and men, because I do not
think it is acceptable simply to dismiss the indictment levelled at us
or the resignations: there are real political questions to be answered
about the reasons for staying with the project.

In essence, the main question is, 'What about solidarity with the
women?' Mike Prior is the only man who has left the Board in the wake
of the resignations of the four women in December 1980. Explaining his
resignation, he offers a description and a diagnosis of the practice of
P&P and the men within it. I differ from his diagnosis in several
important respects,[1] but I also find much to agree with. By the end of
Mike's statement it is clear that his resignation stems from a mixture
of solidarity with the women who left and disgust at the relief at
those resignations he encountered among the men who remained. On the
second point, I can only say that the dominant form of relief which I
encountered was due to the resolution, however unsatisfactory, or a
situation which had been brewing up for some time, with the four women's
resignations quite evidently in the offing for several months: when you
are sliding into a pit, it is unavoidably something of a relief to know
you have finally hit the bottom. But little is to be gained by trying

to argue that my impressions are more or less accurate than Mike's.

As to solidarity, I find this a rather more complex issue than Mike does with his strong gut feeling that he would rather be with them than us. Some may find this claim of complexity irrelevant, an attempt to confuse a clear situation. It may be argued that the men who did not resign can be indicted for that and that alone, the final proof of our awfulness. Seriousness about feminism, perhaps, means we should auto-matically have acted in solidarity with the feminists. Of course, there is a problem in that not all the feminists resigned. But perhaps we should have abided by the majority vote, or perhaps the woman who rem-ained is not feminist enough. But if we are to take our lead from women we shall need to be told which women we should be taking our lead from. If we have to work it out for ourselves, it is specious simultaneously to indict us for not taking our lead from the women.

It is all very well to invoke solidarity as a guide, but when solid-arity is at issue it is usual to ask not just 'solidarity with whom?' but also 'in the name of what?'. In other words, solidarity does not usually imply the abandonment of political discernment. So it is neces-sary to be very specific about asking 'in the name of what' our solid-arity might be invoked.

This requirement also flows from the arguments of the men's editorial in P&P 3. There we rejected the adequacy of sitting quietly nodding our assent as much as we rejected the adequacy of 'adopting' women's struggles from a distance. If those arguments were wrong, then auto-matic solidarity is the order of the day. But then what is being demanded is mute assent and support, not a genuine political engagement with the issues raised by feminism, because political faculties cannot be simultaneously suspended and activated.

In other words, a political engagement by men in the issues raised by feminism means we cannot rest on the terrain of solidarity with women as a moral-political imperative; instead, we must move onto the very different terrain of political discussion and discrimination. Here, a point which is so obvious it ought to be superfluous nonetheless seems relevant to a discussion of solidarity and to understanding the history of P&P: political disagreement is not the same thing as political oppo-sition. More specifically, one can disagree with feminists without that meaning one opposes feminism. Accordingly, it is not good enough to suggest that the answer to my question, 'In the name of what?' is or could be 'In the name of feminism'. As a political ideology and prac-tice, feminism, like socialism, is very far from being a seamless web. At present in the women's movement, there are, effectively competing feminisms: the feminism proclaimed by one group may be unrecognisable as feminism to another group; one set of feminist political strategies may be judged anti-feminist by other feminists; the tone and atmosphere of the movement as a whole has, it seems, become antipathetic to some women who nonetheless continue to regard themselves as feminists. This condition raises problems which are part of the continuing process of a diverse and dynamic political movement. Many points could be made about it, one of the least important of them being the point I want to make here: that in discussing the issues raised and implicated by feminism, disagreement on one item does not necessarily mean disagree-ment across the board; equally, agreement on one item does not neces-sarily mean agreement across the board.

Something more specific than a general appeal to feminism is required
if we are to identify the politics in the name of which other members of
the P&P Board should have resigned when the four women did. Out of the
turmoil of debate and dispute, two printed articles provide the place in
which to seek this more specific identification:
- the women's editorial in P&P 3; and
- 'Feminists - The Degenerates of the Social?' by Fran Bennett, Beatrix
Campbell and Rosalind Coward, their reply to and critique of Paul Hirst's
article in P&P 3.

Much of what I have already said indicates why, whatever my agreements or disagreement at specific points, the women's editorial does not
serve, for me at least, as an adequate political statement. It overloads
the project of P&P by treating it as an exemplar of political collaboration between women and men. Having invited the men to articulate their
commitment to feminism, the authors of the editorial then deny the possibility of an adequate commitment, in apparent ignorance of the arguments in the men's editorial (which was, by the way, completed shortly
before the women's editorial was drafted). It urges men to get it together for themselves and asserts that women must lead in collaboration
between women and men - a demand for the simultaneous activation and
suspension of political enquiry. It treats the men on P&P (and, by
implication, all socialist men) as an homogeneous mass, which is untrue
and unhelpful. But most worryingly of all, it shows a tendency to treat
the concept of patriarchy as a touchstone of feminist commitment. I
suspect I am in a minority on the present Board in being sympathetically
disposed to the concept. But, though I use it in political discussion,
I must admit to doubts about its status, exact meaning and analytic
utility for understanding modern society. Even so, it seems to me to
contain an essential element of truth about relations between men and
women which says something more than 'sexism' does, and which would
probably have to be designated by some other word if 'patriarchy' were
finally eliminated from our conceptual vocabulary in relation to modern
society. But to use the concept as a political criterion for evaluating
commitment to any or all of the feminist project seems to me to be
utterly unacceptable. It is quite on a par with the not unknown practice of describing people as non-socialist if they do not agree with
Marx's labour theory of value. It is particularly inappropriate to give
even a hint of this theoretical policing at a time when the concept of
patriarchy is the subject of a major and important debate within
feminism.

The women's editorial, then, provides nothing in the name of which I
would want to act in solidarity, and it provides much with which I disagree with varying degrees of vigour. This brings us to 'Feminists -
The Degenerates of the Social?'.

As Mike Prior puts it, Paul Hirst's article, 'The Genesis of the
Social', a review of Donzelot's 'The Policing of Families', was the
original proximate cause of the quarrel, the occasion for a resurfacing
of tensions which had been temporarily held in abeyance. It was the
conflict about this article which served to raise the temperature and
led in a direct line to the resignations. It ought to be noted, however,
that it was not a conflict between some who agreed with the views advanced in the final part of Paul Hirst's article and some who did not.
My impression is that where the men on the Board were deemed to have
fallen down was in not fully supporting the attack which was mounted on

the review and its author. The review therefore played a particular role
in the process which led to the resignations, and the reply to it therefore demands particularly careful consideration.

Before considering the main substance of the reply, a preliminary
point is required. 'Feminists - The Degenerates of the Social?' starts
with these two sentences:

'The Genesis of the Social' is an article which has proved
that, for feminists, there is no ready basis for an alliance
with socialists who have criticised so-called reductionist
Marxism. Paul Hirst's review proves, rather, that anti-
feminism and ignorance of the discussions and aim of feminism
is as rampant among socialist men as it ever was.

Similarly, the second sentence of the final paragraph says,

Paul Hirst's article and its assumptions make it quite clear
that feminists who thought they could share a platform with
anti-economistic Marxists were wrong.

It is impossible to leave these sentences unchallenged, for to take Paul
Hirst as typifying in any degree the attitudes of socialist men or even
of 'anti-economistic Marxists' is simply ridiculous. If it is overloading the project of P&P to regard it as a test-case for collaboration
between women and men, it is even worse to use for the same purpose one
article by one man whose positions are far from commanding general assent
among socialist men. Neither men as a whole, nor socialist men as a
whole, nor anti-economistic Marxist men as a whole, nor anti-economistic
formerly-Marxist now-something-else men as a whole, nor the men on P&P
as a whole have homogeneous views about the issues raised in Paul's
review, about the issues raised by socialist feminism or about politics
in general. There are many reasons for refusing the trap of having one's
colours nailed to Paul Hirst's mast by some spurious technique of 'guilt
by association'.

But the three authors do not make this point simply in passing. The
political conclusions of 'Feminists - The Degenerates of the Social?'
depend precisely on the sentences I have quoted. And my point is that
these conclusions are not supported by argument, and, indeed, are not
supportable.

However, this presents me with something of a paradox, for in almost
every other respect the critique of Paul's article is, in my view, extremely strong and at many crucial points virtually unarguable. In
particular, on the question of the standpoints from which histories of
feminism and the family are produced and assessed, on the weak appeal
to 'ordinary women' and the sudden abandonment of an interest in ideology, on the problems in Paul's view of wage militancy, on the general
strategy he advances for the women's movement in relation to the family
and on several other points, the criticisms advanced in the reply are
convincing, welcome and essential.

There is, however, a major problem in the reply, evidenced by the
marked contrast between the arguments about wages (under the heading,
'Feminism from a feminist standpoint') and the arguments about relations
within the family (under the heading, 'The family from several standpoints'). Arguing about wages and the limitations of trade union structures and strategies, the three authors are on firm ground where they
are associated with pioneering critiques of existing practices from a
feminist perspective. But in the arguments about relations within the
family, although the critique of Paul Hirst remains strong, it seems

as if the authors are on unfirm and unfamiliar ground. The analysis of wages and trade unions leads into the exposition of a political strategy, treated briefly but fleshed out with details where appropriate; the analysis of relations within the family leads only to two general asser- tions of the need for transformation - first, for a 'transformation of men's role within the family' and, later, for transformation of 'women's position within the family, and in waged work, AND IN RELATION TO MEN in general'.

The problem is not that I disagree about the need for these trans- formations. It is that the contrast between the two areas of argument starkly demonstrates the lack of thinking about precisely those issues which are at the heart of both Donzelot's book and Paul Hirst's argu- ments. I am reminded of nothing so much as the archetypical male social- ist, holding forth eloquently about women's rights, equal pay, sex dis- crimination and even the right to abortions, but remaining tongue-tied or vague about the implications of the slogan that 'the personal is political'. The contrast between the two areas of argument suggests a kind of feminist economism.

The crucial area of silence, of course, is about issues involving the bearing and rearing of children, the sexual division of labour around parenting and strategies for breaking it down. This silence is not limited to the reply to Paul Hirst; it is a general *relative* silence within feminism. The article by Diane Ehrensaft in P&P 3 points out that the modern women's movement put motherhood on trial early on, found it guilty of oppressing women, and since then has found it hard to say much else. This relative silence risks serious debilitating effects on feminism, which is why Diane Ehrensaft's article is so important.

There is now a minor baby-boom occurring in Britain. One reason for this is that numbers of women who did not have children in their early twenties, often as a result of the direct or indirect influence of fem- inism, have decided to have them as they approach and enter their thirt- ies. Where it has been possible for these women to have children with men, it is not unusual to find that, ine one way or another, the project of parenthood involves breaking down the patterns of family life and division of labour which, by and large, we knew as children. In this, my experience (unreliable guide though my knowledge of my own and friends' experiences is) is that it has been easier to make some inroads into the sexual division of labour than it has been to attack the division between those who are and those who are not the biological parents. In most cases, the latter division can be expressed as being between those who did and those who didn't decide to have the child(ren) in question. Numerous personal accounts testify to the difficulty of breaking this division down - which is not to say that it has universally proven to be totally impossible, nor to suggest that it is ever easy to break down the sexual division of labour between the biological parents.

The difficulties encountered in attacking these divisions are part ideological and emotional, part material and economic. In the terms used in the men's editorial in P&P 3, these problems are possible, appropriate and immediate objects of political struggle. Self-evidently, this struggle, *which is already in progress*, is situated in the field of personal behaviour (of parents and non-parents) and in other fields - national and local government policy on education and the provision of nurseries, factors which constrain the economic feasibility of shared parenting, the structure and timing of meetings of progressive

organisations, and so on. Political strategies in respect of these
issues exist only in the most *ad hoc* and incomplete form. For the
personal politics of parenthood, I am unaware that any strategy as such
exists.   There has been very little political enquiry into the politics
of relations between parents and children.

So: there are political struggles, but a strategy in respect of them
is effectively lacking. For Paul Hirst to call upon feminism to strengthen the role of women within the family is to dabble in irrelevance.
A general call for the transformation of relations within the family is
a little bit less unhelpful, but not much.

Those of us with children are attempting to transform the family.
We need to be told to transform it as much as women need to be told to
get themselves a better deal from society. And in the absence of political strategies for parenthood being debated and developed in the fora
where one would most expect that to happen, the process we are engaged
in is less a struggle and more a kind of flounder.

It is probably clear that I have a personal investment in this issue.
Undoubtedly, this produces a poorly suppressed irritation in what I have
to say about it and about the general relative silence of feminism with
regard to it. Among those with a similar personal investment, I have
encountered a similar irritation. And this irritation tends, necessarily though perhaps not totally logically, towards a dilution of the
immediacy of those feminist truths which previously seemed so self-
evident. Thus, in my own irritated view, by the beginning of the 1980s
it ought to be starkly clear to those without children (as it is to those
with children) that the simple polarity of familialism and anti-familial-
ism is virtually irrelevant to the politics of parenthood and the questions of relations between parents and their children, parents and other
adults, their children and other children, children and other adults,
and between the parents themselves. If this is all feminism has to
offer....

In less irritated vein, of course, this is not all feminism has to
offer. The very critique of the sexual division of labour within the
family is a feminist achievement; whatever its contradictions and in-
completeness, the idea of shared parenting is in large part grounded in
that critique. This is not to say that all the feminist conclusions
from the critique of the family are equally helpful or point in the same
direction: there is one view, for example, which argues for the exclusion of men from parenthood, which seems to me to be a good way of reinforcing exactly that sexual division of labour which is the basic target
of the feminist critique of the family in the first place.[2] It is to
say, however, that, as Diane Ehrensaft's article in P&P 3 also demonstrates, political strategies around this issue begin of necessity from
basic insights developed most forcefully within feminism.

From this starting point I would want to go on to argue that the
process of developing such strategies, and the strategies themselves,
must of necessity involve men as much as women. And in this, arguing
that 'women must lead', as the women's editorial in P&P 3 does as a
general principle, seems to me to start by posing all the important
questions in a way which will ensure that the answers are of precious
little use to people who are actually involved in sharing parenthood.
Indeed, it is if one tries to think in detail about the issues involved
in relations within the family, especially if one recognises the existing political struggles within this field, that the weakness of the
general principle of 'women must lead' is clearest.

One of the achievements of the women's movement has been to reduce
the numbers of men trying to tell women what they feel and what they
ought to feel. Men have been up to that trick for far too long, and it
seems to me that Paul Hirst's article in P&P 3 tries a version of it,
which I find one of the most damning things about it. But the imperative not to indulge in that trick cuts both ways. Women cannot presume
to tell men what we feel, how we experienced our growing-up, the pressures upon us of puberty, sexuality and role-modelling. If it is tried,
and a political strategy of parenthood is evolved on that basis, the
result will be more dabbling in irrelevance. Firstly, it would mean
that an important part of the object of political struggle would be an
unknown; that is, given that men were boys, the experience and evaluation of boyhood is a closed book unless men are in on the political process of developing strategies. Moreover, it runs the risk of weakening
the political drawing power of the consequent strategic perspectives.
Most men seem to have a limited imagination and largely negative picture
of much of the business of caring for children - the part of parenting
usually carried out by the mother. Many men, however, have become
attracted to attempting to share parenthood, not out of a moral imperative to reduce the burden on the mother, but because of its many positive aspects. It is hard to write about this without seeming to ooze
sentimentality, but it needs to be said that there is a lot of fun and
happiness for a man when he starts to mother: there is a kind of love
and intimacy which is quite unavailable elsewhere. There are also the
nappies, the anger, the frustrations and anxieties, but the point is
that there is much else as well. Many men seem to go through their
years of fatherhood experiencing a deep alienation from the children for
whom they are responsible and to whom they often feel a depth of commitment which is unexpressible within the general sexual division of labour
in the family.

In other words, there is a genuine basis for an alliance between men
and women in shared parenthood. The experience of shared parenthood,
with or without a strategy to light the way, is itself an experience
of that alliance in practice. Like all alliances, it involves tensions
and disagreements as well: it is not and cannot be totally unproblematic while society is arranged as it is now. It is nonetheless a
potentially fruitful alliance. I do not see how it can be developed if
the process of developing it subordinates either women or men, elevat-
ing the other sex to the leading role. Returning to the other division
of labour around parenting - that between those who are and those who
are not the biological parents - there may also be a potential alliance
here which can at least *ease* the division. Men and women who do not
want to have children for any one of a wide variety of reasons (or who
do not want to have children yet) may nonetheless want some involvement
with children. It is possible to reduce the concentrated attention of
parents to their children - to give parents some space from, and to
give non-parents some access to, children. And, while this can be
achieved on an individual *ad hoc* basis, it will be easier and more
widespread if political explorations of parenting are directed towards
a strategy for this kind of collaboration as well, because, except for
women who were elder sisters especially in large families (and, much
more rarely, for men who were elder brothers), non-parents tend to have
very little idea of the business of parenting. Again, to the extent
that men without children want, as much as women without children, to

enter such processes, it would hardly make sense if one sex were subordinated to the other in developing strategies around them.

Similar points can be made about a subject which is more sensitive,
at least as far as the suggestion that men could participate in developing strategies around it is concerned. This subject is sex. Beatrix
Campbell's article in *Feminist Review* 5 attempts to open a space for
evolving a feminist politics of heterosexuality.[3] Although she strongly
takes issue with those feminists who identify penetration as the key
symbol and necessarily the indicator of subjugation to male sexual
imperialism, it seems that the attitude to penetration would be, for
her, the keystone of a revived feminist politics of heterosexuality.
Valuable though the article is, not least in breaking out of another
area of relative silence, the immediate designation of penetration as
the key strategic problem presents problems in itself. This is not meant
to deny that women may (or may not - who am I to say?) experience penetration as oppressive, whereas men tend to like it and feel empowered
by it, although I do not think it likely that men's and women's experience of penetration is adequately captured by that oppression/empower-
ment polarity. Certainly, many men do express various degrees of dissatisfaction with the seeming inevitability of penetration and the
machine-like syndrome of performance and sex-by-numbers which surrounds
it, and I have little doubt that many women have equally contradictory
and changing feelings about penetration. Rather, the problem is that
concentrating on penetration seems likely to miss much of what male
heterosexuality is about and to fail to account for various kinds of
sexual imagery which abound in male culture and are not tied to penetration. While penetration is one important element, it may be fruitful
also to question the genital and orgasmic obsession which dominates so
much of male heterosexuality. At the same time, the actual practice of
heterosexuality should surely be placed in the context of the social relations of sexuality and sexual intercourse - their functions and dys-
functions in personal relations, the terms on which sexual connections
are entered and their social meaning.

I advance these views rather tentatively: I am quite prepared for the
possibility that further debate and enquiry will show the perspective I
am suggesting is totally wrong. As the men's editorial in P&P 3 suggested, we are at a painfully early stage in political exploration of these
problems. But what I am not prepared to accept is that a politics of
heterosexuality (except for a politics of rejection) can be developed
if the process of developing it excludes or totally subordinates men.
To propose or even imply that that is possible seems to me to come
dangerously close to being a contradiction in terms.

To return to the starting point for these arguments, I would suggest
that the weakness of 'Feminists - The Degenerates of the Social?' about
relations within the family is a further demonstration of the weakness
of the perspectives advanced in the women's editorial in P&P 3. But I
am not suggesting that a contribution from men to the development of
political strategies around issues first prioritised by feminism will
be either easy or capable of uncritical acceptance by women. To argue
that men can sort out the problems raised but not so far solved by
feminism is as unacceptable as an argument that political strategies for
shared parenthood can be developed if men are excluded from the process
or subordinated in it. Nor am I suggesting that a collaborative development of strategies around these issues will be easy, uncomplicated or

swift. But I am arguing that such collaboration is possible and necessary, and also that it is required of men. Reflecting the arguments of
the men's editorial in P&P 3, I am also arguing that such a contribution
demands something more than the kinds of responses to feminism men have
so far tended to produce.

It now seems clear that this kind of collaboration is not possible with
the authors of the women's editorial in P&P 3. This is to be regretted,
the more so if the positions in that editorial command widespread agreement among socialist feminists, as may indeed be the case. The extent
to which P&P can re-establish itself as a place within which fruitful
debates on these and other issues can be pursued is not clear and depends
on numerous factors, some of them out of the Board's control. It can
only be said that there is a commitment within the current Board to get
to grips with those factors which are within our control.
    For a group of women to say they are fed up with working with men
- a particular group of men, or just men in general - seems to me to be
a reasonable thing to say and to act upon. The frustration of the women
who left P&P with the men who stayed was so clear for so long that, looking back, the only surprise is that they stayed as long as they did. I
find it rather odd that they chose that exact moment to leave, but
essentially I have no quarrel with the fact of their resignations. But
in the way in which they have explained and presented their decision
there is much to disagree with. Despite the problems on the Board, and
despite the shortcomings of some of the attitudes on the Board about
socialist feminism, I find no basis upon which I could have resigned in
solidarity with them. In the end, the problem is that they seem in the
women's editorial to be opposing that kind of collaboration between women
and men which I think is necessary for the further development of political strategies around issues raised by feminism. Indeed, I believe that
to have resigned in solidarity with them would have been an act of political surrender - not a surrender to feminism, but to the kind of false
moralism which blurs political thinking and undermines political engagement with real problems. Such a surrender, into mute assent to feminism,
is incompatible with the kind of engagement by men in the issues raised
by feminism which is, despite its difficulties not only necessary but
urgent.

NOTES

1 The main differences relate to Mike's overstatement of the extent to
   which the men manoeuvred in drafting the editorial, to the exaggera-
   tion of the extent to which we concentrated on the task of drafting
   the paper instead of discussing the issues, to the general implication that there was little if anything to distinguish the attitudes
   of the men, and to the abundant moralism of his statement, especially
   including the reference to Norman Mailer which is just a cheap shot.
   On the first two points, the main manoeuvre was conducted by Phil
   Jones and myself, presenting a lengthy draft for insertion into the
   editorial which took self-criticism further and raised issues of
   sexuality. The point of the manoeuvre was to force discussion of
   these issues, and we were successful in this. To be sure we got the

right effect, we described it as a manoeuvre, though this was probably an insult to the other men's perceptiveness since the whole
exercise was pretty blatant. Mike is right that the issues were not
adequately discussed, but the discussion of them was closer to being
adequate than any other discussion in P&P, and more adequate than
most political discussions in most political fora. Objecting to the
care we took in drafting the editorial seems to me to ignore the outcome which, despite its length and occasional over-elaboration of
arguments, is an extraordinary statement about feminism from men,
especially that group of men.

2 On this issue I have found the work of Nancy Chodorow particularly
informative (although her perspectives are probably not shared by
most other Board members): see *The Reproduction of Mothering: Psychoanalysis and the Sociology of Gender* (University of California Press,
1978). Insights from her work are now entering the debate in Britain,
not only in Diane Ehrensaft, 'When women and men mother', *Politics &
Power* 3, but also in Michele Barrett, *Women's Oppression Today:
Problems in Marxist Feminist Analysis* (London, Verso, 1980) and Ann
Oakley, *Women Confined: Towards a Sociology of Childbirth* (Oxford,
Martin Robertson, 1980).

3 B. Campbell, 'A Feminist Sexual Politics: Now you see it, now you
don't', *Feminist Review* 5, 1980.

Barry Hindess
A Left Strategy for Disaster: A Response to Peter Hain

Peter Hain's argument in *Politics & Power 3* for transforming the Labour
Party into a mass campaigning organisation deserves serious attention.
It represents a view that has gained significant support in sections of
the British left and it has major implications for the future development of the Labour Party. Much of my disagreement with his argument
will be clear from my critique of strategies for a 'left Labour Government' in *Politics & Power 2*, and I shall concentrate here on his central
proposal that Labour should be transformed into 'a *modern* mass party'
(p.188).

To avoid any possible misunderstanding, there are two preliminary
points to be made. First, these short comments have no editorial status:
neither Hain's argument nor my objections to it represent a majority
position within the editorial board of *Politics & Power*. Rather, these
comments are offered in the attempt to sharpen some of the points at
issue in socialist discussion about the future of the Labour Party.
Secondly, I agree entirely with one basic premise of Peter Hain's argument, namely, that any significant move towards socialism in Britain
must involve both parliamentary and extra-parliamentary struggles. I
have argued elsewhere for the unique importance of parliament as a
political arena for socialists and also for the development of popular
forms of control over sections of the state apparatuses and the organisation of production. But I must seriously dispute whether the proposal
to combine both popular and parliamentary struggle within a radically
reconstituted Labour Party represents a viable way forward for socialists
under British political conditions. On the contrary, my view is that the
struggle to reconstruct the Labour Party *as a mass party* (at least in
Hain's sense) would further weaken the already precarious hold of socialist politics in Britain today.

It is important to be clear what is at stake in Peter Hain's idea of
Labour as a mass party. It is not simply that the Labour Party should
both encourage and involve itself in popular politics, developing workplace branches, community newspapers, working with tenants' associations,
and so on. That seems to me thoroughly sensible and desirable. But,
and this is the crucial point at which we part company, Hain wants to
go much further 'and give priority to extra-parliamentary action, *even*

to the point of subordinating electoral politics to it' (p.192 - emphasis
added). That is why his proposals require an absolutely fundamental
change of strategy, and why he argues that 'a totally different attitude
is required' (p.195) from elected representatives in national and local
government. Hain's new model Labour Party should play the central role
in stimulating and coordinating diverse popular struggles into a mass
force for socialism and its struggles for parliamentary change should be
solidly based on that extra-parliamentary strength. In effect, the left
in the Labour Party has to take over the leading role in socialist transformation that the CPGB rather quixotically assigns to itself in *The
British Road to Socialism*, and then bring the rest of the Labour Party
to heel.

Now, there are many problems with that conception of the Labour Party
as a mass party. But, for the purposes of the present short discussion,
let me comment only on two sets of issues: first, the idea of the 'leading role' of the Labour Party in relation to other groups and struggles,
and secondly, the prospects for achieving the kind of reconstituted
Labour Party that Hain advocates and its consequences for parliamentary
and electoral politics.

Consider first the idea of the 'leading role' of the Labour Party.
There is, of course, no disputing the need for party forms of political
organisation in the electoral and parliamentary spheres and few would
deny the importance of coordinating different struggles and strategies.
But many on the left would utterly reject the model of socialist struggle
as organised around the leading role of a single party, questioning
whether the diversity of struggles confronting the left and the different forms of organisation developed within them can be contained within
the logic of any single programme or party organisation.

In recent years the women's movement has been particularly important
in developing that critique of the traditional socialist idea of the
party, of its capacity to play the 'leading role' and the necessity of
subordinating political struggle to its leadership. No doubt that
critique has been developed in part as a response to the appalling way
the organisations of the left (including the Labour Party and the left
within it) have reacted to the demands of the women's movement. But
there is also a more general point to their critique. There are real
and substantial political differences between the interests and objectives of the various groups and movements on the left, between the kinds
of struggles they engage in and the forms of organisation appropriate
to those struggles. Some of these groups or movements may be able to
work together for particular objectives or in particular struggles.
But it would be the purest fantasy to imagine that any party can unify
and overcome within its own organisation the genuine diversity of
political concerns and objectives on the left.

In this respect it is instructive to consider Peter Hain's comments
on the limitations of single-issue politics: 'at the end of the day,
they have come up against power structures which it is simply not
possible to combat within a "single-issue framework"' (p.186). Of
course they have. He is absolutely right to insist that there are
major limitations to single-issue and pressure-group politics. But he
is seriously mistaken about the lesson that should be drawn. The lesson
is not at all that those limitations can be overcome only within an all-
embracing socialist organisation, Hain's revitalised Labour Party. The
point rather is that different strategies, different kinds of struggle,

different organisational structures, and often *different organisations*, may well be needed to pursue different kinds of objectives. That is one reason why people have chosen to work for some of their objectives through single-issue organisations and pressure groups rather than through political parties. Single-issue and pressure-group politics has definite limitations and, within those limitations, particular groups or campaigns may be more or less successful. Exactly the same is true of party politics, whether it be the politics of the Labour Party we know or of the modern mass party that Peter Hain would like to see. Active socialists are needed in the Labour Party and they are needed in extra-parliamentary campaigns and pressure groups, and there will always be practical questions about the connections and interdependencies between struggles in these different arenas. But it is far from clear that those practical questions would be much advanced by the attempt to combine a multitude of heterogeneous groups and struggles within the framework of a single party.

Now consider the prospects for achieving the kind of reconstituted Labour Party that Hain envisages. If socialists are to seriously consider devoting their time and political energies to fighting for such a radical reconstruction of the politics and organisation of the Labour Party then there are several obvious questions to be answered. Is the balance of forces in the labour movement such as to make the struggle for that transformation more than a thoroughly utopian enterprise? What are the obstacles to a mass socialist politics in Britain and are they really largely a matter of the 'parliamentarism' of the Labour Party? What would be the electoral and parliamentary consequences of a serious attempt to transform the Labour Party along the lines of his proposals? He provides remarkably little by way of answer to these questions. But without good and convincing answers socialists in the Labour Party can surely be forgiven for feeling that they have better things to do with their time than to fight for his proposals.

The Labour Party has gone through several changes since its formation out of the Labour Representation Committee over 60 years ago. But it has never come close to being a mass party in Hain's sense, or anything remotely like it. Even at the height of its post-war growth the official figures for individual membership were little more than a million and few party branches at that time could be seriously regarded as thriving centres of local political activity. The Labour Party has always been a more or less organised coalition of diverse political groupings and organisations, reflecting a variety of political concerns and ideologies. And socialism, however understood, has never been the dominant element in that amalgam.

The Labour Party, together with the trade union movement, does indeed provide a space for socialist argument to intervene within the mainstream of British political debate, a space in which the appeal to socialist principles can still have a certain legitimacy and sometimes a limited effect. That space is important and valuable (compare the position of socialism in the USA) but it is also severely constrained. If the ultra-left outside the Labour Party underrate the political importance of that space then Peter Hain's proposals underestimate the seriousness of the constraints upon it. His proposals for a mass socialist party would entail a complete break with the dominant political traditions, organisational forms and working practices of the British labour movement. In effect, the implication is that all these should

be scrapped and the Labour Party should start over again as a totally
different animal. It is not in fact a project for much-needed reforms,
starting from the party's remaining strengths and from the current
political concerns of the major forces that breathe such life as still
survives within the party. It would be remarkable if Hain's suggestions
did not confront 'formidable obstacles' (p.199), from the major unions,
from the overwhelming majority of the PLP, from what remains of the
party's full-time organisation, and probably from a majority of its
active individual membership.

Hain suggests that 'perhaps the most crippling' obstacle to the
creation of a mass socialist politics lies in the Labour Party's commitment to parliamentarism. 'The dominant perspective has been that socialism could be achieved through the ballot box alone' (p.198). Now that
is misleading in at least two important respects. First, in so far as
there has been a 'dominant perspective' in the Labour Party, it has not
been especially concerned with the achievement of socialism at all, let
alone through the ballot box alone. It has been concerned with social
and economic reform (more so at some times than at others), with running
central and local government, with managing the economy and with establishing greater public control over its functioning. Socialism has
provided one form of ideological justification for those objectives,
but it has never been offered as their only justification and rarely,
if at all, as the most important. Many honourable socialists have seen
some of those objectives as important socialist goals; they have often
been right to do so even though their realisation has depended on obtaining significant non-socialist support for the necessary legislation.
But to choose to work for socialist objectives in that way and under
the constraints it involves is a far cry from believing that socialism
can be achieved 'through the ballot box alone'.

It is misleading secondly because of the way it locates the major
obstacles to mass socialist politics as lying *within* the Labour Party.
The Labour Party is first and foremost an electoral agency, competing
for representation in national and local government against other
parties. But why should that 'parliamentarism' be regarded as the
major obstacle to popular involvement in socialist politics? Peter
Hain refers us to Ralph Miliband's *Parliamentary Socialism* where the
answer is all too clear. Labour's parliamentarism is supposed to be an
obstacle precisely because it serves to inhibit realisation of the militant and socialist potential that is imagined to be inherent in the
British working class. Miliband's argument requires a massive act of
faith, shared presumably by Hain, with scant support in British politics
throughout the lifetime of the Labour Party. As always, faith serves
only to obscure more serious problems.

Forms of political involvement raise important issues for socialists,
for the notions of popular democratic control, of communal and cooperative forms of organisation supplanting commodity and bureaucratic forms,
clearly depend on developing forms of popular activity that go well
beyond existing political conditions. There are problems here that I
am in no position to answer, but the primary obstacles to such a popular
politics are surely not to be found in the Labour Party or labour movement alone. Rather they have to be sought in the overlapping forces,
strategies, forms of political calculation and ideologies that constitute
and define the field of politics in Britain - a field that implicates
Labour certainly, but also the Liberals and Tories, the CPGB, SWP and

other minority organisations of the left, the National Front and its more or less close relations, the women's movement, and all the issue organisations and pressure groups. That field imposes real constraints on socialist politics, and it is important that we seek ways of going beyond them. But it also constrains a popular politics of the right - and for that at least we have good reason to be thankful.

What, finally, can we say of the political consequences of the attempt to reconstruct the Labour Party along the lines that Hain proposes, especially in relation to its electoral prospects over the next 10 to 15 years? Perhaps the most obvious objection from within the Labour Party to Hain's proposals would concern the danger that the attempt to subordinate Labour's electoral politics to extra-parliamentary struggle would mean leaving control of government to the Tories for many years to come - a truly frightening prospect under present conditions. That concern seems to me entirely legitimate and I find it astonishing that Hain makes no attempt to discuss it. That apparent disinterest in a serious assessment of the electoral prospects of a reconstructed Labour Party obviously relates to a general tendency throughout his article to discount the importance of parliamentary and electoral politics: the running theme that Labour has been 'far too oriented to parliament' (p.191), the argument that 'real power' does not reside in parliament but that 'effective power, as opposed to the trappings of it, really lies in big business, the multinationals and the private and public bureaucracies which serve them' (p.188) and so on.

I suggested earlier that Hain differs from the non-Labour ultra-left in grossly overrating the strength of support for socialism within the Labour Party and the labour movement generally. But his discounting of parliament in favour of a mass socialist politics (in which a subordinated parliamentary politics is to be incorporated) also overrates the potential for any kind of mass popular politics in Britain today, whether of the left or the right. In that respect he shares with the ultra-left a cavalier disregard of the extent to which parliamentary and electoral politics (with all its strengths and limitations) has taken root in British society and a dangerous underestimation of the importance of what happens in parliament. Of course the powers of parliament are limited. Who but the most blinkered devotees of the 'sovereignty of parliament' (and Labour has more than enough of those) could possibly deny it? But our understanding is not advanced one iota by disputations about 'real power' and where it may be found. Parliament has definite powers and, like all powers, they are subject to definite limitations. Parliament is able to do some things and it is not able to do others. Its limitations provide a social and political space in which other, equally definite, powers are able to be effective. The boundaries of that space are not immutable, and parliament itself is *one* of the agencies that can change them, but their existence means that parliament is not and cannot be all-powerful. But it is not powerless either. To discount it on the grounds that 'real power' lies elsewhere is to discount the major impact that legislation can have in our society.

In his final paragraph Hain tells us, and it is a view that is widely voiced on the left of the Labour Party, that Labour's 'task is not to manage capitalism better' (p.199). That view seems to me dangerously misleading, for it involves a serious misunderstanding of the place socialism occupies within the more or less organised coalition of forces

that is the Labour Party. Socialism is not and never has been the dominant element in that coalition. Labour does provide a significant space
for socialist argument and socialist principles to intervene in British
political life. But that space is very severely limited. Socialists in
the Labour Party must learn to take account of the reality of that constraint and work out ways of going beyond it. But many still persist in
treating Labour as an essentially socialist party perpetually led astray
by a renegade parliamentary leadership. To say that Labour's task is not
to manage capitalism better is to fall into precisely that error. In the
eyes of many of its supporters and its affiliated unions one of the most
important things Labour is in business for is precisely that, to manage
capitalism better. It will do little to advance the cause of socialism,
either within the Labour Party or more generally in British society, if
Labour does not even do that. Of course socialists will want something
more, but the successful management of the British economy is a necessary
and worthy objective for the Labour Party - and one that is by no means
easy to achieve. If Labour could manage that it would be something and,
given the present state of the British economy, we should all be extremely
thankful.

   What most disturbs me about Peter Hain's proposals is that they seem
designed to ensure that Labour does not get the chance to manage capitalism at all. To subordinate electoral and parliamentary politics to the
requirements of extra-parliamentary action is precisely to discount the
importance of government, of all those issues of social and economic
policy that can be tackled only at the level of national politics or
the detailed administration of local government. For Labour as an
electoral agency not to take those issues seriously would be to wash its
hands of the tasks of government and to leave them to other parties.
And it would be to condemn the country to suffer the social and economic
consequences of their actions for the foreseeable political future.